Transitions in Namibia

Which Changes for Whom?

Edited by Henning Melber

NORDISKA AFRIKAINSTITUTET, UPPSALA 2007

Cover:

The restored steam tractor outside the coastal town of Swakop-
mund was made in Germany and brought to the country in
1896. It should replace ox wagons as a means of transport in the
further colonization of Namibia's interior. The 2.8 tons heavy
machine in need of lots of water never managed it through the
sands of the Namib desert. The local colonizers named it after
the German reformer Martin Luther, who in 1521 had declared:
"Here I stand – may God help me. I can not otherwise." Today
a national monument and put behind glass, Namibia's "Martin
Luther" remains an early symbol for the failure of grand visions.

Indexing terms:
  Social change
  Economic change
  Cultural change
  Political development
  Liberation
  Decentralization
  Gender relations
  International relations
  Economic and social development
  Post-independence
  Namibia

Cover photos: Henning Melber
Language checking: Peter Colenbrander
© The authors and Nordiska Afrikainstitutet 2007
ISBN 978-91-7106-582-7
Printed in Sweden by Elanders Gotab AB, Stockholm 2007

Table of Contents

Preface

This volume on social realities in Namibia completes the 'Liberation and Democracy in Southern Africa' (LiDeSA) project undertaken at the Nordic Africa Institute between 2001 and 2006. The chapters in it mainly address topical socioeconomic and gender-related issues in contemporary Namibia and complement the earlier stock-taking publication on Namibian society that focused on aspects of the country's socio-political culture since independence.[1] As before, most of the contributors are either Namibian, based in Namibia or have undertaken extensive research in the country. Their interest as scholars and/or civil society activists is guided by a loyalty characterised not by rhetoric but by empathy with the people. They advocate notions of human rights, social equality and related values and norms instead of being driven by an ideologically determined party-political affiliation. Their investigative and analytical endeavours depict a society in transition, a society that is far from being liberated. Not surprisingly, they explore the limits to liberation more than its advances.

I wish to thank all the authors for their collaborative commitment to this project and for their contributions to a necessary debate, which must take place first and foremost inside Namibia for the best of the country and its people. Thanks also go to Jeremy Silvester and Jan-Bart Gewald, who again served as external reviewers of the draft manuscripts and added to the value of the final texts. I am also grateful for the meticulous language editing so reliably undertaken by Peter Colenbrander, for whom this part of the world is anything but a distant abstraction. I am indebted to Nina Klinge-Nygård, who assisted me over the years in executing my duties at the Nordic Africa Institute. Special thanks are due to Sonja Johansson, Boël Näslund and Karim Kerou, among many other supportive colleagues. They processed the final manuscript in the shortest possible time without compromising the quality of the product. Finally, I extend my heartfelt gratitude to Lennart Wohlgemuth and Karl-Eric Ericsson, director and deputy director during most of my time as research director at the Nordic Africa Institute. They welcomed me from Namibia as part of a team and

---

1. Henning Melber (ed.), *Re-examining Liberation in Namibia. Political Culture since Independence.* Uppsala: Nordic Africa Institute 2003. For other outputs of the project, see the summary report and further bibliographical references accessible on the Institute's website (www.nai.uu.se).

offered me their loyal support and friendship throughout the days we shared as colleagues.

Last but not least, I dedicate my own contribution to this last product of the LiDeSA project to my wife Susan and my daughter Tulinawa, for their love and tolerance during all the years of our family life in Uppsala (which at times suffered considerably from my professional commitments); and to the memory of my brother Rainer (1951–79) and my mother Gretel (1923–2007). They were reunited this very day in the local cemetery between the Atlantic Ocean and the dunes of the Namib Desert, exactly 56 years after my brother's birth and 40 years after we first arrived as German emigrants in this coastal town of then South West Africa. Transitions have many faces, dimensions and meanings.

Henning Melber
Swakopmund/Namibia
9 August 2007

Transitions in Namibia – Namibia in transition
An introductory overview

Henning Melber

"We Africans fought against colonialism and imperialism and successfully overthrew colonialism and white minority rule to achieve genuine social and economic emancipation." Sam Nujoma in his opening address to the congress of the Swapo Youth League, Windhoek, 17 August 2007.[1]

This statement was made by one who should know better: Sam Nujoma, the president of the national liberation movement SWAPO since its establishment in 1960, and Namibia's first head of state, a position he held for three terms from 1990 to 2005. At the time of publication of this volume, he remained in control of an influential faction within the Swapo party, which, through its political office bearers, has exercised political control over the government of the Republic of Namibia since independence. After his retirement from the highest office of the state, Nujoma's personal merits earned him the official title of the Founding Father of the Republic of Namibia.[2] Nonetheless, and with due respect to the 'old man' who over almost half a century has clearly demonstrated an ability to cling to power as a political leader, he has got it wrong in claiming the above achievements. Speaking as a 'political animal,' he either lacks the analytical grasp of social transition and transformation or (more likely) is merely showing that a political project and its rhetoric at times display profound ignorance of social processes (or simply seek to cover up certain class projects by means of such misleading rhetoric).

The implications of such fabrication of a 'patriotic history' were the main focus of the volume that preceded this one, which concentrated mainly on the political culture and ideology cultivated since Namibia's independence and its effects on governance issues and different sectors of society (Melber 2003). The first chapter following the introduction to this second volume serves as a kind of link to these socio-political and ideological dimensions of the Namibian nation-building project. It shows how the liberators use their power of definition in a hegemonic public discourse to reinvent themselves within the heroic narrative that was already being constructed during the anti-colonial struggle. But this rhetoric must be gauged against the achievements claimed by among others the Founding Father, a central figure in the Namibian ver-

---

1. As quoted in "Nujoma Addresses Youth League", *The Namibian,* 20 August 2007.
2. For the politics of transition from the first to the second head of state in more detail, see Melber (2006).

sion of a liberation gospel. This gospel claims that the seizure of political power and the ideological commanding heights included a more profound transition to another society and transformation of colonial structures into a liberated society and economy that benefits the majority among the formerly colonised masses.

Most chapters in this volume are a kind of stock-taking exercise: they examine the extent to which a transition is taking place and the results it has achieved during the 17 years since independence. In so doing, this volume seeks to add to the existing body of knowledge. This new knowledge is by no means confined to the era beginning with Namibia's Independence Day (21 March 1990). Instead, one needs to emphasize that societies are in constant transition as they reproduce (and modify) themselves. The intensity of the transition may change, and the formal end of colonial occupation and foreign rule – inasmuch as political power is transferred to a local agency – are the most obvious points of reference or departure for these new chapters. These milestones are not necessarily complete turning points, but may induce more rapid social change through a more dramatic shift in the organisation of political and social structures, with a resultant direct impact on the fabric and nature of societies.

Social transitions in Namibia have been analysed on many occasions before. This introductory overview cannot provide a complete analysis but it can introduce some of the relevant literature touching on transitions in Namibian society since the 19th century.[3] Brigitte Lau, who headed the National Archives of Namibia until her untimely death, was among those who contributed to insights on early transitions in Namibia with the advent of colonialism (cf., Lau 1987), and John Kinahan, an archeologist with the local authorities, provided an even more historically oriented perspective on social transitions in parts of Namibia and its population (Kinahan 1991). These authors greatly benefited from their direct access to local archives or their own field studies. So did those others who compiled relevant documentary evidence in the true sense by using existing photographic material to document and analyse the visually obvious social changes and power structures induced by colonialism (Hartmann 2004, Hartmann/Silvester/Hayes 1998).

The colonial impact on local and regional modes of production, social reproduction and related aspects of identity has already been explored in numerous analyses, often undertaken in pursuit of an academic degree. Prominent examples of such historical research by local scholars are the thesis by Frieda-Nela Williams (1994) and by Wolfgang Werner (1998), but also by Nampala and Shigwedha (2006).[4] Other insights from a local perspective into historical changes under colonial occupation include Gewald's seminal work (1999 and 2000), which supplements Werner's thesis on the Herero communities. Local analyses on social change in Owambo societies under colonial rule were complemented by the work of Finnish scholars (Siiskonen 1990, Eirola 1992), thereby highlighting in an historical perspective – similar to the academic work linked to the German period of foreign rule – the special relations between the northern

---

3. References are limited to books published in English and ignore numerous relevant journal articles and individual book chapters as well as the additional relevant works existing in German (testifying to the fact that Namibia had been a German settler colony, which resulted in a particular interest among German-speaking scholars that has persisted into the present).

4. Local (especially historical) knowledge production is now reaching a wider audience thanks in part to the publication efforts of the Basler Afrika Bibliographien.

region of Namibia and the Finnish missionaries.[5] The focus on Namibia's northern region previously called Owamboland has also produced scholarly work dealing with the particular impact of Christianity on social transition and transformation (McKittrick 2002) and the effects of environmental change on the organisation of these societies (Kreike 2004, but also Erkkilä/Siiskonen 1992). A good example of how a study on Owamboland-based elites in transition resulted in far-reaching political consequences for the personal future of its author is evident in the case of Gerhard Tötemeyer (1978).[6]

Studies of social organisation and transformation among Namibian social formations other than the Oshiwambo- and Herero-speaking communities are relatively few (see, among others, Kössler 2006 on the Nama). The San or Bushmen communities represent an exception to the general tendency for most analyses to focus on the most relevant (in the sense of most influential) social groups within a country[7]: as the most marginalised indigenous minority group (who are almost viewed as social outcasts), they have achieved relative prominence in the literature (Gordon 1992, Widlok 1999, Suzman 2000, Dieckmann 2007).

The focus on social transformation processes linked to sectoral and regional issues that go beyond specific group identities has been rather limited in historically oriented studies. Among the noteworthy exceptions are Wallace (2002) and contributions to the volumes edited by Bollig/Gewald (2000), Hayes/Silvester/Wallace/Hartmann (1998) and Miescher/Henrichsen (2000), while Emmett (1999) provides insights into the formative stages of modern political resistance to colonial occupation. Analyses of the subsequent politically organised liberation struggle and its internal dynamics are provided by Leys/Saul (1995) and Dobell (1998). A particular trade union perspective within the anti-colonial struggle can be found in works by Peltola (1995) and Bauer (1998), while Becker (1993) explores the gendered perspective. Pendelton (1994) provides a special focus on the most significant urban setting in Namibia and its changes, while Hinz (2003) combines environmental management, ecology and the particular role of local traditional leaders and their control over nature as a resource to present another perspective relevant to the transition of Namibia's society.

Several edited volumes have meanwhile added to the picture of social challenge and reorganisation since independence. Keulder (2000) does so in a historical, state-centred perspective; Melber (2000) looks at socioeconomic realities after a decade of sovereignty; while chapters in Diener/Graefe (2001) offer a wide panorama of relevant studies, as

---

5. This has resulted in a tradition of academic writings, especially from a social anthropology perspective on aspects of the Owambo kingdoms.

6. He obtained access to the field on the basis of his political loyalty to the then South African government occupying Namibia. The results of his interviews, however, originally submitted as a PhD thesis at Stellenbosch, illustrated the generally anti-colonial and anti-South African orientation among the new elite. This was no welcome finding and initially dramatically circumscribed the further career of the author drastically – only to result in a politically very different second career: after Namibian independence he left academia to enter politics and ended up as a deputy minister before his retirement.

7. Which to some extent is also reflected in the prominent role of the German-speaking minority in the analysis of segments of Namibian society (though admittedly mainly in the German literature).

do the contributions in Winterfeldt/Fox/Mufune (2002). All these undertakings have a high degree of local authorial participation.

Finally, one must not omit from this brief overview another form of documenting social transition, namely the personal testimonies of individuals involved in the processes of social change, such as those compiled in the volumes by Becker (2005) and Leys/Brown (2005), and the various literary and poetic narratives, in which the creative writing conveys a political message (cf., Melber 2004). New forms of recorded and published oral history also provide access to testimonies that afford insights into processes of social and political transition and transformation (cf., Namhila 2005).

The contributions to this volume seek to update earlier assessments and to deal with hitherto largely unexplored aspects. They summarise and critically reflect on developments since independence. In doing so, they challenge parts of the dominant narrative of the liberation movement now in political power and control. While Swapo's liberation gospel suggests that the struggle for independence achieved meaningful change for all people in most spheres of life, this volume presents a somewhat different perspective. "We must take time," urged Swapo's President Sam Nujoma in the same speech to the party's Youth League congress in mid-August 2007 quoted above, "to consider where we have come from as party and country, where we are today and where we would like to be as a nation."[8] The chapters below share this motivation and approach, even though they may put forward perspectives or conclusions different from those of the Founding Father.

References

Bauer, Gretchen (1998), *Labor and Democracy in Namibia: 1971–1996*. Athens, Ohio: Ohio University Press

Becker, Barbara (2005), *Speaking Out: Namibians Share Their Perspectives On Independence*. Windhoek: Out of Africa

Becker, Heike (1995), *Namibian Women's Movement 1980 to 1992. From Anti-colonial Resistance to Reconstruction*. Frankfurt am Main: IKO

Bollig, Michael and Jan-Bart Gewald (eds), (2000), *People, Cattle and Land. Transformations of a Pastoral Society in Southwestern Africa*. Köln: Köppe

Dieckmann, Ute (2007), *HaiǁIom in the Etosha Region. A History of Colonial Settlement, Ethnicity and Nature Conservation*. Basel: Basler Afrika Bibliographien

Diener, Ingolf and Olivier Graefe (eds), (2001), *Contemporary Namibia. The first landmarks of a post-Apartheid society*. Windhoek: Gamsberg Macmillan and Nairobi: IFRA

Dobell, Lauren (1998), *SWAPO's Struggle for Namibia, 1960–1991: War by Other Means*. Basel: P. Schlettwein

Eirola, Martti (1992), *The Owambogefahr: The Owamboland Reservation in the Making: Political Responses of the Kingdom of Ondonga to the German Colonial Power, 1884–1910*. Rovaniemi: Historical Association of Northern Finland

Emmett, Tony (1999), *Popular Resistance and the Roots of Nationalism in Namibia, 1915–1966*. Basel: P. Schlettwein

---

8. As quoted in "Nujoma addresses Youth League", *The Namibian*, 20 August 2007.

Erkkilä, Antti and Harri Siiskonen (1992), *Forestry in Namibia 1850–1990*. Joensuu: University of Joensuu

Gewald, Jan-Bart (1999), *Herero Heroes: A Socio-Political History of the Herero of Namibia, 1890–1923*. Oxford: James Currey and Athens, Ohio: Ohio University Press

— (2000), *"We Thought We Would Be Free": Socio-Cultural Aspects of Herero History in Namibia, 1915–1940*. Köln: Köppe

Gordon, Robert J. (1992), *The Bushman Myth. The Making of a Namibian Underclass*. Boulder/San Francisco/Oxford: Westview Press (2nd revised edition with Stuart Douglas, 2000)

Hartmann, Wolfram (ed.), (2004), *Hues between black and white. Historical photography from colonial Namibia 1860s to 1915*. Windhoek: Out of Africa

Hartmann, Wolfram, Jeremy Silvester and Patricia Hayes (eds), (1998), *The Colonising Camera. Photographs in the making of Namibian History*. Cape Town: University of Cape Town Press, Windhoek: Out of Africa and Athens, Ohio: Ohio University Press

Hayes, Patricia, Jeremy Silvester, Marion Wallace and Wolfram Hartmann, Wolfram (eds), (1998), *Namibia under South African Rule. Mobility and Containment 1915–1946*. Oxford: James Currey, Windhoek: Out of Africa and Ohio: Ohio University Press

Hinz, Manfred O. (2003), *Without Chiefs there would be no Game. Customary Law and Nature Conservation*. Windhoek. Out of Africa

Keulder, Christiaan (ed.), (2000), *State, Society and Democracy: a Reader in Namibian Politics*. Windhoek: Gamsberg Macmillan

Kinahan, John (1991), *Pastoral Nomads of the Central Namib Desert. The People History Forgot*. Windhoek: Namibia Archeological Trust and New Namibia Books

Kössler, Reinhart (2006), *In Search of Survival and Dignity. Two traditional communities in southern Namibia under South African rule*. Frankfurt am Main/London: IKO and Windhoek: Gamsberg Macmillan (2005)

Kreike, Emmanuel (2004), *Re-Creating Eden: Land Use, Environment, and Society in Southern Angola and Northern Namibia*. Portsmouth, NH: Heinemann

Lau, Brigitte (1987), *Namibia in Jonker Afrikaner's Time*. Windhoek: National Archives of Namibia

Leys, Colin and Susan Brown (2005), *Histories of Namibia: Living through the liberation struggle. Life histories told to Colin Leys and Susan Brown*. London: The Merlin Press

Leys, Colin and John S. Saul (eds), (1995), *Namibia's Liberation Struggle: The Two-Edged Sword*. London: James Currey/Athens and Ohio: Ohio University Press

McKittrick, Meredith (2002), *To Dwell Secure. Generation, Christianity, and Colonialism in Owamboland*. Portsmouth, NH: Heinemann, Oxford: James Currey, Cape Town: David Philip

Melber, Henning (ed.), (2000), *Namibia – A Decade of Independence, 1990–2000*, NEPRU Publication No. 7. Windhoek: The Namibian Economic Policy Research Unit

— (ed.), (2003), *Re-examining Liberation in Namibia. Political Culture Since Independence*. Uppsala: The Nordic Africa Institute

—(ed.), (2004), *It is no more a cry. Namibian Poetry in Exile and Essays on Literature in Resistance and Nation Building*. Basel: Basler Afrika Bibliographien

— (2006), '"Presidential indispensability" in Namibia: moving out of office but staying in power?' in Roger Southall and Henning Melber (eds), *Legacies of power: Leadership change and former presidents in African politics*. Cape Town: HSRC Press and Uppsala: The Nordic Africa Institute, pp. 98–119

Miescher, Giorgio and Dag Henrichsen (eds), (2000), *New notes on Kaoko*. Basel: Basler Afrika Bibliographien

Namhila, Ellen Ndeshi (2005), *Kaxumba kaNdola. Man and Myth. The Biography of a Barefoot Soldier*. Basel: Basler Afrika Bibliographien 2005 (Live, Legacies Legends; 2)

Nampala, Lovisa T. and Vilho Shigwedha (2006), *Aawambo Kingdoms, History and Cultural Change. Perspectives from Northern Namibia*. Basel: P. Schlettwein

Peltola, Pekka (1995), *The lost May Day: Namibian workers struggle for independence*. Helsinki: The Finnish Anthropological Society in association with the Nordic Africa Institute

Pendelton, Wade (1994), *Katutura: A Place where we stay. Life in Post-Apartheid Township in Namibia: Katutura Before and Now*. Windhoek: Gamsberg Macmillan (2nd revised edition Ohio 1996)

Siiskonen, Harri (1990), *Trade and Socioeconomic Change in Owamboland, 1850–1906*. Helsinki: SHS

Suzman, James (2000), *"Things from the Bush". A Contemporary History of the Omaheke San*. Basel: P. Schlettwein

Tötemeyer, Gerhard (1978), *Namibia Old and New. Traditional and Modern Leaders in Owamboland*. London: C. Hurst

Wallace, Marion (2002), *Health, Power and Politics in Windhoek, Namibia, 1915–1945*. Basel: P. Schlettwein

Werner, Wolfgang (1998), *"No One Will Become Rich". Economy and Society in the Herero Reserves in Namibia, 1915–1946*. Basel: P. Schlettwein

Widlok, Thomas (1999), *Living on Mangetti: 'Bushmen' Autonomy and Namibian Independence*. Oxford: Oxford University Press

Williams, Frieda-Nela (1994), *Pre-Colonial Communities of Southwestern Africa: A History of Owambo Kingdoms 1600–1920*. Windhoek: National Archives of Namibia

Winterfeldt, Volker, Tom Fox and Pempelani Mufune (eds.), (2002), *Namibia Society Sociology*. Windhoek: University of Namibia Press

History and the armed struggle
From anti-colonial propaganda to 'patriotic history'?

Christopher Saunders

A contested historiography is a sign of a healthy and mature democracy. Views of the past inevitably change as the past is seen from new vantage points in an ever-changing present. While certain facts about what happened in the past are incontrovertible, once one moves beyond the bald facts to an interpretation, there are bound to be different views of what happened. As an eminent historian once wrote, history that is worth the name should be "an argument without end," for there are no final truths in history and the process of reinterpretation is ongoing. Yet there are countries where this constant questioning of the past has not taken place, and instead an officially sanctioned view of the past has been imposed, a master narrative that does not admit alternative interpretations. One of the countries that has fallen into that trap is Zimbabwe, with which Namibia had close relations during its liberation struggle. Namibia, fortunately, is not in that situation, and hopefully never will be, but some worrying trends can be detected, as this chapter will illustrate

Two great episodes in Namibian history come to the fore in most contemporary discussions of the country's past: one is the period of colonial warfare against the Germans and the genocide of 1904–07, the other the liberation war of 1966–89. It is with the latter that this chapter is exclusively concerned. Scholars have begun to document how the liberation war has been used for political ends and to write about how it has been memorialised at the Heroes' Acre outside Windhoek and in other ways (most recently Kössler 2007). Here the focus is not on monuments or, say, the use of public holidays and the renaming of streets, but on writing about the past. I present a survey of such writing, conscious that there has been all too little analysis of Namibian historiography in general and hardly any discussion of writing on the liberation war. Given limitations of space, I shall inevitably have to adopt a broad-brush approach and be selective in the examples I cite. A more detailed and comprehensive study will reveal greater complexities and nuances between different works, but I hope that what I say here will prompt others to explore this subject in greater depth. This is no mere intellectual exercise, for it can help us understand current debates and may hold lessons for the future.

Africanist and 'patriotic' history

From the late 1950s, as countries in tropical Africa began to approach independence, old-style Eurocentric writing about the histories of those countries began to be replaced by a new Afrocentric or, as it was usually called, Africanist historiography. Some of this was scholarly and it considered, with appropriate nuance, African resistance to the imposition of colonial rule, African responses to colonialism itself and struggles for independence. Other writing about the past was more overtly political, being clearly designed to buttress the new nations by providing a nationalistic history that would legitimate them and provide them with a necessary history. Such writers tried to trace the history of the new nations from the present back into the distant past, laying emphasis on continuities and the unity of those who challenged the colonial system, and presenting a triumphalist picture of what the nationalists had achieved (cf., Temu/Swai 1981).

From the 1960s, these new forms of historical writing were replicated in those countries in Southern Africa that remained under white minority rule. For South Africa, such writing ranged from the scholarly Afrocentrism of the first volume of the new *Oxford History of South Africa* (Wilson/Thompson 1969) to the more popular, largely uncomplicated history of the African National Congress by Mary Benson entitled *The African Patriots* (Benson 1966). In Zimbabwe too, a nationalist historiography emerged long before the arrival of independence in 1980. The central figure in the development of that was Terence Ranger, who taught at the University College of Rhodesia before being expelled in the 1960s. He then moved to Dar es Salaam, then the United States and Britain, all the time continuing to work on Zimbabwe history himself, and encouraging others to do so, from a standpoint broadly sympathetic to the nationalist movement. In one of his most influential articles, he drew connections between the primary resistance to European intrusion in the late nineteenth century and the modern mass nationalism of his own day, and the argument for continuity was clearly to help give legitimacy to the nationalist movement then seeking power. It resonates with recent attempts to link Mugabe's disastrous policies of the early 21st century with two previous anti-colonial struggles (*chimurengas*) of 1896–97 and 1966–79. Much more recently, however, and reflecting his disillusionment with the way the nationalist project has been hijacked by an oppressive ruler, Ranger has sought to distinguish the nationalist historiography, to which he contributed so much from the 1960s, from what he terms "patriotic history," the unscholarly approach to the Zimbabwean past now propagated, more than a quarter of a century after independence, by the Robert Mugabe regime and its supporters (Ranger 2003).

What Ranger calls "patriotic history" is really not history at all, but myth and propaganda. It does not tell the truth about the past, but emphasises selected aspects of the past to present a picture of a glorious, continuous revolutionary tradition. It rejects academic history writing as an attempt to complicate the story of the past, and, instead, attempts to impose a hegemonic view of the liberation struggle. This writing about the Zimbabwean past is not concerned with the liberation struggle versus the colonial oppressors as one of right against wrong, for the rightfulness of the independence struggle against white minority rule is taken for granted. It stresses, instead, another divide, between those who led the fight and won and those who compromised and should therefore be denounced as unpatriotic and as sell-outs. This categorisation of people into those who were with us and those who were not, relates, of course, to present political battles in Zimbabwe, with those in power trying to legitimise their position by identifying themselves as the true liberators of the country. Others are denounced for not having such liberation credentials or are written out of history.

That the distinction between nationalist and 'patriotic' historical writing is not as clear-cut as Ranger suggests is seen, say, in the work of Ranger's own chief Zimbabwean collaborator, the historian Ngwabi Bhebe, whose work has shifted from the scholarly to what verges on the patriotic (Bhebe 1999, 2004), but Ranger's article may nevertheless serve as a useful starting point from which to pose questions about writing on Namibia's armed liberation struggle. I am concerned here both with writing on that struggle while it continued and with post-independence writing, for writing before independence influenced what came after. From what perspectives has the Namibian conflict been written about? Is Namibia following the Zimbabwean path to 'patriotic' history?

The context

Though Namibia's armed liberation struggle began at roughly the same time as Zimbabwe's, it continued much longer. Zimbabwe entered its brief transition to independence in late 1979, and only in April 1989 did Namibia begin to follow a somewhat similar path. As that month began, and a ceasefire was supposed to take effect, some of the bloodiest battles of the war took place in the war between South African forces and those of the People's Liberation Army of Namibia (PLAN), the armed wing of the South West Africa People's Organisation (SWAPO). Given the time disparity between the two transitions, it is not surprising that much less has been written to date about the Namibian struggle than about the Zimbabwean one. There are other reasons, however, why the body of work on Namibia's liberation struggle remains so small. Namibia's educated elite is minute, and few in that country have had time to devote to writing about the past, while for some Namibians the liberation struggle has remained too painful to write about.

Here I am primarily concerned with writing by Namibians themselves rather than by Western sympathisers, much of whose writing was ephemeral and polemic in intent, though some of the best had lasting value (one example is Herbstein and Evenson, 1989). Before I turn to work sympathetic to the Namibian struggle, however, it is important to note that both before and since independence there has been a large body of writing from the 'other side,' the side of the South African occupation and the forces out to crush the nationalist movement by force. This writing sought to justify, and whitewash, the counter-revolutionary struggle waged by the South African government, and to present those who were engaged in it as performing a necessary task in the combating of terrorism and communism. This literature, which is very heavily focused on the military aspects of the war against SWAPO, comes mainly from South Africans who themselves either fought on the South African side, such as Willem Steenkamp (1989), or were close to those who fought, such as Helmoed-Romer Heitman (1990) and Peter Stiff (2004), or from far-right wing Americans for whom SWAPO was seen as a tool of the Soviet Union (e.g., Norval 1989).[1]

---

1. Steenkamp fought in Angola in the late 1970s. Stiff was a guest of the South African police in northern Namibia in 1989 (Stiff, 2005:429, 481). Norval, an ex-US Marine, was executive director of the Selous Foundation, which also published his *Inside the ANC: The Evolution of a Terrorist Organization* (Washington 1990).

This literature is mostly narrative and anecdotal and not scholarly (despite some use of footnotes). Though these books deserve to be subjected to a detailed critique, here we can merely note that they tend to portray PLAN as weak and ineffectual and as acting on the orders of Moscow. At the same time, and contrary to the suggestion of weakness, such accounts speak of heroic acts of military daring and success by South African and surrogate Namibian forces against a formidable enemy which, despite losing large numbers on the battlefield, nevertheless remained a serious threat. While Stiff makes a brief attempt to look at the war from the viewpoint of two PLAN combatants in his latest blockbuster (Stiff, 2004:347–8), and while some voice is given to those in the South African forces who saw the war as pointless, on the whole this writing is anchored in the idea that the war that the South Africans and their allies fought in northern Namibia and southern Angola was both justified, to prevent a revolutionary take-over in Namibia, and effective. To date there has been no systematic attempt to critique the arguments in such books.

Early writing about the armed struggle

The first major attempt to present a different perspective from that found in such South African history writing, and to promote the nationalist agenda, was *To Be Born a Nation,* produced by SWAPO's department of information and publicity and published by a left-wing British publishing house, Zed Press, in 1981 (SWAPO, 1981).[2] This drew on earlier, slighter accounts from within SWAPO (especially SWAPO 1978), and on the brief history of Namibia written some years before by Randolph Vigne, the leading figure in Friends of Namibia and then the Namibia Support Committee in Britain (Vigne 1975).[3] *To Be Born a Nation* for the first time brought together in book form a detailed account of the colonisation of Namibia and the resistance to it, carrying the story to 1979. The most significant work on Namibia to which it could be compared, Ruth First's *South West Africa*, was written and published before the beginning of the armed struggle, at a time when it was still unclear whether SWAPO or the rival South West Africa National Union (SWANU) would emerge as the leading nationalist movement, and her pioneering study had been, if anything, more sympathetic to SWANU than to SWAPO (First 1963). Vigne's short history had only discussed very briefly the early years of the armed struggle. Now, for the first time, *To be Born a Nation* provided not only a detailed history of Namibia before the armed struggle began , but also an account of how that struggle had developed to the late 1970s, like other nationalist works emphasising the continuities in resistance from precolonial times to the present.

To be Born a Nation was a SWAPO project and no author was identified. Peter Katjavivi, who had set up the SWAPO office in London in 1968 and a decade later moved on to study at Warwick University while remaining a leading SWAPO figure in

2. Zed published many key texts on Namibia in the 1980s, from H. Drechsler's *Let Us Die Fighting* (1980) to Herbstein and Evenson (1989).
3. Many articles on aspects of the struggle appeared in the various SWAPO journals, especially *The Combatant*, the journal of PLAN.

Britain, contributed a foreword, and elsewhere he is described as the book's "editor."[4] The book was launched at the Africa Centre in London on 26 August 1981, the 15th anniversary of the battle of Omugulu-gOmbashe in northern Namibia, the day that SWAPO recognises as the start of the armed struggle. The launch came a day after South African forces had again attacked SWAPO bases in southern Angola, so the literary proceedings were animated by news from the battlefront. In his speech at the launch, Katjavivi modestly admitted that the book was not a definitive account, but said that it aimed "to set the record straight" by countering anti-SWAPO accounts, and that it was therefore itself part of the liberation struggle.[5]

As the title suggested – it was taken, we are told, from a saying in the Mozambique liberation struggle, "to die a tribe and be born a nation" (SWAPO 1981:ii) – this history implied that SWAPO, through its armed struggle, was bringing into being a new Namibian nation. One of the organisation's leading slogans was 'One Namibia, One Nation,' and the book presented SWAPO as embodying the popular will of the Namibian people to oust the occupiers and create an independent nation. *To be Born a Nation* made clear that the armed struggle was the leading form of struggle, and that diplomacy was at best second fiddle to it. SWAPO, as the only organisation involved in the armed struggle against South African rule, represented the Namibian people in their fight for freedom. Such ideas, as we shall see, were to survive in post-independence writing.

While *To be Born a Nation* was the single most important work of history on the liberation struggle to be published before independence, it was not of course the only one. Alfred T. Moleah, a South African exile in the United States, published *Namibia: The Struggle for Liberation* in 1983. In it, he suggested that any attack on SWAPO leadership or policies would be unpatriotic. "Denial of a SWAPO government," he wrote, "is negation of Namibian independence" (Moleah 1983:300). SWAPO's department of information and publicity helped the Namibia Support Committee organise the major international conference on 'Namibia 1884 to 1984' held at the City University of London in September 1984, and not surprisingly the papers that were published in the 800 page volume that emerged from that conference some years later were mostly uncritical of the liberation struggle and did not delve into any of the tensions within it or controversies that dogged it (Wood 1988). And when SWAPO's deputy secretary-general for education and culture collaborated with a German colleague to produce a history text for secondary schools, the epilogue ended as follows: "Since it was founded in 1960, SWAPO has shaped Namibian history … The future of Namibia is bound up with the decisions and actions of SWAPO" (Mbumba/Noisser 1988:291).

All this is of course understandable within the context of the struggle then being fought against South African occupation. Perhaps the most balanced work by a Namibian in this pre-independence period on the liberation struggle post-1966 came from Peter Katjavivi, the activist turned scholar who, after completing a master's degree at Warwick University, moved on to St. Antony's College, Oxford, for a doctorate. After

---

4. See his biography on the United Nations University website: http://www.unu.edu/council/members/katjavivi.html. Richard Moorsom, who was active in the Namibia Support Committee and had completed a master's thesis on Namibia at the University of Sussex, is known to have been one of the main authors.

5. There is a copy of his speech in the Michael Scott Papers, Rhodes House Library, Oxford, Box 34.

he had completed that, he wrote a brief overview for UNESCO of the history of resistance in Namibia from the earliest times to the late 1970s, again emphasising continuities and justifying the armed struggle, and helped edit a book on *Church and Liberation in Namibia* (Katjavivi 1988, 1989). To its credit, his account of resistance did not ignore, as other writing did, the serious crisis that divided SWAPO in the mid-1970s and led to the detention of some of its leading officials (cf., Katjavivi 1988:106–7), though it did not mention the even more serious issue that was only beginning to emerge into the light of day as Katjavivi wrote, concerning torture and other atrocities being perpetrated on SWAPO's detainees in Lubango, Angola.

Of the memoirs of individuals in the struggle to be published before independence, among the most important were the autobiographies of two SWAPO activists. Vinnia Ndadi's *Breaking Contract* (Mercer 1989) and John Ya Otto's *Battlefront Namibia* (Ya Otto 1982) both told the stories of internal resistance leaders who fled into exile to join the externally based struggle. They praise Sam Nujoma as the father figure of the movement, and Ya Otto recalls how he scratched the SWAPO slogan 'One Namibia, One Nation' on the wall of the cell in which he was imprisoned. These activists drew upon their own memories to select historical detail to advance the stories they wanted to tell, stories of great suffering and heroism. While these are striking accounts by extraordinary men, they tell individual stories from the perspective of their authors and are not balanced accounts. To that extent they are, as a literary critic has pointed out, 'myth-making' (Haarhoff 1991, esp. 229). So is the equally striking account that appeared after Haarhoff wrote, Helao Shitywete's *Never Follow the Wolf: The Autobiography of a Namibian Freedom Fighter*, which told of his military training and what happened to him after he returned to northern Namibia as a combatant (Shityuwete 1990).

Such memoirs stressed the unity of the Namibian people under the banner of SWAPO, the popular commitment of the Namibian people to oust the South African oppressor and the heroic nature of the struggle against South African rule. Their publication was designed to help aid the struggle, not only by remembering what had happened but also by encouraging others to support it. As with most work produced in the years of struggle, they served a clear propaganda purpose. While it was widely accepted all over the world that the Namibian liberation struggle was a just one against racism and colonialism, this did not, of course, make such writing good history. It was not 'history' in any real meaning of that word, in that it did not attempt to present a rounded picture or explore the complexities and ambiguities of the struggle. One autobiography critical of SWAPO did appear as the country moved towards independence, but it was slight and as selective from its own perspective as the memoirs of others. It received little attention, not least because its author's party was virtually eliminated in the founding election of November 1989 (Shipanga 1989).

Perspectives after independence

If that, in brief summary, was the state of writing by Namibians about the liberation struggle while it was taking place, what of writing that looks back on the liberation struggle from a post-independence perspective? With the end of the struggle and the advent of independence in March 1990, one might have thought that there would no longer be the same concern by Namibians to show solidarity and to dismiss counter views. It might have been expected that writers would now try to understand what had happened with greater detachment and in fuller complexity. A body of academic literature might have emerged on the liberation struggle by scholars who had not themselves been involved in it and could therefore see it in new perspective. But none of this has happened.

Beyond a few seminar papers [6] and a study of the Cassinga massacre of 1978, the largest single atrocity of the entire apartheid era, by Annemarie Heywood (1996), no scholarly historical writing on the armed struggle has emerged from within Namibia. When more popular works are considered, it was perhaps not to be expected that those who had committed themselves over so many years to a cause would now be any less firm in their commitment to it, or be ready to change their views upon it. They now looked back to the armed conflict as a heroic episode that had brought the new nation into being. They were proud to have participated in that process. They had been socialised in a time of war to be disciplined and suspicious of contrary views, and when others began to advance such views, they were encouraged to close ranks in the face of what they saw as new challenges. While the armed conflict was now over, the struggle, it seemed, was continuing in new ways.

When the process leading to the first democratic election in November 1989 was getting under way, a group of those who had been detained by SWAPO in southern Angola returned to Windhoek after their release as part of the negotiated settlement providing for the transition to independence. On their return, they told of imprisonment and torture in the dungeons of Lubango. The SWAPO leadership had grudgingly admitted that mistakes had been made but would not agree to any enquiry into what had happened (Dobell 1996; Leys/Saul 2003). All SWAPO did was publish a list of those who had fallen in the struggle, with minimal information about the circumstances in which they had died (SWAPO 1996). While this publication was generally welcomed, the list was criticised for being so slight and incomplete, and in the book there was no admission that anyone had died in vain, no attempt to address the pain suffered by those who still did not know what had happened to those who had left to fight and had never returned (cf., NSHR 1996).[7] Some years previously, a group of those related to people who had disappeared had put together a brief account of 'A Struggle Betrayed' (Thiro-Beukes 1986), but it was left to outsiders, people who had been heavily involved in support of SWAPO and its struggle in the 1980s, to write substantial works that began to document what had happened.

Colin Leys and John Saul, Canadian academics who had campaigned for SWAPO for decades, now in the aftermath of independence presented Namibia's liberation struggle as having had negative as well as positive aspects: it was, the title of their book suggested, a 'Two-Edged Sword' (Leys/Saul 1995). Then Siegfried Groth, a German pastor who had worked closely with SWAPO, published *Namibia: The Wall of Silence: The Dark Days of the Liberation Struggle*. When Groth's book appeared, the Namibian

6. Those given at the conference on 'Public History, Forgotten History' held at the University of Namibia, Windhoek, August 2000, have not been published.

7. There was speculation that SWAPO would bring out a second, revised edition of *Their Blood Waters our Freedom*, but this has not appeared.

president, Sam Nujoma, appeared on state television to warn the nation against Groth's "false history."[8] More recent accounts that are highly critical of SWAPO have also been assembled externally. They include the memoirs of Keshii Pelao Nathanael, who now lives in Sweden. A member of the SWAPO Youth League, he had gone into exile, fought and been detained and tortured by SWAPO (Nathanael 2002). And Colin Leys with Susan Brown, now based at the Institute of Justice and Reconciliation in Cape Town, have published a collection of the reminiscences of 11 Namibian activists, only one of whom did not become a critic of SWAPO (Leys/Brown 2005).

In the Leys and Brown book, *Histories of Namibia*, only Ben Mulongeni, who went into exile in 1977 and then studied in Zambia and Bulgaria, plays down the ex-detainee issue. For him, the former PLAN chief of security, subsequently known as 'the butcher of Lubango' was "just a victim of the time he was living in" (ibid, 37). The others were involved in the 'detainee issue' in one or other way, or became critical of the way in which SWAPO sought to stifle any internal organisation that it did not control. Their stories usefully add to our knowledge of SWAPO's actions and authoritarianism, and so of the ambiguities of the struggle, even if the result is an unbalanced set of 'histories from Namibia,' for the collection is far from being a representative sample of those involved. And while such accounts can constitute valuable primary sources, they need to be read critically and sifted by scholars who can assess whether they are accurate in what they remember, or, say, the extent to which they exaggerate to make a point. The life histories reproduced in the Leys and Brown book are not so sifted, and the word 'histories' in the title of the book is therefore misleading in the sense that history should be the critical study of the past, for this is not such a study.

The same is true of writing about the past from other perspectives, whether Ellen Namhila's autobiographical memoir, *The Price of Freedom,* or the collection of brief accounts of the experiences of Namibians in the struggle and after published under the title *Speaking Out* (Becker 2005). Namhila's memoir told the fascinating story of how she left for southern Angola, was among those attacked by South African forces, and eventually settled in Finland. During the struggle she was taught that freedom would come from the barrel of the gun alone, but in her memoir she calls for the full history of the exile experiences of Namibians to be written (Namhila 1997:190, 195). *Speaking Out* includes the story of another woman who survived the Cassinga massacre and of the leading black Namibian journalist in the struggle period. While it is useful to have such accounts, it must be remembered that "the academic lens and personal perspectives of the interviewers and editors facilitates and influences how the life story is told" (Patel/Hirschsohn 2005:x). Autobiographies and life stories are selective in what they say, presenting an individual's point of view, often through the prism of a much later context, and therefore they need to be read critically.

Writing not critical of the now ruling party continued to suggest, as pre-independence writing had, identification between the ruling party, the armed struggle and the nation. Consider Ellen Namhila's recently published life of Kaxumba kaNdola, more commonly known, from being the first accused in the Pretoria terrorism trial of Namibians in 1968, as Eliaser Tuhadaleni, a founding member of SWAPO. When the first

---

8. *The Namibian*, 7 March 1996. Nujoma went on to accuse Christo Lombard, a theology professor who had defended Groth's work, as being an "apostle of apartheid" (ibid).

fighters returned to northern Namibia from training abroad in 1965, they reported to him, we are told by the veteran politician Toivo ya Toivo in the foreword, "because of his self-sacrificing nature, generosity, honesty, and dedication to the liberation struggle" (Namhila 2005:vii). In writing of his support for SWAPO, his long incarceration on Robben Island and his eventual release from imprisonment in 1985, Namhila has chosen to present the reader with huge chunks of primary material, whether from interviews or documentary sources. She does not make it clear on what basis she selected these or alert the reader to the dangers of relying on such sources, especially oral testimony. Her book is a valuable attempt to reconstruct the life of man who had been virtually forgotten, but it is a tribute to a hero and a legend, not a critical account.

In South Africa, many key participants have now written memoirs. The accounts by Ahmed Kathrada, Nelson Mandela and Mac Maharaj of how Mandela wrote what eventually became *Long Walk to Freedom* on Robben Island, and how it was smuggled out, differ, but access to archival documents is now able to reveal more than the writers knew when they penned their accounts and can help resolve differences in what they remembered (*Prisoner*, 2005:172–3). Such a process has not begun in Namibia, where stories, whether of heroes of the struggle or of those who suffered during it, remain unanalysed and are presented uncritically. Writing scholarly studies of the liberation struggle will of course remain very difficult when there is so little documentary material available. SWAPO's own archive, now housed in Windhoek, remains firmly closed to scholars, and there has been no hint of whether it will be opened, and on what conditions.

Nujoma and Namakalu

I turn now to two key books on Namibia's armed struggle: the one by the leading figure in that struggle, the founding president of SWAPO, Sam Nujoma, recently given the title of 'Father of the Nation' by the Namibian parliament, the other the first detailed account of PLAN's operations. Though Nujoma agreed in 1990 to have his life ghost written, the project faltered, but the publication in the mid-1990s of the books by Leys and Saul and Groth, which he and others saw as an attack on SWAPO's record in the struggle, must have encouraged him to bring out his own account to set the record straight from his perspective. His book takes the story of the liberation struggle to independence in March 1990. Unlike other memoirs, it not only draws upon Nujoma's own memory, but uses a considerable range of other accounts of the events it describes, a number of them, in Nujoma's eyes, by opponents in the struggle. Some of the later chapters read almost as if his main purpose was to update *To Be Born a Nation* by continuing the history of the armed struggle to its end.

Oswin Namakulu was trained in PLAN, but like Nujoma, the commander in chief, it seems that he did not engage in actual fighting himself. After holding administrative positions in SWAPO in exile, he returned to northern Namibia and began interviewing PLAN combatants to assemble a descriptive history of PLAN's activities designed explicitly to present what happened in the war from the perspective of those who fought against South Africa. His account ranges over the entire war, from the first armed clash between the two sides, the battle of Omugulu-gOmbashe on 26 August 1966, to the fighting in April 1989. He acknowledges that his book, and its lists of battles and attacks, is far from being comprehensive. Namakalu (2005:159–65) is strangely incomplete. Only in respect of a limited number of engagements does he go into detail. He tells us that he decided to include nothing on Cassinga because it has been written about elsewhere (p. viii). When he deals with the key battle of Cuito Cuanavale in 1987–88, he writes of the Cuban-Angolan forces but does not mention that SWAPO units fought alongside them. He estimates that 75% of his information on PLAN's combat missions from the late 1960s to the mid-1980s came from interviews, "SWAPO documents and PLAN operational reports" (p. viii). Unfortunately for the scholar, he gives no clue as to where these are to be found.

It is *Where Others Wavered*, however, that illustrates better than any other book the problems with much of the recent writing (cf., Saunders 2003; Du Pisani 2007). Its title comes from a statement Nujoma made in 1978, a key year in the Namibian struggle, a statement that he and others often repeated afterwards: "When the history of a free and independent Namibia is written one day, SWAPO will go down as having stood firm where others have wavered: that it sacrificed for the sacred cause of liberation where others have compromised." The title, then, clearly indicates the strong political and polemical purpose of Nujoma's book: to assert and substantiate the heroic role of SWAPO in bringing independence and freedom to Namibia, to praise those who stood firm and to condemn those who did not. Though the sub-title on the cover is 'My life in SWAPO and my participation in the liberation struggle of Namibia,' the book is more about SWAPO and its struggle than about Nujoma's own life and involvement. His identification with SWAPO, "the only effective liberation movement" (Nujoma 2001:267) was, and remains, complete: everything else is subordinated to that. Those who dissented are traitors, on the wrong side of history. His concern to condemn them is shown by his choosing a title that emphasises the wavering of others rather than his own steadfastness and determination.

If his memoir is to be believed, there was never any doubt in Nujoma's mind about the eventual triumph of his cause. His story is of a steady movement towards victory. "We pursued policy with vigour and determination until the final victory," he writes. "The national liberation war was increasingly effective. Every year we made more progress until 21 March 1990 when genuine freedom and independence were achieved" (Nujoma 2001:260). He remained convinced that SWAPO would inevitably defeat the South African Goliath (Nujoma 2001:151), and in the end, of course, was proved right in the sense that South Africa did withdraw and SWAPO was able to come to power. His account is hardly at all self-reflective. Much of it is about events that Nujoma was involved in, or connected to, rather than about his own experiences. There are long descriptive passages dealing with events that he was not present at and which he can have only heard about from others. There is hardly any of the personal detail that enlivens most autobiographies. There is no suggestion that his position as leader was ever under serious challenge, or that there were setbacks, or that any wrong decisions were made. There is hardly anything about the internal history of SWAPO in exile, or about his interaction with close friends or colleagues.

Though Nujoma has maintained since independence that the struggle continues in new forms, one might have expected that he would now view the armed struggle with a certain distance. He still, however, demonises 'the Boers' (racist whites) and cannot bring himself to admit, say, that militarily SWAPO was less effective in penetrating Namibia in the mid-1980s than it had been a few years before, or that there were ever any serious differences of views within SWAPO as to the most appropriate strategy to follow. While there is no doubt that the activities of PLAN were more extensive than the South Africans admitted, Nujoma exaggerates PLAN's military successes. It may have always had a presence in northern Namibia, but it did not have a mechanised brigade there, and PLAN combatants were not "effective and permanently fighting in all the regions inside Namibia at all times" (Nujoma 2001:271, 389).

Namakalu is more critical of mistakes made by PLAN. He admits that one of the early fighting units in northern Namibia was equipped only with axes and hunting knives and that others had no arms at all, that there was an acute shortages of medicines and food as well as weapons, and that though SWAPO's secretary of defence was ordered to open a second front in Angola at the Tanga conference, this was not done effectively (Namakalu 2005:12, 35, 45–6). He also mentions a number of friendly-fire incidents in which members of PLAN were killed and refers to the problems and suspicions caused by the Koevoet practice of posing as PLAN combatants, wearing PLAN uniforms and using "the same methods and approaches as genuine PLAN fighters" (Namakalu 2005:47, 108, 158). But despite such admissions, his book presents the war as a heroic one, and – as we will see – decisive in bringing about independence.

One of the weakest sections of Nujoma's book relates to the crisis of April 1989, when over 300 SWAPO fighters lost their lives in northern Namibia. Whereas by 1979 the forces of the Zimbabwean liberation armies had established a significant presence in the rural areas of Zimbabwe, PLAN had not been able to achieve anything comparable. Visiting Mugabe in Harare, Nujoma was, it seems, advised to tell his forces to insist that they should be placed in bases during the transitional period, as the Zimbabwean guerrilla forces were in 1979, despite the fact that there had been no agreement on SWAPO bases in Namibia in the transitional period. None of this is clarified in Nujoma's account, which blames the tragedy on the West and the South African foreign minister, Pik Botha. Nujoma believes that Botha persuaded the Reagan administration to reduce the size of the United Nations Transitional Assistance Group (UNTAG) force in Namibia, as a result of which there were no UN troops in the north on the day the Western plan was at last implemented. Nujoma implies that there was a conspiracy to provide a setting in which the PLAN fighters in northern Namibia could be massacred (Nujoma 2001:286, 395ff.) No-one who has made a detailed study of these events will be convinced by such an interpretation, which at a minimum fails to explain why the SWAPO leadership did not anticipate what might happen if there were no UN forces in place in the north when the armed PLAN fighters emerged.

When writing of the 1960s, Nujoma emphasises how important it was for him to assert the claims of South West Africa/Namibia to independence at a time when many lumped SWAPO with the African National Congress of South Africa and did not distinguish their separate freedom struggles against the same rulers. Again and again, he stresses the need in the 1970s and 1980s to reject any idea of a Bantustan solution for Namibia (e.g., Nujoma 2001:157) and to insist on 'genuine independence,' which meant, in his eyes, the total removal of South Africa from Namibia and SWAPO taking power. Very reluctantly, he and SWAPO had to accept in mid-1978 that Walvis Bay would not be included in the new Namibia and that its future would need to be negotiated after independence.

That SWAPO was the only Namibian party to engage in an armed struggle, and so in effect constituted the liberation movement, is one of the key ways in which the Namibian struggle differs from the Zimbabwean and other Southern African liberation struggles. From the mid-1960s, having decided not to launch an armed struggle, SWANU never posed any effective challenge, and yet SWAPO pressed to be recognised as the 'sole and authentic representative of the Namibian people,' and won such recognition, first from the Organisation of African Unity and then from the UN General Assembly (Nujoma 2001:157). Unlike leaders of other liberation movements in Southern Africa, Nujoma did not have to worry about being outflanked from the left or being overtaken by another organisation. He did not need to bargain with others and define positions to differentiate SWAPO from a rival. But in SWAPO there was never much space for democratic debate. The 'sole and authentic' doctrine caused many problems in the negotiations over the future of Namibia, for it seemed to suggest that SWAPO did not believe in the multiparty democracy it claimed it wanted to see installed in Namibia, and it buttressed the authoritarian tendencies seen in the ruling party after independence.

In perhaps his greatest distortion, Nujoma dismisses as of little account the detainee scandal of the early 1980s that did so much damage to SWAPO. He writes of SWAPO advancing "from strength to strength" in the late 1980s. All he says about the detainees is that their detention was legitimate, because they gave information to the South African Defence Force and so were in some sense responsible for the massacres at Shatotwa and Cassinga. He fails to deal with the allegation that the SWAPO leadership itself knew in advance of these raids but did not warn those in the camps. He merely says that "if we are accused of ill-treating detainees, this was very little compared to the killing, cruel torture and brutal treatment the apartheid South African regime inflicted on our people over so many years," and adds "we prefer to leave that sad history behind us and concentrate on national reconciliation ..." (Nujoma, 2001:357). No wonder, then, that in 2006, when war veterans protested in Windhoek that they had been forgotten, he was reported to have said that he would shoot any veterans who continued to demand more from the state (*Legalbrief,* 4 September 2006).

The centrality of the armed struggle in the years of exile meant that SWAPO became dominated by a military culture, strongly hierarchical, authoritarian and closed. This was aided by the almost constant rumours of spies at work and by evidence of actual spies. Nujoma devotes considerable space to the various traitors and spies who, he claims, infiltrated the movement over the decades. The deputy chief of SWAPO's military wing at the beginning of the armed struggle not only turned out to be an agent of the South African security forces but – even more astonishingly – was allowed to remain in SWAPO even after he had been exposed. It seems that he betrayed Toivo ya Toivo and others, who were to spend decades in jail, and was able to tip off the South Africans that the commander of SWAPO's military wing was crossing the Zambesi by boat, which led to his death in May 1967 (Nujoma 2001:163; Namakalu 2005:esp. 7, 13).

A decade later, Shipanga is the prime traitor and quisling, who worked "hand in hand with apartheid South Africa." All Nujoma says to substantiate this is to claim that Shipanga attempted to get West German support in a bid to take over the leadership

(Nujoma 2001:246). Nujoma allows no recognition of the possibility that Shipanga was also, to cite the title of his memoir, *In Search of Freedom*, nor does he acknowledge the damage done to the movement then and later by this episode, which, as Leys and Saul have shown in detail, arose from the disaffection of the Youth League leaders and the disillusionment of many of the fighters in the camps with the SWAPO leadership (Leys/Saul 1994). Of Shipanga and other 'reactionaries,' Nujoma merely says "we simply asked them to leave" (Nujoma 2001:247). He makes no mention of their detention first in Zambia and then in Tanzania. He seems to justify what was done to them by saying that their "numbers were very small. Fewer than a hundred were involved." He merely continues: "There was really no uproar at all ... the armed liberation struggle continued with intensity" (Nujoma 2001:247). So Nujoma fails to tackle the charges made against him and his organisation, but brushes them aside and provides a bland and highly distorted account that fits with SWAPO's refusal to deal with such issues since independence. Nujoma has added his authorial voice to the 'wall of silence' that SWAPO erected (cf., Leys/Saul 1994; Dobell 1996).

Sensitive to the charge that SWAPO was not democratic in its practices in exile, Nujoma makes the astonishing claim that in the exile years there were "democratic elections every 5 years for the leadership of the Party" (Nujoma 2001:246). But only two 'consultative' conferences took place in the decades of exile, and none at all in the 1980s, the years of the 'spy drama.' Suggesting that SWAPO was democratic in its practices in exile is an example of reading back into history what he wants to find there. As SWAPO has never encouraged open discussion within its ranks, it is not surprising to find no sense of debate in his book, of alternatives weighed, of difficult decisions taken. Critics are not only dismissed as waverers and traitors: he writes of "the elimination of some puppets like Chief Elifas" (Nujoma 2001:251) as if assassination was fully justified.

The armed struggle was decisive and victorious

Though Nujoma gives much space in his memoir to the intricacies of the diplomatic activity in which SWAPO engaged, for both him and Namakalu the armed struggle is presented as being decisive in winning the goal of independence. As the war was fought to free Namibia from South African occupation, and that goal was achieved in March 1990, it is easy to say that the war was victorious and to see those who fought it as responsible for that victory. But for all the symbolic significance of the armed struggle, was it the war itself that brought independence? Might it not even be that the way the war was fought contributed to the long delay before that goal was reached?

There is certainly much myth in the way Nujoma portrays the war. Omugulu-gOmbashe was not, as he portrays it, a military victory for the liberation forces (cf., Namhila 2005, especially 67), for the South African police attacked and routed the SWAPO guerrilla fighters. In August 1990, on the first occasion on which he and others could gather at the site of the battle after independence, he said: "Now it is a fact of history that the armed struggle initiated at this place became the decisive factor in bringing about freedom and independence." In his book he writes: "It was the armed liberation struggle that more than anything else motivated the Namibian people to support the struggle waged by SWAPO" (Nujoma 2001:268). Like Nujoma, Namakalu claims that, despite occasional setbacks, PLAN grew ever stronger and more effective and won victory after victory. His last page sums up the central problem with his book and Nujoma's. The whole page is devoted to this single sentence: "Glory to the Heroes and Heroines of the Namibian National Liberation Struggle" (Namakalu 2005:188).

Though South Africa would never have been persuaded to leave Namibia without the armed struggle, that struggle was not nearly as significant in bringing about independence as the works by Nujoma and Namakalu suggest. Only very recently has Nujoma begun to acknowledge that Namibians within the country who did not have guns also made a major contribution to the outcome (see Kössler 2007:382). And what he says in his autobiography of his almost ceaseless diplomatic activity while in exile is itself testimony to the significance of the role played by the international community and those in the outside world who gave SWAPO support.

Conclusion

Such works give partial, highly selective versions of the past, designed to help legitimise the present order. In not revealing more about the inner history of the struggle, they reflect the dominant culture of SWAPO, which is open only within circumscribed limits and is dismissive of critics. Namibia's armed struggle had its heroic aspects, but deserves to be written about dispassionately. Writing that suggests those who did not agree with the SWAPO leadership can be written out of history is propaganda, not history.

I have tried to show that much of the writing on the Namibian liberation struggle since independence has been as flawed as the polemical writing designed to further the struggle when it was still being waged. There is clearly the danger that in Namibia, as has happened in Zimbabwe, this kind of 'history' will become hegemonic and that a dogmatic line will be laid down concerning what happened in the past, allowing no alternative and critical voices. Fortunately, in the Namibian case, such voices, if muted, continue to be heard and there is still some tolerance of alternative perspectives. Two archival/digital projects now under way may help promote scholarly writing on the liberation struggle from within the country.[9] Unfortunately for the writing of such history, the history department at the University of Namibia, always short-staffed, has never been headed by a professorial Namibian specialist. Peter Katjavivi became the University's first vice-chancellor, then followed Dr Zed Ngavirue, another Oxford graduate, in taking up a diplomatic post.[10] Namibia has had no Terence Ranger-like figure to help galvanise scholarship within the country from outside. One of the consequences is that much of the history of the liberation struggle, and especially how it impacted 'ordinary' people in the various regions of Namibia, remains to be told. Will the future bring a flowering of academic and critical work on the Namibian liberation struggle? Or will Namibia follow the Zimbabwean road, with those in power seeking to replace anything

---

9. The Aluka digital project (www.aluka.org and Isaacman et al, 2005) and the Archives of Anti-colonial Resistance and the Liberation Struggle project (Archives: 2005).

10. I do not mention Zedekia Ngavirue's 1972 thesis, not published until 1997, because *Political Parties and Interest Groups in South West Africa (Namibia)* did not concern the post-1966 armed struggle.

worthy of the name of history by the kind of propaganda that Ranger generously calls "patriotic history"? Time will tell.

References

Archives of Anti-Colonial Resistance and the Liberation Struggle, (2005), *Annual Report 2003–04*. Windhoek: AACRLS

Becker, Barbara (2005), *Speaking Out: Namibians Share their Perspectives on Independence*. Windhoek: Out of Africa

Benson, Mary (1966), *The African Patriots: The Struggle for a Birthright*. Harmondsworth: Penguin

Bhebe, Ngwabi (1999), *The ZAPU and ZANU Guerrilla Warfare and the Evangelical Lutheran Church in Zimbabwe*. Gweru: Mambo

— (2004), *Simon Vengayi Muzenda and the Struggle for and Liberation of Zimbabwe*. Gweru: Mambo

Dobell, Lauren (1996), 'Namibia's Wall of Silence,' *Southern Africa Report*, 11 (4) July

Du Pisani, Andre (2007), 'Memory Politics in "Where Others Wavered. The Autobiography of Sam Nujoma",' *Journal of Namibian Studies*, I (1)

First, Ruth (1963), *South West Africa*. Harmondsworth: Penguin

Groth, Siegfried (1995), *Namibia: The Wall of Silence: The Dark Days of the Liberation Struggle*. Cape Town: David Philip

Haarhoff, Dorian (1989), *The Wild South West. Frontier Myths and Metaphors in Literature Set in Namibia, 1760–1988*. Johannesburg: Witwatersrand University Press

Heitman, Helmoed-Romer (1990), *South Africa's War in Angola*. Gibraltar: Ashanti

Herbstein, Denis and John Evenson (1989), *The Devils are Among Us: The War for Namibia*. London and New Jersey: Zed

Heywood, Anne-Marie (1996), *The Cassinga Event*. 2nd ed. Windhoek: National Archives of Namibia

Isaacman, Allen, Premesh Lalu and Thomas Nygren (2005), 'Digitization, History, and the Making of a Postcolonial Archive of Southern African Liberation Struggles: the Aluka Project,' *Africa Today*, 52 (2)

Katjavivi, Peter (1986), 'The Rise of Nationalism in Namibia and its International Dimensions,' unpublished D.Phil. thesis, Oxford University

—(1988), *A History of Resistance in Namibia*. London: James Currey for UNESCO

— et al. (eds), (1989), *Church and Liberation in Namibia*. London and Winchester: Pluto

Kössler, Reinhart, (2007), 'Facing a Fragmented Past. Memory, Culture and Politics in Namibia,' *Journal of Southern African Studies*, 33 (2) June 2007, pp. 362–82

Leys, Colin and Susan Brown (eds), (2005), *Histories of Namibia*. London: Merlin

Leys, Colin and John Saul (1994), 'Liberation without Democracy; the SWAPO Crisis of 1976,' *Journal of Southern African Studies*, 20 (1) March

— (eds), (1995), *Namibia's Liberation Struggle. The Two-Edged Sword*. London: James Currey

— (2003), 'Lubango and After: "Forgotten History" as Politics in Contemporary Namibia,' *Journal of Southern African Studies*, 29 (2) June

Mbumba, Nangolo and Norbert Noisser (1988), *Namibia in History. Junior Secondary History Book*. London: Zed

Melber, Henning (2005), 'Namibia's Past in the Present: Colonial Genocide and Liberation Struggle in Commemorative Narratives,' *South African Historical Journal*, 54, pp. 98–111

Mercer, Denis (ed.), (1989), *Breaking Contract. The Story of Vinnia Ndadi*. London: IDAF (first published in Canada, 1974)

Moleah, Alfred T. (1983), *Namibia. The Struggle for Liberation*. Wilmington: Delaware

Namakalu, Oswin (2005), *Armed Liberation Struggle. Some Accounts of PLAN's Combat Operations*. Windhoek: Gamsberg Macmillan

Namhila, Ellen (1997), *The Price of Freedom*. Windhoek: New Namibia Books

Namhila, Ellen Ndeshi (2005), *Kaxumba kaNdola. Man and Myth – The Biography of a Barefoot Soldier. Lives, Legacies, Legends*. Vol. 2. Basel: Basler Afrika Bibliographien

Nathanael, Keshii Pelao (2002), *A Journey to Exile: The Story of a Namibian Freedom Fighter*. Aberystwyth: Sosiumi

National Society for Human Rights (1996), *Critical Analysis. SWAPO's 'Book of the Dead'*. Windhoek: NSHR

Norval, Morgan (1989), *Death in the Desert: The Namibian Tragedy*. Washington: Selous Foundation

Patel, Y. and P. Hirschsohn (2005), (ed.), *Married to the Struggle. 'Nanna' Liz Abrahams Tells Her Life Story*. Bellville: n.p. *A Prisoner in the Garden. Opening Nelson Mandela's Prison Archive*. Johannesburg: Penguin

Ranger, Terence (2004), 'Nationalist Historiography, Patriotic History, and the History of the Nation: the Struggle Over the Past in Zimbabwe,' *Journal of Southern African Studies*, 30 (2) June, pp. 215–34.

Saunders, Christopher (2003), 'Liberation and Democracy: A Critical Reading of Sam Nujoma's "Autobiography"' in H. Melber (ed.), *Re-examining Liberation in Namibia. Political Cultures since Independence*. Uppsala: Nordiska Afrikainstitutet

— (2006), 'Review Article', *Social Dynamics*, December

Shipanga, Andreas (1989), *In Search of Freedom: The Andreas Shipanga Story as Told to Sue Armstrong*. Gibraltar: Ashanti

Shityuwete, Helao (1990), *Never Follow the Wolf: The Autobiography of a Namibian Freedom Fighter*. London: Kliptown Books

Steenkamp, William (1989), *South Africa's Border War*. Gibraltar: Ashanti

Stiff, Peter (2004), *The Covert War: Koevoet Operations in Namibia, 1979–89*. Alberton: Galago

SWAPO, Department of Information and Publicity (1978), *Information on SWAPO: An Historical Profile*. Lusaka: SWAPO

—(1981), *To Be Born a Nation*. London: Zed

SWAPO (1996), *Their Blood Waters Our Freedom: Glory to the Heroes and Heroines of the Namibian Liberation Struggle*. Windhoek: SWAPO Party

Temu, A. and B. Swai (1981), *Historians and Africanist History: A Critique*. London: Zed

Thiro-Beukes, Erika, Attie Beukes and Hewat Beukes (1986), *Namibia. A Struggle Betrayed*. Rehoboth: Akasia

Vigne, R. (1975), *A Dwelling Place of Our Own: The Story of the Namibian Nation*, 2nd ed. London: IDAF

Wilson, Monica and Leonard Thompson (1969), *The Oxford History of South Africa*. Vol. I. Oxford: Oxford University Press

Wood, Brian (ed.), (1988), *Namibia 1884–1994: Readings on Namibia's History and Society*. London: Namibia Support Committee

Ya Otto, John (1982), *Battlefront Namibia*. London: Heinemann

Commercial land reforms in postcolonial Namibia
What happened to liberation struggle rhetoric?

Phanuel Kaapama

Namibia has a total geographical area in excess of 800 000 square kilometres and a population estimated in 2007 at two million people. Although the country has a very low population density, most of this land mass comprises semi-arid rangeland, with low rates of rainfall and infertile soils, making it unsuitable for large-scale agricultural production. This has created a condition of land scarcity that has over the years remained a source of social tension and indirectly a potential source of violent political conflict. Access to and control of agricultural land ownership have equally remained a key feature in the Namibian processes of social differentiation and state formation from precolonial times through the era of colonial rule. Moreover, some scholars and practitioners share the perspective that given the structural sociopolitical and economic legacies from the past, land remains at the heart of the postcolonial processes of state consolidation, in particular the realisation of the objectives of the policies of national reconciliation and nation-state building.

These views are predicated upon a number of factors, such as the fact that the land use and ownership patterns bequeathed to the postcolonial state continue to be manifestations of the legacy of colonial injustice perpetuated against the indigenous populations by successive colonial administrations since the 1880s. These injustices resulted from the fact that the policies and programmes of these governments were geared to ensuring that the patterns of agricultural land use and ownership during this historical episode reflected a number of socioeconomic distortions. For instance, a large part of the country's best agricultural land, comprising ranches and farms, was exclusively owned by white commercial farmers. A 1976 study cited in a UNIN (1985:31–2) report made the following two observations in this regard. First, that 48% of these commercial farms were owned by absentee landlords who visited periodically and left day-to-day operations and management in the hands of white local supervisors. Second, the report alluded to the "over-concentrated" agricultural land ownership structure, in terms of which it was estimated that in the early 1970s close to 40% of the commercial farms in the eastern cattle-rearing district of Gobabis were owned by 16% of that area's farmers.

Another factor contributing to the heightened status of the postcolonial land reform agenda was the fact that mass mobilisation and public galvanisation campaigns of the forces of liberation were premised not only on ending colonialism as a system of foreign domination, but also strongly pledged the creation of an environment that would enable the disenfranchised people of Namibia to engage in socially just processes of national development. Such environment was largely sketched in terms of prioritising measures to redress the inequalities created by Namibia's colonial past, such as the skewed distribution of commercial agricultural land ownership.

The purpose of this chapter is to revisit the thrust of the liberation struggle's political and economic ideological outlooks with a view to contrasting these critically against the policies and programmes being pursued by the postcolonial Namibian government. In this process, the chapter will reflect critically on the dominant political and economic discourses and their respective influences on the content of commercial agricultural land reform.[1]

Articulation of the land question in the context of the nationalist struggle for liberation

The South West Africa Peoples' Organisation (SWAPO), founded on 29 April 1960, became the leading movement in the nationalist struggle for the liberation of Namibia. SWAPO emerged out of the Owamboland People's Organisation (OPO), which was founded in 1957 to protest against the deplorable working conditions in the contract labour system that was enforced by the South African colonial government in Namibia. SWAPO waged its nationalist struggle on three fronts. First, there was the political front based on the political mass mobilisation of the Namibian people in support of its cause for the liberation of Namibia. Second, there was the diplomatic front that culminated in SWAPO's recognition by the UN in 1972 as the 'sole and authentic' representative of the Namibian people's aspirations for independence and statehood. Third, there was the military front, launched on 26 August 1966.

SWAPO adopted a number of ideological blueprints to provide political guidance to the struggle, as well as to guide the articulation of its vision of the postcolonial processes of economic reconstruction and national development. Among these, the most instructive was the 1976 SWAPO Political Programme, which was akin to the main body of contemporary socialist thought. It explicitly stated that one of the goals of the movement was to unite all Namibian people, particularly the working class, the peasantry and progressive intelligentsia into a vanguard party capable of safeguarding national independence, as well as of building a classless and non-exploitative society based on the ideals and principles of scientific socialism (Kiljunen 1981:185, 189). In this context, classlessness was explained "as a social arrangement that requires the fundamental change of thought, custom and approach to the ownership of the means of production and decisions as to the distribution of the collective output of society" (UNIN 1985:23).

SWAPO predicated its embrace of the socialist ideological outlook upon its perception that the colonial practices and values in the territory were based on the degrading principles of racial discrimination and remorseless economic exploitation of the black working class and peasantry, practices entrenched through the mechanism of apartheid capitalism. These colonial socioeconomic practices ensured the perpetuation of a vicious

---

1. The text is an extract from my PhD project with the University of Witwatersrand in Johannesburg/South Africa, which is jointly funded by the University of Namibia and the Volkswagen Foundation's Funding Initiative for Collaborative Research in Sub-Saharan Africa.

circle of poverty and deplorable living conditions for the black majority, who were seen merely as tools for the maximisation of profit for the colonial economy, and could be discarded when they were deemed no longer useful for that purpose. In view of these negative images, SWAPO argued that the free market system was particularly unsuited to the postcolonial process of national reconstruction. Hence, in the quest to reverse the above socioeconomic patterns of colonial exploitation it was deemed imperative for the government of an independent Namibia to pursue development strategies capable of securing the full well-being and all-round development of all the Namibian people (UNIN 1985:1, 24).

Angula (1990:34) observed that the peasantry constituted the real force capable of resisting the forces of colonialism, given their relatively independent means of livelihood (in comparison with urban workers). Thus the former constituted the decisive force in the progress and subsequent outcome of the struggle for national liberation. Consequently, it comes as no surprise that SWAPO's economic development blueprint gave extensive prominence to the transformations required to stimulate the development of rural areas. For instance, the UNIN (1985:36) report stressed that the systems of agricultural land ownership and organisational structure in independent Namibia would be influenced primarily by a political ideology oriented towards ending the colonial structure and modes of production based on the exploitation of indigenous African peasants and farm labourers by white settler farmers. In this regard, the report proclaimed that under the SWAPO-led government of an independent Namibia the state would become the absolute owner of all agricultural land, although there was to be relative accommodation of a number of other forms of ownership of the means of agricultural production.

The stated long-term goal of the postcolonial SWAPO-led government was the establishment of fully fledged state farms based on the model of large-scale socialist farming enterprises, in which the means of production and the resultant output would be owned by the state. This form of ownership was deemed particularly suitable for a number of reasons: first, in the context of specialised activities such as plant and/or animal breeding, as well as seed, horticultural and nursery production; second, state ownership would be in the best interests of the country by ensuring the quality of agricultural export commodities and the cost-effectiveness of their production; and third, reshaping the agricultural system would achieve greater social equity. The report was cognisant of the widespread failure of state farming in other African countries: hence it advocated safeguarding against potential pitfalls by providing for the necessary management skills and the political mobilisation of the peasantry (UNIN, 1985:60–1).

The second set of agricultural land use and ownership patterns proposed in the SWAPO blueprint were cooperatives based on the combination of private ownership of land with emphasis on joint cultivation and/or sharing of farm support services, as well as collectives and communes. It was argued that these forms of ownership would serve as the nucleus for integrated social and economic development, since they were deemed to embody higher forms of political and economic organisation in which the means of production and patterns of distribution of outputs were designed in ways that enabled realisation of benefits for the whole community. Moreover, these forms of collective ownership were described as more favourable to the reversal of the colonial socioeconomic relations based on exploitation, as well as for provision of large resource bases for accumulation from below. However, the document was also cautious about the prospects for success of production and distribution cooperation based on traditional communalism. It pointed out, in this regard, that in some transitional societies the means of ownership readily fell under the control of emerging political and economic elites, who might be inclined to manipulate the transitional system for their parochial self-aggrandisement at the expense of the welfare of the general society. Moreover, the document placed particular emphasis on the need to balance the spirit of group solidarity with the concept of individual responsibility. Consequently, it advocated raising the sociopolitical consciousness of the community as a whole through educational, political and organisational self-reliance mechanisms (UNIN 1985:62–4).

The third form of agricultural land ownership proposed in the UNIN (1985:64) economic development blueprint for an independent Namibia was individual family farms on land units leased from local communities. In this regard, rights of ownership were to vest in individuals and could be passed on from one heir to another. The report gave cognisance to both the advantages and drawbacks of such a smallholder sector, by citing its most significant strength as the ability to provide higher yields, as well as to generate significant employment in comparison with the capital intensive large-scale agricultural production. On the negative side, it was noted that this form of ownership tends to be incapable of ensuring an optimal combination of resources adequate credit and long-term capital, and tends to experience managerial and entrepreneurial weakness. The report, however, rightly noted that some of these weaknesses are attributable to the lack of appropriate technical packages, partly because of inadequate adaptive research on this form of agricultural land ownership and use.

The SWAPO blueprint, however, also alluded to a number of potential constraints on the realisation of the radical economic transformation programme envisaged by the liberation movement. These included the fact that the postcolonial government was bound to inherit an entrenched and sophisticated capitalist system, with an ingrained racist character and in all likelihood underpinned by diametrically opposed forces directed from inside and outside the country. It therefore noted that although the broad political framework would immediately change at independence, inherited institutional arrangements, with their goals, structures, methodologies, rules and personnel might persist in the reinforcement of existing socioeconomic disparities (UNIN, 1985:24–5).

In view of these potential constraints, the documents proposed structuring the post-independence efforts for national reconstruction in three phases. In the immediate post-independence period (the first year of independence), the attention of the postcolonial government would be primarily on instituting appropriate contingency measures to mitigate the impact of possible impediments and obstructions from the retreating pro-colonial forces. For instance, in the context of land, the report hinted at the possible mass exodus of white farmers. Consequently, a two-pronged strategy was envisaged. First, measures would be instituted for the immediate reversion of abandoned land to the state, to be administered either as state farms, cooperatives and collectives and/or a combination of these options. Second, the new government would engage in dialogue with the departing white farmers to ensure the smooth transfer of ownership. Such dialogue could entail offering incentives and compensation packages to farmers who handed over their ranges intact to the incoming administration. However, the report noted that SWAPO was fully aware that this strategy might create room for the white farmer community to advance unreasonable demands that might subvert progress towards a non-racial and non-exploitative society. Moreover, it cautioned that these short-term measures might lead to delay in formulating and implementing parallel long-term strategies to realise a desirable state of socioeconomic affairs. Nevertheless, the report gave an assurance that "a SWAPO government was unlikely to accede to any demand that compromises its social policy" (UNIN, 1985:26–7, 55, 56, 59).

It was expected that the second phase, covering the medium-term timeframe (the first five years of independence), would see government's attention shift towards the introduction of measures to realise social justice in the context of a broad-based non-exploitative agricultural development strategy. In this regard, the report noted that:

> … since the colonial structure and mode of production were based on the exploitation of the Africans by the white settler farmers … any continuation of extreme inequalities with minor reforms would … manifestly fail to meet popular expectations forged over decades of suffering and anti-colonial struggle.

Therefore the key objective of SWAPO's economic development was the total transformation of the undesirable historical, structural, ideological and political parameters that had, over the years, led to the perpetuation of conditions of socioeconomic underdevelopment. It envisaged that the necessary structural changes would be undertaken in the context of a comprehensive rural development strategy with a view to restoring the land to the tillers. It was also envisaged that these undertakings would effect a series of positive changes in the living standards of the low-income rural masses. Furthermore, the report cautioned against the emergence of a privileged bureaucratic class and advocated deliberate measures to safeguard against the situation elsewhere in postcolonial Africa where prominent politicians, public servants and urban-based economic elites manipulating the system to appropriate large areas of the best farming land to themselves (UNIN, 1985:27–8, 56).

The third phase (covering the timeframe beyond the first five years of independence) was to be devoted to achieving long-term growth, as well as the full realisation of the objectives of social and distributive justice. This was to be done on the basis of a series of systematic schemes to adjust incentives, land tenure systems, agricultural production patterns and farm inputs, as well as by organising the peasantry into associations, cooperatives and other economic group activities.

The nature of the independence transition and its implications for land reforms

After the successful implementation of UN Security Council Resolution 435 in 1989, which paved the way for the independence of Namibia (eventually attained on 21 March 1990), SWAPO, having won the highest number of votes in the 1989 transitional national elections, established the first postcolonial Namibian government.

However, as the UNIN (1985:25) report had correctly anticipated, the manner in which independence was attained had major implications for the implementation of the transformation-oriented socioeconomic development agenda envisaged by the liberation movement. In particular, the report noted that the direction and progress of the postcolonial rural development initiatives would hinge on the extent to which the incoming government had the wherewithal to implement its declared political commitments to eradicate injustices, inequality and exploitation (UNIN, 1985:55).

In this regard, the nature of the independence transitional process placed a number of constraints on the pursuit of postcolonial transformation in the domain of commercial agricultural land as envisaged in the SWAPO economic and social blueprint. For one thing, the strategies outlined in SWAPO's economic development blueprint were overly premised on the anticipated mass exodus of the white population and the subsequent abandonment of land. However, because of the nature of the dynamics that unfolded during the transition to independence and its immediate aftermath, only a handful of white farmers left the country.

Second, another key factor in the transition to independence that reputedly precluded pursuance of the radical socioeconomic transformation envisaged by SWAPO was the Security Council's imposition of the 1982 constitutional principles. These represented a number of constitutional preconditions for an independent Namibia that would have to be met if the country was to be admitted into the community of independent nations. Thus, article 16 (1) of the constitution of the Republic of Namibia states that:

> All persons shall have the right in any part of Namibia to acquire, own and dispose of all forms of immovable or movable property individually or in association with others and to bequeath their property to their heirs or legatees: provided that Parliament may by legislation prohibit or regulate as it deems expedient the right to acquire property by persons who are not Namibian citizens.

However, article 16(2) further states that: "The state or a competent body or organ authorized by law may expropriate property in the public interest subject to the payment of just compensation, in accordance with requirements and procedures to be determined by Act of Parliament."

Thus, as cautioned in the UNIN report (1985:55), the post-independence government would only be able to institute its anticipated transformatory agenda if the post-independence constitutional framework was exclusively formulated and adopted by the representatives of the Namibian people, acting freely, without preconditions that entrenched the rights of private ownership of the principal means of production. Therefore, in the eyes of the descendants of the victims of settler colonialism the international community's imposition of the 1982 constitutional principles is seen as an alibi to safeguard vested socioeconomic interests that were established through colonial theft and plunder and as providing an inappropriate basis for pursuing meaningful national reconciliation based on principles of restorative justice and for promoting equitable and sustainable national development processes. Proponents of this view draw on the observation by Moyo and Hall (2004:2) that while some countries with historic problems over land were supported by their former colonial masters to resolve these disputes, reparation and restitution for colonial losses in Africa have not been adequately addressed either academically or in the aid packages that are extended to these countries. The key players in the Western Contact Group that sponsored the 1982 principles have come under a barrage of criticism for having acted in bad faith by clandestinely prioritising the protection of the vested interests of their economically privileged land-owning kith and kin.

It is equally important to acknowledge that the Namibian transition to independence coincided with the ascendance of the neoliberal governance model. Not only was this model seen as a viable idiom for state design and reconstruction, but also its adoption became a prerequisite for the accommodation of emerging and/or reformed states within the context of the international politics of development aid, aid that was instantaneously needed to kick-start their reconstruction and development processes (Okoth-Ogendo, 2000:46–7). Thus, the need to embrace the principle of economic neo-liberalism is said to have arisen from these geopolitical shifts at the global level.

Perhaps in anticipation of these constraints, the central message of the SWAPO political programme was significantly watered down. The SWAPO election manifesto (1989:1–2) for the crucial 1989 transitional elections embraced the ideals of solidarity, freedom and justice as the beacons to guide the movement towards the future and constituted the thrust of SWAPO's philosophy of government. The document elaborated on these ideals as follows. Solidarity: in view of the fact that the struggle was not only to liberate the black majority from colonial domination but also to emancipate the whites from the narrow and dehumanising confines of class and race privilege, the SWAPO government pledged to institute "concrete actions to promote fraternal and human social relations, in particular to address the essential needs of all Namibian people who find themselves in a difficult social and economic plight." Freedom: SWAPO pledged that a SWAPO-led government would uphold the wide array of democratic rights and freedoms, including the right to property, and went on further to state that "in a liberated Namibia under a SWAPO led government, freedom will mean an opportunity for all Namibian people to realise their potential … and [will direct] the development of our society in a way that creates the necessary material requirements and achieves higher forms of social consciousness." Justice: The manifesto was highly critical of the policies and social practices perpetuated by the colonial ruling class, which it accused of being "responsible for the division of the Namibian society into two distinct social groups: the landless and property-less black majority, on the one hand, and the propertied and privileged white minority, on the other." On this basis, it committed a SWAPO-led government to the task of ensuring that social justice and equality for all would be the fundamental principle governing the decision-making process in an independent Namibia. The manifesto further stated that "in order to bring about social justice and heal the wounds of colonial oppression, the SWAPO led government will not only restore the Namibian people's lost political and legal rights, but will also effect a fundamental social, industrial and economic change."

With regard to land reform, the 1989 manifesto reaffirmed the movement's commitment to redressing the imbalances created by colonial policies of land allocation on a racial basis, but also made provision for private land ownership in addition to the three forms of land ownership stipulated in the UNIN economic blueprint cited earlier (SWAPO 1989:9–10).

The implications of these ideological changes were explained by the then SWAPO secretary of information and publicity and later minister of information and broadcasting, Hidipo Hamutenya, in an address to the Windhoek regional conference of the Namibia National Students Organisation (NANSO) two months before independence (January 1990). He affirmed SWAPO's conviction that socialism was "seen and embraced by the victims of oppression and exploitation as the only saviour which can deliver them from the hardships imposed by colonialism." He noted, however, that the prospects for socialist transformation in Africa and in particular Namibia did not appear that bright at that time. He predicated these doubts on the fact that the goal of socialist transformation and the application of socialist concepts to African situations had suffered from both theoretical inadequacies and practical drawbacks. These had led to the adoption of notions such as African socialism "which are used to cover up the contradiction between the politicians' public espousal of socialism and the lack of it with regard to the economic policies of African countries, which call themselves socialist." However, he insisted that there were prospects for and the promise of successfully pursuing the desired socioeconomic transformation, provided the right foundations were laid. In particular, he strongly refuted claims that socialism and democracy were inherently irreconcilable by insisting that the latter needed to be an essential part of the former. Hence, he argued, the democratisation of Namibian society was necessary before the process of socialist transformation could commence.[2]

Postcolonial commercial agricultural land reforms: Prospects and challenges

The 1991 national conference on the land question

Immediately after the attainment of independence, the new Namibian government convened the landmark 1991 National Conference on the Land Question. It was attended by 500 delegates representing the broad spectrum of sociopolitical, economic and cultural interests from all corners of the country. The purpose of the conference was to provide a consultative platform for fostering national consensus on the volatile issue of postcolonial land reforms. This was done with a view to providing, based on broader public input, a solid basis for the formulation of policy on land reform and the preparation of a programme of action.

The conference adopted 24 recommendations in the form of consensus resolutions that have since served as fundamental guiding principles for government policy. It was noted by Harring and Odendaal (2002:31) that although these recommendations were not legally binding on the Namibian government, they nevertheless have remained highly influential in the shaping of all subsequent major land reform principles, policies and programmes.

The consensus resolutions included a statement acknowledging that "there was injustice concerning the acquisition of land in the past and something practicable must be done to rectify the situation." Other consensus resolutions included the adoption of the principle of Willing-Seller Willing-Buyer (WSWB), which according to Moyo et al. (2004:1) implies that those holding land ownership rights retain full discretion in deciding when and how to make their land available for sale, while prospective buyers (be they individuals or the government acting on behalf of the state) can only contemplate acquiring commercial agricultural land when it is offered for sale. Hence, under the WSWB regime of agricultural land reform, the rights and interests of existing landown-

---

2. 'Socialism Can Work: But We First Need to Democratize Our Society,' *The Namibian,* 15 January 1990.

ers are fully protected, as they are neither compelled to sell against their will nor at a price with which they are not fully satisfied.

However, it was noted by Latiff (2005:1) that the WSWB principles are a value-laden concept referring to an imaginary ideal rather than actual practice. The meaning of the concept will be influenced by the context within which it is applied. As a result, the application of WSWB principle can often become an ideological battleground by assuming the status of a non-negotiable issue among landowning classes and becoming an object of contempt for the landless and their sympathisers.

Some commentators have noted that in the Namibian context the decision of the land conference regarding the adoption of WSWB derived from Article 16 of the Namibian constitution. This would account for its subsequent infusion into the Agricultural (Commercial) Land Act (Act No. 6 of 1995), which structures the legal processes for the redistribution of commercial land in Namibia. However, the Act reserved government's preferential rights to purchase land that comes on to the market at the expense of other bidders who may be willing to pay a higher price or be the seller's buyer of choice. However, this provision was not fully adhered to, as it was circumvented by some land owners who opted to convert their farms into business entities (e.g., closed corporations) and later traded them as a corporate concession to preferred buyers, including foreign nationals. The loophole was addressed in the Second Commercial Agricultural Land Reform Amendment Act.

The provision that accords preferential rights of purchase to the state has come in for criticism especially from propertied interest groups and neoliberal economists, who construe it as hindering free trade in agricultural land and blame it for preventing the realisation of the real monetary value of the land by sale or by bonding at the bank. Proponents of this view argue that if one takes all farms in Namibia, about 5,000 at 5,000 hectares each at a price of N$ 500 per hectare in the year 2006, their combined value would be about N$ 12.5 bn. However, if ownership of this land could be traded freely without with land reform constraints between any willing-seller and any willing-buyer from anywhere, the same land would be valued at N$ 50 bn. It is further argued that the negative impacts of these constraints are also manifested in the reluctance of potential investors to put their money in eco-tourism and other land-based business ventures, for fear that they will not be allowed to sell the land and all its added fixed assets for the highest price possible. As a result, agricultural land reform stands accused of having created a situation whereby "the largest amount of capital available for the country's prosperity remains locked away in untradable land."[3]

The suitability of the WSWB principle has come under increasing scrutiny from those sympathising with landless groups, who blame it for resulting in procrastination in the land reform process in view of the apparent reluctance of landowners to dispose of their land to the state for the resettlement of landless peasants and farm workers. Those sharing this concern reiterate the view that their apprehensions concerning the WSWB principle cannot be taken lightly, since the same principle has failed spectacularly in Zimbabwe, where it operated for close to two decades after independence. The Southern African Regional Poverty Network (SARPN) (2003:8–9) attributed this failure to the

---

3. 'Multimillionaire Dreams of Turning Namibia into a Game Park,' *The Namibian,* 14 September 2006.

fact that although the willing-buyer side of the equation was there most of the time, progress was hampered by the absence of the willing-seller side of the bargain.

In this regard, Kaumbi (2004:93) took issue with the argument that the WSWB principle derived from the Namibian constitution by pointing out that the relevant article expressed itself on the issue of the payment of fair and just compensation where private property is expropriated by the state, and therefore does not mention the WSWB principle. He further reasoned that the mere fact that the Namibian constitution makes provision for the state to expropriate private property where such action is deemed to be in the public interest in itself signifies a departure from the WSWB principles defined above. He thus concludes that the attribution of WSWB to the constitution, one of the foremost reasons for the lack of timely implementation of necessary structural changes to the landownership pattern, could be construed as a blatant misinterpretation of the constitution. Harring et al. (2002:11) share this view by noting that article 16 of the constitution does not require WSWB, for it clearly sanctions expropriation of land without regard to the willingness of individual sellers. Furthermore, they hint that article 16 must also be read in the context of the constitutional obligation to affirmative action, as stated in Article 23(2):

> Nothing contained in Article 10 hereof shall prevent Parliament from enacting legislation providing directly or indirectly for the advancement of persons within Namibia who are socially, economically or educationally disadvantaged by past discriminatory laws or practices, or for implementation of policies and programmes aimed at redressing social, economic or educational imbalances in the Namibian society arising out of discriminatory laws or practices …

This apparent discrepancy is a probable reflection of the delicate political ground the government was treading in the process leading to the passage of the Commercial Agricultural Land Reform Act, in particular its need to keep the confidence in the economy of commercial farmers and potential investors.

The UNIN (1985:55–6) report gave the assurance that SWAPO was not only aware of, but also prepared to deal with the transitional pitfalls that could result in the manipulation of the system by those yielding economic power with a view to retaining control over the means of production. A SWAPO government, it pledged, "was unlikely to accede to any demand that compromises its social policy." The opposite, however, seems to be the case. Although the WSWB principle has been hailed by some powerful international institutions and their local proxies, it has remained a thorn in the flesh of those whose ancestors lost land to the settler colonialism pursued by successive colonial administrations and of all those who engaged in and/or supported the nationalist struggle for the liberation of Namibia. Rather than helping to resolve conflicting claims and interests in the agricultural land reform process, the application of WSWB principles seems to have solidified social tensions between those benefiting from the status quo and those who sees themselves as victims of the perpetuation and sanctioning of colonial land theft.

The land resettlement programme

At independence, the Namibian government initiated the land resettlement programme under the auspices of the Ministry of Lands, Resettlement and Rehabilitation (MLRR). This was the agency entrusted with acquiring land on behalf of the state for the resettlement of landless small-scale farmers on a leasehold basis. The operational procedure of this scheme is rather simple, in that upon the state's acquisition of commercial agricultural farmland the deed of ownership is registered in the name of MLRR, which assumes responsibility for regulating the property rights in respect of the land in question. The programme seems to be primarily informed by a welfarist slant on social reforms, in the sense that it is undertaken mainly with the view to providing previously disadvantaged persons with the indirect means for acquiring agricultural land. The primary rationale of this programme is to facilitate upliftment of the beneficiaries so they can achieve acceptable levels of social and economic development in order to support themselves (Harring et al., 2002:99). Thus,in view of its underlying principles, it may be concluded that of the two postcolonial commercial agricultural land reform initiatives, the land resettlement programme seems to come closest to the three forms of agricultural land ownership envisaged in the SWAPO economic blueprint for an independent Namibia.

In order to illustrate the complexities underpinning the implementation of the resettlement policy, Harring et al. (2002:96) outlined the three processes involved. First there was the process to earmark resources for acquiring sufficient land for resettlement. Second, there is the selection of beneficiaries, a process that can become politicised and is fraught with possibilities for fraud and which therefore requires utmost transparency in order to preserve the integrity of the land reform programme. Third, there is the institutionalisation of effective and efficient support mechanisms for the resettled farmers in order sustain the productivity of the land as well as the viability of the resettlement programme.

Nevertheless, the implementation of the land resettlement programme seems to be riddled with numerous challenges that have greatly contributed to procrastination and delays in its implementation. downgrading of the ability of this programme and of government initiatives for integrated rural development and poverty reduction to have the desired positive impact on the targeted populations. For instance, MLRR has been unable to attain its anticipated target for the redistribution of 9.5 million hectares of land (approximately 25% of the total commercial agricultural land) within the five-year period (2000–05) of the Second National Development Plan (NDP 2). In this regard, Harring et al. note (2005:96) that only 90 farms were acquired in the first ten years of independence. At this pace, government would acquire only 900 farms in 100 years, or less than 20% of the total number of commercial farms in Namibia.

Harring et al. (2002:97) further note that MLRR acquires isolated farms as they are offered for sale, charging that this piecemeal approach to land reform is unlikely to be effective. Instead, they advocate the adoption of alternative broad and transparent approaches consistent with a similarly broad programme of agricultural development, which would entail the proactive identification of major regions within which to acquire blocks of farms for resettlement purposes.

Moreover, it is alleged that the process of allocating farmland through the resettlement programme has become highly politicised and is therefore wanting in transparency (SARPN 2003:21). As a result, it is alleged that the 'economics of affection' have found expression in the ties of political patronage, which are being exploited by some political office bearers and bureaucrats as elaborate avenues for preferential treatment of party stalwarts, as well as of friends and relatives of the ruling elite. In this regard, Horsthemke (2004:88) has alluded to the absence of sound criteria for the selection of the beneficiaries of resettlement programmes, resulting in few checks and balances against rent seeking and free-riding behaviour. Van den Brink has cautioned against excessive centralisation in the planning and administration of the processes for selecting beneficiaries, resettling them and providing them with infrastructure and other support services, as this may spawn costly and paternalistic bureaucratisation (Van den Brink, 2002:18).

Testimony of this are the controversies ignited by allegations of maladministration of the resettlement process in the Omaheke, such as fact that poor farm workers and their families faced with threats of eviction were brushed aside, while MLRR opted to allocate land to high ranking civil servants and political office bearers, despite their high salaries, which meant they could easily afford to acquire farms through the affirmative action loan scheme (AALS).[4] These glitches resulted from a number of policy oversights, such as the absence of a framework for dealing with the farm workers on farms acquired by the state for redistribution, or even with regard to farm workers already on farms that are reallocated to new owners under the government's land resettlement scheme. Moreover, although the national resettlement policy of 1997 originally identified five main target groups for resettlement, including evicted farm workers, in the 2001 white paper on the national resettlement policy, farm workers and other landless peasants were moved down a few notches on the priority list of targeted beneficiaries in the sense that the new criteria included all Namibian citizens who were socially, economically or educationally disadvantaged by past discriminatory laws and practices, irrespective of their present socioeconomic status (Werner 2004:20).

In another instance, an MLRR official in the Omaheke region himself became a beneficiary of the scheme for whose administration he was responsible when he was allocated a resettlement farm. To make matters worse, he opted to lease his newly acquired farm to the previous white owner of the farm, as well as to two other persons who later accused the official of having misled them into believing that they were jointly resettled on this farm.[5]

These malpractices occurred despite the fact that the SWAPO economic blueprint advocated safeguards against the possible disproportionate influence of the privileged bureaucratic and economic classes that could lead to abuse by prominent politicians, public servants and urban-based economic elites in their efforts to appropriate large areas of the best farming land for themselves (UNIN 1985:56). MLRR is empowered to allocate user rights to targeted beneficiaries on a leasehold basis, with a view to provid-

---

4. 'Government Official Threaten to Boot Farmworker' and 'Nothing Wrong With Land for the Privileged,' *The Namibian,* 20 and 21 November 2002.

5. 'Resettlement Story Sparks Panic in Omaheke' and 'Land Abuse Exposed,' *New Era,* 27 and 28 March 2007.

ing the recipient with relatively secure property rights. For instance, the beneficiaries can use, bequeath, mortgage and modify the property, although these user rights are supposed to be closely regulated by the state.

According to the MLRR, resettlement beneficiaries are entitled to 99-year leasehold agreement, which is supposed to be registered with the deeds office upon its formal certification. The importance of clearly stipulated and understood legal rights with regard to land derives from the fact that land confers on the beneficiaries the sense of ownership, as well as the social status that accompanies land ownership. However, it was noted by Harring et al. (2002:100–1) that while the MLRR may have attempted to meet its legal obligations, most of the resettlement beneficiaries who interacted with their study team were not fully aware of their legal rights to the land they occupied. For instance, were the legal rights conveyed to beneficiaries through these 99 year leases renewable? Would the families of the direct beneficiaries inherit these properties as a matter of right or would the MLRR have a role in approving such transfers? these leases be sold or traded? If used as collateral for loans, could these leases be foreclosed by banks and other financial institutions? Could beneficiaries be ejected from their leases for bad behaviour, etc? In this regard, the informants hinted that although in theory land leases given to beneficiaries could be used as collateral, in reality it has proven difficult for them to access loans from both commercial and developmentally oriented financial institutions by using their allocated land as collateral.

The problem of legally defined land rights needs to be looked at as part of a bigger problem that has faced many landless Namibians since the pre-independence era, in particular the socially disenfranchised poor segments. It has been noted by Harring et al. (2002:101) that the legal status of most landless Namibians is less than the legal status of their economically privileged counterparts, who generally own their land in freehold. Thus, most landless Namibians often hold a legally undefined usufructuary interest in communal areas, or undefined squatters rights in the hundreds of informal peri-urban settlements scattered across the country.

Moreover, the process of resettlement brings together groups of settlers from different communities and different parts of the country, often speaking different languages and possessing varying human and socioeconomic capabilities. According to Harring et al. (2002:96), immense social effort is required to organise these diverse individuals into functioning new communities. Clearly defined, understood and enforced land rights are a necessary ingredient in the social stabilisation of these newly forged communities.

Another expressed concern relating to land resettlement is the economic viability of the programme. Such concerns mainly arise from the fact that the price of commercial agricultural land in Namibia has continued to increase in relation to the profit that can be made from commercial farming activities. Sherbourne (2004:8) urged government to resolve the economic dilemma by deciding either to continue subsidising the unprofitable land reform programme or, alternatively, to simply allow those who can afford to farm to reap the benefits of the agricultural land reform process. However, it has been noted by Harring et al. (2002:30–1) that the colonial dispossession of land from indigenous African communities from which the postcolonial structure of land tenure in Namibian derives was not a market-driven exercise, but was also a heavily subsidised government enterprise. Thus, one must balance the argument that land reform is expensive with the cost of seizure borne by the original owners of the land, as well as the cost of converting the land into the commercial farms that they are today. However, the duo of scholars expressed their doubts as to whether land reform is the most socially or economically efficient way to advance affirmative action and/or welfare schemes designed to uplift and improve the living conditions of the masses of poor people in Namibia.

Kaumbi, by contrast (2004:93), argues that during both the anti-colonial resistance and the subsequent nationalist liberation struggle local indigenous people paid for the land with their blood. He therefore insists that although postcolonial land reform may be costly, this brutal reality dictates that this cost must be incurred sooner or later in order to avoid repetition of this cruel fate.

Some critics hint at the potential danger arising from the policy to convert large economically viable agricultural units into smaller re-demarcated and partitioned farming units for the purpose of resettling landless households. For instance, its was noted by Harring et al. (2002:98) that given the country's aridity, most available agricultural land has a low carrying capacity for livestock production, while the small plots intended for crop cultivation are equally unlikely to provide meaningful employment for the resettled farmers. It is also feared that the small size of the resettlement allotments present the threat of overgrazing that could ultimately lead to land degradation and the subsequent reduction of the productivity of the land

Some commentators have, however, noted that the greatest impediments to the productivity of small landholding units under the resettlement programmes arise from the inadequacy of the support being extended to resettled farmers. As a result, resettled peasants, farm workers and pensioners with limited sources of income are unable to productively utilise their newly acquired land. This is despite the fact that SWAPO's pre-independence economic development blueprint acknowledged a number of potential weaknesses that could undermine the viability of smallholding units, such as the inability to combine resources and to attract adequate credit and long-term capital, as well as managerial and entrepreneurial weaknesses. These challenges were, however, attributed to the lack of adequate research on agricultural production based on small landholdings. Moreover, the MLRR's 1997 draft white paper on resettlement limited support to beneficiaries of the resettlement programmes to the first five years of resettlement. This assumed that over this period they would acquire the necessary experience and self-confidence to sustain themselves. However, this provision was reformulated in the 2001 white paper, which stated that the duration of support would be determined progressively in accordance with the types of resettlement and the categories of beneficiaries. Moreover, Harring et al. (2002:13) noted that moneys made available through annual budget appropriations are primarily earmarked for land acquisition, with little provision being made for infrastructural and training needs and other related empowerment programmes for resettlement beneficiaries. The Second Commercial Agricultural Land Reform Amendment Act was enacted in May 2001 to ease the constraints imposed by these allocational discrepancies.

In this regard, Harring et al. (2002:98–9) refer to the Skoonheid resettlement project. Started in 1993, it had no elaborate scheduled development plans for achieving sustainability, with the result that seven years after its commencement the beneficiaries remained heavily dependent on monthly food handouts from government. Consequently, Harring et al. cautioned against beneficiaries developing dependency syndromes and emphasised the view that sustainability was only achievable through systematic schemes to provide resettled farmers with the necessary human, technical and infrastructural operating capital. In their view, such schemes could be implemented over a longer period of ten to 15 years, provided they were subjected to independent monitoring and evaluation processes and provided MLRR was willing to intervene and restructure failing projects.

However, looking at some of the challenges that have bedevilled the land resettlement programme since its inception, it seems that government has been unable to institute a fully integrated and effective package of intervention that combines the allocation of land with the corresponding agricultural and other support services. This implies that the current difficulties being experienced by resettled farmers cannot be seen as reflecting any inherent inferiority in small landholding agricultural production. This misconception is attested to by Harring et al. (2002:98), who note that although the perception that resettlement beneficiaries are loafers is echoed by parliamentarians, in their own field study of ten resettlement projects they came across people desirous of making a living but frustrated by the lack of adequate support. They warn against the danger of some resettlement projects becoming rural slums and dumping grounds for poor people.

The alleged abuses and inefficiencies cited above cannot be looked upon lightly, since they may lead to the substitution of hope and enthusiasm by frustration and disillusionment and ultimately foment class and ethnic conflicts.

The Affirmative Action Loan Scheme (AALS)

The patterns of commercial agricultural land tenure inherited from the colonial dispensation had been structured by government subsidised-loans for commercial agricultural land acquisition and development (Harring et al., 2002:17). Thus, in its quest to redress the racially skewed commercial agricultural land ownership patterns, the Namibian government amended the pre-independence Land Bank Act (No. 13 of 1944) through Agricultural Bank Amendment Act 27 of 1991. Section 46 (1) (a) of the latter empowered the minister responsible for the agricultural and rural development sectors to provide funds

> … for the purpose of enabling any person who undertakes to carry on farming or other agricultural operations to acquire with a view to such person's advancement contemplated in Article 23 (2) of the Namibian Constitution or otherwise, agricultural land or enabling any such person to carry on farming or other operations on any agricultural land occupied by him/her, whether or not such land is the property of such a person.

Subsequently, in 1992 cabinet introduced the AALS under the auspices of the Agricultural Land Bank of Namibia to promote several land and agrarian reform objectives. First, it was to promote private agricultural land ownership for previously disadvantaged Namibians to enable them to become fully fledged commercial farmers, capable of penetrating the lucrative agricultural commodities export markets. Second, it was to encourage the relocation of farmers with many livestock from communal areas to commercial farmland, thereby freeing up land for those with fewer livestock, as well as relieving the pressing problems of overgrazing and desertification on communal agricultural land (Sherbourne 2004:14–15).

In this regard, AALS was designed to encourage agrarian capitalist change by dispersing capital on favourable terms to previously disadvantaged emerging farmers to enable them to acquire land through market-based mechanisms. Hence, contrary to its redistributive-inclined liberation struggle ideology, the SWAPO-led government opted for top-down accumulative agricultural land reform. The presupposition here was the parallel development of medium- and large-scale black autarkic farming units capable of penetrating the lucrative commercial agricultural sector, previously the exclusive preserve of a handful of white commercial farmers.

Concerns abound regarding the apparent inclination of the emerging black elite not only to amass more than one farm but also to choose farmland closest to markets and with good soil and water. The poor landless peasants and workers, meanwhile, are left to languish as a result of artificial scarcities of land. This is the situation described by Moyo et al. (2004:5, 11) as a generalised but locationally narrow form of land concentration from below, based on internal processes of local agrarian and power differentiation.

Moreover, discontent is also being expressed about AALS's possible role in raising the price of commercial agricultural land, and its consequent indirect contribution to the current snail's pace of the resettlement programme. Sherbourne (2004:14, 16), based on his review of commercial farmland transaction data at the office of the registrar of deeds, noted that the average prices paid by AALS farmers have been much higher than for other buyers. As a result, he has expressed the need for a critical examination the ways in which the current scheme has supported the subsidisation of land acquisition by the emerging economic elite, as this may be contributing towards the upward spiral of commercial agricultural land prices to the detriment of broader-based land reforms.

He (2004:17) has also expressed the fear that the strategy of encouraging previously disadvantaged persons to venture into commercial agricultural farming on the assumption that such ventures are inherently profitable could prove to be unsustainable in the long run, and may amount to what he terms "setting them up for failure." He explains this concern through a hypothetical illustration of a formerly disadvantaged beneficiary of the AALS who takes out an investment loan of N$ 2.5 m for land and livestock, as well as infrastructural improvement and equipment. The potential annual income of such a farmer is estimated to be N$ 280,000, whereas his/her annual loan repayment is estimated at N$ 313,000. Sherbourne concludes that the profitability of such a typical farming venture would remain but a distant dream (Sherbourne 2004:9–10). Given the high cost of land, he goes on to argue that profitability in the commercial agricultural sector will only be possible where the prospective farmer does not have to purchase the land but acquires it as an inheritance or gift. His conclusion is that the current forms of land reform in general, and AALS in particular, could end up being the exclusive preserve of the rich urbanised black elite with the wherewithal to subsidise their newly acquired farms from their other, principal sources of income.

Some of the above conclusions seem to be seriously flawed and contradictory in a number of respects. For instance, the hypothetical illustration totally overlooks the fact that some AALS beneficiaries are drawn from the ranks of already established and successful farmers in the communal areas, who had, over the years, been able to accumulate productive capital in the form of livestock, equipment, savings etc. Consequently, they may not find themselves in the financial predicament envisaged by Sherbourne. Secondly, Sherbourne (2004:14) notes elsewhere in his paper that full-time farmers accounted for 41% of the AALS beneficiaries by October 2003. Furthermore, this group enjoys favourable terms, such as a three year grace period, after which the interest payments on their loans gradually rise over six years before reaching the AgriBank's normal lending rate. One is therefore flabbergasted as to how he arrived at some of his conclusions. Thirdly, elsewhere in his paper Sherbourne (2004:14) also notes that a casual drive through Namibia's commercial agricultural farmlands suggests a trend towards diversification in land use, including tourism, trophy hunting, game lodges, wildlife photography and adventure sports. This suggests that traditional commercial farming is no longer seen as the optimum form of land use. Since nothing prevents previously disadvantaged farmers from also diversifying land use patterns on their newly acquired farms, one is therefore left to wonder why Sherbourne believes that the emerging commercial black farmers are being set up for failure.

The Commercial Agricultural Land Tax Act

As pointed out by Atwood (Lund 2000:14), different people acquire and/or hold on to farmland for different reasons, some of which can lead to poor utilisation of land and hence culminate in the reduction of national economic output, as well as the role of land in the social reproduction of society. For instance, the primary interest of prospective and current landowners in their land may be as an investment portfolio with high potential for appreciation, or as a hedge against inflation, a tax shelter, or as a means for accessing subsidised credit. The taxation regime in place in Namibia is being blamed for encouraging people to purchase and/or hold on to agricultural land for reasons other than its productive potential, since they are allowed to offset farming losses against the profits from their other business ventures. Therefore, it is argued that some people buy farms to reduce their tax liability. As Moyo et al. note (2004:12), such loopholes can be exploited to conceal land underutilisation.

For instance, Harring et al. (2002:7) estimated that as much as 60–80% of Namibian commercial farms are not profitable and are very heavily in debt and only about 30% of all farmers are essentially debt free. They attribute this to the heavy subsidisation of the Namibian commercial agricultural sector during the era of colonial rule, as well as the fact that commercial agricultural land was not taxed prior to 2005. These circumstances contributed to the tendency of individual farmers to continue to manage unprofitable farms. They note that any effort to tax agricultural land would likely force most commercial farms out of business – and put these farms in government hands

In addition, Sherbourne (2004:14) has observed that some of Namibia's economic elite tend to acquire farms merely as places to visit occasionally with a view to enjoying a rural lifestyle in contrast to the urban lives that they have become accustomed to.

These tendencies are also blamed not only for the exorbitant escalation of prices of farmland, but also for the misallocation of resources, and hence the reduction of society's aggregate welfare through the disproportionate redistribution of wealth and income in favour of a small economic and political elite at the expense of the economically disenfranchised majority. For instance, Moyo et al. (2004:7) point to the trend whereby large tracts of farms are concessioned and sold to private investment companies, as well as the consolidation and conversion of farmland into large-scale conservancies for exclusive wildlife use and other nature-based economic activities. Although these land use patterns are justified by those involved as promoting the sustainable use of natural resources in fragile areas, critics point to the fact that in some cases they perpetuate the exclusion of landless segments of society from what is at times their only available source of livelihood. A classic example of this situation is the much publicised dream of the South African-based property developer and owner of the 65,000 hectare Erindi Game Lodge near Omaruru, Gert Joubert. On the pretext of a promise to attract 2 to 3 million tourists to the country every year, he proposed turning the whole of Namibia into a vast game park across which animals could migrate freely, while the only internal fences would be those around towns and villages.[6]

As Moyo et al. (2004:7) observe, such schemes could undermine integrated rural development strategies, since farmland ends up being directed away from locally articulated development goals more relevant and beneficial to the specific interests of the inhabitants of rural areas, particularly the poor.

In view of the challenges regarding the availability and acquisition of agricultural land by the state for resettlement purposes alluded to above, the Technical Committee on Commercial Farmland (TCCF), instituted by government in November 1991 in line with the consensus resolutions of the national land conference, advocated the principle of horizontal equity by recommending the gradual phasing-out of tax concessions favouring the commercial agricultural sector, including the land tax exemption for commercial farms (Harring et al. 2002:32–4). This recommendation was embodied in the Land Valuation and Taxation Regulations of 2001, which in turn were adopted in terms of the 1995 Commercial Agricultural Land Reform Act. This Act empowers the minister responsible for lands to impose "a land tax to be paid by owners of agricultural land and prescribe the rate, methods of calculation and the time and manner of payment or collection of such tax and penalties for any failure to pay such tax or to comply with any provision of such regulation." The primary objective of the regulations is to provide for the taxation of commercial agricultural land in proportion to its estimated value, and they are intended to increase the cost of holding on to unused or underused agricultural land. In particular, they are intended to discourage the tendency of some current and prospective landowners from of holding on to land for egotistical reasons. In addition, it is anticipated that agricultural land taxation will raise funds for the Land Acquisition and Development Fund, as proposed in both the First and Second Agricultural (Commercial) Land Act, Acts 6 of 2000 and 2 of 2001 respectively (Harring et al. 2002:13).

However, such land taxation policies, as a form of property tax, have generally been criticised in neoliberal economic literature. For instance, Barzel (1993:29) argued that property taxes tend to promote inefficient resource allocation, since the value of the property subjected to these types of tax diminishes compared to what it should be in the absence of the tax. From this perspective, property taxes stand accused of distorting the allocation of resources, leading to their inefficient utilisation, in the sense that expansion of production would produce a net gain, whereas the tax levy creates a wedge that prevents the realisation of that gain, because the marginal units will be valued at more than cost.

---

6. 'Multimillionaire Dreams of Turning Namibia into a Game Park,' *The Namibian,* 14 September 2006.

Conclusion

This paper has highlighted not only the pre-independence national development out-look of SWAPO as a liberation movement, but has also shed light on a number of factors that may have necessitated compromise on the initial commitments to realise social equity within the context of land reforms initiatives. Moreover, the paper has attempted to demonstrate how the principles underpinning commercial agricultural land reforms, and the policies and programmes they helped nurture, has tended to perpetuate the concentration of land in the hands of both white and black economic elites.

In this regard, there seems to be ample evidence to substantiate the observation by Moyo et al (2004:3) that agricultural land reform processes in several Southern African countries, including Namibia, are largely modelled on neoliberal economic principles, even though those principles do not offer coherent articulation of the purpose of land reforms in the local, national and regional socioeconomic development context. By implication, therefore, the ideological underpinnings of postcolonial Namibia's commercial agricultural land reform processes reinforce the pre-independence extroverted model of economic accumulation from above.

As a result, it is becoming increasingly evident that the socioeconomic trends generated by these reforms are gradually fostering socioeconomic conditions capable not only of hardening social differentiation within the previously disadvantaged community, but also of promoting social polarisation between those benefiting from the perpetuation of the socioeconomic status quo and those enduring continued economic disenfranchisement and social marginalisation.

In this regard, the postcolonial process of national reconciliation is also fiercely criticised for being more effective at fostering mutually beneficial ties between economic and political elites across the racial divide. For instance, Kossler and Melber (2001:149) lament the fact that the policy of national reconciliation seems to have "laid and still lays" the main onus of forgiveness and concessions on the shoulder of the black masses, while preserving the spoils of the postcolonial political and economic dispensation for a handful of previously disadvantaged individuals who have graduated into to the echelons of state power from the ranks of the liberation struggle and have thereby been most fortunate in gaining admission to the exclusive socioeconomic club of the privileged minority white group.

As noted by Mudge (2004:101), although Namibia has made some inroads with its various land reform initiatives, these have thus far not significantly benefited the poor and the needy. This predicament warrants the unyielding pleas for a socially equitable settlement of the land question as a prerequisite for sustained peace and political stability in Namibia. As a result of the persistent land hunger being endured by the landless masses, Farring et al. (2002:31) noted that there are strong feelings of resentment and betrayal about the fulfilment of the liberation struggle promises. This underscores the need for critical introspection by and between the various stakeholders involved and/or affected by the agricultural land reform processes, with a view to precluding the radicalisation of the rural poor, such as peasants and farm workers. In this regard, Horsthemke (2004:87) noted that failure to take advantage of postcolonial political stability may create room for politically opportunistic behaviour: the frustrations of the peasants and farm workers, as well as of the descendants of colonial genocide and of war veterans, could be manipulated by competing political interests to threaten the very foundations of peace and political stability in the country.

Wole Sonyika (Hunter 2004:4) rightly cautioned that the persistence of socioeconomic injustice constitutes an enduring threat that one day could rock the foundations of what may initially have seemed like a remarkable process of reconciliation. Thus the time may come when Namibia will be forced to rethink its handling of the socioeconomic challenges that are being generated by the present neoliberal economic agricultural land reform model. The socioeconomic and political realities around the land question in Namibia are far from being sustainable. This situation calls for serious policy-oriented research that arises from and speaks to the contexts, needs, aspirations and insights of prevailing local realities, and seeks workable solutions that transcend the parochial and elitist factional interests served by the present agricultural land reform policies and programmes.

References

Angula H.K. (1990), *The Two Thousand Days of Haimbodi ya Haufiku*. Windhoek: Gamsberg Macmillan

Barzel Y. (1993), *Economic Analysis of Property Rights*. Cambridge: Cambridge University Press

Farring S.L. and W. Odendaal (2002), *"One Day We Will All Be Equal ... "*: A Socio – Legal Perspective on the Namibian Land Reform and Resettlement Process. Windhoek: Legal Assistance Centre

Horsthemke O. (2004), 'Land Reform in Namibia: Opportunities and Opportunism,' in J. Hunter (ed.), *Who Should Own the Land? Analysis and Views on Land Reform and the Land Question in Namibia and Southern Africa*. Windhoek: Konrad Adenauer Stiftung/Namibia Institute for Democracy, pp. 87–91

Hunter J. (2004), 'Who Should Own the Land? Introduction,' in J. Hunter (ed.), *Who Should Own the Land? Analysis and Views on Land Reform and the Land Question in Namibia and Southern Africa*. Windhoek: Konrad Adenauer Stiftung/Namibia Institute for Democracy, pp. 1–7

Kaumbi U. (2004), 'The Land Is Ours,' in J. Hunter (ed.), *Who Should Own the Land? Analysis and Views on Land Reform and the Land Question in Namibia and Southern Africa*. Windhoek: Konrad Adenauer Stiftung/Namibia Institute for Democracy, pp. 92–94

Kiljunen K. (1981), 'The Ideology of National Liberation,' in R. Green, M.L. Kiljunen and K. Kiljunen (eds), *Namibia the Last Colony*. Essex: Longman

Kössler R. and H. Melber (2001), 'Political Culture and Civil Society: On the State of the Namibian State,' in I. Diener and O. Graefe (eds), *Contemporary Namibia: The First Landmark of a Post Apartheid Society*. Windhoek: Gamsberg Macmillan

Latiff, E. (2005), 'From Willing Seller, Willing Buyer To A People-Driven Land Reform', *Programme For Land and Agrarian Studies*, Policy Brief No. 17, September

Lund, C. (2000), 'African Land Tenure: Questioning Basic Assumptions', International Institute for Environment and Development (IIED), *Drylands Issues Paper* 100

Moyo S. and R. Hall (2004), *Conflict and Land Reform in Southern Africa*, Paper delivered at Centre for Conflict Resolution (CCR) policy seminar on the Political Economy of Post-Apartheid South Africa and its Conflict Management and Economic Role in Africa, Cape Town, 30 July–1 August 2004

Mudge D. (2004), 'Land Reform in Perspective,' in J. Hunter (ed.), *Who Should Own the Land? Analysis and Views on Land Reform and the Land Question in Namibia and Southern Africa.* Windhoek: Konrad Adenauer Stiftung/Namibia Institute for Democracy, pp. 100–03

Okoth-Ogendo, H.W.O. (2000), 'The Quest for Constitutional Government,' in G. Hyden, D. Olowu and H.W.O. Okoth-Ogendo, *African Perspective on Governance.* Trenton NJ: Africa World Press, pp. 33–60

Sherbourne R. (2004), 'A Rich Man's Hobby,' in J. Hunter (ed.), *Who Should Own the Land? Analysis and Views on Land Reform and the Land Question in Namibia and Southern Africa.* Windhoek: Konrad Adenauer Stiftung/Namibia Institute for Democracy, pp. 8–10

Southern African Regional Poverty Network (SARPN) (2003), *Seeking Ways Out of the Impasse of Land Reform in Southern Africa:* Notes from an Informal Think Tank Meeting, Pretoria, South Africa, 1–2 March 2003 http://www.sarpn.org.za/documents/10000287/P294_Final_Impasse_Land.pdf downloaded 8 September 2003

Swapo of Namibia (1989), *Swapo Election Manifesto.* Windhoek: SWAPO

United Nations Institute for Namibia (UNIN) (1985), 'Economic Development Strategies for Independent Namibia,' in N.K. Duggal (ed.), *Namibia Studies Series* No. 9, Lusaka: UNIN

Van den Brink, R. (2002), *Land Policy and Land Reforms in Sub –Saharan Africa: Consensus, Confusion and Controversies*, A Presentation to the Symposium on Land Redistribution in Southern Africa, Burgers Park Hotel, Pretoria, South Africa, November 2002

Werner, W. (2004), 'Promoting Development Among Farm Workers: Some Options for Namibia,' in J. Hunter (ed.), *Who Should Own the Land? Analysis and Views on Land Reform and The Land Question in Namibia and Southern Africa.* Windhoek: Konrad Adenauer Stiftung/Namibia Institute for Democracy, pp. 19–45

Between politics and the shop floor
Which way for Namibia's labour movement?[1]

Herbert Jauch

Despite the prominent role played by Namibian trade unions in the country's liberation struggle, and regardless of the fact that the labour movement is still the strongest organised force among Namibia's 'civil society' organisations, trade unions seem to have lost much of their popularity and political influence in recent years. Due to Namibia's large rural population and the underdeveloped manufacturing sector, trade unions might seem to represent only a minority of the population. However, as pointed out by Mbuende (1986:177–9), there are close links between the Namibian peasantry and the industrial working class as a result of the contract labour system, whose legacy is still visible today. Workers' wages contribute significantly to the survival of family members in the rural areas and Namibia's industrial workers bear a substantial burden caused by the widespread unemployment, about 37% nationwide (Ministry of Labour 2005:3). Over the past two decades a permanent urban working class has emerged, but most workers in formal-sector employment share their income by way of remittances to members of their extended families in urban and rural areas. The labour force surveys of 1997, 2000 and 2004 revealed that almost half of Namibia's national household incomes are derived from wages and salaries (Ministry of Labour 2001, 2002 and 2006).

Despite its small population of less than 2 million people, Namibia has about 30 trade unions grouped into two federations and several unaffiliated unions. The largest trade union federation is the National Union of Namibian Workers (NUNW), which represents 60,000–70,000 workers. The NUNW played a key role during Namibia's liberation struggle and continues to be affiliated to the ruling SWAPO party. The second trade union federation is the Trade Union Congress of Namibia (TUCNA), which was formed in 2002 by unions that rejected NUNW's party-political link (Jauch 2004:38–47)

This article sketches some of the challenges faced by the Namibian labour movement 17 years after independence, with particular emphasis on the question of trade unions and politics. It is argued that Namibia's trade unions are at a crossroads today and that the choices made now will have a lasting impact on the future and the relevance of the labour movement in the years to come.

---

1. This article draws extensively on the author's earlier publications in 2002 and 2004.

The socioeconomic environment

Seventeen years after independence, Namibia is still characterised by huge socioeconomic inequalities that are largely a reflection of its colonial apartheid history, but also of the class stratification that has taken place since independence. Namibia has relatively limited financial resources in both the government and the private sector to conduct frequent surveys on social-economic developments. However, the Central Bureau of Statistics (CBS) under the National Planning Commission (NPC), the Bank of Namibia and the ministry of labour all conducted several national surveys on which this paper draws.

Namibia's population of about 1.8 million people is relatively young. More than half the population is less than 25 years of age and more than 40% is less than 15 years old. In 2004, only 37% of the population lived in urban areas compared to a rural population of 63%. These figures are changing steadily due to the increasing urbanisation that has taken place since independence. In 2000, the average Namibian household had 5 members with an average size of 5.6 members in rural areas and 4.2 members in urban areas (Ministry of Labour 2002:26).

Economically active population

In 2004, 888,348 Namibians were 15 years or older and the labour force survey classified 493,448 (56%) of them as economically active. The bulk of those classified as economically inactive were students (41%), followed by 'home-makers' (25.3%), retired and old people (25.9%) and those affected by illness and disability (6.9%). There was a gender discrepancy, as males are dominant among economically active Namibians accounting for 63.7%, while most of the economically inactive Namibians (51.7%) were women (Ministry of Labour and Social Welfare 2006:3, 38).

Although the number of jobs in the agricultural sector has declined steadily over the years, it is still the largest sector in terms of employment in Namibia, accounting for 102,636 (or 26.6%) jobs in 2004 (see Table 1). It is, however, important to point out that this figure included about 36,000 communal/subsistence farmers, 490 commercial agricultural employers and 5,765 'own account' self-employed agricultural workers. There were 42,620 farm workers on private farms and 2,034 workers on public farms (ibid:53).

Other important employment sectors were the public sector (19.6%) and especially the service sectors, which accounted for about 35% of all formal sector jobs. On the other hand, manufacturing has remained severely underdeveloped in Namibia and accounted for only 6% of employment (see Table 1).

Overall, there were 86,161 employees in the public sector (including parastatals) and 194,516 in the private sector. The total number of employees thus stood at 280,677 in 2004, while there were 12,209 employers outside the agricultural sector and 37,441 'own account' self-employed workers (Ministry of Labour and Social Welfare 2006:53).

TABLE 1: EMPLOYMENT BY SECTOR (1988–2004)

Industry	1988		1997		2004	
	No.	%	No.	%	No.	%
Agriculture	34,398 (commercial farms)	18.6	146,899 (commercial & communal farms only)	36.6	102,636	26.6
Fishing	1,673	0.9	6,771	1.7	12,720	3.3
Mining & quarrying	10,062	5.4	6,592	1.6	7,563	2.0
Manufacturing	9,442	5.1	25,983	6.5	23,755	6.2
Electricity, gas & water supply	1,273	0.7	4,576	1.1	6,151	1.6
Construction	12,657	6.9	19,801	4.9	19,605	5.1
Wholesale & retail trade, repair of motor vehicles, hotels and restaurants	29,394	15.9	36,803	9.1	67,027	17.4
Transport, storage & communication	7,880	4.3	13,480	3.4	15,861	4.1
Finance, real estate and business services	4,325	2.3	28,061	6.8	16,956	4.4
Government service including administration, defence, education, health, social work and social security	38,098	20.6	56,974	14.2	75,863	19.6
Other community, social & personal services (including domestic work)	35,589	20.6	53,065	13.1	36,713	9.5
Other			2,135	0.6	479	0.1
TOTAL	184,791	100	401,203	100	385,329	100

Sources: Department of Economic Affairs 1988; Ministry of Labour 2001 and 2006.

Table 1 shows significant changes in employment patterns between 1988 and 2004. Overall, there was a shift away from the primary sector (such as agriculture and mining) towards the tertiary sector. The manufacturing industries remained fairly stagnant and insignificant in terms of employment, despite various government attempts to boost this sector. This presents the classical picture of a neocolonial economy, characterised by a jump from the primary sector to tertiary industries without the foundation of a significant manufacturing sector as a basis for industrial development.

The importance of wages and salaries

About half of all Namibian households (47%) relied on 'wages and salaries' as their main source of income. In urban areas, this figure was as high as 74%. These figures indicate the critical importance that wages and salaries have for the survival of Namibian households. This is further emphasised by the fact that 68% of households in the country (82% in urban areas) lack a secondary source of income (Ministry of Labour and Social Welfare 2006:36–7).

Employment and unemployment

The Namibian government's unemployment definition is based on three criteria, namely:
- being without work,
- being available for work, and
- seeking work.

The 'strict definition' of unemployment excludes from the ranks of the unemployed those individuals (15–65 years old) who are without jobs and available for work, but who are *not* actively seeking work. The 'broad definition' of unemployment on the other hand regards every person who is 15–65 years of age and without work but available for work as being unemployed, whether he/she is looking for work or not. The labour force survey of 2004 presented unemployment figures for both definitions as follows.

Unemployment in Namibia according to the 'broad definition' stood at 36.7%, whilst the 'strict definition' resulted in an unemployment rate of 21.9%. Using the 'strict definition' of unemployment in the context of the Namibian labour market is problematic. The criterion 'actively seeking work' for classifying the unemployed may not be accurate, as many unemployed people may have stopped looking for work, not because they do not want to work, but simply because they may be demoralised and have given up hope of finding a job. Others may not bother to seek work as they witness the fruitless efforts of their friends and relatives. Thus, the criterion 'not seeking work' may not be relevant in labour markets that are characterised by mass unemployment.

TABLE 2: UNEMPLOYMENT – BROAD DEFINITION (2004)

	Overall percentage	Percentage among women	Percentage among men
Nationally	36.7	43.4	30.3
Urban areas	29.0	33.8	24.4
Rural areas	44.7	53.0	36.5
Caprivi region	51.1	58.6	44.0
Erongo region	34.3	41.7	28.9
Hardap region	28.0	39.2	17.9
Karas region	26.8	36.3	20.2
Kavango region	44.4	47.4	41.3
Khomas region	24.2	26.7	21.9
Kunene region	40.1	56.8	25.9
Ohangwena region	64.2	66.7	60.7
Omaheke region	18.9	29.3	13.0
Omusati region	64.6	64.6	64.7
Oshikoto region	35.0	39.4	30.7
Oshana region	31.2	34.0	27.5
Otjozondjupa region	28.8	45.8	16.4

Source: Ministry of Labour and Social Welfare 2006

Namibia's unemployment has regional, gender and age dimensions. In 2004, the rural unemployment rate (44.7%) was significantly higher than the rate in urban areas (29%). Unemployment also had a gender dimension, as significantly more women (43.4%) than men (30.3%) were unemployed. Young people were especially hard hit, as 65% of those between the ages of 15 and 19 and 57% of those aged 20 to 24 years were unemployed. On the other hand, the unemployment rate was significantly lower (16–21%) among those between 45 and 59 years of age (ibid:3, 66 and 68).

Unemployment in Namibia is of a long-term nature, as 56% of the unemployed have been jobless for two years or more. Another 17% have been unemployed for 1–2 years while only 5.3% of the unemployed population has been without a job for less than three months. There was no significant difference between men and women regarding the duration of unemployment. However, there was a difference between urban and rural areas as the unemployed in the rural areas tended to be out of jobs for longer than those in the urban areas. Long-term unemployment (two years or more) in rural areas affected 60.5% of the unemployed compared to 49.9% in urban areas (ibid:69).

Unionisation rates

Accurate statistics on trade union membership rates are difficult to find as only a few unions have computerised membership database systems. Most unions rely on their files and on membership-fee deduction records of employers to count their members. A trade union survey carried out by the Labour Resource and Research Institute (LaRRI) in 1998–99 revealed a unionisation rate of about 50% among employees in formal sector employment (LaRRI 1999:11). These figures were updated and indications are that the highest levels of unionisation are found in the public sector (75–80%), the mining and energy sectors (67%), the textile industry (63%) and the food, fishing, hospitality, wholesale and retail sectors (49%). On the other hand, unionisation levels are low among domestic workers, farm workers and in the banking and insurance sectors (see Table 4). Likewise, only about 10% of workers in the small business sector are organised by trade unions (Karuuombe 2002:47).

The labour force survey of 2004 put the unionisation rate among employees in the public and private sectors at 29%. This figure is significantly lower than those provided by trade unions and their accuracy would have to be established by examining the trade union membership records. This is very difficult at present because of the lack of accurate, computerised database systems. It is thus also impossible to determine the exact number of women in trade unions. It is estimated that 35–40% of union members are women, roughly in line with women's share in the formal labour market. Women are, however, underrepresented in decision-making structures and hardly any occupy the key positions of general secretary or president.

Working conditions and minimum wages

The majority of Namibian workers fall into the category of unskilled and semi-skilled workers. With the exception of a few sectors where strong trade unions managed to negotiate reasonable working conditions (e.g., mining, fishing and the civil service),

TABLE 3: ESTIMATED UNIONISATION RATES, 2004

Sector	*Approximate number of employees*	*Estimated unionistaion rate (signed-up members)*[2]	
Agriculture	44,600	9,000	(20%)
Manufacturing, building and construction	27,000	10,500	(39%)
Mining and energy	6,700	4,500	(67%)
Food, fishing, wholesale, retail and hospitality	45,000	22,000	(49%)
Textile	8,000	5,000	(63%)
Public service, parastatals and municipalities (excluding army, police and teachers)	80,000	60,000	(75%)
Teachers	15,000	12,000 (	80%)
Domestic work (private households)	21,500	3,500	(16%)
Banking, insurance, real estate and business services	15,500	4,500	(29%)
Transport, communication and security	14,000	3,500	(25%)
TOTAL	277,300	134,500	(49%)

Sources: LaRRI 1999; Jauch 2004, Ministry of Labour and Social Services 2006; Updates from trade unions (2004). These figures do not include communal farmers and unpaid family labour.

these workers usually earn below N$ 1,000 per month[3] (US$ 143) and enjoy very few benefits. The only benefits that are compulsory by law are social security payments for workers who work more than two days per week.

Workers at labour brokers, known as labour hire companies, experience the poorest working conditions. Workers there earn between N$ 2 and N$ 5 (US$ 0.28–0.71) per hour without benefits and job security. Wages are also extremely low for domestic and farm workers, who often earn cash wages of only N$ 300–500 per month (US$ 42–71). Likewise, until recently Namibian textile workers at the Malaysian company Ramatex earned wages of only N$ 600–800 per month (US$ 85–114) (Jauch and Shindondola 2003:19–20).

The Namibia Farmworkers Union (NAFWU) managed to reach an agreement with agricultural employers to implement a national minimum wage of N$ 429 (US$ 54) per month in addition to food and housing. This national minimum wage came into effect on 1 April 2003 but was only implemented on most of the country's commercial farms. On communal farms, the average monthly wage was only N$ 201–250 (US$ 28–35) per month (Karamata 2006:3).

On the other hand, well-qualified and experienced professionals and managers earn huge salary packages that compare favourably with the best in the world when the costs of living are taken into account. Managers in the civil service earn packages of about N$

---

2. Signed-up membership refers to the number of workers who applied for union membership and received their membership cards. The number of paid-up members (whose membership fees are received by unions on a monthly basis) is likely to be about 20% lower than the signed-up membership.

3. The Namibia dollar (N$) is pegged to the South African rand and the exchange rate stood at around US$ 1 to N$ 7 in July 2007.

250,000–400,000 per year (US$ 35,000–57,000), while some managers in parastatal companies earn up to three times that amount.

These enormous differences in payment have created a four-tier labour market:

1. a small elite enjoying a standard of living comparable to first world countries;

2. a significant group of formal-sector workers with permanent jobs and low to middle incomes;

3. a growing group of casual workers and 'labour hire' workers who are the victims of a labour market that virtually forces them to accept any job under any conditions; and

4. unemployed workers who turned to the informal economy, to sex work or to crime as a last resort.

Trade unions and politics

The NUNW played a prominent role during the liberation struggle and in the public policy debates after independence. Its history is in many ways similar to that of Congress of South African Trade Unions (COSATU), as both played a critical role in terms of mass mobilisation during the liberation struggle. After decades of intense repression, the NUNW unions emerged from the mid-1980s onward as key players in the economic and political arena. They linked the struggle at the workplace with the broader struggle for political independence and formed links with other social and political organisations such as the Namibia National Students Organisation (NANSO) and the South West Africa People's Organisation (SWAPO). The NUNW understood its role as that of a social movement, which could not address workers issues separately from those affecting the broader community. Exploitation at the workplace was thus linked to the broader struggle against racial and political oppression.

Most of Namibia's trade unions were established inside the country after the mid-1980s. Although several attempts to form unions had been made before, they were suppressed by the colonial regime time and again. However, the earlier efforts laid the foundation for the later emergence of the National Union of Namibian Workers (NUNW) and its affiliates (see Peltola 1995:167–97; Bauer 1997:69). Community organising surged inside Namibia from 1984 onwards, focusing on the crisis in housing, employment, health, education and social welfare. In the absence of trade unions, workers began to take their workplace problems to social workers at the Roman Catholic church and the Council of Churches in Namibia (CCN). At that time, the umbrella of the churches provided political activists with a shield under which they could start organising workers. Unlike trade unions, which had been crushed by the colonial state, churches were able to operate across the country. By 1985, workers and community activists had formed a Workers Action Committee in Katutura, which became the forerunner of trade unions (Bauer 1997:70).

During the mid-1980s, South Africa's National Union of Mineworkers (NUM) began to organise workers at Namibia's Consolidated Diamond Mines and Rossing mines in Oranjemund and Arandis. They linked up with the Workers Action Committee and formed the Rossing Mineworkers Union by April 1986. This union later became the

Mineworkers Union of Namibia (MUN) (loc. cit.). The MUN and other NUNW-affiliated unions provided workers with an organisational vehicle through which they could take up workplace grievances as well as broader political issues, which were always seen as linked to the economic struggle.

Another factor that contributed to the emergence of trade unions inside Namibia was the release of Namibian political prisoners from 1984 onwards. Some returned to Windhoek and began working for the SWAPO structures again. A decision was taken to reactivate the NUNW inside Namibia and by April 1986 a Workers Steering Committee had been formed. It incorporated the Workers Action Committee and all other efforts to organise workers around the country. Fieldworkers began organising different workplaces and in September 1986 the NUNW's first industrial union was launched, the Namibia Food and Allied Workers Union (NAFAU) led by John Pandeni, one of the former Robben Island prisoners (loc.cit.). Shortly afterwards, the Mineworkers Union of Namibia (MUN) was launched, led by another former Robben Island prisoner, Ben Ulenga. In 1987 the Metal and Allied Workers Union (MANWU) and the Namibia Public Workers Union (NAPWU) were launched, followed by the Namibia Transport and Allied Workers Union (NATAU) in June 1988, the Namibia National Teachers Union (NANTU) in March 1989, the Namibia Domestic and Allied Workers Union (NDAWU) in April 1990 and the Namibia Farmworkers Union (NAFWU) in May 1994 (LaRRI 1999:3). In 2000, the Namibia Financial Institutions Union (NAFINU) was launched as the first NUNW union catering to white-collar workers, while the Namibia Music Industry Union (NAMIU) joined in 2001. These unions constitute the affiliates of the NUNW today.

The exiled and internal wings of the NUNW were merged during a consolidation congress held in Windhoek in 1989. At that time, the NUNW unions inside Namibia had already established themselves and were a formidable force among grassroots organisations. They enjoyed huge support even beyond their membership and played a critical role in ensuring SWAPO's victory in the elections of 1989.

The NUNW maintained its links with SWAPO after independence through its affiliation with the ruling party. This link has led to heated debates both within and outside the federation. While the majority of NUNW affiliates argued that a continued affiliation would help the federation to influence policies, critics have pointed out that the affiliation would undermine the independence of the labour movement and that it would wipe out prospects for trade union unity in Namibia.

Trade unions outside the NUNW have repeatedly stated that they differed fundamentally from NUNW over the question of political affiliation. They charged that NUNW could not act independently and play the role of a watchdog over government as long as it was linked to the ruling party. There was also a growing public perception that NUNW was merely a workers' wing of the ruling party, although the NUNW and its affiliates have on several occasions been vocal critics of government policies. They criticised government on issues such as the slow process of land redistribution and education reform and self-enrichment by politicians. However, developments since 2004 point to an increasing influence of the ruling party over the NUNW and its affiliates, as will be discussed below.

Challenges after independence

The achievement of independence in 1990 had a tremendous impact on the labour movement and required a redefinition of the role that trade unions wanted (and were able) to play. The function of political mobilisation, which had taken centre stage before independence, was taken over by SWAPO, whose leadership returned to Namibia in 1989 and became the government after independence. Given the close structural links between the NUNW unions and SWAPO as well as the fact that most union leaders played a prominent role in the party as well, there was a widespread expectation among workers that the SWAPO government would be a 'workers' government.' A few years before independence, leading SWAPO intellectuals like Kaire Mbuende had argued that the interests of workers and peasants constituted the dominant position in SWAPO (Mbuende 1986:199). However, once in power SWAPO did not pursue revolutionary working class politics and instead maintained the predominantly capitalist structure of the economy, while introducing the notion of social partnership into labour relations. Trade unions were expected to define a new role within this framework and although the NUNW had previously called for radical change, it accepted the new framework with little resistance.

Social partnership?

Once in office, the SWAPO government embarked upon a path of reforming Namibia's colonial labour relations system. The overall aim was to move towards a new system of 'social partnership' governed by the Labour Act passed in 1992. Tripartite consultations and collective bargaining were seen as critical for the implementation of this new labour dispensation. The government envisaged an improvement in the living and working conditions of Namibian workers to be brought about by a combination of successful economic policies and successful trade union engagement with the private sector. The government defined its own role merely as that of a 'referee,' trying to create a level (and enabling) playing field for collective bargaining between business and labour.

However, the consultative process leading to the formulation of the Labour Act was driven by government as the dominant partner, which decided on the scope of the consultations. Unlike in a corporatist, institutionalised arrangement – such as in the classical cases of postwar, social democratic Sweden and Germany – where capital, labour and state jointly formulate socioeconomic policies (Sycholt and Klerck 1997:88), social partnership in Namibia did not take the form of a joint decision-making process. In the process of drafting the Labour Act of 1992, for example, government consulted with labour and capital but reserved the right to make the final decision without trying to achieve consensus with the social partners.

The Labour Act of 1992 constituted a significant improvement compared with the previous colonial labour legislation. It extended its coverage to all workers, including domestic workers, farm workers and the public services. The new law encouraged collective bargaining, entrenched basic workers' and trade union rights, set out the procedures for legal strikes and provided protections against unfair labour practices (Bauer 1993:11). However, the act fell short of some of the expectations of trade unions, which felt that employers had unduly influenced the law through 'behind the scenes' lobbying.

The act did not make provision for minimum wages (as SWAPO had promised in its 1989 election manifesto) and it did not guarantee paid maternity leave. Payment during maternity leave was only introduced with the Social Security Act of 1996. Other key demands of the NUNW that were not accommodated in the Labour Act were the 40-hour working week and 21 days of annual leave for all workers (Jauch 1996:91).

Overall, post-independence labour legislation constituted a significant improvement for labour, but it also served to reduce worker militancy by shifting the emphasis away from workplace struggles to negotiations between union leaders and management. Bargaining issues in Namibia were (and still are) narrowly defined and usually deal with conditions of employment only (Klerck and Murray 1997:247). The trade unions' main function was thus narrowed to being the representative of workers in a tripartite arrangement. While this enabled trade unions to win improved working conditions in well-organised sectors like mining, fishing and the public service, collective bargaining remained almost meaningless for vulnerable workers such as farm workers, domestic workers and security guards. Despite the introduction of national minimum wages in 2003 and 2005 for farm workers and security guards, these workers are still exposed to highly exploitative practices. The ongoing adversarial nature of labour relations, coupled with racial polarisation in many workplaces and huge wage gaps, are further obstacles to the notion of social partnership.

Trade unions are also confronted with a threat of a dwindling membership base due to the increasing 'casualisation' of work. In an attempt to cut labour costs and to curb trade union influence, employers in various economic sectors, including retail, fishing, mining, hospitality and manufacturing, resorted to temporary and casual work contracts for low-skilled workers. The emergence of labour hire companies (labour brokers) in the late 1990s in particular, highlighted the threat of 'casualisation' to workers' incomes, job security and benefits. By 2006, over 12,000 workers were already employed through labour hire companies, which retained a significant part of workers' earnings as their fees and deprived them of the benefits enjoyed by permanent workers. Due to the insecurity of their contracts and their shifts between different workplaces, trade unions found it very difficult to recruit and represent labour hire workers (see Jauch and Mwilima 2006). Thus trade union membership has become increasingly narrow in focus, covering permanent workers in 'traditional' sectors such as the public service, mining, fishing, construction and retail, while unions are unable to reach tens of thousands of workers in precarious working conditions on farms, in private households, at labour hire companies and in the informal economy.

Against the background of huge imbalances in terms of economic power between capital and labour, the state's chosen role as 'neutral referee' and creator of an enabling environment for collective bargaining effectively benefited business interests. Business representatives went as far as describing worker militancy as an obstacle to job creation and economic development. Such sentiments were even echoed by some government officials and politicians, which was just one indication that the close political ties between labour and SWAPO did not prevent the entrenchment of a pro-capitalist state after independence. This process was also assisted by the lack of political clarity on the side of trade unions regarding the development of a different social order after independence. Notions of worker democracy, worker control and social transformation that had just emerged in the late 1980s had not been developed into a coherent concept within the labour movement at the time of independence.

Conservative economic policies

Perhaps the biggest challenge facing labour after independence was to define an effective strategy for influencing broader socioeconomic policies in favour of its working class base. This task proved to be extremely difficult in the face of an onslaught by the neoliberal ideology that was usually portrayed as the only practical policy option for Namibia and other countries in the region. Klerck accurately described the Namibian government's response to globalisation as:

> … an open-ended encouragement of foreign investment; the marital stance towards the International Monetary Fund and World Bank; the confinement of social transformation to an extension of representative institutions; a tendency to reduce black empowerment to increasing the black entrepreneurial classes; and a failure to conceive of an economic policy that departs in substance from that of the colonial powers (1997:364).

IMF and World Bank advisors have become regular visitors to Namibia and 'assisted' with the country's public expenditure review and with 'training' high-ranking staff members of government economic institutions. Local economists by and large seem to be trapped in the neoliberal dogma and continue to promote the very policies (e.g., structural adjustment programmes) that have caused severe social hardships in other SADC countries. The Namibian government's increasing slide towards neoliberal policies manifested itself, for example, in the introduction of Export Processing Zones (EPZs) and privatisation programmes. Opposition to such policies by the labour movement was frequently countered by accusations that trade unions were still living in the (ideological) past and that trade unions were obstacles to economic growth and job creation. In the absence of a comprehensive alternative development strategy by labour, trade unions were forced on the defensive on several occasions and found themselves sidelined in economic policy formulation.

A divided labour movement

The year 2006 in particular revealed deep-seated divisions within the Namibian labour movement. Failure to live up to the proclaimed ideal of 'one country, one federation' and 'one industry, one union' resulted in a multitude of trade unions. In some industries, three or more trade unions compete with each other for membership, for example in the fishing and security industries. Even at federation level, the NUNW now faces a significant rival. The Namibia People's Social Movement (NPSM) and the Namibia Federation of Trade Unions (NAFTU) merged in 2002 to form the Trade Union Congress of Namibia (TUCNA), which has 14 affiliates with a combined membership of about 45,000. The TUCNA unions focus predominantly on workplace issues and are less engaged with policy issues than the NUNW, which represents about 70,000 workers. The main dividing line between the two federations is the question of the NUNW's affiliation to SWAPO, which the TUCNA unions reject.

Party-political conflicts

The influence of SWAPO politics on the NUNW has repeatedly come into the lime-light during the past two years. Following the crystallisation of 'camps' within the rul-ing SWAPO party during its extraordinary congress in 2004 (which decided on the party's presidential candidate), the NUNW and its affiliates were drawn into the battle. Although there were no significant ideological differences between those in SWAPO who supported Hidipo Hamutenya and those who supported Sam Nujoma, rival camps began to emerge within the union federation. In the run-up to the NUNW's congress in 2006, the former acting secretary-general of the NUNW, Peter Naholo, who was regarded as part of the 'Hamutenya group,' was removed from his post in December 2005. This set the stage for the months to come as trade union leaders mobilised inten-sively with a view to ensuring that candidates loyal to their own 'camp' would be elected at congress in April 2006 (New Era, 4 April, 10 April, 11 April, 20 April, 26 April & 28 April 2006; Republikein, 31 March 2006). During the congress, this battle for po-litical control overshadowed proceedings despite the many labour, social and economic issues that workers had raised during their regional conferences in preparation for the congress. As the 'Nujoma group' among the NUNW congress delegates gained the up-per hand during the congress deliberations, an unprecedented step was taken to cancel individual elections for each leadership position. Instead, congress endorsed the list of candidates that the 'Nujoma group' had proposed.

In the aftermath of the NUNW congress, the political divisions lingered. Some lead-ers of the Namibia National Teachers Union (NANTU) openly criticised the NUNW congress as undemocratic and in violation of constitutional provisions. The union even suspended the payment of NUNW membership fees in protest. Other NANTU lead-ers, however, disagreed with their colleagues and engaged in a battle for control of the teachers' union (New Era, 18, 24 and 26 May 2006). During the NANTU congress in September 2006, those who were seen as being part of the 'Hamutenya group' received only about one-third of the congress votes and lost their leadership positions. Once again, the 'Nujoma group' had gained the upper hand.

Ideological contradictions

Besides being drawn into intense party-political battles, Namibia's trade unions also experienced a loss of vision. The statements and practices of several trade unions during the past few years revealed deep-seated ideological contradictions. Sentiments of radical nationalism and liberation, for example on the land issue, were mixed with an accept-ance of neoliberalism as the ideology of the 'free market.' As trade union leaders entered (and continue to enter) company boards as part of a poorly defined union investment strategy, their views (and interests) increasingly converged with those of government and business. Also, some trade union leaders are now occupying management posi-tions in the public and private sectors, which contradicts the principle of worker control within unions. These developments point to a lack of clarity regarding the working class base of the labour movement and whose interests it is meant to serve. Nationalist and 'populist' sentiments are still dominant and only a few union leaders advance positions based on a class analysis.

Worker control?

There is also an increasing lack of accountability within unions, which need to reintroduce the practice of mandates and report-backs to their members before taking major decisions. This applies to wage negotiations and policy interventions alike. Unions need to reverse the increasing trend towards becoming 'leaders' organisations' and instead return to the practice of grassroots democracy and worker control. An encouraging development in this regard was the strike at the Malaysian textile company Ramatex in October 2006. Under pressure not only from a ruthless company management that constantly threatened relocation but also from the Namibian government, which granted Ramatex special privileges and protection, the recognised trade union (NAFAU) failed to improve workers' extremely poor conditions of service for four years. Following the resignation of many disillusioned Ramatex workers from the union, NAFAU managed to reinvigorate itself after its congress in September 2006. The union finally resorted to utilising its members' dedication as a source of power. Frustrated by Ramatex's unwillingness to accommodate even the most modest demands, the union finally held a strike ballot among its members in early October 2006. Over 90% of the Namibian Ramatex workers voted in favour of a strike and on 13 October the factory came to a standstill. In an impressive show of determination, over 3,000 young, predominantly female workers chanted and danced with their placards, indicating that they would not return to work unless their demands were met.

Faced with the prospect of huge losses and the pressure of delivering on time to its clients in the US, the company management responded within hours and indicated its willingness to improve its previous offers. On the second day of the strike, an agreement was reached which paved the way for significantly improved wages and benefits and thus constituted a victory for the Ramatex workers. Throughout the strike, the union leadership consulted the striking workers outside the factory building. Workers were briefed and asked to approve the proposed agreement before it was signed. This was a significant departure from the widespread practice of union leaders negotiating agreements behind closed doors and informing their members through the media.

Conclusion

Namibia's labour movement stands at the crossroads today as it tries to redefine its role 17 years after independence. Workers and their trade unions had to realise that the changes after independence did not lead to the expected socioeconomic transformation. There are signs that the labour movement lost its vision and now struggles to develop a strategy about how to play a meaningful role in the process of social change. Deep political divisions, not only between NUNW and its rival federation TUCNA, but also within the NUNW itself, worsen this dilemma. These divisions may serve individual political interests but undermine the potential power of the Namibian labour movement as a whole. A multitude of trade unions that are unable to work with each other cannot provide Namibian workers with the strong organisational base needed to advance a working class agenda.

Although it can be argued that trade unions' participation in tripartite arrangements does not necessarily conflict with the larger goal of bringing about social transformation, collective bargaining and tripartite consultations alone are certainly insufficient to address Namibia's huge socioeconomic inequalities. In order to become an engine of social change, trade unions will have to deepen their roots in Namibia's working class constituency and articulate its interests beyond the workplace. This implies that the labour movement will need to develop effective strategies for influencing policies, particularly in the economic arena, which is shaped by neoliberal dogma.

Despite its current weaknesses, the Namibian labour movement still has the potential to become (again) a key organisation in the quest for socioeconomic justice. Like trade unions elsewhere in Africa (see Kester and Sidibe 1997), Namibian unions have a long experience of struggle, a massive potential for organisation and action and an expectation to benefit from independence and democracy. Trade unions have structures (although sometimes weak) all over the country and a significant membership base that is only matched by the country's churches. Provided that unions can strengthen their internal capacity and achieve the level of rootedness in their working class constituency that they had in the late 1980s, the labour movement can become the driving force for more fundamental socioeconomic social change. This will also require that trade unions intensify and cement their links with other progressive organisations that represent socially disadvantaged groups.

Namibia's trade unions face two possible scenarios today. Provided they can meet the challenges outlined above and redefine their role as 'struggle organisations' with a specific class base and a strategic agenda, they are likely to play a central role in the fight for the interests of the Namibia's disadvantaged majority. Failure to seize this opportunity will result in Namibian unions gradually losing their mass base while union leaders are absorbed with bargaining issues, party-political careers, union investments and tripartite participation without addressing (and challenging) the fundamental socioeconomic structures that uphold the continued skewed distribution of wealth and income.

References

Bauer, G.M. (1993), 'Defining a role: trade unions in Namibia,' *Southern Africa Report*, Vol. 8, No. 5, pp. 8–11

— (1994), *The labour movement and prospects for democracy in Namibia*. PhD thesis, University of Wisconsin, Madison

— (1997), 'Labour relations in occupied Namibia,' in G. Klerck et al. (eds), *Continuity and change: Labour relations in independent Namibia*. Windhoek: Gamsberg Macmillan

Department of Civic Affairs and Manpower (1988), *Manpower survey*. Windhoek: Department of Civic Affairs and Manpower

Jauch, H. (1996), 'Tension grows: labour relations in Namibia,' *South African Labour Bulletin*, Vol. 20, No. 4, pp. 90–93

— (2002), 'From liberation struggle to social partnership: The challenge of change for the Namibian labour movement,' in V. Winterfeldt, T. Fox and P. Mufune (eds), *Namibia-Society-Sociology*. Windhoek: University of Namibia Press

— (2004), *Trade unions in Namibia: Defining a new role?* Windhoek: FES and LaRRI

— and N. Mwilima (2006), *Labour hire in Namibia: Current practices and effects.* Windhoek: LaRRI

— and H. Shindondola (2003), *Ramatex: On the other side of the fence.* Windhoek: LaRRI

Karamata, C. (2006), *Farm workers in Namibia: Living and working conditions.* Windhoek: LaRRI

Karuuombe, B. (2002), *The small and micro enterprise (SME) sector in Namibia: Conditions of employment and income.* Windhoek: JCC and LaRRI

Kester, G. and Sidibe O.O. (1997), 'Trade unions, it's your turn!' in G. Kester and O.O. Sidibe (eds), *Trade unions and sustainable democracy in Africa.* Aldershot: Ashgate

Klerck, G. (1997), 'The prospects for radical social transformation,' in G. Klerck et al. (eds), *Continuity and change: Labour relations in an independent Namibia.* Windhoek: Gamsberg Macmillan

— A. Murray and M. Sycholt (1997), *Continuity and change: Labour relations in an independent Namibia.* Windhoek: Gamsberg Macmillan

— and M. Sycholt (1997), 'The state and labour relations: Walking the tightrope between corporatism and neo-liberalism,' in G. Klerck et al. (eds). *Continuity and change: Labour relations in an independent Namibia.* Windhoek: Gamsberg Macmillan

Labour Resource and Research Institute (1999), *Understanding the past and present – mapping the future: The National Union of Namibian Workers (NUNW) facing the 21ˢᵗ century.* Windhoek: LaRRI

— (2003), *Namibia: Labour market and socio-economic indicators.* Windhoek: LaRRI

Mbuende, K. (1986), *Namibia, the broken shield: Anatomy of imperialism and revolution.* Malmö: Liber

Ministry of Labour (2001), *The Namibia labour force survey 1997: Final report of analysis.* Windhoek: Ministry of Labour and National Planning Commission

—(2002), *The Namibia labour force survey 2000: Final report.* Windhoek: Ministry of Labour and National Planning Commission

Ministry of Labour and Social Welfare (2006), *Namibia labour force survey 2004: Report of analysis.* Windhoek: Ministry of Labour and Social Welfare

Murray, A. and G. Wood (1997), 'The Namibian trade union movement: Trends, practices and shopfloor perception,' in G. Klerck et al. (eds), *Continuity and change: Labour relations in an independent Namibia.* Windhoek: Gamsberg Macmillan

Mwilima, N. (2006), *Namibia's informal economy: Possibilities for trade union intervention.* Windhoek: LaRRI

Peltola, P. (1995), *The lost May Day: Namibian workers struggle for independence.* Helsinki: The Finnish Anthropological Society in association with the Nordic Africa Institute

Liberated economy?
A case study of Ramatex Textiles Namibia

Volker Winterfeldt

"The ultimate foundation of this entire economic order ... is in effect the structural violence of unemployment ..."
(Pierre Bourdieu, *The essence of neoliberalism*)[1]

The backdrop

At the Namibian government's invitation, the Malaysian multinational Ramatex Berhad group opened a subsidiary in Namibia in mid-2002 amid general applause. Ramatex is an integrated textile manufacturer offering a range of textile products from yarn to knitted garments. The Namibian branch went into production in the capital Windhoek as an Export Processing Zone (EPZ) enterprise. Ramatex Textiles Namibia profits from both its EPZ status and the advantages derived from the US African Growth and Opportunity Act of May 2000. AGOA I allows tariff preferences for imports from southern Africa countries into the US[2]. On Namibia's side, such a good haul of Foreign Direct Investment (FDI) is not only seen as a success story in itself, it also serves as a persuasive showpiece, pointing out to other potential global investors the way to a profitable Namibian future.

As a Namibian EPZ company, Ramatex capitalises on ample tax and tariff exemptions and is granted preferential treatment in capital and currency matters by way of legislation. EPZ Act No. 9 of 1995 exempts companies from any sales or value added tax payable in Namibia and from all customs or excise duties for goods imported into the EPZ or manufactured in the EPZ. Corporate income is not taxed and capital invested protected from expropriation. Companies are not subject to foreign exchange controls, including the repatriation of capital and profits, and are authorised to hold foreign currency accounts with local banks. In the interests of developing a skilled national labour force, the act entitles EPZ companies to apply for the reimbursement of 75% of the costs incurred in training Namibian citizens employed by such com-

---

1. In *Le Monde diplomatique*, December 1998:issue: http://mondediplo.com/1998/12/08bourdieu

2. Incorporated in the US Trade Act of 2002, the act was amended and signed in August 2002. AGOA II expands preferential access for imports from beneficiary sub-Saharan African countries to "knit-to-shape or wholly assembled apparel articles." In particular, it grants "lesser developed beneficiary country status" to Namibia. Thus Namibian EPZ-companies are allowed "to use third country fabric in qualifying apparel ... regardless of origin of fabric and regardless of origin of yarn." <http:www.agoa.gov/agoa_legislation/AGOII_summary.pdf>

pany[3]. In addition to the competitive advantages derived from such stipulations, the Namibian government offered Ramatex most favourable investment conditions with regard to industrial site, labour supply, energy, water, and political and administrative handling. Thus, it convinced the Malaysian investor to relinquish a similar but less profitable invitation by the Eastern Cape regional government in South Africa.

In attracting foreign investment such as Ramatex's, Namibia pins its hopes on employment generation, dissemination of professional skills and technological advancement. The chronic shortage of productive Namibian capital has shaped the country's planning for socioeconomic development and higher standards of living since independence. Thus, since 1990 developmental policies have attached great importance to the attraction of foreign capital, from which a pivotal contribution to industrialisation and accelerated growth is expected. Article 99 of the Namibian constitution laid the foundations. The Foreign Investments Act No. 27 of 1990 provided for liberal investment conditions and allowed for the institution of the Namibia Investment Centre (NIC) in the Ministry of Trade and Industry (MTI). Since then, as the EPZ Act exemplifies, promoting an environment conducive to FDI has become a major political concern. The Namibian government extends a plain invitation to global investors. Its economic policy rationale aims at combining the internal mobilisation of Namibia's natural and social resources with foreign capital resources. The economic impact of export-led industrialisation, it is hoped, will spur development and eradicate poverty.

Economic liberalism vs. social equity: The developmental dilemma

As this quick glance has already shown, Ramatex's certification in 2001 as a Namibian EPZ company did not come out of the blue. Again, in 2004 the nation's most prominent policy document of the new millennium, *Namibia Vision 2030,* stays true to the spirit of the outgoing millennium. Though markedly attenuated by a stronger orientation towards the national workforce as a developmental resource basis[4], it reproduces the familiar neoliberal fundamentals with regard to FDI. The remarkable partnership between Namibia's political elite and the Malaysian investor exemplifies, in several of its aspects, an essential intellectual trait of *Vision 2030*: the combination of the vision of socioeconomic justice on a national scale with the merciless dictates of profitability emanating from global economic liberalism. Conceptually, such conflicting paradigms rather represent the reconciliation of the irreconcilable.

The case study of Ramatex also substantiates the hypothesis that the post-independence economic policies of the South West Africa People's Organisation (SWAPO) party government unequivocally dissociate themselves from the vision of a 'liberated economy', which the former liberation movement had formulated at the time of the struggle for national and social emancipation. Whatever the official wording of vision-

---

3. Cf. sections III.5.1.a. and b.; III.7.2.; VI.16.1.; VIII.25.1. of EPZ Act No. 9 of 1995. Republic of Namibia, *Government Gazette* No. 1069.

4. *Vision 2030* speaks of "people-centred economic development," while "the creation of a diversified open market economy," to be based on the "competitiveness in the export sector," represents the vision for the promotion of Namibia's globalised macroeconomic environment. Republic of Namibia, Government of, Office of the President (2004):9, 33.

ary or policy documents, in actual practice social progress is increasingly devised as a function of capitalist market forces only. The crude reality of the dictates of the neoliberal globalised market economy has long replaced the vision of a liberated independent economy. Henning Melber's (2003) diagnosis of self-inflicted *limits to liberation* found in Namibia's political governance and political culture must, sadly, be extended to the economic realm as well.

To shed light on Namibia's developmental policies, it is appropriate to inquire into the implementation of Ramatex's investment and production scheme, looking critically at both sides of this partnership. For years, in public statements by stakeholders this scheme has been promoted as being sustainable in terms of its contribution to social and economic development, as well as from an environmental perspective and in respect of international relations. Only recently, against the backdrop of exacerbated industrial relations at Ramatex, have a few critical comments been voiced.

There is sufficient circumstantial evidence to believe that Namibia's practical engagement with the Malaysian company should not be painted in just rosy colours. On the contrary, on closer examination, the developmental impulse seems to prove rather small. Moreover, it has to be offset against the saddening helplessness of politics so far, which failed in transforming into social benefits what little impulse there may have been. The evidence of the past five years appears to push the year 2030 to an even more distant future.

The analysis of the Ramatex example will inquire into the *social limitations* of the neoliberal *economic* initiative. Employment creation will have to be assessed in terms of the generation of actual purchasing power on an individual level. On a macroeconomic level, Ramatex's investments will have to be weighed against the investment costs incurred by the state and the municipality of Windhoek in accommodating entrepreneurial demands. The social costs of allowing a conflictual employment situation will have to be looked into in terms of exploitation of labour, industrial relations, corporativism and social freedom.

Liberal economics assumes that globalisation is the most efficient tool to counter marginalisation. Its critics argue that globalisation takes place in an economic world characterised by power differentials. Ironically, a look back at the historical example of the very first classical advocates for global liberalisation, the Manchester textile lobby, demonstrates the Janus-faced reality of liberalism right from its beginnings: While India and the world were to open their markets to industrial textiles from England, the representatives of Manchester capital lobbied for (and obtained) legislative tariff barriers against the import of India's famous silk fabrics.

In a more general mode, therefore, the analysis of Namibia's experience with Ramatex will have to test the consistency of the above landmark assumption of the neoliberal discourse: To whose advantage is such a process of globalisation, based as it is on the superiority of extremely mobile international capital? Can the idea of an equal partnership between the potent investor and the marginalised economy materialise? Can globalisation show the way forward to social equity? Or is globalisation, as it often was in the past, the best tool to further marginalise the underdeveloped economy? One might even ask how 'liberal' – in the classical understanding of the concept, calling for the complete abstention of state involvement in the economy – is an economic policy that involves the state as an active political, administrative and infrastructural guarantor for foreign investments?

A preliminary conclusion: The new (or not so new) economic rationale of liberalism is characterised by neglect of genuine social responsibility. Contrary to its claim, liberalism does not halt marginalisation Nor can it prevent further exacerbation of internal social structural inequalities and contradictions of a dependent economy and society in the globalisation process in the long run. On the contrary, economic and social marginalisation comes along with globalisation, as long as the conditional framework of globalisation follows the well-established pattern dictated by the capitalist accumulation process over the past five centuries.

Ramatex in Namibia – analysis of an unequal partnership

The players (1): The Namibian authorities

The first news of a major Malaysian textile manufacturer being certified by the government as an EPZ company was divulged by the NIC in July 2001 (*Namibia Economist,* 29/6/–5/7/2001). This followed a heated public debate between the MTI and representatives of the labour movement only months after a critical stocktaking of the first quinquennium of the EPZ policy. Already in late 1999, the Namibian Economic Policy Research Unit (NEPRU) had critically reviewed the EPZ concept. Disturbed by the poor achievements of Namibia's foreign investment policies throughout the 1990s, the analysts emphasised that EPZ policies had to meet certain conditions to be successful. They voiced concern at the early withdrawal of several EPZ companies, questioning their economic agenda (*New Era,* 1–8/4/1999). NEPRU, in the 1990s an important advisory voice to the Namibian government, pointed to the discrepancy between the generous incentives Namibia grants foreign investors and their relatively meagre response. NEPRU criticised the legislative and political framework. It suggested the removal of administrative barriers and the streamlining of procedures for handling EPZ companies (the 'one-stop-shop'; NEPRU (October and December 1999). NEPRU's review, on the other hand, also considered labour issues to be the crucial drawback to Namibia's investment climate. In particular, it took aim at the limited supply of an educated workforce, at rigid labour market regulations and the unstable labour relations in the country's highly unionised formal sector.

In March 2000, the Labour Resource and Research Institute (LaRRI), an institution often addressed as the *think tank* of the Namibian labour movement, published a study critical of EPZ. The report set off the initial expectations of the MTI against the actual state of affairs in the EPZ regime. Of the envisaged 25,000 new jobs (LaRRI 2000:38), a mere 405 had materialised (*Namibia Economist,* 18/–24/2/2000). MTI challenged this figure, indicating employment at about 1,000 EPZ workers (*The Namibian,* 26/4/2000). Still, the MTI's Offshore Development Company (ODC) had to confirm that only 405 of a projected total of 1,145 workplaces had been created so far[5]. The ODC also calcu-

---

5. Republic of Namibia (1999):3. The ODC had been established in May 1995 by the government of Namibia in execution of the EPZ Act as a marketing and management umbrella company for the EPZ regime. See Part IX.26. of the Act.

lated the nominal total capital of the 80 companies that had been granted certificates since the inception of the EPZ programme: it amounted to approximately N$ 8.5 bn. Since only 18 of these companies had actually started operations, EPZ capital totalled N$ 280 m[6]. LaRRI's examination of the firms in operation confirmed a lower amount of only N$ 130 m[7].

Whichever evidence is taken as a basis, whether a total of US$ 21 or 45 m (calculated on the basis of the figures given above at the current exchange rate of N$ 6.25 per US$), the inference remains the same: the invitation Namibia had extended globally for FDI had not yet paid off. In 1990, the country had taken a general "policy decision to embark on an export driven industrialization" (Republic of Namibia (1995b):5). The policy had been implemented based on an uncompromising liberalisation of trade and investment regulations. The EPZ regime had added to it, extending the tax holiday granted to foreign investors indefinitely, and had made an effort to create the necessary institutional and management structures. Yet, as Namibia's founding President Nujoma admitted at the launch of the ODC in 1995, "success in attracting new investments … had been less than satisfactory" (*The Namibian*, 30/5/1995).

It is against this background of a still unsatisfactory outcome of FDI policies – and in view of a critical phase in the development of the GDP, which had considerably decreased since the mid-1990s – that the MTI decided to take the bull by the horns when approaching Ramatex. The company proposed an investment of N$ 1.2 bn[8] for a Namibian EPZ-certified branch, ten times the amount of all previous EPZ investments. The Namibian side offered a conspicuous package of incentives. In addition to the profitability-oriented EPZ advantages, in particular exemption from corporate, sales and other taxation, duties and levies[9], the MTI presented an extremely competitive cost-cutting arrangement for infrastructural support.

Ramatex was granted a 99-year lease on an industrial plot of 43 hectares in Windhoek's Otjomuise district (*The Namibian*, 28/9/2001). While the leasehold was valued at N$ 16.9 m (*New Era*, 28/4/2005), the city of Windhoek placed the land at Ramatex's disposal "for a nominal fee" (*AZ*, 30/5/2003), as both city Mayor Matheus Shikongo and the city's former CEO Martin Shipanga confirmed. It emerged from the ranks of the city council that the nominal fee amounted to a monthly N$ 1[10]. Subsequently, at

---

6. As of 30 December 1999, of 80 companies 41 still were "in process" to start operations, 21 had withdrawn. All in all 113 companies had applied for an EPZ certificate. Republic of Namibia (1999):1–3.

7. LaRRI (2000):45. In January 2006, Minister of Trade and Industry Immanuel Ngatjizeko reported that 177 enterprises had been granted EPZ status so far, of which only 25 were fully operational. Their investment totalled N$ 5.2 billion in July 2005, generating 6,976 "new direct jobs." *New Era*, 26/1/2006.

8. *The Namibian*, 16/5/2002. In a later statement, Ramatex's Executive Director Albert Lim mentioned a sum of N$ 1.1 billion (*The Namibian*, 29/8/2002).

9. The picture concerning corporate taxation is ambiguous. In compliance with its EPZ status, Ramatex would be indefinitely exempted from taxes on profits realised in Namibia. The EPZ Act of 1995 had removed the limitations stipulated by the Foreign Investments Act of 1990. The United Nations Notes on Namibia report a 99-year tax exemption. IRIN News Briefs 8 February 2005. However, the Namibian media repeatedly referred to a 20-year tax holiday. *Namibia Economist*, 29/6/–5/7/2001; *AZ*,5/9/2002.

10. N$ 1,188 for the duration of the lease, or US$ 150.

Ramatex's insistent request, the leasehold had to be extended to a total of 160 hectares (*Republikein*, 30/5/2003). The industrial site, situated in one of Windhoek's pristine hilly and rocky areas, had first to be graded at the city's expense (*Namibia Economist*, 29/6–5/7/2001). The city also built an access road at a cost of N$ 1.5 m (*New Era*, 28/4/2005). Ramatex was given free electricity, water and sewage infrastructure[11] up to the factory site, as well as preferential rates for water and electricity[12]. In return, the company was under contract with the city to build a waste-water reclamation plant on its premises, thus taking responsibility for the purification of the highly polluted water used in the industrial dyeing process (*AZ*, 1/3/2005). NamPort, the parastatal company managing Namibia's only deep-sea harbour Walvis Bay, guaranteed free wharfage[13]. Indirectly, Namibia's incentives package also included the cost of building a new container terminal. The decision had to be taken to enable TransNamib, the parastatal transport company, to handle the transportation of 30 containers daily between Windhoek and Walvis Bay[14].

In total, the infrastructural support provided directly to Ramatex out of the capital Windhoek's coffers amounts to N$ 106.12 m[15]. To this, N$ 17 m for TransNamib's new Windhoek terminal can be added, though the terminal obviously does not cater exclusively to Ramatex[16]. The city had entered into an agreement with the Namibian

---

11. *Namibia Economist*, 29/6/–5/7/2001. *The Namibian* (28/9/2001) reports that in an agreement signed between the city of Windhoek and Ramatex at the end of September 2001 "the City authority and Government will each spend N$ 30 million for electricity, water and sewerage infrastructure at the complex." *New Era* estimates "free infrastructure at N$ 27 million" (*New Era*, 28/4/2005).

12. *AZ*, 5/9/2002. *New Era*, the government-owned weekly, reports Minister Hamutenya stating that "he had a meeting with the two chief executive officers of NamWater and NamPower [both parastatals servicing water and electricity nationwide] as well as the mayor of Windhoek to give just a small discount on water, electricity and on land to be bought by the company." 13/–15/7/2001. The 'small discount' on water tariffs, as it transpired in 2004, was a rebate of approximately 50% of the full municipal rate. The price of N$ 3.52 charged by the municipality was below cost recovery (*The Namibian*, 2/7/2004). The rebate on electricity was such that the N$ 0.185 per kilowatt/hour the municipality charged Ramatex forced the capital's electricity department to overspend its budget in 2004 by N$ 4.3 m in subsidising Ramatex's consumption of electrical energy (*The Namibian*, 25/2/2005. *AZ*, 1/3/2005).

13. *Namibia Economist*, 29/6/–5/7/2001. However, NamPort benefits from port charges. On the other hand, Namibia's economy is not commissioned to handle ocean freight for Ramatex, which is taken over by the US-American Gulf Africa Line. GAL ships "about 700 containers of textile and apparel every month" to the States (*Namibia Economist*, 20/–26/7/2001).

14. Initially, TransNamib's capacity was limited to about half of this number. In September 2002, Ramatex complained about capacity-related bottlenecks created by TransNamib and NamPort. TransNamib, insolvent as it was at that time, decided to invest N$ 17 m in a new and modern container terminal in Windhoek. The sum had to be made available to the parastatal by government (*AZ*, 5/9/2002; 6/9/2002. *The Namibian*, 5/9/2002).

15. Statement of Hafeni Nghinamwaani, the then strategic executive of the department for economic development of the city of Windhoek. The money comes from the city's capital development fund (*Namibia Economist*, 5/–11/2002; *AZ*, 1/4/2002). In April 2005, *The Namibian* divulged some details of the package: the first 43 hectares of the industrial plot were valued at N$ 16.9 m, the access road at N$ 1.5 m, subsidised electricity and free infrastructure were estimated at N$ 27 m, subsidised free water supply and infrastructure at N$ 39 m, the sewage system at N$ 17.3 m (*The Namibian*, 1/4/2005).

16. LaRRI, in an excellent study of the working and social conditions at the Ramatex factory that caused quite a political stir, concludes: "Based on the assumption that Ramatex and its subsidi-

authorities obliging the government to reimburse the capital city half the costs incurred in serving Ramatex. The state proved quite slow in honouring the contract[17].

Last but not least, the issue of the reimbursement of costs incurred in the vocational training of Namibian employees of Ramatex has to be addressed. The wording of the EPZ Act entitles Ramatex to a refund of up to 75%. It would be quite surprising if Ramatex had not seized this financial opportunity, given that the firm is forced to employ most of its Namibian workforce first on a trainee basis due to the lack of a sound vocational background. Moreover, the Act makes the development of labour skills a condition for granting EPZ status[18]. However, official statements on the matter have been strictly avoided. On the contrary, whenever they rated the significance of Ramatex's economic venture for Namibia's economic progress, stakeholders regularly emphasised the multiplier effect of the skills transfer made possible by the employment generated by the company. Also, in September 2004, the permanent secretary in MTI, Andrew Ndishishi, revealed vague government plans to facilitate the future training of Ramatex workers at public expense, in order to obviate the need for the Malaysian company to continuously resort to the employment of foreign workers (*The Namibian*, 15/9/2004).

What the permanent secretary withheld, however, was the fact that the Namibian authorities had already started financing the training of Ramatex workers as from the 2002–03 financial year. Since then, the Namibian state budget had provided an annual N$ 500,000[19]. To date, the state revenue fund has subsidised Ramatex for the vocational training of its employees to the tune of N$ 2.05 m. This subsidy is all the more surprising given that the firm is under an obligation to self-finance the training of its workers in full. Ramatex had signed a contractual statement on the matter in 2001 in return for the incentives package granted by the city of Windhoek (*AZ*, 1/3/2005).

The players (2): The multinational conglomerate

Ramatex Berhad, Ramatex Namibia's parent company, is Malaysia's largest and only fully vertically integrated textile manufacturing enterprise. It produces mainly for the export markets of the developed capitalist world. The group, registered on the Kuala Lumpur stock exchange since 1996, employs 45,000 workers (*Namibia Economist*, 29/6/–5/7/2001). Founded in 1982, the company expanded into China in 1997. It is

---

aries will employ about 7,000 Namibian workers at the end of 2003 with an average wage of N$ 500 per month, and given the expenses of about N$ 120 million in public funds to set up infrastructure for the company, the following calculation can be made: The financial support that Ramatex received from the Namibian government is equivalent to the salaries of all worker for 34 months – almost 3 years!" LaRRI (2003):39.

17. Until April 2005, the city had received only N$ 19.8 m from the state (*The Namibian*, 1/4/2005).

18. Republic of Namibia (1999), Parts VIII.25.(1)–(3) and II, 3(e).

19. Under budget vote 27/04/045 (respectively, for 2005–06, N$ 550,000 under budget vote 10/10/45). Government of Namibia (2003), p. 379 and Government of Namibia (2004), p. 384: Budget vote 27, Higher Education, Training and Employment Creation, Main Division 04: Vocational and Technical Training, Item 045: Ramatex. Government of Namibia (2005), p. 151: Budget vote 10, Education, Main Division 10: Vocational Education and Training (VET), Item 45: Ramatex. See also: Sherbourne (2005):6.

controlled by the Ma family, which owns 59% of the shares. Branches operate in Singapore, Cambodia, China, Mauritius and Namibia[20].

Ramatex Textiles Namibia (Pty) Ltd. is certified as a Single-Factory Export Processing Zone. It counts four subsidiaries, all located in Windhoek's Otjomuise district: Flamingo Garments, Rhino Garments, Tai Wah and Lichen Apparel. The Otjomuise factory operates a spinning mill (ring spun), two dye houses and 2 knitting mills (Cotton News 2003:3). Its production is directed towards the EU, the Middle East and mainly the east coast of the US, favoured by the AGOA stipulations. The plant was built with imported prefabricated materials[21]. The means of production, as well, were imported, partly by falling back on machinery from the South African subsidiaries. To date, all the raw materials and semi-processed goods are imported into Namibia, as the country does not produce sufficient cotton of its own to satisfy Ramatex's demands. Ramatex's monthly production totals N$ 50 m[22].

Prior to their closure in October 2003, Ramatex operated three factories in Dimbaza, King William's Town, not far from East London in the Eastern Cape province, South Africa. With the prospect of considerably reducing its capital costs in Namibia, the parent company decided to terminate the operations of Tai Wah Textiles South Africa and May Garments Company South Africa (LaRRI 2003:8). Trade union calculations show the following comparison of average salaries paid by Ramatex: N$ 625 in Namibia, N$ 809 in Mauritius, N$ 1,184 in South Africa and N$ 1,398 in Malaysia.

Originally, Ramatex South Africa had entered into negotiations for expansion with the Eastern Cape regional authorities, presenting its plans for the employment of an additional 18,000 workers. The provincial authorities offered a 100-hectare factory site on flat land for R 250,000 in Buffalo City, supported by Buffalo City's Mayor Sindisile Maclean. The company was granted a tax holiday for six years, approved by the SA ministry for trade and industry. However, the South African cabinet opposed further privileges demanded by the Malaysian subsidiary. As a result, Ramatex SA was on the lookout for alternatives, criticising the Eastern Cape government's incentives for not being "strategically fit for Ramatex's investment criteria and vision"[23]. One of the SA subsidiaries apparently turned down an offer from Lesotho (*AZ*, 14/3/2002). Eventually, the attractiveness of Namibia's incentives package lured the concern to Otjomuise. The South African factories closed down after just two and a half years. This fact points to the extreme mobility of international textile capital. Ramatex Namibia went into production in mid-2002, only one year after successfully concluding its negotiations with the Namibian authorities, a development marked by the official inauguration on 14 June 2001 (http://www.windhoekcc.org.na/Default. aspx?page=120).

---

20. *Der Standard*, 30/6/2005. International Textile, Leather & Garment Workers' Federation (no year of publication), Mollet 2001:94. <http://www.ramatex.com.>

21. *The Namibia Economist* reported the arrival at Namibia's international harbour Walvis Bay of "forty two containers containing prefabricated materials to be used in building the plant ... Port authorities said this week that they are expecting 600 to 700 more containers" (20/–26/7/2001). See also: *The Namibian*, 28/10/2005.

22. As of the second half of 2003. *AZ*, 27/10/2003. The MTI agencies, Namibia Investment Centre and Offshore Development Centre, in December 2003 estimated a monthly volume of production of about N$ 28 m (InvestDevelop – Namibia's Investment Newsletter, 8/12/2003:2).

23. Dispatch online, 21/6/2001.

Ramatex Namibia had intended to go into production in September 2001, but construction work started only in August 2001. At first, MTI announced the employment of 18,000 workers (*New Era,* 13/–15/7/2001), whereas the concern planned for 15,000, 8,000 of them to be taken on in the first three years (*Namibia Economist,* 20/–26/7/2001). However, only by March 2002 had the first 1,000 workers completed their training at the Windhoek Vocational Training Centre (LaRRI 2003:11). At peak times, Ramatex's workforce amounted to approximately 8,000 employees (*AZ,* 27/10/2003). Currently, after the closure of Rhino Garments at the end of 2005, the number of workers has levelled out at 6,500.

The company again postponed the start of its garment production to April 2002 (*AZ,* 24/4/2002), waiting for further liberalisation of imports into the US through AGOA II, which eventually became US law in August 2002 (<fDiMagazine ForeignDirectInvestment>:1.8.2002). Namibia had been presented its original AGOA I certificate only in December 2001 (*AZ,* 11/12/2001). In this agreement, the country had not been listed as a *Lesser Developed Country* (LDC). Thus, Namibian exporters were restricted to purchasing their raw materials and semi-finished products either from America or from specific African countries. In the meantime, Namibia continued negotiating for its LDC-status. Namibia's reclassification under AGOA II would allow the company to procure the bulk of its production-related imports directly from its own plants in Malaysia. Eventually, Ramatex went into apparel production in June 2002, once the US House of Representatives had successfully passed AGOA II legislation (http://www.grnnet.gov.na/News/Archive/2002/April/ Week4/ramatex.htm).

On several occasions, Ramatex brought into play its remarkable economic heft in negotiations for further support from the Namibian side. The concern demanded a spatial extension of its lease in September 2002 to be used for industrial expansion. Initially, the city of Windhoek reacted reluctantly to the company's demand for more land. As a result, Executive Director Albert Lim bypassed the municipal authorities and approached Prime Minister Gurirab directly. Quite uncouthly, Lim hinted at the possibility of disinvestment[24]. The Namibian government mediated between the two parties. Eventually, the city bowed to the pressure from both sides and placed two more industrial plots at Ramatex's disposal free of charge[25].

Some of the initial hopes for forward linkages for Namibian entrepreneurship seemed to materialise. Jesaya Nyamu, Hamutenya's successor as minister for trade and industry, particularly emphasised increased revenues in the transport sector (*The Namibian,* 28/3/2003). Undoubtedly, employment creation has to be added on the company's credit side, as well. After all, Ramatex has become the biggest single employer in Namibia's private sector economy. Some hopes, on the other hand, did not come to much. After receiving the second portion of land for free from the city of Windhoek in 2002, the firm announced its plans to establish its own subsidiaries to complement the textile sector: a factory for plastic and carton packaging, another manufacturing elastic bands, facilities for producing garment labels, buttons, and zips, as well as a printing

---

24. "We are now faced with the dilemma of whether to move to Malawi or Botswana for expansion" (*The Namibian,* 5/9/2002).

25. 5 ha in July 2002 and 112 ha in May 2003. In total, Ramatex's leasehold amounts to 160 ha. (*AZ,* 25/9/2002; 30/5/2003).

house. Also, the firm considered setting up department stores for about 10,000 employees on its premises, as well as a sports centre (*New Era*, 23/–26/9/2002). By mid-2007, none of these ambitious plans had materialised. On the contrary, the only additional use made of the industrial plot was an improper one, as Ramatex erected buildings for residential purposes (*AZ*, 25/9/2002). Windhoek officials complained to the government, to no avail.

Despite its importance as an employer, Ramatex's contribution to boosting the purchasing power of Namibia's formal sector is clearly limited by the low level of salaries paid to the production workers, mainly female. Moreover, there are reasonable doubts as to the positive effect of Ramatex's economic activity on the country's public funds. The wage structure agreed to between management and trade union, coming into effect on 1 February 2003, shows that the annual income levels of the company's African workforce remain below the taxation threshold.

In the first two years of its existence in Namibia, the Malaysian company displayed a certain liberal nonchalance in complying with the laws and policies of the host country. These are some of the issues on public record:

- no publication of an environmental impact assessment report, as required by Namibian environment-related policies;
- issuing a written demand to female workers to undergo pregnancy tests as a prerequisite for employment;
- no registration as a factory with the ministry of labour;
- withholding contributions to the social security commission funds until August 2002 (*The Namibian*, 12/7/2002;
- denying the union(s) access to the premises for the purpose of unionising, thus denying workers the right of collective bargaining (ibid.);
- setting up residential units within an industrial area, as well as lined ponds, without an approved plan, without written permission from municipal authorities, and against their written wishes to stop building activities (*AZ*, 25/9/2002): such residential units contravene a clause in the EPZ Act precluding residence in an EPZ;
- violation of quality standard regulations ISO 14,000 and SABS regarding industrial sewage; violation of regulations concerning the installation of electrical cables;
- feeding cheap industrial power into the electrical net of residential units built on Ramatex's premises (*The Namibian*, 23/1/2002).

On 18 May 2005, after several months during which rumours were regularly brushed aside by the Namibian authorities as unfounded, Ramatex Textiles Namibia closed down its Otjomuise subsidiary Rhino Garments and 1,600 workers were retrenched (<http://www.laborrights.org/press/namibia_tex-tiles0505.htm>: 19/5/2005). Their meagre retrenchment packages, the fruit of weeks of negotiations between trade union and management, granted workers a severance allowance equivalent to one week's salary "in appreciation of their service", in addition to a lump sum of N$ 300[26]. Ramatex accused the Namibia Food and Allied Workers' Union (NAFAU) of having plotted with the

---

26. One and a half weeks for workers with a minimum of two years service, plus N$ 375 (*New Era*, 17/5/2005).

Brussels-based International Textile Garment and Leather Workers' Federation (IT-GLWF) to stage an abstention campaign among American consumers, which allegedly curbed orders from the US market. In January 2005, the ITGLWF in an open letter had turned to Namibia's founding President Sam Nujoma, MTI, the ministry of labour, as well as to the International Labour Organisation (ILO), complaining of "appalling labour practices and workers' rights abuses". The same letter of complaint reached several major US chain stores such as Sears, KMart, ShopKo, OshKosh B'Gosh Inc. and Children's Place. The appeal attracted considerable attention from the general public in Namibia and the commercial world in the US.

However, Rhino Garment's closure may well have been motivated by other considerations, such as the expiry of the International Multi-Fibre Arrangement (MFA) and the Agreement on Textiles and Clothing (ATC) on 1 January 2005, and the power game initiated by the company's management to send a message of intimidation to its employees in the remaining three Otjomuise subsidiaries. Based on the first bilateral agreements signed in the 1960s, the MFA in 1974 and (on MFA's expiry in 1994) the ACT in 1994 had governed the international textile sector, restricting textile and clothing imports from low-wage economies. Strict quotas favoured producers in the industrialised world. For Ramatex, this meant two things: in future, the outlet in its classical metropolitan markets would narrow, as competition with other low-wage producers from developing economies, especially from China, stiffened. On the other hand, being itself well placed as a producer in China and in other Asian countries, the multinational mother conglomerate benefited from the scrapping of quotas. Since the US has already signalled that AGOA's validity would be extended to 2015, Ramatex Namibia, though facing stronger competition, could still avail itself of its preferential treatment on the US market as an *African* producer – reason enough to carry on production in Namibia for the time being, while threatening to close shop.

The combination of all these factors may have induced Ramatex Textiles Namibia to send a message of intimidation to its remaining workforce of 6,000 by closing down Rhino Garments after three years of strained industrial relations in all the Otjomuise factories. The intention was not difficult to decipher: since the signing of the first wage agreement in 2002, Ramatex workers had not received any salary increase. Salary negotiations were protracted for years and only concluded in October 2006 when the union finally mustered its courage and prompted workers to down tools. Even then, after being forced to make remarkable concessions, Ramatex insisted on publicly voicing the possibility that it could transfer its production any day now, and altogether, to other African countries.

The players (3): The Namibian workers and trade unions

Ramatex's workforce represents the weakest link in the tripartite game between the state, the multinational company and labour. In mid-2004, the company employed approximately 8,000 workers, thus becoming the biggest single private employer in post-independence Namibia. Around 1,900 of them were Chinese, Malaysian, Filipino and Bangladeshi nationals, the first three groups also serving as trainers on the job and supervisors. Considering the restrictive immigration policy of the Namibian government, their number appears rather surprising.

In September 2002, after some months of training Namibian workers on the job and paying them extremely low salaries, a three-tier salary scheme was adopted. It is based on skills, piecework[27], and in actual practice, nationality. Both Namibian and Asian workers earn a basic salary. Where the piece rate is met, a piecework wage is added. Wages differ markedly between Namibians and their Asian fellow workers in better job positions, the Namibian workforce being at a disadvantage. Their wages, on account of the minimal rating of their professional skills, hardly exceed the basic salary.

Until 31 August 2002, Ramatex paid N$ 1.76 per hour to a trained worker (*The Namibian*, 30/8/2002). The new salary scheme again put trainees into the lowest salary bracket. Until October 2006, they earned an hourly wage of N$ 1.50, whereas workers were paid N$ 3.00, quality controllers N$ 3.50 and supervisors N$ 4.00 (LaRRI 2003:19). On the basis of the contractual nine-hour shift calculated for 23 work days per month, monthly salaries in the respective categories amount to N$ 301.50, N$ 621, N$ 724.50 and N$ 828. In actual practice, Ramatex's employees are asked to work on Saturdays (paid overtime at a rate of 1.5) and occasionally on public holidays (double time). Even then, a supervisor's salary, the highest category, would not be subject to taxation. In comparison, the minimum wage introduced in 2004 for commercial farm workers, traditionally one of the most underprivileged employee groups in the formal labour sector in Namibia, is fixed at N$ 421 in cash and additional N$ 250 in kind, that is at N$ 671. Correspondingly, annual salaries of Ramatex workers in the respective categories amount to N$ 3,726, N$ 7,452, N$ 8,694 and N$ 9,936. Thus, wages range between a monthly US$ 48 and US$ 133[28], with an average calculated at US$ 90. The only contribution deducted from the workers' salaries and apportioned to a public fund is the monthly premium paid to the social security commission.

Ramatex introduced a complex six-step recruitment and training procedure. Workers are only taken on probation, a period covering approximately 3 to 6 months at the company's discretion. During this time they qualify only for a trainee salary[29]. Wages do not provide for medical benefits or for any housing or transport allowances (*The Na-*

---

27. Cf. "Flexible Remuneration Scheme," clauses 2.1 and 2.2 of template "Letter of Appointment" from Flamingo Garments. Ramatex Textiles Namibia (Pty) Ltd (2002a):1.
28. Calculated at a rate of 6.25 Namibian dollar per US dollar (April 2006).
29. A leaflet handed out to applicants outlines the "Recruitment Procedure." It states the following steps: Applicants register with the ministry of labour, which according to the trade union, compiles a list of applicants and communicates it to the company (step 1). An interview follows (step 2). Passing the interview, the applicant is admitted to a training programme after a "test period" of 3–5 days (step 3). Once taken into the training programme, she/he signs a training agreement and undergoes further training for two weeks until the next evaluation. Passing the evaluation, 10 more weeks of training ensue (step 4). Step 5 consists of a performance appraisal. As far as step 6 is concerned, the leaflet remains ambiguous. It states: "Sign contract after three months and salary increased [sic!]." This may imply that now, after three months, a contract is signed. It may also mean that after an initial 3 months of training, another 3 months of trainee status are required before the worker is granted a worker's salary of an hourly N$ 3. LaRRI's study confirms that training periods in individual cases may span even more than half a year. Training takes place either at the Windhoek Vocational Training Centre, and/or on the job at Ramatex. With regard to the recruitment procedure, Ramatex's management corroborates workers' information that the ministry of labour keeps a database of applicants (cf. LaRRI 2003:15–16).

mibian, 24/4/2003). The latter, as a rule, is of substantial significance for every employee in Windhoek. In the capital, as in all the urban centres of southern Africa, apartheid had not only segregated black workers in distant townships but also hindered the development of a public transport system. Today, the municipality lacks the means to provide sufficient public transport[30]. Forced by their meagre wages to economise, the (mainly female) workers have to walk long distances in an unprotected and unsafe area that has since become a focus for crime.

Working conditions are reported to be problematic in various ways. At the height of the first recruitment wave at the beginning of 2002, Ramatex demanded pregnancy tests at the applicant's own expense. The firm refused to appoint pregnant women. A public outcry followed, condemning the employment practice as a violation of Namibian labour laws. The company's management first denied any such measure, then admitted to having issued a letter prescribing the pregnancy test and eventually revoked it[31]. Employees also complained of health and safety issues, especially skin rashes caused by dyes (LaRRI 2003:22–4). When their complaints were taken up in media reports, Ramatex reacted with a full-page advert questioning the reliability of the report (*New Era*, 5/–11/7/2002).

Initially, staff was denied the right to collective bargaining. The company forbade unions from entering the premises to enlist members (*The Namibian*, 8/7/2002). Only on 2 October 2002 did Ramatex and the Namibia Food and Allied Workers Union (NAFAU) signed a recognition agreement. The document emphasises the "concept of freedom of association" and grants the union collective and exclusive bargaining rights. In its turn, NAFAU committed itself to answering for the legality of all industrial action[32]. Under such a corporativist scheme, the union is under a legal obligation to assist in law enforcement in cases of industrial action. In mid-2003, nine shop stewards represented the workers at the four subsidiaries in Otjomuise (*The Namibian*, 2/6/2003).

Various seeds of conflict created a delicate situation. As a result, since the inception of production five so-called 'wild cat' strikes have brought Ramatex to a temporary halt. This sparked off conflict between the trade union and workers and prompted action

---

30. Private taxis cater for most of the capital's commuters. Normally, Namibian companies either provide transport to and from work or pay transport allowances on top of the salary. As a result of the habitational structures of apartheid, the vast majority of Ramatex's workers live in Katutura, Windhoek's African town centre, and the northwestern districts, at a distance of at least seven to eight kilometres from their workplace. Thus, working in Otjomuise requires paying two taxi fare stages. At the current rate of N$ 6.5 per stage, transport costs amount to N$ 26 per day, or approximately N$ 650 to 700 per month. Comparing such expenses with the salaries indicated above sheds light on the plight of Ramatex's workforce.

31. Ramatex's demand was allegedly aimed at avoiding later applications for maternity leave. The minister of women's affairs and child welfare condemned management's demand as discriminatory and infringing the country's Labour Act (*New Era*, 1/–3/3/2002). Executive Director Albert Lim countered that "no employee had been forced to undergo pregnancy tests." (*The Namibian*, 14/3/2002). The same newspaper (26/6/2002) claimed to be in possession of a letter to employees from Ramatex, which confirmed the allegation. Calle Schlettwein, the permanent secretary at the ministry of labour, declared the request for pregnancy tests illegal. In July, Ramatex admitted to having issued the letter demanding pregnancy tests to applicants in February 2002, stating that the letter had been revoked (*New Era*, 5/–11/7/2002).

32. Clause 11 of the recognition agreement between Ramatex Textiles Namibia (Pty) Ltd and the Namibian Food and Allied Workers Union. Ramatex Textiles Namibia (Pty) Ltd (2002c).

by government officials, who accused the employees of sabotaging Namibia's efforts to attract foreign investment. While two of the strikes involved only the Namibian labourers, the other three engaged the Asian employees.

The first downing of tools in protest against new contracts occurred on 28 August 2002 and involved approximately 100 discontented workers (*The Namibian*, 29/8/2002). For several weeks, the atmosphere at Ramatex had been disturbed by the protraction of the recognition talks between the union and the company and by widespread confusion over contracts aimed at introducing productivity-related piece rates. In that difficult situation, Namibian officials intervened. They asserted the government's official political stance, countering the workers' demands. A large delegation of members of the National Council, the second chamber of the Namibian legislature, visited the Ramatex plant in Otjomuise, publicly expressing their satisfaction with the company's achievements. The NIC headed by David Nuyoma accompanied them (*New Era*, 16/–18/8/2002). Only a minority of workers went on strike, but Ramatex reacted by locking out all 1,500 employees (*The Namibian*, 30/8/2002), who then staged a demonstration at the ministry of labour. The strike was called off after both NAFAU and the ministry intervened. Subsequent negotiations between the union and the company resulted in the salary scheme coming into effect on 1 September 2002. However, locked-out workers had to reapply for their jobs (*New Era*, 30/8/–2/9/2002).

The second occurrence involved about 3,000 textile workers on 15 April 2003. Their action over wage increases and transport allowances again met with a total lock-out by the company, this time for two weeks. NAFAU intervened, mediating between management and labourers as Namibian riot police entered the factory. Ramatex declared the dismissal of the initiators of the strike. It rejected all claims for higher wages, citing its fears for the multinational's competitiveness "under the Charles Darwin Economic Theory" (Executive Director Albert Lim in *The Namibian*, 23/4/2003) as a pretext. On 29 April, employees resumed work. They were again forced to sign new contracts and 416 workers remained suspended for allegedly masterminding the strike (*The Namibian*, 8/5/2003). The strike yielded no result, meeting multiple resistance. In a concerted move, management and Namibian officials dismissed the industrial action as "economic sabotage"[33]. Likewise, the union labelled it as illegal (*The Namibian*, 22/4/2003). Above all, the strikers' bargaining power was severely weakened by the fact that the company countered their action by recruiting workers for its newly opened subsidiary Rhino Garments. Every day, for about a week, some 1,000 workers flocked to the gates, prepared to accept any salary as long as they could gain employment (*Namibia Economist*, 9/–15/5/2003).

The high rating that Ramatex's initiative had gained in the economic policies of the Namibian government showed again in October 2003. The Namibian trade unions' research arm, the Labour Resource and Research Institute (LaRRI), published its critical assessment of labour issues at the multinational's Namibian affiliate. The in-depth report received great attention from the media. In response, MTI's Jesaya Nyamu denied that Ramatex's labour relations could be classified as exploitative (*AZ*, 24/10/2003). Just

---

33. State President Nujoma on Labour Day 2003. He condemned the strike as illegal, called one of the worker activists a "spy" (*AZ*, 2/5/2003). Previously, David Nuyoma had stated that the illegal strike sent the wrong signal to potential investors (*AZ*, 24/4/2003).

a week after the publication of the report, President Nujoma started a media offensive in support of Ramatex and ostentatiously visited Otjomuise (*AZ, 27/10/2003*). Nahas Angula, then minister of higher education, presently Namibia's prime minister, justified the company's wage structure as reflecting the workers' low productivity levels (*The Namibian, 5/11/2003*).

To this day, industrial labour relations have hardly improved. Conflicts continue at the company's premises. In December 2003, Ramatex's 500 Filipino employees brought their grievances about "poor wages, cramped living conditions and health concerns" (*The Namibian, 17/12/2003*) before the public. The conflict simmered at low intensity until July, when the workers again took action, finally forcing the company to honour some of their requests. In January 2004, a majority of the 1,000 Chinese workers downed tools, both Malaysian Chinese and Chinese workers from the mainland's People's Republic (*Asian Labour News, 5/2/2004*). The case of the 416 Namibian workers who had been suspended after the industrial action in April 2003 kept the interest of the media alive during the first half of 2004 (*New Era, 26/1/2004*). The employees, while still waiting for a disciplinary hearing to be instituted by Ramatex as prescribed by the procedural stipulations of the Namibian Labour Act, had taken their case to court.

In August and September 2005, the sad saga of the 438 Bangladeshi workers at Ramatex swept through the press. The company finally managed to get the labourers deported from the country by the Namibian authorities, after hiring them overseas only a few months before. The Namibian unions' umbrella organisation, the National Union of Namibian Workers (NUNW), and NAFAU threatened to stage a general strike but were overtaken by the swift action of the state in rescinding the Bangladeshis' work permits. In October 2004, the infection control unit of the Katutura state hospital in Namibia's capital Windhoek informed the city of Windhoek and the general public of its investigations into the alarming rate of skin infections among factory workers at Ramatex[34].

In January 2005, the ITGLWF's boycott appeal sent a shock wave through the public, forcing government, Ramatex and NAFAU to engage in tripartite discussions in the following weeks (*The Namibian, 31/3/2005*). In April 2005, Bishop Zephania Kameeta of the Evangelical Lutheran Church of the Republic of Namibia (ELCRN) gave his view on the questionable effects of globalisation on Namibian society. Bringing his high moral repute to bear, he publicly exhorted the Namibian churches to take a stand (*AZ, 29/4/2005*). In the meantime, the first media rumours about Rhino Garment's closure shook the public.

The second half of 2005 and the early part of 2006 were marked by the protracted dispute over the long overdue salary increase. Since the first salary agreement, Ramatex labourers had kept working for the same monthly pay. NAFAU asked for salary increases from N\$ 3 an hour to N\$ 6.50 for the lower income bracket and from N\$ 4.50 to N\$ 8.50 for supervisors. The company smugly let its employees know that it had opened four new factories in China, and then countered the union's demand by offering an increase in the hourly pay rate of 10 Namibian cents. NAFAU, well aware of the predicament of the workers who might be caught between an insufficient income and

---

34. Media reports spoke of "more than 20 cases of skin irritation a day, and the numbers appeared to have increased over the last two or three months" (*The Namibian, 22/10/2004*).

no income at all in the not unlikely case of total disinvestment by Ramatex, offered to lower its demand to 50 cents. Management raised its offer by a further 5 cents, maintaining that the Namibian staff's miserable productivity did not allow for more.

Following these skirmishes in December 2005, Namibia's Prime Minister Nahas Angula intervened to try to end the deadlock in January 2006, to no avail (*The Namibian*, 26/1/2006). Months of rumours followed during which the Malaysian company engaged in a scathing censure of the productivity of its Namibian workforce. The textile multinational created the impression that it had already made the firm decision to cease its operations altogether. Its threat of final closure seemed to be corroborated in May 2006 when details of a letter addressed to the Namibian government filtered through. Ramatex's management had offered its Namibian subsidiary to the Namibian state for sale at an asking price of above N$ 500 m (*The Namibian*, 15/5/2006). The executive director of the Ramatex Berhad group, Albert Lim Poh Boon, stated his intention to close shop by 30 May 2006 should the Namibian partner not show immediate interest (*AZ*, 17/5/2006).

Ramatex's assertion of the uncompetitive productivity of its local workforce weighed heavily in the public debate, as it touched on a sensitive nerve, Namibia's want of a skilled industrial labour force. Resulting from tried and tested apartheid practices of prevented industrialisation, Bantu education and bonded migrant labour in colonial times, the country's post-colonial economy indeed experiences marked vocational shortcomings. Against the neoliberal backdrop of economic policies aiming to attract FDI, such want is seen as a major handicap with the potential to scare off international investors. Ironically, the blame is laid on the Namibian labourers.

Ramatex's case, on the other hand, is hardly verifiable. Not being a listed company in Namibia, no audit reports are made available by the company, which makes it difficult to establish the facts (*The Namibian*, 17/5/2006). Herbert Jauch, LaRRI's director and researcher, undertook to question the company's assertion closely. In a study of Africa's clothing and textile industry focusing on Ramatex Namibia, he related the value of Namibian exports to the US in the years 2002–04 to the estimated labour costs incurred by Ramatex. The findings are startling: labour costs, including both the Namibian and Asian labour force in Ramatex's service, total approximately 10% of Namibian export value (Jauch 2006:216–7). Even taking only the strictly AGOA-related statistics for total Namibian imports of textiles and apparel to the US in 2004 as a basis for a similar calculation, Ramatex's labour costs would barely exceed 15% of the customs value of the company's Namibian exports to the US[35]. Whatever the accuracy of the contention about low productivity levels, these certainly cannot be put forward to explain the (alleged) lack of profitability in Ramatex's case.

---

35. http;//www.agoa.info/?view=country_info&country=na&stay=trade. This AGOA website indicates a volume of Namibian textile and apparel imports into the US in 2004 classified under AGOA and GSP (Generalized System of Preferences) of US$ 161.193 m. The lack of any Namibian textile industry other than Ramatex makes it likely that the exports listed above are to be ascribed to Ramatex only. The company's labour costs of US$ 24.8 m are then related to the export value.

The Namibian government reacted to the company's blackmail by setting up a high-level technical committee of cabinet ministers and the NUNW[36]. As an alternative to the proposed takeover, a "turnaround plan" intended "to salvage the situation" (*New Era*, 22/5/2006) was soon announced. It included:

- the provision of N$ 13 m by the Namibian state to finance the water reclamation plant that Ramatex (in 2002) had contractually agreed to build and pay for[37];
- the refund of vocational training costs. However, the plan avoided mentioning the fact tha such refunds had been regularly provided for in the nation's annual budget legislation since 2002;
- the promise to induce the parastatals NamPower and NamWater, as well as the municipality of Windhoek to grant Ramatex preferential tariffs for electricity and water. Possibly, the promise was made in view of the expiry of the favourable terms Ramatex had enjoyed since 2002;
- the assurance that the trade unions would be reminded of their national obligation to contribute to industrial peace;
- the firm intention to mobilise the Southern African Customs Union (SACU) and the Southern African Development Community (SADC) to negotiate for Ramatex's preferential treatment in southern African and European markets (*New Era*, 22/5/2006).

The Malaysian multinational, staging yet another uncompromising tactical move, rejected the government's offer. Instead, it renewed its bid to sell the business to the state. Concurrently, it began removing all equipment from its Otjomuise spinning and knitting factories, relocating the machinery to its overseas subsidiaries (*AZ*, 2/6/2006). Though it refrained from any direct intervention, this last move might have prompted the Namibian government to begin opposing Ramatex's pressure. The authorities launched a series of routine audits and checks intended to establish the company's compliance with environmental and AGOA rules. At the beginning of June 2006, the government finally rejected Ramatex's offer of a buy-out (*AZ*, 7/6/2006).

The state's negative response marked a turning point. Ramatex indicated its willingness to reconsider the generous incentives programme offered by the government. By the end of June, it resumed negotiations with NAFAU on the disputed salary increase. Company and unions decided to set up a joint committee tasked with monitoring productivity (*AZ*, 4/7/2006). Thus, for the first time in months, Ramatex sent a signal that it indeed intended to maintain production in Namibia. In August 2006, media reports revealed secret negotiations between government officials and Ramatex Berhad's executive director, Albert Lim, flown in from Kuala Lumpur. This time, the talks excluded the unions. It transpired that Lim pressurised the Namibian government to grant work visas in considerable numbers to allow the entry of additional Asian employees to Namibia. The request was again motivated by the Namibian staff's alleged productivity

---

36. On the government's side, the committee included the permanent secretary of the ministry of finance, Calle Schlettwein, as a chair; the representatives of MTI, the ministry of foreign affairs, the attorney general's office and of ODC (*The Namibian*, 15/5/2006; 22/5/2006; 30/6/2006).

37. Criticised for the environmental damage caused by its production process, Ramatex had pledged N$ 25 m for the construction of the plant in a full-page newspaper advert in 2002.

backlog, provoking harsh reactions from NAFAU and the NUNW (*The Namibian,* 11/8/2006).

The last act, for the time being, took place in October 2006. The inconclusive wage negotiations, government's pliability in complying with the multinational's request to employ a foreign workforce and especially the unrest among the Namibian labourers at Ramatex induced the unions to call for a strike ballot. Nine out of ten workers voted for industrial action (*The Namibian,* 11/10/2006). Concurrently, the city of Windhoek announced its decision to take charge of the factory's waste management at Ramatex's expense, after publishing the devastating findings of the city's investigation into water pollution in Otjomuise. However, the city also confirmed the company's release from its contractual obligation to build a water reclamation plant[38].

On 13 October 2006, Ramatex workers downed tools. Two days of abstention from work combined with the state's refusal of a take-over and the recent hard line taken by the municipal authorities induced the company to eventually make remarkable concessions:

- a salary increase of 36.7%, from N$ 3 to N$ 4.10 per hour;
- a monthly housing allowance of N$ 150;
- a monthly transport allowance of N$ 100;
- an annual bonus of 60% of the monthly salary.

In addition, the parties to the wage settlement agreed to the introduction of a medical aid scheme, to which the company is to contribute 70%, and to the establishment of a pension fund, to which both employee and employer are to pay in a contribution at the rate of 5% of the employee's salary. The agreement became effective on 1 October 2006, 49 months after the first salary agreement (*New Era,* 16/10/2006). Combining salary and benefits, the pay cheque of a Ramatex worker would currently amount to approximately N$ 1,100[39], an increase of 43% over the previous salary. In return, Ramatex Namibia was granted a rebate of N$ 13 m for the water reclamation plant as well as permission to bring additional Asian labourers into the country.

The current situation indicates that – despite all threats of total disinvestment – Ramatex Textiles Namibia intends to make the most of AGOA and the preferential treatment that flows from it. The multinational's line of approach reveals a two-pronged strategy. For as long as AGOA facilitates access to the US-market for apparel, Namibia's EPZ environment, as well as the country's affordable labour costs, seem to make up for the possible skills shortages of its labour force. At the same time, spinning and knitting production have been shifted to the Asian branches of the Ramatex Berhad Group.

---

38. *The Namibian,* 12/10/2006. The plant is now constructed under the responsibility of the city, and (partially) financed with the N$ 13 m made available by the state.

39. Calculated, as was done in calculating the previous average salary of N$ 621, on the basis of a contractual 9-hours working day for 23 days a month. Thus the basic salary amounts to N$ 848.70. Housing and transport allowances bring the salary to N$ 1098.70. Adding one-twelfth of the annual bonus to the monthly salary brings the monthly pay cheque to N$ 1,141.35. Of the monthly basic salary, 5%, that is N$ 42.44, has to be deducted for the employee's contribution to the pension scheme, resulting in a salary of N$ 1098.70. Deductions for medical aid are not taken into account in this calculation. The annual salary of N$ 13,200 still ranges below the Namibian tax threshold of N$ 20,000. No tax, therefore, accrues to the state from salaries of trained Ramatex workers.

Ramatex's threat-and-smile strategy points to the fact that the profitability of its entrepreneurial activities in Namibia is not determined solely by the productivity of labour. The political landscape shaped by the Namibian government's FDI-friendly policies, offering the company massive opportunities for saving capital costs over the past five years, as well as the preferential market access facilitated by Namibia's AGOA certification, are of equal if not greater importance.

The players (4): The Asian workers

Ramatex Namibia has always been secretive about the number of foreign workers of Asian origin it employs. Information supplied by NAFAU representatives and government officials level out at approximately 1,900 in mid-2004 (*The Namibian*, 15/9/2004). Detailed media reports add up to a higher total. They estimate the Chinese workforce at 1,000, 800 of them Malaysian and the rest from mainland China (*Asian Labour News*, 5/2/2004). A further 750 are Filipinos and some 510 were recruited in Bangladesh (*AZ*, 10/9/2004). Before the dismissal of Rhino Garment's 1,600 employees, the total number of foreigners represented roughly a quarter of Ramatex's workforce. To date, figures indicating the number of the additional Asian 'trainers' admitted to Namibia on the basis of the negotiations in mid-2006 have not been released. It transpired that the Namibian factory runs separate human resource departments for its Namibian and foreign employees. The foreign workforce is requested to sign contracts of three years' duration before entering the country (*The Namibian*, 17/12/2003). The company holds the foreign workers' passports, ostensibly for safekeeping (*Asian Labour News*, 5/2/2004).

Time and again, cultural conflicts are reported to have affected working relationships between Malaysian management and Asian supervisors on the one hand and the African workforce on the other. The Asian superiors are accused of cultural arrogance (LaRRI 2003:25–7), whereas management complains about the low performance and lack of discipline of African workers, which they ascribe to considerable deficiencies in work ethic that is culturally not up to Asian standards (*The Namibian*, 23/4/2003). However, positions are not at all as clearly entrenched as may seem to be the case. Ramatex's productive workforce of Asian origin, though privileged compared with its African counterparts, proved a hard nut for management to crack. Several labour disputes prominently involving its Asian employees rocked the company.

On 10 May 2003, about 700 Chinese Malaysians remained in their hostels built on the premises, demanding wage increases and better conditions of service. At first, Ramatex, the NIC and the ministry of labour denied that there had been any industrial action at all[40]. Subsequent information alleged that only 216 Asian workers had gone on

---

40. *The Namibian*, 13/5/2003. In parliament, Deputy Labour Minister Rosalia Nghidinwa referred to Ramatex's explanation that the stay-away occurred on a weekend, when workers were not on duty. Therefore, it could not have been a strike. Moreover, the date coincided with the Buddhist full moon religious festival (*The Namibian*, 16/6/2003). However, in 2003 the 'Wesak' festival started only on 15 May, 5 days after the work stoppage (ibid.). As to the closure of the plants over weekends, the contract template of Flamingo Garments states under clause 7.2: "As the company's operation is continuous, it operates for 24 hours and 7 days per week and you may work on shifts. You should not refuse such shift work." "Letter of Appointment" from Flamingo Garments. Ramatex Textiles Namibia (Pty) Ltd (2002a):1. Mocks Shivute, permanent secretary

strike. Seven were dismissed together with three managers accused of mishandling the work stoppage that officially had not taken place[41]. The Asian workers resumed work on 13 May, without any information being released as to the compromise they had obviously reached with management.

Half a year later, in December 2003, after two Filipino workers charged with having contracted Hepatitis C were sent home, 700 fellow workers, mainly Filipinos, reacted with a petition. Ramatex's management had classified hepatitis as a sexually transmitted disease (STD) and refused to honour the medical bill. The petition complained about working and living conditions. It emphasised the low monthly basic wage paid out in Namibian dollars, equivalent to US$ 200. The adverse exchange rate translated into approximately N$ 1,400, while at the time of signing their contracts, the salary in Namibian currency amounted to N$ 2,400 to 2,600. The workers demanded payment in US currency, which their contract provided for as an option (*The Namibian*, 17/12/2003). They also turned to their embassy in South Africa. A Filipino diplomat, Consul-General Oscar Orcine, then visited Namibia in January 2004 to discuss the grievances with Ramatex officials after the company had not responded to official letters. He was given the cold shoulder by the Malaysian management. The dispute remained unresolved until, in July 2004, the Filipino workers decided to partially down tools, refusing to work overtime. On 26 July, Ramatex eventually gave in to the demand, promising to pay monthly salaries in US dollars (*The Namibian*, 21/1/2004; 20/7/2004; 27/7/2004).

In the meantime, unrest amongst ethnic Chinese workers from Malaysia and nationals of the People's Republic over poor contract conditions had become apparent in December 2003. The unrest led to industrial action, with a majority of the 1,000 Chinese employees refusing to work as from 8 January 2004. They demanded a reduction of their contract term from three to two years, and the implementation of their contractual claim to be reimbursed for medical expenses. Though accepting the workers' demand, the company suspended the Chinese workforce for 17 days without pay, as it was low season (*Asian Labour News*, 5/2/2004). Officially, this move was motivated by the wish to afford workers unpaid leave for the celebration of the Chinese New Year (*The Namibian*, 14/1/2004). In early February 2004, a group of 80 mainland Chinese workers quit, severing their contracts and leaving for home, indignant at the working and living conditions at the factory. A further 150 followed their example (*The Namibian*, 14/1/2004).

During the first two weeks of August 2004, news confirmed that Ramatex had dismissed 66 of its 438 Bangladeshi workers for allegedly poor work performance. The dismissed had been hired in August 2003, whereas the majority of the Bangladeshi employees had just come to work in Namibia in July 2004 (*The Namibian*, 5/8/2004; 10/8/2004). As the dismissal of the 66 implied the cancellation of their work permits, the workers challenged their imminent deportation in court, claiming their dismissal had been unfair and in breach of the labour law. They were allowed by the court to stay

---

of the ministry of information and broadcasting, stated in a press release that the workers had merely been "released from work to allow them to celebrate their own national religious festival, just as we celebrate Christmas, Easter and other religious holidays" (*New Era*, 1/6/2003).

41. According to Ramatex's management, the company at that time employed 525 foreigners, 460 of them as trainers and 65 as part of the management team (*The Namibian*, 16/6/2003).

in the country and fight their case. The company reacted by offering to reinstate the workers at a lower salary, US$ 120 instead of their previous monthly pay of US$ 200 (*The Namibian*, 24/8/2004)

The affair had far-reaching implications, as the public had been alerted to the dire labour relations at Ramatex over a long period of two years. The municipality of Windhoek was called in, as neighbours informed city officials of the apparently intolerable housing conditions of Bangladeshi workers. They were accommodated in a private house in Windhoek West. More than 300 tenants shared a small space including a garage, with unsuitable sanitary facilities. The property had been rented by Desmond Gertze, a local representative of Bay Eastern Overseas Ltd., an agency under contract to Ramatex for the supply of 2,000 Bangladeshi workers (*The Namibian*, 10/9/2004; 25/8/2004). Desmond Gertze, a Rehoboth resident and brother of Neville Gertze, the Namibian high commissioner in Malaysia, had entered an equal partnership with a certain Hanif to form Saujana Blossom Import and Export Namibia, a Namibian-Bangladeshi joint venture. Saujana Blossom acted as Namibian pendant of Bay Eastern Overseas, and was Ramatex's accommodation-service provider for the workers from Bangladesh[42]. The alleged family connections sparked suspicions in the media that the high commissioner was involved not only in providing work permits to the Bangladeshi workers in Malaysia. Neville Gertze was also said to be indirectly linked with the recruitment of workers and the provision of their accommodation in Windhoek (*The Namibian*, 10/9/2004; *New Era*, 15/9/2004).

The high commission's procurement of work permits was commonly assessed as violating Namibian immigration regulations, as most of the workers were unskilled (*AZ*, 10/9/2004). The ministry of home affairs criticised the high commission, which had granted work permits instead of work visas, again in violation of the Namibian Immigration Control Act. However, in laying the sole blame on High Commissioner Gertze, the ministry omitted to mention that in a letter written to Ramatex, dated 30 April 2004, MTI had already acknowledged the factory's request to employ expatriates. Based on previous negotiations between Gertze and Ramatex's Albert Lim Poh Boon, the ministry had given the green light to the company to employ foreign workers for a period not exceeding two years. The NUNW suspected "high-level corruption in the granting of work permits"[43].

These events resulted in a generally critical stance being taken by the Namibian authorities, stakeholders and the public. The municipality turned to the courts to obtain an injunction against Saujana Blossom's illegal building renovations at the notorious 'Hotel Ramatex', made to accommodate tenants in large numbers in an unsuitable building. Various representatives of political parties and trade unions condemned the constant violations of workers' rights in what was perceived as a 'sweatshop'. The NUNW, together

---

42. According to information given by Willy Gertze, Neville's and Desmond's father. In an interview, father Gertze added that his nephew, the Windhoek municipality's strategic executive for finance Roger Gertze, "had no role to play in the accommodation of foreign workers," though he had "been approached for 'advice' on the city's building procedures" (*The Namibian*, 14/9/2004; *AZ*, 13/9/2004; *New Era*, 13/9/2004).

43. *The Namibian*, 21/9/2004. The umbrella organisation claimed that its investigations brought to light the sum of "US$ 21 m in undocumented payments ... made in the instance of the Bangladeshi workers" (*The Namibian*, 13/9/2004).

with the Namibian Red Cross, opened an account for legal aid expenses for the workers. Living conditions of Ramatex workers were widely perceived as a "humanitarian crisis of a scandalous nature" (*New Era,* 14/9/2004). They were equated with "apartheid practices such as single-sex dormitories, and ethnic and racial divide-and-rule techniques" (The Star [South Africa], 13/10/2004). On the other hand, the authorities also had to put up with critical questions from the media. Why had a substantial Namibian delegation consisting of stakeholders of MTI and the city of Windhoek, who in July 2003 had visited the CEO Albert Lim at his invitation at Ramatex's headquarters in Kuala Lumpur, not managed to persuade the company of the need to respect Namibian EPZ and labour laws (*AZ,* 14/9/2004)?

After serious riots at the factory on the occasion of the visit of Alif Hossain, the managing director of Eastern Overseas flown in to account for the evident mess, the company eventually decided to terminate all contracts with its Bangladeshi workforce. Repeatedly, the workers had vehemently protested against their living conditions. They also complained about substantial deductions from their salaries not provided for in their contracts. As a consequence of their dismissal, their work and residence permits had to be rescinded by the Namibian authorities. By mid-September 2004, all workers from Bangladesh, with the exception of the first group of 66 allowed to fight their case in court, were removed from Namibia.

The Bangladeshi migrants had invested US$ 3,500 each for their recruitment by Bay Eastern Overseas[44]. In a letter detailing the demand for recruits, Ramatex stipulated that the immigrants would be hired for two years and paid a monthly salary of US$ 120, based on a 48-working-hour week. Medical services in Namibia were to be granted free of charge, as well as accommodation and transport (*The Namibian,* 21/9/2004). The final contract signed by the workers, once in Namibia, formally provided for a monthly salary of US$ 200. The company deducted US$ 70 for accommodation, US$ 45 for the provision of canteen food and another N$ 20 for transport (*New Era,* 13/9/2004; *The Namibian,* 14/9/2004).

The Bangladeshi employees had been made to foot the bill. Once again, the unskilled workers represented the weakest link in the tripartite scenario linking state, capital and labour. In a thoughtful opinion piece, LaRRI's Jauch summarised the deportation of the Ramatex workers as a classic example of human trafficking that capitalised on the globalisation of unemployment and poverty. Contradictory and conflictual as it may be in the Namibian case, the interaction between multinational conglomerate, shady agencies and authorities reflects both the crude logic of the present-day neoliberal economics of globalisation and the tragic irony of Namibia's developmental hopes, hooked as they are to foreign investment.

The players (5): Room for manoeuvre?

In particular, Ramatex's environmental attitude raised questions among the general public about the actual room for manoeuvre that both the Namibian authorities and civil society enjoyed. To date, the firm still has to publish an adequate report on its

---

44. *The Namibian,* 10/9/2004. It appears that Ramatex also paid for the service rendered for recruitment, i.e., a sum of US$ 580 per recruit (*The Namibian,* 13/9/2004).

Environmental Impact Assessment (EIA). For over four years the factory has operated production processes based on water, like dyeing, so-called 'wet processing', which are strictly regulated by international and Namibian norms, and which are to be publicly monitored. Namibia's environmental policies, though not yet integrated into an Environmental Act as such, prescribe the report of an investigation into the environmental impact to be a public document. It is a binding prerequisite for decision-making previous to the establishment of a project of this order of magnitude (*The Namibian*, 25/1/2002).

To date, there is only contradictory information as to whether or not Ramatex did carry out an adequate EIA. In early March 2002, three-quarters of a year after the start of construction work at the factory site, Ramatex's Lim stated that an EIA had already been completed. His statement followed a public confrontation between Namibian environmentalists and municipal and government authorities. Earlier in January 2002, MTI Minister Hamutenya, assisted by NIC Director David Nuyoma, had ruled out the possibility that Ramatex would "start operating unless its environmental systems on waste disposal, recycling and sewage meet municipal requirements". According to the media, an environmental document assessing the textile project was due at the end of that month. The MTI maintained that it had been produced by "an Australian consultancy", whereas the environmental department of the city of Windhoek indicated that it originated from Malaysia. It transpired later that the Malaysian document, prepared by a company named Perunding Environmental Planning Consultancy, merely provided a general picture of the industrial production processes at the Otjomuise factory, not an assessment of their impact (*The Namibian*, 23/1/2002; 25/1/2002; 14/3/2002; 5/4/2005; 4/5/2005).

To add to the blurred picture, Ramatex's Albert Lim maintained in October 2003 that a team of Danish consultants had recently finalised an assessment. He stated that the company could not disclose its contents because of its "trade-sensitive information" (*The Namibian*, 27/10/2003). Indirectly, his statement revealed the helplessness of the Namibian authorities. Contrary to the EPZ Act (Part V, 14.5.a), they had not insisted on the assessment of the environmental impact as a precondition for issuing an EPZ certificate in 2001. Nor did they now insist on the publication of the alleged report. Already at the beginning of December 2001, Earthlife Namibia, a branch of the environmentalist NGO Earthlife Africa, had alerted four ministries, the municipality, Ramatex and the trade unions by writing of their concerns. Earthlife demanded details of the EIA report now that the company had been certified. The reactions of the officials concentrated rather on condemning the request. The environmentalists were accused of putting at risk the country's developmental efforts to attract foreign investors[45]. Ironically, a year later, the phalanx of critics split. Minister Hamutenya condemned the city

---

45. Martin Shipanga, the city's CEO, suspected a South African plot behind Earthlife's environmental concerns, since SA had lost Ramatex to Namibia (*AZ*, 19/12/2001). Minister Hamutenya reacted with an open letter published in *The Namibian* on 1 February. He condemned Earthlife's "propaganda charade, dressed up as environmental concerns," their environmental concerns being "subversive to government development efforts and harmful to the national image." A few days later, President Nujoma joined in the harsh critique (*AZ*, 4/2/2002). The mayor of Windhoek, Matheus Shikongo, accused the NGO of the sabotage of Ramatex. (*The Namibian*, 1/2/2002).

for producing "a subjective account of Ramatex's environmental status" (*The Namibian*, 28/3/2003).

From the start, the city had been in an awkward position. The city council felt that it had to seize this seemingly golden opportunity for the industrial development of the capital, which promised to give fresh impetus to the labour market. The city's executive therefore warmly welcomed Ramatex. On the other hand, a large part of the financial and practical burden resulting from the incentives package offered by the government to Ramatex fell on the municipal budget. This included N$ 106 m for infrastructural services, 160 hectares of municipal land free of charge and carrying the considerable costs of urban development for the several thousand migrant jobseekers who flooded the town in two major waves in January 2002 and May 2003, when Flamingo Garment and Rhino Textile started recruitment of trainees (*AZ*, 28/9/2001; *The Namibian*, 15/1/2002; *Namibia Economist*, 9/–15/5/2003). In the meantime, the state watched from the sidelines, being itself a debtor to the city to the tune of N$ 30 m for infrastructural developments (*The Namibian*, 28/10/2005).

As well, Ramatex's water consumption constitutes a substantial portion of Windhoek's total consumption[46]. Shortly after Ramatex went into production, the municipality had to declare a sizeable price increase in order to reduce consumption (*AZ*, 1/8/2002). Whether this was just a coincidence or not, Windhoek's residents were asked to pay for the increase, whereas the firm had been granted preferential rates as part of the initial incentives package. The preferential rates granted to Ramatex amounted to only 48% of the rates payable by other industrial water consumers (*AZ*, 2/7/2004).

In April 2004, Windhoek's residents were also called on to pay for an environmental audit the city council decided to conduct at the Otjomuise factory. Numerous concerns had been raised about the evident water pollution. Towards the end of 2003, preliminary tests indicated that toxic substances from the factory might have seeped into one of Windhoek's major aquifers. The following months revealed the extent of systematic contamination. The 'wet processing' for the purpose of dyeing textiles produces several thousand cubic metres of polluted waste water and 1.9 tonnes of toxic salt daily (*The Namibian*, 30/1/2004; 28/9/2004). The capital city has no facility for its safe disposal.

To this day, the company has not built the required plant for waste water treatment, as had been stipulated in the contract between the city and Ramatex. In the absence of such a plant, Ramatex temporarily stores the water in large evaporation/oxidation ponds. Filled beyond the limits of their capacity, the ponds overflow, dumping pollut-

---

46. Windhoek's consumption in the financial year 2001–02 amounted to 19.465 m cubic metres. As far as Ramatex's consumption is concerned, the picture is not clear. The percentages published by the media vary considerably from 4.3% (i.e., 840,000 cubic metres, according to the city council) to 3% (according to Martin Shipanga, the city's CEO), to 2.7% or 3.6% (according to the city's chief environmentalist). In January 2002, Ramatex had stated that its water consumption would amount to 1,440 cubic metres of water per day. This figure adds up to the abovementioned 2.7%. In March 2004, the municipality of Windhoek recorded a water consumption of 27,000 cubic metres, in April 2004 of 53,671, in May of 47,000, corresponding – throughout the year – to 2.6% of the capital's total consumption. In October 2005, a consumption of 2,000 cubic metres per day was indicated by the media, i.e., 3.7% of the capital's total consumption (*AZ*, 1/8/2002; *The Namibian*, 23/1/2002; 2/4/2003; 2/7/2004; 12/10/2004; 28/10/2004). Initially, Hafeni Nghinamwaani, the then strategic executive of the department for economic development of the city of Windhoek, maintained that the Ramatex plant "will not use potable (tap) water, but instead use semi-purified water." *Namibia Economist*, 5/–11/4/2002.

ants into the groundwater as well as into the Goreangab Dam, one of Windhoek's major water reservoirs. The factory has also been accused of sprinkling excess waste water on to open areas of its premises. Residents in the neighbourhood of the works complained not only of the stench emanating from the disposal of the waste water on the premises but also recorded irritation to their skin and respiratory tracts. In violation of municipal regulations, the company hired a private contractor to dispose of the sludge that forms in the ponds (*The Namibian*, 21/12/2004; 4/11/2005).

Several injunctions by the City fell on deaf ears. Caught in this environmental predicament, the municipality called in the Namibian government. After difficult negotiations, an interministerial technical committee agreed on the decision that the city was to build the recycling plant for Ramatex. The costs, estimated at N$ 13 m, are to be borne by the state (*AZ*, 28/12/2005).

Conclusions: Liberalisation of social equity

The case study cannot but raise sceptical questions as to the developmental rating of Ramatex's Namibian initiative. Enticing as the prospect of export-led industrialisation[47] may seem, the structure within which it is to take place sets narrow limits to its economic implementation, and even narrower ones to its potential for the social progress of the majority of the population.

The *players* involved in this game of skewed give and take are unequal in power. Their actions follow rules dictated by their respective contrasting economic, political and social interests, but they are also shaped by the conditions set by the neoliberal imperatives of the global economy. Where the international mobility of capital invariably outdistances the mobility of labour, tripartite relations between multinational capital, state and labour are all the more skewed, right from the outset, where poverty provides the national setting for the labour market in a developing economy.

Acting within these structural constraints, the invitation that the *Namibian government* extends to international capital becomes logical. It is driven by the interest to overcome the national economy's dependence on the export of mineral resources and its related negative global terms of trade. The drain of natural and social resources in colonial times has left the country's post-independence economy with insufficient capital means for their processing, and with a skewed social structure.

The *Namibian stakeholders,* on the other hand, not only just identify with, and execute, the government's developmental policies, but also, to an increasing extent, their attitudes reflect their elitist perceptions and interests, both economic and social. They form an emerging bourgeois class, more and more affluent, which in the new post-colo-

---

47. In debating the industrialisation strategy for developing economies based on a case study of Ramatex, Endresen and Bergene advocate small-scale industrialisation where production first serves the national market and then selectively approaches the world market. Cogently arguing their case, the authors point to the paradox in developmental policies of EPZ-based textile industrialisation: "Host governments subsidise heavily to keep them [the textile multinationals], which paradoxically makes it easier for them to leave and relocate production." (Endresen and Bergene 2006:89.) However, in the specific case of Namibia, the extreme limitations of a national market with a population of just about 1.8 million of whom only one-tenth are taxpayers representing worthwhile purchasing power, are also to be considered.

nial setting of Namibian society steps to the side of the traditional white middle classes and capitalist entrepreneurship. Together, they nurture vested capitalist interests, which tend to dupe other classes' developmental aspirations. Thus, in adopting neoliberal paradigms, both Namibian policies and Namibian political actors come to accept the social costs of economic development and, as the case study shows, to neglect the social damage. In departing from pre-independence visions of social equity, a characteristic theme of the liberation struggle, present-day Namibian developmental strategies of financial de-regulation reflect the class-shaped, capitalist restructuring of Namibian society.

Ramatex's demanding and ruthless attitude may seem extortionate due to the sheer extent of its economic power, and it certainly is. But the multinational conglomerate also submits to the force of circumstances, finding itself compelled to establish optimal conditions of profitability in order to compete in the fierce global textile market. As a result, the multinational's economic might cannot but call into doubt the expedience of any unreserved liberalisation of capital imports. Much as the import of capital in principle may be expected to have spin-off effects, in Ramatex's Namibian case they do not materialise.

The endeavours of *Namibian labourers* inevitably collide with any regime of maximised profitability. As well, they clash with the efforts of a set of national policies that aim at establishing an attractive investment climate without being in a position to attach strings to it that may be beneficial to the country. Too weak is their position as an unskilled workforce, too easily replaceable the individual employee, given the inexhaustible reservoir of internal labour migrants in an economy ruled by poverty and more and more de-regulated by 'flexible' labour relations. Where, on top of that, national politics bow to economic power to the extent of ignoring the country's immigration rules, allowing a substantial influx of an un- or semi-skilled *foreign industrial workers,* the vulnerability of its own internal migrants becomes even more pronounced. Last but not least, the *trade unions'* room for manoeuvre has been narrowly restricted by Ramatex's short-sighted managerial arrogance, and, arguably, by their own close political affiliation to the ruling party and government. The company successfully manages to play the actors involved in the game off against each other – different government institutions, municipal bodies, national and foreign workforces, civil society and the public. Labourers and their corporate representatives are in a desperate position.

Contrasting economic and social interests, cultural conflicts over work ethos, different rules of the game for each player and unequally distributed power: the case study of Ramatex cannot but question the developmental impact of such policies of de-regulation and of such generous incentives as were granted to attract the Malaysian company. Where investment is imported in kind, no additional capital circulates in the host economy; no related expansion of investing or commercial activities ensues. Where the productive employment of capital goods yields commodities exported without customs revenue, the host country cannot capitalise on them. Where the internal market is not given impetus, the host country cannot profit. Where exemption from taxation does not stand the national budget in good stead, the only benefits are to be expected from employment of labour. Where the state's budget finances most of the costs for vocational training, it might be inappropriate to speak of skills transfer, as we rather witness internal skills generation. Where the additional purchasing power of salaries barely satisfies the most basic needs, further productive incentives for the internal market are few and far from sustainable. Where fiscal revenue from salaries does not accrue, owing to small annual incomes below the taxation threshold, there is no positive effect on the national income.

Does this hold out the prospect of social progress, as measured against the principles of social equity? The liberal discourse, whether in its classical or its present shape, boldly rests on the *glorification of the principle of social retardation*: first comes the successful individual, the entrepreneur, then (if all goes well, and always to a lesser extent) society, that productive majority actually instrumental in creating economic wealth. First come, first served. The liberal economic ideology is *not* the epitome of social responsibility. It is class-biased, and so is its concept of development.

The introductory remarks to this case study pointed to the contradictory paradigmatic body of Namibia's *Vision 2030* document. It attempts to harmonise harsh economic liberalism and the tempting vision of social welfare within the difficult framework of a developing society. The analysis of Ramatex's Namibian operations shows that neoliberal economic orientations, seen in the long term, tend to affect or even negate collective structures based on social solidarity. Conversely, any vision of social welfare must make the preservation and promotion of collective structures of social solidarity the focal point of accelerated sustainable development. Certainly, *Vision 2030* warns of the dangers of unbalanced globalisation to a much greater extent than the relevant Namibian legislation and policies of de-regulation do. Yet, this conceptual contradiction still remains central to the document – and unresolved.

References

Cotton News from Sub-Saharan Africa (2003), *Namibia, Botswana, South Africa, Lesotho and Senegal – a special issue of the Cotton Importer,* Update from the Cotton Board. Memphis, Tennessee, USA

Endresen, Sylvi B. and Ann Cecilie Bergene (2006), 'Labour standards and the question of industrialisation strategy. An African example,' in H. Jauch and R. Traub-Merz (eds), *The future of the textile and clothing industry in sub-Saharan Africa.* Bonn: Friedrich Ebert Stiftung, pp. 80–95

ETI Forum (Ethical Trade Initiative) (2004), *MFA phase-out – who gains? who loses?* London, 27 October 2004

Gurirab, Theo Ben (1988), 'Namibia in the context of imperialism,' in B. Wood (ed), *Namibia 1884–1984: Readings on Namibia's history and society.* London and Lusaka: Namibia Support Committee and United Nations Institute for Namibia, pp. 4–13

Institute for Public Policy Research (2003), *IPPR Economic Outlook – One lump or two?* (by Robin Sherbourne). Windhoek, February 2003

International Textile, Leather & Garment Workers' Federation, *Targeting Multinationals Project – Ramatex Berhad profile.* (No date or place of publication.)

Jauch, Herbert (2000), 'Export Processing Zones and the quest for sustainable development: a Southern African perspective,' *Environment & Urbanization,* Vol. 14, No. 1

— (2006), 'Africa's clothing and textile industry: the case of Ramatex in Namibia,' in H. Jauch and R. Traub-Merz (eds), *The future of the textile and clothing industry in sub-Saharan Africa.* Bonn: Friedrich Ebert Stiftung, pp. 212–26

Labour Resource and Research Institute (LaRRI) (2000), *Export Processing Zones in Namibia – taking a closer look.* Windhoek, March 2000

— (2003), *Ramatex – on the other side of the fence.* Windhoek, October 2003

Melber, Henning (2003), 'Limits to liberation – an introduction to Namibia's postcolonial political culture,' in H. Melber (ed), *Re-examining liberation in Namibia – political culture since independence.* Uppsala: Nordic Africa Institute

Mollet, Andrew (2001), 'Profile of Ramatex – a Malaysian group with investments in China and South Africa,' *Textile Outlook International,* January 2001

Namibia Investment Centre / Offshore Development Company (2003), *InvestDevelop – Namibia's Investment Newsletter: Smart partnerships drive development forward,* Issue 11, 8 December 2003, Windhoek

Namibian Economic Policy Research Unit (NEPRU), *Quarterly Economic Review* No. 23, October 1999, Windhoek

— *Quarterly Economic Review* No. 27, December 1999, Windhoek

— *Quarterly Economic Review* No. 44, March 2002, Windhoek

South West Africa People's Organisation (2004), *Vision, life and times of Hifikepunye Lucas Pohamba.* Windhoek (election pamphlet)

Ramatex Textiles Namibia (Pty) Ltd (2002a), *Flamingo Garments (Proprietary) Limited: Letter of Appointment* (template)

— (2002b), *Recognition Agreement between Ramatex Textiles Namibia (Pty) Ltd and the Namibian Food and Allied Workers Union,* 2 October 2002, Windhoek

— (2002c), *Recruitment Procedure* (leaflet)

Republic of Namibia (1990a), *Government Gazette* No. 2, Windhoek, 21 March 1990: Constitution of the Republic of Namibia

— (1990b), *Government Gazette* No. 129, Windhoek, 28 December 1990: Foreign Investments Act No. 27 of 1990

—(1995), *Government Gazette* No. 1069, Windhoek, 18 April 1995: Export Processing Zones Act No. 9 of 1995

Republic of Namibia (1995b), Government of, Ministry of Trade and Industry: *EPZ Business Plan for proposed Offshore Development Company.* Windhoek, April 1995

Republic of Namibia, Government of, Ministry of Finance (2003), *State Revenue Fund – Estimate of revenue and expenditure for the financial year 1 April 2003 – 31 March 2004.* Windhoek

—(2004), *State Revenue Fund – Estimate of revenue and expenditure for the financial year 1 April 2004 – 31 March 2005.* Windhoek

— (2005), *State Revenue Fund – Estimate of revenue and expenditure for the financial year 1 April 2005 – 31 March 2006.* Windhoek

— Republic of Namibia, Government of, Ministry of Trade and Industry, Offshore Development Company (1999), *EPZ Progress Report of December 1999*

Sherbourne, Robin (2005), 'National Budget 2005/06: The continuity candidate's budget,' in *Intitute of Public Policy Research (IPPR) Opinion* No. 17, May 2005, Windhoek

Newspapers

Allgemeine Zeitung (AZ)
Namibia Economist
New Era
Republikein
The Namibian
Windhoek Observer

Websites

<http:www.agoa.gov/agoa_legislation/AGOII_summary.pdf>: *US Trade Act of 2002*

<http;//www.agoa.info/?view=country_info&country=na&stay=trade>: *US imports from Namibia, textiles and apparel*

<http:www.asianlabour.org/archives/000772.php> (2004): *Asian Labour News* – an online database of news about workers in Southeast Asia and China and the issues that affect them: Mainlnd workers at Malaysian factory in Namibia call it quits – 5 February 2004

<http://derstandard.at/druck/?id=2092228>: *Der Standard online: Ironie der Globalisierung*

<http;//www.dispatch.co.za/2001/06/21/easterncape/AAINCENT.HTM>: *Eddie Botha: Call for review of tax incentives*

<http://www.fdimagazine.../AGOA_extension_to_boost_US-Africa_textile_trade.htm>

<http://www.foei.org/trade/activistguide/mfa.htm>: *The Citizens' Guide to Trade, Environment and Sustainability – Multi-fibre Arrangement (MFA) and the Agreement on Textiles and Clothing (ATC)*

<http://www.grnnet.gov.na/News/Archive/2002/April/Week4/ramatex.htm>

<http://www.grnnet.gov.na/News/Archive/2005/february/week2/agreements_rpt.htm>: *Joint press statement by the Government, NAFAU and Ramatex – February 2005*

<http;//www.irinnews.org/print.asp?ReportID+45451>: *UN Office for the Coordination of Humanitarian Affairs – Namibia: Textile industry faces multiple challenges*

<http;//www.itglwf.org>: website of the International Textile, Garment and Leather Workers' Federation

<http://www.laborrights.org/press/namibia_textiles0505.htm>: *UN Integrated Regional Information Networks – Namibia: Textile sector stumbles as foreign owners pull out*

<http://www.namibweb.com/tin.htm>: NamibWeb.com – The online guide to Namibia: Incentives for Investors

<http:www.namibianembassyusa.org/Trade%20&%20Investment/profiles.php>: Official website of the Embassy of the Republic of Namibia in Washington, USA

<http;//www.queensu.ca/samp/migration>: *February 2005*

<http://www.ramatex.com.>

<http://www.sadocc.at/news/2005/2005-105.shtml>: *Southern Africa Documentation and Cooperation Centre – Uncertain future for the country's textile industry – 22 April 2005*

<http://www.un.namibia.de/UN-arch/2005/un_05_02.php#news02>: *IRIN News Brief*

<http://www.windhoekcc.org.na/Default.aspx?page=120>: *City of Windhoek – Ramatex investment in the City of Windhoek*

Old ties or new shackles?
China in Namibia

Gregor Dobler

One of the first things you see of Namibia when you drive into the country from Angola on Oshikango's main road (after passing large billboards promoting the frequent use of Tafel Lager, Coca Cola and Safe Ryder condoms) are the large red letters on the brown wall of a new warehouse complex, welcoming you to 'China Town.' China Town is one of two large complexes currently under construction in Oshikango by Chinese investors (the other is called 'China Village'). Together, they will add about 70 new Chinese shops to the 20 odd already in existence in Oshikango.[1]

China Village and China Town are very real symbols of China's growing presence in Africa. Both shop owners and investors are Chinese, the complex was built by Chinese construction companies, and the new shops' prospective Angolan clients will pay for the Chinese goods with petrodollars in turn earned largely from exports to China.[2]

Symbolic as they may be, the new shops are just a small example of China's growing influence in Africa. The People's Republic re-entered the African scene only towards the turn of the millennium, but since then the country's engagement in Africa has been growing at a truly amazing pace and China's rise as an economic and political power is likely to change Africa's international relations more profoundly than any other major trend since the crumbling of the Soviet Union and the end of apartheid. China's high need for raw materials and the equally high output of the country's immensely competitive export industry have profoundly altered terms of trade and thus affected the distribution of wealth both between and within many African countries, while the political engagement accompanying economic expansion has changed the African diplomatic landscape.

In Oshikango's China Village, three major trends of China's growing influence on African countries are visible in a nutshell: Africa is supplying China with commodities for its expanding industries while importing more and more goods manufactured by these industries. China's economic engagement is accompanied by financial aid that has contributed to the creation of a market for Chinese industries – most visible in the con-

---

1. The construction of China Town had started slightly earlier, in 2004. The investment was made by the pioneering 'Chinese' businessman in independent Namibia, ironically a Taiwanese national who had already built Windhoek's China Town. China Village was built by another long-standing expatriate mainland Chinese businessman for about N$ 25 m.

2. According to ITC trademap data (UNCTAD), China imported 25% of Angola's total oil exports in 2003, with oil exports making up 99.9% of total Angolan exports to China (Goldstein et al. 2006:32). The IMF's Direction of Trade data state that 36% of total Angolan exports went to China in 2004 (Goldstein et al. 2006:30), while oil accounted for 91.7% of Angola's overall exports.

struction sector, where the market share of Chinese companies has been rapidly growing throughout Southern Africa.

These three elements – commodity export, competition in the construction industry and the import of manufactured goods by Chinese migrant entrepreneurs – will be used in the current article as examples to assess China's role in the Namibian economy. The aim of this overview is neither to praise China's growing presence as a South-South alternative to neocolonialism nor to deplore it as new economic imperialism. Instead, the article intends to show the extent to which the Namibian economy is already linked to the Chinese. The real question will not be whether to applaud or condemn the Chinese influence, but how to channel it in ways that benefit Namibia instead of cementing its old role in global structures of economic and political dependency.

Before concentrating on Namibia, however, it is useful to review some of the major trends in China-Africa relations.

China in Africa: Some major trends

During the Cold War years, China's interest in Africa was largely political. The People's Republic was trying to overcome its political isolation through links with the continent's socialist governments and liberation movements. Economic benefits for China were mostly small or negative. China-Africa cooperation rested largely on a rhetoric of anti-imperialistic solidarity symbolised by the Bandung conference in 1955: the 'Afro-Asian bloc' was seeking to counter the dominance of Western colonial countries.

Since Chinese economic reforms triggered an unprecedented economic boom based on manufacturing, China's interests in Africa have shifted from the political arena to the economic.[3] The main motivation is the increasing need for the raw materials of industrial production. Today, China is the world's largest producer of personal computers: even in 2001, 50% of all cameras, 30% of all air conditioners and 25% of all washing machines were manufactured in China.[4] In order to sustain an average annual economic growth of around 8%, China needs to secure the import of a wide array of commodities and it is mainly due to Chinese demand that world market prices for virtually all commodities have risen sharply over the last years. Between 2000 and 2003, China contributed 76%, 95%, 99% and 100% of the increase in global demand for aluminium, steel, nickel and copper respectively (Kaplinsky, McCormick, Morris 2006:5). The most visible example of growing Chinese demand, however, is oil. China changed from a net exporter of petrol to a net importer in 2001 and has since been seeking new import markets in African countries such as Sudan, Chad and Angola. Today, the country procures 28% of its oil and natural gas from Africa (*CCS China Monitor* 04, 2006:3).

On the other hand, Chinese exports of manufactured goods to African countries have been increasing tremendously. Imports from China still represented only 6.5% of African imports in 2004, but this figure was only 1% in 1990. Since 2000, African

---

3. For an overview, see e.g., Alden 2005; Goldstein et al. 2006; Humphrey, Messner 2006; Kaplinsky, McCormick, Morris 2006, Lyman 2005; Payne, Veney 1998; Shinn 2005.
4. www.worldbank.org/transitionnewsletter/octnovdec02/pgs4-6.htm (14 Oct 2005).

imports from China have shown average annual growth rates of 33% (Goldstein et al. 2006:7f.).

China's increasing demand for commodities and its high output of cheap manufactured goods have shifted terms of trade in favour of countries exporting raw materials and importing manufactured goods – among them many African countries. They profit from higher export gains and cheaper import prices. Without the appropriate policy measures, however, China's emergence may cement the dependency of many African countries on the export of raw materials – an economic position that tends to come with high vulnerability due to price volatility and with high inequality due to corruption and rent-seeking.

The main losers in the shift in the terms of trade have been countries exporting manufactured goods. In Africa, the textile sector has suffered most severely from Chinese competition on third markets after the trade barriers for Chinese textile imports to the US and the EU were partially lifted in 2004 (see Volker Winterfeld's article on Ramatex in this volume).

While China used economic aid to gain political benefits during the Cold War years, this relation has shifted today. The People's Republic promotes its trade interests by political means: high profile diplomacy and the rhetoric of anti-colonial solidarity are still omnipresent 50 years after Bandung. Chinese foreign policy in Africa relies on a large number of embassies and on many high-profile visits to and from Africa. Chinese foreign ministers have been visiting African countries every year since the late 1980s, and Chinese presidents have made frequent official visits to the continent. Whenever Chinese diplomats meet their African counterparts, both sides stress mutual friendship and common interests as formerly colonised developing countries. As the Chinese Africa policy issued in early 2006 puts it, "Sharing similar historical experience, China and Africa have all along sympathized with and supported each other in the struggle for national liberation and forged a profound friendship." The Chinese government stresses "African countries' independent choice of road"[5] and does not link aid to political conditionalities – apart from the acceptance of the 'one China principle,' prohibiting official relations to Taiwan.[6] This policy of non-interference paved the way for substantial oil deals with Sudan and infrastructure projects and military deals in Zimbabwe when these countries where internationally isolated and shunned by both Western donors and multinationals.

All in all, China has been very successful in establishing and maintaining the rhetoric of mutual solidarity and South-South cooperation. This insistence on common interests and historic friendship often masks very tangible economic and political advantages for China. Its political impact in Africa, however, is considerable – all the more as it comes with real benefits, like debt relief, diplomatic cooperation in the international arena and an increasing amount of development assistance.

---

5. The Africa policy is available on various official internet sites; a handy pdf version was prepared by the Institute for Security Studies: http://www.iss.co.za/af/regorg/unity_to_union/pdfs/chinaafrica/afrpolicyjan06.pdf (26 May 2006).

6. China has been quite successful in enforcing its Taiwan policy in Africa. In 2000, only eight African states still had official relations with Taiwan. Liberia (2003) and Senegal (2005) have since sided with China, leaving only Burkina Faso, Chad, The Gambia, Malawi, São Tomé and Principe and Swaziland.

China-Namibia diplomatic ties are no exception to the general trend. They are rooted in Chinese support of SWAPO and the liberation struggle before 1990. In 1964, when Moscow and Beijing were competing for allies among Africa's left wing liberation movements, Sam Nujoma was invited to Beijing: he came back with funds he used to buy a Land Rover for SWAPO's exile work and with high esteem for the Chinese leadership (Appolus 2004). SWAPO was officially allied to Moscow and never really changed sides, while the rival SWANU movement was on China's side for some time (Gibson 1972:120–31). In spite of these rivalries, relations between the People's Republic and SWAPO remained good (for a detailed analysis, see Taylor 1997). China's support in the UN Security Council for Namibia's case against the South African occupation and the detachment of military instructors to train SWAPO's PLAN combatants in Tanzania are often evoked by politicians from both sides, as is the fact that China was one of the first countries to establish diplomatic relations with the newly independent state in 1990. Still today, SWAPO party sees China as a natural ally and as a partner in the struggle for economic independence from neocolonialism.

Over the years, Sam Nujoma has visited China 12 times, often accompanied by important trade delegations. On his last official visit in 2004, he was presented with the Chinese translation of his autobiography – a well-received symbolic gesture typical of Chinese-African diplomatic relations. Jiang Zemin came to Namibia in 1996 and other high-level representatives of both countries exchange visits on a regular basis. On all these occasions, both sides have stressed mutual friendship and the common struggle for a more just world system, often mentioning stronger South-South ties as a means to improve African lives. As He Shijing, Chinese chargé d'affaires in Namibia, put it, "We both faced a common task and struggle against imperialism, but now have a similar one which is for the economic development of our countries."[7]

Primary sector commodities

Although Namibian exports rely heavily on primary sector commodities, direct Chinese involvement in the Namibia raw material market has until now not been very prominent. While Chinese firms are concluding deals with commodity exporters all over the continent, no major contracts have been negotiated with Namibian producers yet. This is partly due to the tight control over Namibia's mineral production through established distribution networks and long-term contracts. In 2003, 41% of overall Namibian exports were diamonds, exclusively controlled by Namdeb, a joint venture between De Beers and the Namibian government, and 15% consisted of other mineral products (mainly copper, uranium and zinc) stemming from large mines mostly owned and controlled by overseas firms (Directorate of International Trade 2005:4).

As there are no known oil reserves in Namibia, Chinese interests in this field have so far been confined to neighbouring Angola. The most substantial Namibian exploration deal of recent years, however, included a Chinese contractor. In February 2005, Circle Oil (an oil company based in Limerick, Ireland, and listed on the London Stock

---

7. *New Era*, 16/06/2003. The statement was made on the occasion of a donation of $ 30,000 to SWAPO party by the Chinese Communist Party, earmarked for printing and distribution of party materials.

Exchange Alternative Investment Market) announced an agreement by which China Shine H F, a Chinese state-owned company was said to take over 72% of Circle Oil's prospecting licence (later upgraded to an exploration licence) covering most of northern Namibia: Circle Oil was to retain 18% and the Namibian state-owned NAMCOR 10%. High expectations were somewhat dampened when it turned out that China Shine would pay its share not in cash but by drilling at least three wells and acquiring seismic data, but still, the company's budget for the Namibian project was announced to be over $ 1 bn and 2,000 workers were expected to start work on the ground in late 2005. In June 2006, however, the deal was still not finalised and Circle Oil was negotiating with other possible investors, as China Shine had not yet fulfilled its commitments and no work had started on the ground.[8]

In 2004, Namibia's Rössing mine became the first Western producer to export uranium oxide to China. The mine increased its output to counter the negative effects of the weak US dollar and found a willing buyer in China's national nuclear industry. So far, the amounts exported have been rather small (106 tons in 2004, *Allgemeine Zeitung,* 14/7/2005 and 109 tons in 2005, *Republikein,* 7/6/2006), but as China is planning to increase its nuclear power-generating capacity from 6 GW to over 30 GW by 2020 while a second Namibian uranium mine is scheduled to become operational in late 2006, uranium oxide exports from Namibia to China may increase in the future.[9]

The most important field of primary sector exports to China is less publicised, as it does not involve mineral resources: Chinese firms have invested in joint ventures in Namibia's fishing industry since independence and in 2003 about 80% of Namibian exports to China consisted of fish and fish products.

Overall, the export of Namibian primary sector commodities to China (as indeed Namibian exports to China as a whole) is rather insignificant if compared to, for example, Angolan exports to China. The indirect effects of China's emergence on the Namibian primary sector economy, however, are large. As outlined above, commodity prices have risen sharply over the last years mainly due to the increasing Chinese and Indian demand. World market copper prices, for example, rose by 58% in 2004 (Goldstein et al. 2006:31), largely triggered by rising demand from China (and, to a lesser degree, from India). This should have profited Ongopolo Mining and Processing, the principal Namibian copper producer, after a strong South African Rand had negatively affected the company in the years before 2004. The expansion process took longer than expected, however, and the debts amassed while financing new production sites proved fatal for the company. Amid allegations of mismanagement, Ongopolo was taken over by the British company Weatherly International in June 2006.

World market prices for other minerals produced by Namibia – mostly uranium, zinc, gold and marble – have risen sharply since 2004, helping the Namibian economy to achieve a growth rate of 5.9% in 2004.[10] The commodity boom has triggered inten-

---

8. See, among others: http://www.circleoil.com/site/news/press_release28012005.htm; http://www.circleoil.com/site/news/press_release03022006.html; http://www.circleoil.com/site/documents/Interim_Report_%20June302005.pdf (all 26 June 2006).

9. http://www.altonsa.co.za/rossing/reports/Rossing%20Stakeholder%20Report%202004.pdf (26 June 2006)

10. Increase in real GDP. This exceptionally high figure is partly due to a 39% increase in diamond production after the extension of the Elisabeth Bay mine and an increase in offshore mining

sive prospecting activity in the country. New mining sites for zinc, uranium, copper and gold have become operational or are scheduled to become operational in the near future, while the projected life of existing mines is constantly extended due to higher marginal gains. Rössing, for example, has announced that the uranium mine's projected life has been extended from 2009 to 2016.

Due to the rise of China in the world economy, terms of trade become more favourable for commodity exporters such Namibia (just as they became less favourable after the end of the Soviet Union, when exports from the former Soviet Union increased competition and made prices crumble). Depending on the political and economic framework, however, this can be a mixed blessing. Income from mining is not sustainable, but will cease over time: it will only provide the means for sustainable growth when it is used to further the economic potential of a country in other sectors. Unlike the export of manufactured goods, however, the export of primary commodities creates income without any constructive effort, often tempting elites to seek quick rents rather than to invest in sustainable economic development. Commodity exports thus often increase vulnerability from external factors without benefiting larger portions of the population.

This is aggravated when world market demand and prices for a commodity are volatile. Many economists have voiced concern about China's effect on commodity price volatility. China is regarded as a swing producer, quickly adapting its export production to changes in the price for manufactured goods. Due to the size of the Chinese economy and its high importance for global commodity demand, shifts in the country's production can quickly affect world market prices (for a more detailed discussion, see e.g., Goldstein et al. 2006:31).

It is too early to assess the effects of China's rise on the 'resource curse' and on the vulnerability of the Namibian economy. One thing, however, is clear: when a country's dependency on commodity exports increases, the economic policy framework must become more intelligent and more resourceful. Partly due to China's growing weight in the world economy, the relative importance of commodity export for the Namibian economy is increasing. It remains to be seen if economic policy follows, translating improving terms of trade into improved livelihoods for the majority of Namibian citizens.

Construction industry

Many export contracts in the mining and energy sector have been facilitated through active Chinese diplomacy in Africa. The same channel has been decisive for infrastructure projects and for the Chinese construction industry in general. Chinese building contractors have often made their first appearance on African markets through public projects funded by Chinese government loans or grants (for an early assessment of the strategies, see Bräutigam 1983). It has, of course, long been common for Western governments to link development assistance to contracts for the donor country's industry and it comes as no surprise that China is imitating the practice. It seems, however, that

---

activity; but other mining grew by 30.5%, profiting from the fact that a new zinc mine became operational (http://www.bon.com.na/docs/pub/economic%20outlook%202005–06.PDF, 26 June 2006).

China is playing the game more skilfully – and in some cases more ruthlessly – than Western donor countries.

The list of public contracts awarded to Chinese companies and backed by Chinese government money is long. In Angola, China today accounts for over 60% of the country's foreign loans. From 2002 to early 2006, Angola received $ 5.5 bn in Chinese loans and an additional $ 3 bn was granted in June 2006 (*CCS China Monitor*, 04/2006:16; *The Namibian*, 27/06/2006). The major part of that sum has been awarded through the Chinese Eximbank for a credit line for reconstruction, guaranteed by oil exports. The building projects financed with the amount are mostly carried through by Chinese firms – among many others, hundreds of kilometres of road construction, a $ 3 bn oil refinery in Lobito (*CCS China Monitor* 03/2006:19), 44 15-floor buildings in Cabinda and 5,000 additional apartments in a village nearby.[11] Copper mining by China-based Pan Asia Oasis Inc. is also profiting from a $ 211 m loan from the Chinese government to rebuild roads leading to the area.[12]

Chinese help for its own industry not only comprises loans and guarantees, it also includes logistical and political support. In Mozambique, for example, the Chinese embassy is actively informing Chinese construction companies of upcoming tenders. Partly due to this promotion of tender opportunities, a third of Mozambique's current road construction projects (approx. 600 km of roads) are carried out by Chinese road contractors (Bosten 2006:5f).

While projects of that size have so far been absent in Namibia, a large variety of prominent public construction contracts have gone to Chinese companies. China Jiangsu International Namibia Ltd. was responsible for the construction of the supreme court in Windhoek (1994–97), the new police and prison training college in the same city (1996–97) and the new magistrate's court in Katutura (1997–99). China Beijing Corporation for International Economic Co-operation built 102 houses in Katima Mulilo in 1999, funded through an interest-free Chinese government loan. Northern Tannery in Ondangwa, built in 2000–02 and shut down in 2006, was financed by the Chinese government as well and constructed by China Nanjing International Namibia Construction (*The Namibian*, 14/06/2000). The private Chinese firm New Era Investment was responsible for, among many other public projects, the new town council building in Helao Nafidi Town, inaugurated in April 2006 by President Pohamba.

The most prominent instance of Chinese involvement in public construction projects is the new State House on the outskirts of Windhoek. As with Heroes' Acre, the main contractors are North Korean firms. After the Chinese government donated N$ 55 m

---

11. "The planning and projection of the city's project is expected to match Asian and European urban concepts while utmost care will be taken to ensure that it falls within the lifestyle and architectonic characteristics of the country, Ju Lizao, a representative of the Chinese firm said. This urbanisation project will create 4,000 local and 1,000 Chinese jobs at minimum cost while ensuring quality. The project is expected to span over 30 months." *CCS China Monitor*, 03/2006:18.

12. *CCS China Monitor* 10/2005:23. These loans and grants widen the political margin for the Angolan government, allowing non-compliance with Western and international donor agendas. A Chinese soft loan of $ 2 bn to Angola came after Western donors postponed a donors' conference meeting due to concerns about corruption. The loan came with a grace period of 5 years and is repayable over 17 years at 1.5%. It is bound to be spent on Chinese contracts – and helped China outbid India on an oil deal. (Kaplinsky, McCormick, Morris 2006:30).

for the construction of State House in 2002 ("with no strings attached," as a spokesman of the Namibian government told the press), a Chinese company was given a share in the project without public tender. In May 2005, another generous grant by the Chinese government for the building of the new State House was announced, but its amount was not disclosed. In April 2006, during the budget debate in parliament, it surfaced that the presidential home attached to State House would be wholly donated by the Chinese government and built by Chinese companies. It was announced that the Chinese government would tender for the construction in China (*The Namibian*, 21/04/2006), thereby possibly introducing new players to the Namibian market.

While Chinese construction companies came into the Namibian market in the late 1990s by tendering for public projects often backed by Chinese government money, they have since moved into the private sector and are making life very difficult for the remaining Namibian and South African construction companies. Chinese companies' market share is estimated to be "anywhere between a third and two thirds of the construction market" (*Insight Namibia* 04/2006:19) and it is growing. The main reason for the Chinese success is pricing: Chinese firms are undercutting Namibian competitors on a regular basis. Experts say that profit margins on government construction projects have declined from 30% to 10% or 15% due to Chinese companies (*Insight Namibia* 04/2006:20) – a reduction that simultaneously saves public funds and creates local unemployment. Chinese contractors claim that their success is due to hard work, reliability and efficiency, while local construction companies were characterised by inflated profit margins, the frequent missing of deadlines and low productivity prior to the arrival of international competitors.

Local companies reply by accusing Chinese firms of unfair competition. Industry representatives such as the CIF (Construction Industry Federation) have claimed that Chinese firms profited from preferential treatment in the allocation of tenders and that government was unwilling to force Chinese companies to comply with Namibian labour laws. They even spread rumours that convicts were used as forced labour on the construction sites in order to cut costs. Allegations of political protection and favouritism are difficult to prove or disprove. While it is not unlikely that political influence and corruption play a role in large public contracts (government infrastructure projects are notoriously prone to corruption worldwide), I have not come across any tangible proof of rigged tenders or unfair competition. At the very least, these allegations are an indicator of the growing resentment against Chinese competitors among local businesspeople.

All in all, while Chinese competition makes life difficult for the Namibian construction industry, Chinese competition seems to have had a favourable effect on productivity and efficiency in the sector and lowered construction costs in the country. Chinese firms should, however, be more rigorously supervised as to their compliance with Namibian labour laws, and, where public tenders are concerned, preferential treatment of local firms or stricter regulations regarding the employment of local workers should certainly be considered.

Chinese migrant entrepreneurs

China shops

In everyday life, the most striking aspect of China's growing importance for Namibia is the omnipresence of Chinese shops in the country, selling everything from tractors to sports bags, from camping tables to pirated perfumes. There is no Namibian town without its China shop, and in many larger villages the only shop selling anything other than sugar, cooking oil, soap and beer is owned by a Chinese migrant. All of these migrants have come from China since 1990, looking for business opportunities outside the highly regulated and crowded Chinese economy.

The following overview is informed by a case study in Oshikango, the main trading post on the Angolan border – a special situation, as most shops in the town are living off the offshore wholesale trade into Angola (for more details see Dobler 2005, 2007, 2008).[13] Many aspects, however, from trade organisation to the difficulties with work permits, are general features of the life of Chinese migrants in Namibia.

Oshikango is a small but vibrant town on the border with Angola. Due to the town's position on the main road linking Namibia to Angola, it is also the main trade hub between the two countries. Large warehouses sell all kinds of imported goods wholesale to Angolan traders. Most of the warehouses operate offshore – the goods are imported 'in bond' for export to Angola, without paying Namibian import duties and taxes on them. The most important goods traded in Oshikango are used cars, beer and liquor, furniture, white goods and clothing articles. Chinese shops mainly deal in clothing, textiles, shoes, electronics and all kinds of cheap consumer goods, but also in motorcycles, furniture and small tractors.

Oshikango is the ideal place to do business in the Angolan market without actually investing in Angola. Political and economic conditions are stable and foreseeable, and an excellent road (and in the near future a railway line) links the town to the Southern African ports of Durban, Cape Town and Walvis Bay. Many investors are still reluctant to invest in Angola: they fear political interference and insecurity, and are unwilling to comply with the more demanding Angolan rules for foreign investments (like the obligation to form a joint venture with an Angolan partner). Since about 2003, however, Oshikango has lost some of its appeal. Apart from infrastructure development in Angola, giving viable in-country alternatives to Angolan wholesalers, this is mainly due to the strong Rand and to the enforcement of Angolan import duties. A large part of the Angolan economy functions on a US-dollar basis. While one US dollar would buy 13 Rands/Namibian Dollars in 2003, it was worth only N$ 6.2 in early 2006, significantly lessening Angolan buying power in Oshikango.[14] An even heavier blow came in 2004, when Angola employed the British firm Crown Agents to supervise the custom's office in Santa Clara, the Angolan border post opposite Oshikango. Before that, import

---

13. Thirteen months of fieldwork were carried out in 2004 and 2006, focusing on economic and political transformation in the border boom town. To protect my informants, who partly entrusted me with rather sensitive business information, I have tried to make them unrecognisable in my descriptions. This accounts for my often rather vague ascription of citations.

14. Consequences for Angolan clients are not as heavy as one might expect, as many imports to Oshikango are also paid in US dollars, particularly used cars, furniture and all kinds of Chinese goods. Beer and liquor sales, however, have been highly affected by the strong Rand.

duties and consumption taxes, introduced in 2002 and amounting to up to 60%, were often avoided through bribery. As this practice continues at other border posts, many Angolan traders make large and costly detours in order to import goods purchased in Oshikango through the Katwitwe or Calueque border posts.

Most Chinese-owned shops in Oshikango sell wholesale to the Angolan market. They import large quantities of goods: many shops receive up to ten 40 foot containers of merchandise per month. For larger quantities, the goods are usually ordered directly from the factory, while lesser quantities are bought through wholesalers in China. The ability to deal with Chinese suppliers and government offices and to find new articles or better suppliers for the same article is the main asset Chinese traders in Oshikango have. "The problem is to bring the things here. Once they are here, selling is easy. Angolans buy everything," a trader told me. The cultural skills necessary to buy successfully on the cheap Chinese market (obviously including language skills) makes them exclusive and prevents Namibian competition. The cultural skills for selling in Oshikango are acquired by most migrants on the job – including rudimentary English and Portuguese.[15]

Due to their access to Chinese markets, the migrant entrepreneurs can undercut prices for comparable goods produced elsewhere. You can buy leather belts for N$ 5, radio cassette players for N$ 40 or soccer shoes for N$ 45 (Namibian retail prices, including all taxes). Quality is poor for some goods, but not for all: Chinese traders often complain that Angolan and Namibian customers do not perceive differences in quality and only compare prices.

The profit margins of the first Chinese traders were very high, but competition quickly led to lower margins. Chinese shops in Oshikango are fierce competitors for each other. They do not fix prices, nor are they shy to copy successful business ideas from their neighbours. Whenever new merchandise introduced by one of the shops is selling nicely, other shops are quick to order similar items and sell them at lower prices. Even brands established by one of the larger traders have been pirated by his colleagues through different Chinese factories.

The Chinese migrants come to Namibia to create a living for themselves and to escape the constraints of the Chinese domestic economy. They expend a lot of energy, hard work and creativity on their business, and many of them are very successful. However, their work benefits not only themselves and their families, it is also of enormous relevance to the Chinese economy. Today, Chinese migrant entrepreneurs are living in every country of the world, and in every African town there are Chinese shops selling goods produced in the People's Republic. The single shops are often small, but collectively they form a highly efficient network of sales outlets for Chinese industries largely independent of government initiatives. The Chinese government has certainly changed emigration rules and created greater room for business initiatives and its diplomats are constantly busy with securing the favours of foreign governments, but the main input for Chinese shops comes from the migrant entrepreneurs. If there is today no country in

---

15. There is, however, a generational gap here: while the older Chinese migrants often do not speak any foreign language before coming to Namibia, many of the young have a good working knowledge of English. This reflects the enormous improvements in the Chinese education system in the last two decades.

the world where Chinese goods do not form part of people's everyday life, that is largely due to these migrants.

Starting from a very low basis, Namibia's imports from China have grown at a staggering pace since approximately the turn of the millennium. According to ITS trade data, Namibian imports of manufactured goods from China have grown from $ 132,700 in 1996 to $ 1.5 m in 1999, $ 9.3 m in 2002 and more than $ 20 m in 2003. As the growth rates reflect the process of adjustment due to China's integration into the world markets, they will eventually slow down when China's relative weight in the world economy is reflected by its weight on the Namibian market. Until that point is reached, however, both Namibian businesses and traditional exporters on the Namibian market will have to live with constantly declining market shares and dwindling margins.

Problems of legality

For most Chinese nationals in Namibia today, getting a work permit is the single most essential prerequisite for success in business. "When we are here, we can always make money in some way or the other. If we have to go back to China, it is much more difficult." The days when one could easily get a work permit for establishing a retail shop are over. Chinese shops are present in every Namibian town, and both the public and politicians are growing more and more concerned about the negative effects on local industries and on the locally owned retail trade. It has even become difficult for shop owners to get work permits for relatives as assistants in their businesses, and a new migrant without connections (and more often than not without the necessary language skills) does not have a realistic chance on his own to get a work permit issued. There are, however, still several options for new migrants.

Perhaps the most common option is to pay established Chinese businessmen in Namibia who act as immigration brokers. They take charge of the necessary documents and provide both housing and a work place for the new arrival. Their charges can amount to well over N$ 100,000. Most of that sum is gradually paid back by working for the broker. After about three or four years, when they have paid back the broker's fees, new arrivals have also acquired the necessary skills and local knowledge to start a business of their own.

A second option seems to be more common still. Instead of paying a broker for the whole package, new migrants (either people with business experience elsewhere and some capital, or new business partners or relatives of Chinese living in Namibia) only pay for the service of a well-connected Chinese person who assists them in getting their work permit. Informants differed as to the price of this service, but the average sum mentioned was about N$ 20,000. All informants were convinced that part of that sum went to senior Home Affairs officials, the rest to the broker, but they were unclear about the respective shares.

While migrants complain about the rising sums involved, they accept them as the unavoidable entrance fee into a new world of opportunities. They are taught the rules of the game by their predecessors and they care more about the outcome than about legality. None of these rules are made by them, anyway. If they are concerned about the lack of legality, it is because it heightens both their risks and the leverage of the brokers. "You know, people talk so much about corruption. You can't just go there and give money to an officer. If he doesn't know you, he will not take it, and maybe arrest you. So there are only very few people who know those in charge for a long time, they are friends, and they know, if I take money from this one, it will be okay."

With work permits becoming scarcer or more expensive, more and more Chinese entrepreneurs are looking for alternative, cheaper ways to come by them – or simply ignore the risks of illegality. There are Chinese citizens who have been living in the country for years on a long expired tourist visa, relying on their luck not to get caught. A more promising way for creative entrepreneurs is to serve – or to do lip service to – the penchants of their host country's officials. While the Namibian government has gradually realised that there may be enough Chinese retail shops in Namibia, they are still keen to attract investors for manufacturing. More and more Chinese are thus thinking about establishing production facilities in Namibia. There is, for example, a Chinese firm producing duvets for export in the otherwise more or less manufacturing-deserted Oshikango Export Processing Zone (EPZ) park. Nothing could be more welcome to Namibia, even if the cotton, the textiles and the sewing machines are imported from China. I was at first puzzled why anyone should care to sew duvets in Namibia instead of importing them from China at lower costs. The answer, at least according to the general consensus of Chinese pavement radio, is simple: the main outcome of the venture is not duvets, but work permits. "With such a workshop, you will get work permits for maybe 20 or 30 technicians. Two or three of them actually work there, the rest is working somewhere in a shop."

The shops the additional migrants are working in often have no connection to the manufacturing business. Work permits have actually become just another commodity, a source of income for Chinese businessmen established in Namibia. Many of them are now busy establishing all sorts of manufacturing plants in order to sell the opportunity of legal employment to fellow countrymen. They typically spend about N$ 50,000 for the import of machinery, money easily recovered by the selling of three work permits.

Chinese who have been in the country for some time and are keen on establishing their own businesses usually keep a close watch on government policy. When President Pohamba in a speech urged Namibians to enhance computer skills and infrastructure, a young Chinese took it as a sign that a computer service and training centre could meet with the favour of Home Affairs. "Everybody talks about manufacturing. But service is, I think, good too. It is good for Namibia. And you don't need so much money. If you import machines, even if they don't work, just for show, you have to pay a lot of money for transport. With computers, that could work. I can still do some business at the same time."

Immigration laws are a field of state administration in which migrants all over the world are likely to become criminal at one point or another. Most of those who have tried to get a work permit or a new ID card from Home Affairs will probably understand, if not approve of, the temptation for somebody who is neither proficient in the language nor familiar with the system to get his papers in a more expeditious way. Illicit activities of Chinese nationals in Namibia are not limited to immigration offences, however. There are indicators that organised crime in Namibia has its Chinese face, too. Chinese shops in Windhoek are paying for 'protection': the gangs who control that business are equally involved in international drug dealing into and through Namibia, in cigarette smuggling and in the human trafficking of illegal prostitutes from South Africa to Namibia. In the north, Chinese nationals are involved in large-scale illegal currency deals, privately buying US dollars earned in the cross-border trade from local businessmen and reselling them at slightly higher rates in South Africa. I was unable to establish the source of the funds used for these currency deals, but due to the high risk involved, there is some likelihood of reinvestment of illicit gains and of money laundering.[16]

Economic benefits?

The business opportunities in Namibia certainly benefit the Chinese migrant entrepreneurs. But how much does their work benefit the Namibian economy and the Namibian people? To answer this question (and to decide what stance the Namibian government should adopt towards Chinese businesses), it is useful to distinguish short-term effects from long-term hopes and aims.

In the short run, the presence of Chinese shops makes some goods more accessible to the average consumer. Clothing, blankets, mattresses or shoes have become a lot cheaper – not to mention the plethora of unnecessary gadgets one can buy in China shops all over Namibia. Upper class consumers may raise a dismissive eyebrow at the quality, or argue that many of these items are rather useless. But for many people, a cheap radio of inferior quality at an affordable price looks more convincing than one of superior quality that is beyond their means, and even 'unnecessary' material possessions can create a strong feeling of exclusion if you are not able to afford them.

In addition to that, Chinese businesses create employment for Namibians. Once Oshikango's China Village is completed, around 200 Namibian people will find a job there. Most China shops in Namibia actually employ at least some people – shop assistants, store hands or security guards. Most of these jobs are for unskilled workers, however, and there have been many complaints about ill-treatment of workers.

In the short run, while Chinese shops benefit some of the more vulnerable Namibians, it is doubtful whether these benefits outweigh the losses experienced by existing businesses and, most importantly, the export of profits earned to China where they can no longer fuel the Namibian economy. The real issues, however, emerge in a long-term perspective. Throughout history, migrant entrepreneurs, and especially foreign shop owners, have been accused of parasitism and exploitation. But history equally abounds with examples of the constructive economic role played by migrant entrepreneurs who come into a country with capital, energy and new skills. What really mat-

---

16. Most of these allegations, however, rest on informed hearsay only. While some Chinese nationals were convicted in Windhoek and Walvis Bay for, among other things, cigarette contraband, drug dealing, armed assault and attempted murder, neither major structures of organised crime nor its links to South African gangs have so far emerged in court cases. The most prominent case judged in court involved a charge of heroin dealing and a burst from an illegally owned R4 automatic rifle in the upmarket Windhoek Country Club resort (See *The Namibian*, 13/08/2004, 11/11/2004). When, in 2003, smuggled cigarettes for over N$ 15 m were seized, "Police said it suspected that the source was a well organised syndicate from China. Contraband cigarettes are normally transported from China to Durban in South Africa before being shipped to Walvis Bay and back to South Africa." (*The Namibian* 6/02/2003).

ters for the Namibian economy is not whether the Namibian government should grant more or less work permits, or whether Chinese shops compete with existing ones owned by Namibians. The real question is whether the self-interest of Chinese migrants can be channelled into directions that will create genuine development, skills transfer and added value that stays within the Namibian economy.

Deborah Bräutigam (2003) has shown how, in the case of Mauritius, Chinese businessmen have moved from trade into manufacturing, creating the germs of successful indigenous industrialisation. This has not happened in Namibia yet and there are not many signs that it is about to happen. Government is certainly trying to push Chinese investors in that direction, but I know of only two or three 'real' Chinese manufacturing investments in Namibia, compared to hundreds of Chinese shops and a growing number of Potemkin villages in the manufacturing sector. Trade is still easier, more lucrative and less risky than manufacturing – not only for Chinese migrants. But competition among shops is already tough and profit margins will decline further. Many established Chinese shop owners are already looking for different markets where they can swim ahead of the crowd (two of them told me they wanted to move to Iraq as soon as the situation becomes a bit more stable; for a parallel example see Haugen and Carling 2005). If Namibia can offer them alternative investment opportunities outside trading, they might be induced to put their formidable energy, and their money, into projects that really further economic development.

Conclusion

This overview of the role China plays for the Namibian economy is far from exhaustive. I have concentrated on primary commodities, the construction industry and retail trade by migrant entrepreneurs only, leaving many other issues aside. There are many further fields where China's growing presence has large consequences for Namibia – from military cooperation, technical assistance and cultural exchange programmes to traditional Chinese medicine or the growing number of twinning agreements between Namibian and Chinese towns, let alone diplomatic ties at government level.

But even such a short review, bound to be outdated soon, shows how much the balance of the world economy has already shifted towards China. Africa (and the world) will have to face this fact, instead of wishing it did not happen. Only then can African countries implement policy measures that will allow them to benefit from the Chinese boom. More favourable terms of trade may, of course, make a crucial difference to commodity exporters, but unless China's role is rendered more constructive through economic legislation and diplomacy, Oshikango's China Village could become a symbol for the revamping of the old economic world system with a different trade partner – once again reducing African countries to the export of raw materials and the import of manufactured goods.

Notwithstanding that danger, China's emergence can create real possibilities. Quite apart from its interest in raw materials, there are signs that China is really willing to contribute to development in Africa, from the surge of donor moneys coming from the People's Republic to the willingness of the Chinese government to reduce textile exports to Southern Africa in order to protect local industries. On a local scale, the immense energy and creativity of Chinese migrants in Namibia could certainly be put to more constructive use than to obtaining and selling work permits, or the import of broken machinery for false manufacturing sites. African governments will not change China's role in the world economy nor the leverage that comes with it, but policy measures they implement now may contribute to transforming its consequences and may determine whether China's emergence will reshuffle the cards in Africa's international economic relations or simply change the players.

References

Alden, Chris (2005), 'China in Africa,' *Survival* Vol. 47, No. 3, pp. 147–64

Appolus, Emil (2004), 'Reminiscences of Times Gone By,' *New Era*, 3/12/2004.

Bosten, Emmy (2006), China's Engagement in the Construction Industry of Southern Africa: The Case of Mozambique. Paper for the Workshop 'Asian and Other Drivers of Global Change', St. Petersburg, Russia, 19–21 January 2006 http://www.ids.ac.uk/asiandrivers (June 2006)

Bräutigam, Deborah (1983), 'Doing Well by Doing Good,' *The China Business Review,* Vol. 10, No. 2, pp. 57–58

— (2003), 'Close Encounters: Chinese Business Networks as Industrial Catalysts in sub-Saharan Africa,' *African Affairs,* Vol. 102, pp. 447–67

Directorate of International Trade (2005), *China Market Study.* Windhoek: Minstry of Trade and Industry

Dobler, Gregor (2005), *South-South Business Relations in Practice. Chinese Merchants in Oshikango, Namibia.* http://www.ids.ac.uk/asiandrivers (June 2006)

— (2007), 'Solidarity, Xenophobia and the Regulation of Chinese Businesses in Namibia,' in C. Alden, D. Large and R. Soares de Oliveira (eds), *China Returns to Africa.* London: Hurst

— (2008), *The Way to Consumption. International Commodity Flows and Trade Networks in Oshikango, Namibia* (forthcoming)

Gibson, Richard (1972), *African Liberation Movements.* London: Oxford University Press

Goldstein, Andrea, Nicolas Pinaud, Helmut Reisen and Xiaobao Chen (2006), *The Rise of China and India – What's in it for Africa.* Paris: OECD

Hart, Gillian (1996), *Global Connections: The Rise and Fall of a Taiwanese Production Network on the Southern African Periphery.* Berkeley: Institute of International Studies

Haugen, Heide O. and Jorgen Carling (2005), 'On the Edge of the Chinese Diaspora: The Surge of Baihuo Business in an African city,' *Ethnic and Racial Studies,* Vol. 28, No. 4, pp. 639–62

Humphrey, John and Dirk Messner (2006), *The Impact of the Asian and other Drivers on Global Governance.* http://www.ids.ac.uk/asiandrivers (June 2006)

Kaplinsky, Raphie (2005), *Globalization, Poverty and Inequality.* Cambridge: Polity Press.

—, Dorothy McCormick and Mike Morris (2006), *The Impact of China on Sub-Saharan Africa.* http://www.ids.ac.uk/asiandrivers (June 2006)

Kößler, Reinhart (2005), It's 'Capitalism, Stupid! Die Wirklichkeit der Süd-Süd-Kooperation,' *iz3w,* No. 287, pp. 18–21

Kojima, Kiroshi (2000), 'The "Flying Geese" model of Asian Economic Development: Origin, Extensions, and Regional Policy Implications,' *Journal of Asian Economics,* Vol. 11, No. 4, pp. 375–401

Lyman, Princeton (2005), *China's Rising Role in Africa. Presentation to the US-China Commission.* 21 July, 2005 http://www.uscc.gov/hearings/2005hearings/written_ testimonies/05_07_21_22wrts/lyman_princeton_wrts.pdf (14 October 2005)

Payne, Richard J. and Cassandra R. Veney, (1998), 'China's Post-Cold War African Policy,' *Asian Survey,* Vol. 38, No. 9, pp. 867–79

Shinn, David H. (2005), *China's Approach to East, North and the Horn of Africa. Testimony before the U.S.-China Economic and Security Review Commission 'China's Global Influence: Objectives and Strategies.* 21 July 2005 http://www.uscc.gov/hearings/ 2005hearings/written_testimonies/05_07_21_22wrts/shinn_david_wrts.pdf (14 October 2005)

Taylor, Ian (1997), 'China and SWAPO: The Role of the People's Republic in Namibia's Liberation and Post-independence Relations,' *The South African Journal of International Affairs,* Vol. 5, No.1, pp. 110–22

Xiang, Biao (2003), 'Emigration from China: a Sending Country Perspective,' *International Migration,* Vol. 41, No. 3, pp. 21–48

Poverty, politics, power and privilege
Namibia's black economic elite formation

Henning Melber

In Namibia ... we are clear ... No exploitation of man by man.
That will not be allowed here. Namibia's first head of state, Sam Nujoma,
during an interview (Nujoma 2003:XIII)

The Policy of National Reconciliation has served our people well. Instead
of retributions and backlash, we have created a stable society where our
people work together for the achievement of our common goals of economic
development and the improvement of the living standards of all our people.
Namibia's second head of state, Hifikepunye Pohamba, in his address to the
nation on the 17th anniversary of independence, 21 March 2007

Ever since independence, the government of Namibia has held the exploitative and discriminatory nature of the century of firm occupation under German and South African
settler colonialism and its infamous apartheid system as being responsible for the gross
inequalities characterising the postcolonial social order. Indeed, the inherited socioeconomic structures placed a heavy burden on the erstwhile freedom fighters of the South
West African People's Organisation (SWAPO of Namibia) after they had seized legitimate political power and, subsequently, as the Swapo party, assumed ever greater and
ultimately absolute political control over the country (cf., Melber 2007). The challenges
ahead were by no means eased by the compromises made at the outset to secure the
final stage of the decolonisation process and a transition and transfer of political power
under an arrangement of controlled change. After all, the way to independence required
acceptance of the socioeconomic structures in existence by constitutionally endorsing
the status quo in terms of ownership and property rights. As part of the negotiated settlement, the scope of social change was confined to reforms within this constitutional
framework guided by a policy of 'national reconciliation.'

Notwithstanding these limitations on politics claiming to be guided by the notion
of fundamental emancipation, from the mid-1990s onward the liberation movement
democratically consolidated its position by securing a two-thirds majority in parliament
and complete control over the institutionalised political decision-making process. The
former comrades in the struggle were now political office bearers confronted with the
mammoth task of social delivery of reforms to the previously colonised and marginalised majority. After all, the anti-colonial movement's proclaimed goals and perspectives
were not only those of fighting the oppressive and exploitative system of apartheid colonialism. The liberation struggle was at the same time about creating conditions for a
better life after apartheid, not only in terms of political and civil rights, but also of the

inextricably linked material dimensions of human well being and a decent living for those previously marginalised and excluded from the benefits of the wealth created (to a large extent by them!).

Given the scale of chronic poverty existing at independence, the formulation and implementation of a rigorous strategy to achieve a coherent and cohesive social protection policy might have been expected to be at the forefront of postcolonial efforts to secure further emancipation. Government's responsibility to its electorate would, in those circumstances, have been reflected in concerted attempts to transform the socio-economic environment in order to combine further exploitation of the country's natural resource base with redistributive interventions in the interests of the majority of the population. Article 23(2) of Namibia's constitution, which was adopted in early 1990, entrusts elected law-makers in parliament with passing legislation aimed at redressing "social, economic or educational imbalances in the Namibian society arising out of past discriminatory laws or practices." But as the social reality presented in this chapter documents, painfully little has changed since then in terms of correcting the scandalous inequalities.[1]

Poverty and wealth

In terms of conventional econometric measurements for income inequality (the Lorenz curve and its related numerical index, the Gini coefficient), Namibia ranks in the top category of countries with the deepest social divides. Based on data in the mid-1990s, Namibia had a Gini coefficient of 0.701, not only an extremely unequal distribution of income, but the highest such coefficient for all countries for which it had been reliably calculated.[2] The deep internal socioeconomic divides are along both regional-ethnic as well as class lines. Geographical disparities were exacerbated by the legacy of the migrant labour system, which during the 20th century had promoted the rural-urban bias and the further and lasting marginalisation of whole regions (cf., Frayne 2005; Tvedten 2004; Winterfeldt 2002). Economic data and statistics gathered since independence

1. See also earlier versions of this considerably updated and revised text, which offer additional information on related aspects (Melber 2005c and 2006).
2. See for background information on measuring inequality in the Namibian context, Hastings (1999). The Gini coefficient can range in theory from 0 to 1, where the former would indicate that every person has exactly the same income (total equality), and the latter case would indicate that one individual received all income (total inequality). Notably, the degree of (in)equality measured does not allow for any conclusions to be drawn about the absolute amount of per capita income. This is illustrated by the fact that Namibia has the highest Gini coefficient, while in the mid-1990s the (generally poorer) Bangladesh had one of the lowest Gini coefficients, at less than 0.3. In contrast to Bangladesh's status as a Least Developed Country, however, the average annual per capita income of Namibia of the order of $ 2,000 places it in the lower middle-income country category. So much for the contrast between aggregated data and social realities! Not surprisingly, Namibia has one of the widest discrepancies between its ranking in terms of average annual per capita income and its Human Development Index. As the resident representative of UNDP pointed out during the launch of Namibia's first Human Development Report, Estonia in 1996 had a lower per capita income than Namibia but ranked 48 positions higher in terms of human development. Except for the oil enclaves of Qatar, Kuwait, Oman and Gabon, Namibia had the highest disparity between its real GDP per capita and human development rankings (Adei 1996:3).

confirm that the luxury which a small elite enjoys contrasts with the abject poverty of the majority of the people. A large-scale National Household Income and Expenditure Survey (NHIES) undertaken during 1993–94 concluded that "there are vast disparities between a small, wealthy minority and a big majority of which many live below the poverty line" (Central Statistics Office 1996:4). According to the report, 10% of the households (amounting to 5.3% of the population) accounted for 44% of private household consumption while the remaining 90% of households (amounting to 94.7% of Namibia's population) consumed 56% (ibid., p. 15). The figures also show that, in economic terms, the average Namibian does not exist. The notion of an average income becomes rather meaningless when half the population survives on approximately 10% of such fictive average income while 5% of the population enjoys an income more than five times higher than this abstract average. As a direct result of the inequalities, more than 40% of households were rated below the poverty line, and, sadly, Namibia has the highest malnutrition level of any country in the world with an average per capita income above $ 1,000.[3] The Namibia occupational wages survey of 2002, tabled in parliament in June 2006, shows the gross income inequalities in salaried employment: 14.9% of employees earn below N$ 600 (about $ 100) a month, while only 0.1% of employees earn above N$ 33,000 (about $ 5,500) a month, with the majority of salaries ranging between N$ 1,000 and N$ 5,000 (Dentlinger 2006).

As the first Human Development Report (HDR) published for Namibia in 1996 by the local UNDP office concluded: "Namibia is one of the worst performers in the world in terms of human development levels relative to national income" (UNDP 1996:73). With a Human Development Index (HDI) of 0.573 in 1996, the report commented with regard to the country's ranking in the world that "considerable advances still have to be realized before Namibia rises from its current position of 116th (out of 174) to its GDP ranking of 79th" (ibid., p. 74).

According to the social and demographic indicators presented in an overview table in a recent IMF assessment (2005:30), the latest available World Bank figures at the time suggested a GDP per capita (in constant 1995 prices) of $ 2,184 for 2004, while figures from the latest household income and expenditure survey undertaken by Namibian authorities highlight the unabatedly scandalous degree of skewed income distribution: the wealthiest fifth of the population controls 78.7% of income share, while the poorest fifth has to live on a mere 1.4%. Even neighbouring South Africa (with a GDP per capita of $ 4,020) has a less radical social divide, the corresponding figures being 66.5% and 2.0% respectively, hence indicating a broader band of social strata between the extreme haves and have-nots. Little, as the data suggest, has actually changed since independence in terms of the general distribution of wealth and poverty among the country's population, of which too many live in destitution.

---

3. Studies based on the available data offer further evidence of the magnitude of the challenges arising from the massive scale of poverty (cf., Hansohm, Presland 1998; NEPRU 1999; Schade 2000 and 2004).

Official planning for development

Towards the end of the first decade of Namibia's independence, a number of stocktaking exercises had started to summarise various aspects of socioeconomic and institutional development.[4] Namibia's planning policy emerged hand in hand with the establishment and consolidation of the structures of a sovereign Namibian state. The First National Development Plan (NDP 1), the essential framework document for the country's development strategy and capital investment programme for 1995–96 to 1999–2000 (National Planning Commission 1995) identified and highlighted four major development objectives:

a) a 5% annual growth rate for the economy;

b) the creation of ample opportunities for employment;

c) the reduction of inequalities in income distribution; and

d) the design of economic and social programmes to help alleviate poverty and to help vulnerable groups in society.

These four main aims are closely interrelated. However, only economic growth had a regular and comprehensive monitoring system, and the targeted average growth rate was not met. The other three aims were not regularly or systematically measured, but the figures and data available from a variety of sources (as unreliable, erratic, and even contradictory as they might at times be) suggest they were not met.

Efforts to draft the Second National Development Plan (NDP 2) were delayed, with policy guidelines formulated only towards the end of NDP 1 (National Planning Commission 1999). Instead, new parallel parameters were created with the introduction of a 'Vision 2030,' announced by the head of state and described by the National Planning Commission Secretariat (NPCS) as "the country's first long-term vision" (ibid., p. 27). It was obviously unclear at that stage to what extent 'Vision 2030' was supposed to replace, substitute, modify or simply augment NPCS efforts to formulate a comprehensive development strategy. There is, of course, a marked difference between a vision and a plan. While equity in development was highlighted by NPCS as a principal and strategic goal of 'Vision 2030,' the challenge remained to put forward the necessary steps to realise it. After a delay, NDP 2 was presented as the country's strategic development blueprint for the period 2001–02 to 2005–06 (National Planning Commission, undated [2002]). It identifies ambitious aims, but admits that most goals of the previous plan had not been met. The point of departure of the vision is "sustainable and equitable improvement in the quality of life of all people in Namibia" (ibid., Vol. 1, p. 50). NDP 2 lists the following national development objectives: poverty reduction, employment creation, promotion of economic empowerment, economic growth, reduction of inequalities in income distribution, reduction of regional development inequalities, promotion of gender equality and equity, enhancement of environmental and ecological sustainability and combating the further spread of HIV/AIDS (ibid.).

Even more ambitious is the long-term 'Vision 2030.' It was officially launched on 2 June 2004, i.e., six years after President Nujoma had initiated the blueprint as his brainchild. It declares as its aim placing the quality of life of all Namibians on par with

---

4. These include Halbach (2000), several contributions to Melber (2000), as well as the annual subchapters on socioeconomic developments for 1990 to 2000 in Melber (2002).

people in the developed world by 2030. According to this vision, Namibia will within the next 25 years be

> a healthy and food-secured nation in which all preventable, infectious and parasitic diseases are under secure control; people enjoy a high standard of living, good quality of life and have access to quality education, health and other vital services. All of these translate into long life expectancy and sustainable population growth. (Republic of Namibia 2004:20)

Ignoring for a moment its missing sense of reality, 'Vision 2030' indeed highlights a true dilemma: it names the challenge the government has to reckon with if it is to retain its legitimacy and credibility among the electorate:

> The goals of the Namibian struggle for independence were framed in terms of social justice, popular rule and socioeconomic transformation, thus the legitimacy of the post apartheid system of governance rests on its ability to deliver transformation or, at any rate, to redirect resources to address the socioeconomic causes of poverty and potential conflict ... Continued prevalence of widespread poverty would, in the eyes of those affected, imply government's unwillingness to change the status quo, or its inability to improve their economic conditions. Therefore, the challenge calls for a functioning social-democratic framework, underpinned by a robust and sustainable system of equitable social provisioning for the basic human needs of all citizens, in terms of, among others, education, health, housing, water, sanitation, land, etc. (Office of the President 2004:174–5).

As a 'sub-vision' it is declared that "Namibia [should develop] a significantly more equitable distribution of social well-being, through the sustainable utilization of natural resources in a mixed economy, characteristic of higher income countries, primarily through stronger growth and poverty-reduction" (ibid., p. 177).

The separate design of a poverty reduction strategy was based on a cabinet decision taken at the end of 1998. Since its adoption and proclamation (Republic of Namibia undated and 2002), little has been recorded in terms of monitoring achievements. Thus the picture emerges of a government eagerly compiling assessments and drafting strategic plans, but failing to achieve the declared goals set out in these documents. Despite visible initiatives by ministries to design policy-oriented development blueprints through a variety of official documents, a lack of any coherent development strategy remains a striking feature, as, even more clearly, does the failure to translate existing concepts into concerted action. In the words of the country report of the Swedish development agency:

> On the whole, several development policies, plans and structures are in place in Namibia for the Government to take on a more coherent and efficient poverty reduction programme, but all too often, efforts seem more to be focused on reviewing plans rather than implementing them. (Sida/Embassy of Sweden, Namibia 2004:6)

The outgoing representative of the local EU office expressed a similar view in public when he vacated his office in mid-2006. He identified poor planning, misjudgments and haphazard decision-making by government as a source of concern. In an interview published by the state-owned newspaper, he maintained that government executed "development plans without proper planning and the necessary research needed for the implementation of its socioeconomic projects" (quoted in Philander 2006). Such criticism, combined with the increase in graft scandals and corruption, was also reflected in

Namibia's international ranking. The global competitiveness report released at the end of September 2006 by the World Economic Forum (WEF) saw Namibia drop from 79th to 84th rank (Katswara 2006). In the UNDP Human Development Index (HDI) released in mid-November 2006, Namibia retained 125th position. But the country, with a marked spread of 50 ranking points as between these two indices, was again among those that displayed the greatest discrepancies between the (higher) rank in per capita income and the (lower) rank in HDI, a discrepancy that testified to the extreme inequalities. Nothing had actually changed for the better in comparison with the data presented in the first report of 1996. Ranked according to children under weight for age, Namibia ended third last among the countries of Southern Africa (24% for the age group under 5 years). Given the country's relative resource wealth compared with some of the neighbouring states, this is nothing less than a scandal. When an IMF mission held local Article IV discussions during November 2006, the published final statement warned that "more determined efforts [were] needed to reduce poverty so as to maintain social cohesion" (International Monetary Fund 2006).

Transition without transformation

Since independence, the Republic of Namibia's balance sheet for both the politically institutionalised culture (cf., Melber 2003a) and the culture of the political institutions (Melber 2005b) as well as socioeconomic performance (cf., de Waal et. al. 2002) has been at best mixed. "One Namibia, two nations" reported a local journalist, who quoted the first HDR presented by the local UNDP office: "Given the right policies, Namibia could translate its high per capita income into improved living standards for the majority of the population at a faster rate" (Sutherland 1996). A decade later, a UN country assessment warned of an unfolding humanitarian crisis due to the combination of HIV/AIDS, food insecurity and the ineffective delivery of critical social services to the most vulnerable groups (Dentlinger 2005). And a report by the World Bank on the (lack of) achievements in expanding so-called human capital noted:

> Inequalities inherited at independence persist, despite major efforts to eradicate them. They are evident in the distribution of access, learning outcomes, and resource inputs. These inequalities ... represent a threat to national cohesion, peace, and political stability, and a failure to realize the productive potential of a large proportion of the population. (Marope 2005:xviii)

While the international financial institutions and potential foreign investors praised the Namibian tax system for its efforts to be internationally attractive and competitive, that system has actually failed to use its potential to induce redistribution of wealth in any way. In contrast to "the prevalence of redistribution as a guiding motive in the design of tax systems in developed countries," Namibia seems to be similar to most other less developed countries, in which "poverty and/or inequality considerations have generally been of secondary importance, at best, in ... fiscal reforms" (Gemmell, Morrissey 2005: 31f.). Instead of such indifference, which has the ultimate consequence of favouring the better off once again, "redistribution as an effect should be targeted deliberately, and not be treated as an automatic by-product of political and economic reform" (Nel

2005:36). While taxation has been of little interest in the literature so far (cf., Hansohm et al. 2002), there is sufficient evidence that the current tax system ignores the considerable profit-generating activities on the margins of the formal economy in the prosperous parts of an 'informal' but highly successful business sector (operating particularly in the ruling Swapo party's home base in the Northern Owambo-speaking regions) and "has not been utilised as a redistributive mechanism to any significant extent" (Rakner 2001:142). The mere fact that it took 16 years after independence before even the still predominantly white commercial farmers were taxed on their land illustrates the point.[5]

An analysis of the first 15 state budgets since independence saw "little reason to believe that public spending is becoming more equitable and more focused on the poor," but "that public spending is becoming more rather than less inequitable" (Mbai, Sherbourne 2004:1). Even worse, there were reasons for "a strong suspicion that public spending is increasingly being channeled to more privileged groups in society employed in activities that bring little in the way of return through higher economic growth, such as in defence, paramilitary security, intelligence and poorly performing parastatals" (ibid., p. 13f.). This critical local assessment concluded that "it is quite possible that poverty and inequality have worsened and that the national budget has done little to offset this trend" (ibid., p. 4).

"Do We Have Cause for Celebration?" asked the editorial of the independent English local daily on the occasion of Namibia's 'Heroes Day' celebrated on 26 August 2005 to mark the 39th anniversary of the beginning of the armed struggle by SWAPO in 1966. Its sober conclusion: "Our goals of a just and equitable society seem far out of reach; our stated aims of bridging the gap between rich and poor diminish even further and only serve to further widen the rift between the haves and the have-nots" (*The Namibian*, 25 August 2005). In preparation for the UN summit discussing the achievements in regard to the millennium development goals, the Namibian NGO Forum (NANGOF) tabled a shadow report that contrasted with the official government position. It spelled out the challenges being confronted, including destitution and abject poverty, and expressed "grave concern regarding the performance of government." NANGOF called "for a critical review of the policies, strategies and approaches and structural tools adopted to remedy the situation with major emphasis on their dysfunctionalities and capacity gaps in adequately responding to the problem" (quoted in Kakololo 2005).

Declared efforts to eradicate inequalities have to be critically scrutinised and questioned in relation to the visible outcome so far under the given constraints of a framework limiting social change to government-induced reform policies. As a partial result of a combined approach of "national reconciliation" and "affirmative action" (Schmid 2002), the class structure has been slightly modified and the privileged segment of society became less exclusive in terms of pigmentation. However, as the sobering results of an assessment for the period 2000–04 suggests, "very few changes occurred in the composition of senior management. Based on the available data, it seems that white

---

5. Some suggest that one reason for such delay may be the fact that by the mid-1990s a considerable number of cabinet members and other lawmakers had already acquired commercial farms themselves.

men even increased their disproportionately large share of senior managers to almost 60%." (LaRRI 2005:19)[6]

Instead, so-called Affirmative Action (AA) measures were a convenient vehicle to cover up unlimited access to resources by those who were able to abuse their strategic positions: "Corruption and nepotism under the disguise of affirmative action will destroy the reputation of the policy," warned the same report. "Affirmative action must not become a new form of discrimination but an instrument to overcome the legacies (and still widespread practice) of racism and gender discrimination" (ibid., p. 110). Instead of pursuing a policy aiming at structural changes, however, the blatantly racist power structures and property relations have merely been gradually replaced by a more colour-blind class agenda. Like the "comrades in business" (Adam et. al., 1997) in neighbouring South Africa, the "colour of business" (Adam 2000) by means of Black Economic Empowerment (BEE) serves the class interests of a new bureaucratic elite from the ranks of the erstwhile liberation movement. These liberators profitably cashed in on their access to the country's resources through the political and public service offices they secured at and after independence. The results have been sobering for the country's still underprivileged majority. On behalf of the organised labour force, the Mineworkers Union of Namibia (MUN) expressed public concern over the state of BEE. The union declared that it "was not happy to witness a process where only the elite was in the driving seat" (*The Namibian*, 7 September 2005).

Greed and graft

A stock-taking exercise undertaken by a local NGO on reported cases of corruption since independence, reached the conclusion that "Namibia as a small economy has substantial volumes of corruption," which in most cases "involve Government agencies … where more resources are available and where controls are weakest" (NID 2005:20). Despite fairly positive rankings so far, Transparency International also notes a decline of the country on its index over the last years. According to its corruption index presented in early November 2006, Namibia dropped from 47th to 55th rank (*The Namibian*, 7 November 2006). Obviously, the anti-corruption crusade introduced by Namibia's second head of state since 2005 has had no visible results so far.

Soon after taking office, President Hifikepunye Pohamba used a rally in commemoration of Cassinga Day for 'a national alert' on corruption, asking for support for his government's drive to root out graft. He claimed that those who fought for independence and freedom did not sacrifice their lives so that other Namibians could enrich themselves through corruption, but for the country to be developed for the benefit of all Namibians. He warned that greed had become akin to colonialism. Those guilty of

---

6. According to the Namibian Employers' Federation (NEF), the Affirmative Action Act has so far resulted in a few well-educated Namibians from the so-called previously disadvantaged group using their status "to hop from one job to another in search of greener pastures" (Tjaronda 2006). This conclusion tends to overlook, however, the fact that (still predominantly white) Namibian private companies showed little enthusiasm for supporting a structured transfer of skills to enhance internal upward mobility among employees.

corruption not only eroded the national fabric, but also looted resources that could be used to alleviate poverty and create jobs:

> We fought against the colonialists because they were treating us badly, but now we have chased them out, there are people from our own society, our brothers and sisters, black people, who are colonising other fellow black Namibians and their Government by stealing the money of the public and enriching themselves … My government is not going to tolerate corruption, tribalism and nepotism and I am calling upon all Namibians who are practising these things to stop doing so immediately. (Quoted in Shivute 2005)

Looking at the evidence since then, the call seems not to have been heard. At about the same time, the deputy director in the office of the auditor general publicly shared his frustration at the lenient checks and balances in public accounting and transparency when he stated that instructions were "totally ignored without any fear" by top civil servants, including permanent secretaries (Maletsky 2005). This has been confirmed with the emergence of several high profile cases of misappropriation of public funds. In one case, N$ 100 m disappeared abroad over several years in a 'black box' by means of a shady investment transaction by top officials of the Overseas Development Corpora-tion (ODC). The money was supposed to enhance foreign direct investment through an export processing zone scheme. In the meantime, it has become known that since 2003 another N$ 30 m went "missing" (Hofmann 2006). ODC was actually expected to import capital instead of exporting it.

A second case suggested that investments by the Government Institutions Pensions Fund (GIPF) into dubious black empowerment projects resulted in losses amounting to N$ 650 m (Grobler 2005a). Government officials subsequently corrected the report: according to their estimates the losses would total "only" some N$ 350 m. In another case of publicly known scandals, even more spectacular because of the involvement of high political office bearers, N$ 30 m was transferred for speculative purposes from the Social Security Commission (SSC) to a private financial institution (Avid) without any guarantees. The institution had good political connections but its reputation has been increasingly tarnished by its inability to pay the money back.[7] A spectacular court case investigating the financial operations of the investment firm had since mid-July 2005 dramatically disclosed a network of politically well-connected 'comrades.' Their shady business practices seemed to illustrate in textbook fashion the infamous prevailing 'fat cat syndrome,' and attracted the interest not only of the media but of the wide audience drawn to the court room, who at times tended to turn the hearings into a Hollywood drama. The most prominent fraud saga to date in Namibia's post-independence history escalated just two days ahead of the annual Heroes' Day public holiday in 2005 when the accused key witness shot himself in the presence of policemen after being arrested, while a deputy minister resigned from the office he had been sworn in to only five months earlier (cf., reports in *The Namibian*, 25 August 2005).

---

7. A presidential commission of inquiry started a probe into SSC in 2002, after it became known that brokers and middlemen tasked with investing SSC funds took cuts worth millions of dollars in state pension money. The Avid deal took place after the launching of the investigations, which have kept the police busy for four years with no findings or other information released. See: 'SSC Inquiry Probe Inches Forward.' In: *Insight Corruption Tracker*, July 2007. According to the same source, a total of 62 persons from the SSC were accused of fraud by June 2007.

Even the secretary of the Swapo party's Elder Council found harsh words at a press conference for these scandalous disclosures, which he likened to a monster of avarice and avidity, which "is eating the national cake greedily, excessively, with impunity." As he concluded: "Corrupt practices have become the order of the day" (quoted in Shigwedha 2005). Namibia's prime minister shared similar sentiments when he commented on the squandering of the several hundred millions from the GIPF pension funds on get-rich-quick schemes masquerading as BEE. These, he dismissed as "just asset-stripping" contributing to an even bigger rich-poor-divide: "We have to be careful, otherwise we are going to end up having a class war in this country," he warned (quoted in Grobler 2005b).

Based on experiences so far, the chairperson of the standing committee of the Namibia Chamber of Commerce and Industry (NCCI), diagnosed "a culture of envy and jealousy" spreading among black empowerment stakeholders and players in the country. This culture, he continued, contributed to the economic failure of schemes (quoted in Sibeene 2006). The relatively excessive remuneration of managers in parastatals and municipalities (often with salaries twice that of the head of state) is another indicator of an – at times unashamed – self-enrichment strategy by members of the new elite. They base their access to the country's public purse on political or public sector offices and benefit from direct preferential treatment. In an act of voluntary transparency, the Development Bank of Namibia (DBN) disclosed in its annual report the remuneration it offered. In 2005, its CEO earned "a hefty N\$ 1.1 m in total, which consisted of a N\$ 716,609 pensionable salary, a bonus of N\$ 257,960 and company contributions to pension and medical aid of N\$ 163,101. The bonus was up by a whopping 85% on the previous year's."[8]

During the year, of 94 loan applications submitted, seven loans were granted: among the recipients were two other parastatals, a town council, two companies with strong political connections (involving the ex-deputy foreign minister in the one case and the director general of the NPC in the other case),

> and one to a company which was on the verge of liquidation only to be bought up and saved by a foreign company (Ongopolo Mining and Processing). The remaining loan was extended to Namibia Poultry Industries for which no information is presented in the report … while both the chairperson's and CEO's reviews mention the positive aspects of most of the loans, no mention is made of the loan to Ongopolo or to Namibia Poultry Industries, the two largest loans the bank has made. Of course the key question is why did it take the Development Bank to make these loans rather than a normal commercial lender?[9]

---

8. 'Nice Work if You Can Get It.' In: *Insight,* August 2006, p. 15.

9. Ibid. The special case of Ongopolo's transfer to the multinational mining company Weatherly International merits detailed presentation, but would exceed the limitations on the length of this chapter. Suffice it to point to the interview with the new CEO in the same issue of the magazine. Financed a few years earlier as a BEE project, Ongopolo sold for liquidity reasons but has since turned out to be a profitable investment for Weatherly. As its CEO stated in the interview: "I guess we knew more about the company than some of the directors," one of whom was, by the way, the former trade union leader who features prominently in the fuel deal reported below. The new CEO also stated his intentions to establish "a school for miners as there's been no training whatsoever in the workforce for the last five years" (i.e., since the takeover as a BEE enterprise) and the aim to bring "a number of essential functions, that for some crazy reason were outsourced, back into the company." Quoted from: "For Us it's Make or Break." Ibid., pp. 10–13.

During a labour case in court, it emerged in late 2006 that the monthly salary of the former chief executive officer of the Agricultural Bank of Namibia (employed there between 1997 and January 2004) amounted to N$ 83,000. The claimant, who described this as a "mid-range" and "moderate" package, initially demanded N$ 6 m in compensation for what he considered unfair dismissal by the parastatal. As he explained to the Windhoek district labour court, he could have expected that at the end of his contract he would be reappointed for another five-year-period as Agribank CEO (Grobler 2006b). While the claimant was not very successful in squeezing out more money after his contract properly came to an end, the CEO of the Walvis Bay municipality – who reportedly had a similar monthly salary of between N$ 85,000 and 92,000 (Kraft 2007) seemed more successful. As it emerged in July 2007, the city's director of 12 years resigned at the end of March 2007 after he had renewed his five-year contract in 2006. The municipal council accepted an accelerated resignation, which allowed the CEO to vacate his office within a week, and, for unknown reasons, agreed to a golden handshake of close to N$ 2.8 m (Hartman 2007).[10]

Given this undisguised and unashamed greed, it hardly comes as a surprise that one Swapo MP suggested in all seriousness during a debate in the National Assembly that the current speed limit of 120 km/h on all Namibian roads be modified. Sedan cars, he said, such as Volvo, Mercedes Benz, Camry and the like, "whose speedometers go over the limit of 180 km/h, should be allowed a limit of up to 160 kilometres per hour." He urged the need for this "based on the simple fact that if one has experiences driving any of these cars, you will agree that you are likely to fall asleep driving at 120 km/h, because the car does not seem to be moving" (quoted in Weidlich 2007). As a result of the hunt for money and status, exemplified by such weird and misguided conceptions of 'special treatment' presented during a parliamentary debate (thereby vindicating the adage that the fantasy of satire is surpassed only by reality), differences in salary packages created a three-tier labour market. A study by the trade union-affiliated research institution LaRRI empirically illustrated the radically segmented workforce, which is composed of "a small elite enjoying a standard of living comparable to first-world countries, a significant group of formal sector workers with permanent jobs and low-to-middle incomes and a growing number of casual, informal and unemployed workers" (Katswara 2005).

The notion of national reconciliation, proclaimed as a guiding principle for the consolidation of postcolonial Namibia, to a large extent translates into a pact between old and new elites, whereby the latter are coopted as the beneficiaries into existing struc-

---

It should be mentioned that a year later the same magazine reported much less critically on the 2006 annual report presented by the DBN and applauded its CEO for his transparency and accountability. This contrasted favourably with general attitudes and practices and DBN is the only parastatal to report its CEO's annual income (which increased only marginally) as well as the remuneration for its non-executive directors. As the article concluded: "Namibia can be thankful that the DBN is not turning into yet another opaque and inefficient parastatal accountable to no one but itself. Yet if the DBN can do it, there is absolutely no reason why others can't do it too." 'The exception to the rule.' In: *Insight*, August 2007, p. 17.

10. Reportedly, the reasons he gave to the media for his resignation were private and linked to his intention to finalise his Ph.D. thesis. When the information about the golden handshake leaked out at a council meeting in July, the municipal authority took the view that this arrangement was an entirely internal affair (Kraft 2007).

tures. Looking at the balance sheet, government itself realised by mid-2006 that BEE as hitherto practised – and later termed BBEE (Broad Based Economic Empowerment) –had failed to produce the desired results. As the cabinet announced, "economic empowerment through schemes such as Affirmative Action loans, fish quota allocations, land resettlement and employment equity must reflect positive changes in the lives not only of a few individualists" (Maletsky 2006). Addressing a media briefing on the issue, Prime Minister Angula "bemoaned the fact that some of the beneficiaries sold their fishing quotas to buy expensive cars which they later crash" (ibid.). The so-called Namibianisation of the fisheries sector is indeed a case in point. It had to a large extent translated into the privatisation of natural resources and the siphoning off of profits by allocating fishing quotas to comrades – who generate income by transferring the utilisation of the quota to companies that are pro-forma Namibian but in fact internationally managed and owned, while spending their share of the deal on non-productive, consumptive purposes (Melber 2003b).[11] As a result, Namibia ends up among those cases where

> in the absence of property-rights protection, societies with a more unequal distribution of wealth and characterized by a small fraction of people who can afford entry into rent seeking will also be ones with greater social polarization and entrenched rent seeking by few at the expense of the majority. (Chakraborty, Dabla-Norris 2005:20)

This absence of property rights protection is documented in the Namibian case most conspicuously by the unscrupulous looting of state finances, as the case of the Namibia Development Corporation (NDC) exemplifies. Transformed as a public development agency from the former apartheid era (established originally in the 1970s as a "Bantu Investment Corporation") into a state-funded BEE institution (what an irony!), its liquidation was decided by cabinet in early 2007 due to its massive losses. NDC had, among other things, lent N$ 55 m to the ODC as investment capital without any realistic hope of returns. As it emerged during a parliamentary committee hearing, the NDC liquidation also opened windows of opportunity for prominent BEE-lenders seeking to avoid the repayment of the credits received earlier. The BEE transactions by NDC had amounted to some N$ 24 m in credits, of which NDC was able to secure some N$ 3 m by early 2007. Among the recipients were prominent wealthy black businessmen. According to one opposition MP during the parliamentary committee hearing discussing the case, these would not only be able to repay the loans, but could purchase the whole of NDC (Hofmann 2007).

The politics of class

The new rhetorical impetus by the Pohamba government has so far not had much impact on the social realities or even in terms of visible change of policy. On the contrary, more revelations of self-enrichment schemes at the expense of the public purse and individual consumers have hit the headlines. Another "horde of black economic em-

---

11. A similar translation of 'affirmative action' into further privileging the new elite can be seen in the current redistribution policy misleadingly labelled as land reform (necessary and overdue but still absent) (Melber 2005a).

powerment groups in Namibia"[12] has since mid-2006 come under heightened scrutiny by the newly established Anti-Corruption Commission (ACC). The three-year deal in question was about importing, as of 2005, 450,000 metric tons of fuel per year (half of Namibia's annual fuel supply) from the South African energy company Sasol, for which the Namibian state oil corporation NamCor (National Petroleum Corporation of Namibia) awarded a tender to a BEE outfit called Namibian Liquid Fuel (NLF). This joint venture between Sasol and the Namibian black empowerment company Philco Twenty siphoned off a whopping windfall profit for the transport of the fuel, which NamCor could have organised itself to keep fuel prices lower. As it later emerged, NLF was only set up in October 2004 on the initiative of Sasol in response to the advertised tender, which called for a joint venture with a local company. Ownership was divided between Sasol (49% of shares) and the Philco Twenty conglomerate (later renamed Petronam) of local individuals representing firms that existed on paper without any proper offices (51% ownership). The ultimately awarded tender amounted to N$ 800 m per annum (or N$ 2.4 bn in total) for the three-year period of the contract (which, according to unconfirmed reports, has in the meantime been extended to five years). Further financial details were withheld for reasons of 'national security,' since fuel supply is considered of strategic relevance.

When information on the deal leaked, a press conference was arranged in July 2006 to counteract the negative reports. By any standards, this backfired, since the questions by the journalists brought more dubious information to light (see Grüllenbeck 2006a and 2006b; Grobler 2006a; and Amupadhi 2006). Philco Twenty Ltd. had as its main Namibian beneficiaries a former trade union leader (holding 14%), a former deputy director of the ministry of finance and economic advisor in the office of the president (12%), another State House employee (10%), the former secretary of state in the office of the president and an investment broker (8% each). Interestingly, a South African citizen who had never resided in Namibia was also a member of the Namibian BEE club (8%). NLF refused to answer why this was the case. In all the details of the transaction, i.e., from the purchasing to the transport of the fuel from Durban to Namibia, the Namibian company was involved on paper only. The fuel tanker and its crew were hired from the South African petrol company Engen. During the media briefing, the former trade unionist declared in defence of the deal that the shareholders were "just black entrepreneurs who needed the money and took advantage of a given situation" (quoted in Grobler 2006a).

The newly appointed executive secretary to the Namibian BEE company, previously assistant to the former prime minister and special advisor to the minister of justice and state attorney, justified the involvement of Philco Twenty as a BEE-initiative in a striking manner. As he explained to the local German daily, the reason lay in established economic knowledge. According to this view, every society requires a layer of rich entrepreneurs. In Namibia, these are still the old elites, who export capital or circulate it among themselves. Wealth is in this way never redistributed. The creation of a rich level of previously disadvantaged people consequently amounts to BEE policy. Only

---

12. Quoted from the subheading of a report entitled "The Mother of all Empowerment Deals" published in the local monthly magazine *Insight,* March 2006, pp. 28–9. This revealed an intimate network of higher ranking officials and their relatives as "an intricate web" (ibid., pp. 30–1) involved in the deal.

they can, through new investments, redistribute the wealth of the old elites. Namibians should not envy them but welcome their engagement (quoted in Grüllenbeck 2006a). In an interview with *Insight* magazine, the former trade union leader confirmed a similar social engagement rooted in the affirmation of the existing system, as long as black entrepreneurs were receiving their 'fair share':

> As entrepreneurs we have got certain needs to satisfy, our potential to develop and families to feed. As an entrepreneur wanting to succeed I always strive to get involved in the mainstream of the economy of the country – whether it's for myself, the country at large, or for some of the broad-based beneficiaries.[13]

Another prominent BEE activist (who incidentally also performs as a popular stand-up comedian) publicly held a similar view at around the same time. In an opinion piece, he defended the new state-supported income-generating activities as a kind of tit for tat:

> It doesn't take a genius to figure out that there are more white Namibians who continue to benefit financially from the political stability created in this country when it comes to amassing wealth. And I say good for them. I admire them and I am learning from them. They make use of their connections and take advantage of well-worn loopholes in the system. That's what business is all about: taking advantage of financial opportunities that might present themselves. My beef is that when black entrepreneurs do the same, they are purported to be corrupt! (Jacobs 2006)[14]

A popular school of thought, possibly finding additional concrete evidence in the details of the Namibian case study presented here, holds the view that "it is the concentration of economic and political power in the hands of narrow privileged groups that produces inequalities and poverties" (Miller 1996:581). The privatisation of public resources results firstly in political-administrative power as personalised power, secondly in politics as a kind of business enterprise and thirdly in vertical clientele relationships of a neopatrimonial nature: "In sum, the result is authoritarian and incompetent states that rarely respond to public pressure" (Wilson et al. 2001:10). But it also results, after an incubation period, in growing dissent among the formerly supportive ordinary people, who had assumed that life after independence might be at least a bit better in material terms than before.

---

13. Quoted from "Sasol Don't Want Free Riders", *Insight*, August 2006, p. 21. A commentary on the NFL deal in the same issue (entitled "Low Risk, High Returns") asks if "BEE in Namibia will be defined as the art of doing little more than exploiting political links and then watching the money coming in?" and ends: "Unless there is a clear understanding of BEE and a set of regulations, those with the right political links will be in pole position to receive government guaranteed loans, state-linked business contracts and individual jobs, thus swelling the bellies of a small group of the ruling elite." (Ibid., pp. 22 and 23).

14. By the way, after almost a year of investigation the ACC came to the conclusion in July 2007 that there was no case of corruption involved. As if to add insult to injury, the findings of the ACC report were first announced to the public by NLF (*The Namibian*, 20 July 2007). For the necessary critical analyses of this whitewash, see the various background articles in *Insight*, August 2007. A summary report on this, the biggest black empowerment deal in Namibia to date, can be found in the same issue and is entitled 'Namibia's own OILigarchs.' It concludes that "the whole deal looks like little more than a way of enriching the lucky few who own no assets, possess no expertise and add no value. Namibia's own oligarchs." (p. 15) The fact that several among the lucky few continue to hold full-time higher positions in the public service was not considered by the ACC to be a conflict of interest.

The ongoing exclusion of the impoverished and marginalised from the benefits of the country's wealth and resources, however, is no longer only the result of the structural legacy of apartheid, as is so conveniently claimed by the new postcolonial elite. To that extent the official position, which continues to put the blame squarely on settler colonialism alone, is misleading and shying away from the real issues at stake. In her weekly column, the editor of the autonomous local English daily *The Namibian*, summarised the current challenges by pointing out that

> the term 'previously disadvantaged' … is being misused to the advantage of those who already have more than enough … We'd do better to concentrate on efforts on the 'presently disadvantaged' because only then will we make a real difference in our very economically divided society. (Lister 2005)

The current rent-seeking strategy of a minority among the erstwhile colonised majority, cashing in on its politically consolidated base by abusing its control over state assets and deciding upon their allocation, has recently been challenged even in the state-owned daily newspaper:

> There is simply no reason, for example, why the fishing sector cannot be revamped and reorganized to benefit society at large instead of the small clique that have access to the fishing quotas year in year out. The absence of a progressive policy in this regard cannot be blamed on the policy of national reconciliation, nor the liberal constitution, nor on nation building, or on the nature of transition to independence etc. It is simply a question of a country, perhaps unconsciously, following the wrong policies. (Kaure 2005)

Put slightly differently: the visible results of the state's policy direction on the Namibian postcolonial reality so far do not indicate a serious political will to serve the poor. It's not about redistribution of relative wealth, or tackling chronic poverty by means of social protection, it's all about self-enrichment, capitalism and class. In other words, it's business as usual. As the assessment of the trade union-affiliated local think tank warned:

> Affirmative action does not necessarily eradicate socioeconomic inequalities. Instead, inequalities may merely be shifted from the basis of race, ethnicity or gender to the basis of class. Affirmative action may promote the redistribution of opportunities in favour of previously disadvantaged groups, but it's not the principal mechanism to redistribute wealth or to overcome poverty. (LaRRI 2005:11)

But even if one accepts the notion of a capitalist class project as the necessary point of departure, Namibia's postcolonial development has not yet produced any meaningful 'patriotic bourgeoisie' (if something like that still exists in these neoliberal times of global capitalism). What has been emerging instead, is at best a crypto-capitalist, petty-minded self-enriching new black elite, which expends its energy on exploiting the public purse. As a critical political commentator concluded in one of his many opinion articles, "what we have done so far is to create a truly parasitic class that depends on public resources to lead an un-earned lifestyle" (Kaure 2006).

In the absence of a meaningful, profit-generating industrial sector, in which capital would be accumulated through a combination of value-adding manufacturing and the profit margins created by the wage labour producing such commodities, surplus generation has relied on the privatisation of natural resources (mainly in fishing, mining, agriculture and tourism) or benefits generated by access to privileges in the public sector and the state-owned enterprises (in particular public utilities such as water and electricity, but also telecommunications and transport). Public procurement and other outsourcing activities by those in control of state agencies turn 'affirmative action' and 'black economic empowerment' into a self-rewarding scheme based on 'struggle credibility and credits' among the activists of the erstwhile liberation movement. Through such practices, the skewed class character of Namibia's society has hardly changed since independence. Cooption into the ruling segments of an existing socioeconomic system is very different from social transformation. Both AA and BEE in their current form continue to cultivate human and natural exploitation for the benefit of a few at the expense of far too many. As the veteran opposition politician Hitjevi (Gerson) Veii, former president of the first Namibian liberation movement SWANU and political prisoner on Robben Island, categorically stated during a fund-raising event for his party:

> While the intention of Affirmative Action and Black Economic Empowerment was to reduce the imbalances created by apartheid colonialism, these concepts are being hijacked by ruling elites to destroy our much anticipated class struggle. (Quoted in Matundu-Tjiparuru 2006)

The losers of such non-transformation of the inherited economic, political and ideological foundations of society are all marginalised Namibians. The response by the postcolonial state to the demands of the ex-combatants for integration is a case in point. A recent case study concluded on a note that also applies to government-supported elitist self-enrichment schemes for a privileged few who benefit by occupying the political commanding heights of the formally sovereign Namibian state:

> The paradox could be precisely that while the reach of 'the state' is extended and deepened, this does not happen equally. The state is there more for some than for others and its languages have more resonance for some than for others. Furthermore, this process is conditional on the localisation and vernacular forms of state intervention. This leads to two questions. First, could the very way in which state power is extended and deepened perhaps contain the seeds of its destabilisation? And second, will the state-citizen relations thus formed outlive the particular persons who have forged those relations? (Metsola/Melber 2007:105)

The bio-political techniques, which are instrumental in such containment policy, ultimately face the challenge that the eradication of poverty would mean the elimination of the poor in the sense of their visible presence in the dominant society. Such a pseudo-solution would in the last round of the battle, which cannot be won by those holding on to power and privilege, culminate in Zimbabwe's 'Operation *Murambatsvina*.' The Shona word translates as 'sweep out the dirt' or 'clean out the rubbish' and entailed in practical terms the brutal removal by the state's police and army of the urban poor from the streets and dumping them in the urban outskirts and rural hinterlands. The innocent victims were guilty of being poor and those people made homeless were estimated to amount to one million. They had been targeted since 2005 by the central government and its 'security organs' because of the informal trade and housing schemes they had established as a means of survival in the face of their suffering under a policy that had failed since independence. As the Zimbabwean artist Hosiah Chipanga put it in one of his popular songs: "*Vatadza kupedza urombo, zvino vavakuda kupedza isu varombo*"

("They have failed to eliminate poverty, now they want to eradicate the poor")[15] – but only to realise, that sooner or later, this does not work.

References

Adam, Kanya (2000), *The Colour of Business: Managing Diversity in South Africa*. Basel: Schlettwein

Adam, Heribert, Frederik van Zyl Slabbert and Kogila Moodley (1997), *Comrades in Business*. Cape Town: Tafelberg

Adei, Stephen (1996), *Launching of Namibia Human Development Report 1996*. Address by Resident Representative UNDP Namibia, 17 July

Amupadhi, Tangeni (2006), 'Namibia to Investigate Sasol Role,' *Mail & Guardian*, Johannesburg, 30 June to 6 July

Central Statistics Office (1996), *Living Conditions in Namibia. Basic Description with Highlights. The 1993/1994 Namibia Household Income and Expenditure Survey. Main Report*. Windhoek: Republic of Namibia/National Planning Commission

Chakraborty, Shankha and Era Dabla-Norris (2005), *Rent Seeking*. Washington DC: International Monetary Fund (IMF Working Paper 05/43)

de Waal, Johan, Herbert Jauch, Henning Melber and John Steytler (2002), 'A Social Assessment of Namibia's Economic Achievements since Independence – a Round-table Debate,' in V. Winterfeldt, T. Fox and P. Mufune (eds), *Namibia – Society – Sociology*. Windhoek: University of Namibia Press, pp. 3–25

Dentlinger, Lindsay (2005), 'Namibia Remains 'the Most Unequal Country' in World,' *The Namibian*, Windhoek, 15 September

— (2006), 'Jobless Rate Officially 36.7%,' *The Namibian*, 14 June

Frayne, Bruce (2005), 'Rural Productivity and Urban Survival in Namibia: Eating Away from Home,' *Journal of Contemporary African Studies*, Vol. 23, No. 1, pp. 51–76

Gemmell, Norman and Oliver Morrissey (2005), 'Distribution and Poverty Impacts of Tax Structure Reform in Developing Countires: How Little We Know,' *Development Policy Review*, Vol. 23, No. 2, pp. 131–44

Grobler, John (2005a), 'Bad Investments Cost GIPF N$ 650 m,' *The Namibian*, 29 August

— (2005b), '"Rotten apples" could Foment Class War: PM,' *The Namibian*, 7 September

— (2006a), 'BEE Fuel Deal still Murky,' *The Namibian*, 13 July

— (2006b), 'N$ 83 000 a Month "Modest" Says ex-Agribank CEO as Labour Case Wraps Up,' *The Namibian*, 16 October

Grüllenbeck, Stefan (2006a), 'BEE auf dem Weg zur Farce,' *Allgemeine Zeitung*, 13 July

— (2006b), 'Lesen Sie das bloss nicht!' *Allgemeine Zeitung*, 14 July

Halbach, Axel J. (2000), *Namibia – Wirtschaft, Politik, Gesellschaft nach zehn Jahren Unabhängigkeit*. Windhoek: Namibia Wissenschaftliche Gesellschaft

Hansohm, Dirk and Cathy Presland (1998), 'Poverty, Inequality and Policy in Namibia. The State of Knowledge and the Way Ahead in Poverty Research,' in *In Search of Research. Approaches to Socioeconomic Issues in Contemporary Namibia*. Windhoek: Namibian Economic Policy Research Unit

---

15. I owe this quote to my former colleague Amin Kamete.

—, Klaus Schade and Maano Nepembe (2002), 'Taxation, Expenditure and Accountability: Lessons from Namibia,' *IDS Bulletin*, Vol . 33, No. 3, pp. 58–66

—, Klaus Schade and Arne Wiig (2001), 'Trade Policy, Poverty and Inequality in Namibia,' in F. Wilson, Nazneen Kanji and Einar Braathen (eds), *Poverty Reduction. What Role for the State in Today's Globalised Economy?* London/New York: Zed, pp.164–95

Hartman, Adam (2007), 'N$ 2,8 m Handshake for Walvis CEO, *The Namibian*, 19 July

Hastings, Thomas (1999), *The Role of Remittances in the Namibian Economy*. Windhoek: Namibian Economic Policy Research Unit (NEPRU Occasional Paper 15)

Hofmann, Eberhard (2006), 'ODC-Loch wird immer grösser,' *Allgemeine Zeitung*, 5 July

— (2007), 'Volksvermögen zerrinnt,' *Allgemeine Zeitung*, 13 April

International Monetary Fund (2005), *Namibia. Staff Report for the 2004 Article IV Consultation*. January 27 (released as IMF Country Report 05/97)

— (2006), *Statement by IMF Staff at the Conclusion of the 2006 Article IV Consultation Discussions to Namibia*. Press Release No. 06/252, November 14

Jacobs, Lazarus (2006), 'To BEE or Not To BEE?' *The Namibian*, 4 August

Kakololo, Emma (2005), 'Nangof Calls for More Action on Poverty,' *New Era*, Windhoek, 15 September

Katswara, Tonderai (2005), 'Wide Salary Gap between Workers, *The Namibian*, 12 April

— (2006), 'Namibia's Drop in Economic Rankings "Cause for Concern",' *The Namibian*, 2 October

Kaure, Alexactus (2005), 'Determinism or Human Agency – Which Way Namibia?' *New Era*, Windhoek, 15 July

— (2006), 'Living in a Parasites' Paradise,' *The Namibian*, 7 July

Kraft, Kirsten (2007), 'Die Katitit Klausel,' *Allgemeine Zeitung*, 20 July

LaRRI (2005), *Namibia's Affirmative Action in Employment. An Assessment 2000–2004*. Windhoek: Labour Resource and Research Institute (LaRRI)

Lister, Gwen (2005), 'Political Perspective,' *The Namibian*, Windhoek, 24 June

Maletsky, Christof (2005), 'Top Govt Bean Counter Spills some Beans on Corruption,' *The Namibian*, Windhoek, 12 May

— (2006), 'Cabinet Ppproves Amendments to BEE Policy,' *The Namibian*, Windhoek, 27 June

Marope, Mmantsetsa Toka (2005), *Namibia Human Capital and Knowledge Development for Economic Growth with Equity*. Washington DC: World Bank (Africa Region Human Development, Working Paper Series 84)

Matundu-Tjiparuro, Kae (2006), 'Reflections of Veteran Politician,' *New Era*, 7 August

Mbai, Julia and Robin Sherbourne (2004), *Have Priorities Changed? Budget Trends Since Independence*. Windhoek: Institute for Public Policy Research (IPPR Briefing Paper 32)

Melber, Henning (ed.), (2000), *Namibia: A Decade of Independence 1990–2000*. Windhoek: Namibian Economic Policy Research Unit

— (2002), *Namibia 1990–2000. Eine analytische Chronologie*. Windhoek: Namibia Wissenschaftliche Gesellschaft

— (ed.), (2003a), *Re-examining Liberation in Namibia. Political Culture since Independence*. Uppsala: Nordic Africa Institute

— (2003b), 'Of Big Fish and Small Fry: Rent-Seeking Capitalism Made in Namibia – The Case of the Fishing Industry,' *Review of African Political Economy*, No. 95, pp. 142–49

— (2005a), 'Land & Politics in Namibia, *Review of African Political Economy*, No. 103, pp. 135–42

— (2005b), 'People, Party, Politics and Parliament: Government and Governance in Namibia,' in Mohamed Salih (ed.), *African Parliaments Between Governance and Government*. Basingstoke/New York: Palgrave Macmillan, pp. 142–61

— (2005c), 'Namibia's Post-colonial Socioeconomic (non-) Transformation: Business as Usual?' *Nord Süd aktuell*, Vol. 19, Nos. 3&4, pp. 306–21

— (2006), *Breeding Fat Cats. Affirmative Action, Black Economic Empowerment, and Namibia's Post-Colonial Elite Formation*. Copenhagen: Danish Institute for International Studies (DIIS Working Paper No. 2006/29)

— (2007), 'SWAPO is the Nation, and the Nation is SWAPO.⊠Government and Opposition in a Dominant Party State. The Case of Namibia,' in Katarina Hulterström, Amin Kamete and Henning Melber, *Political Opposition in African Countries. The Cases of Kenya, Namibia, Zambia and Zimbabwe*. Uppsala: Nordic Africa Institute (NAI Discussion Paper 37), pp. 61–83

Metsola, Lalli and Henning Melber (2007), 'Namibia's Pariah Heroes. SWAPO ex-Combatants Between Liberation Gospel and Security Interests,' in Lars Buur, Steffen Jensen and Finn Stepputat (eds), *The Security-Development Nexus. Expressions of Sovereignty and Securization in Southern Africa*. Uppsala: Nordic Africa Institute and Cape Town: HSRC Press, pp. 85–105

Miller, S.M. (1996), 'The Great Chain of Poverty Explanations,' in Else Oyen, S.M. Miller and Syed Abdus Samad (eds), *Poverty: A Global Review. Handbook on International Poverty Research*. Oslo/Stockholm/Copenhagen/Boston: Scandinavian University Press, pp. 569–86

Ministry of Labour/Republic of Namibia (2002), *The Namibia Labour Force Survey 2000: Final Report of Analysis*. Windhoek: Republic of Namibia/Ministry of Labour

Namibia Institute for Democracy (2005), *Actual Instances of Corruption as Reported in the Namibian Print Media 1990–2004*. Windhoek: Namibia Institute for Democracy

National Planning Commission (1995), *First National Development Plan 1995/1996–1999/2000*. 2 volumes. Windhoek: Government of the Republic of Namibia

— (1999), *Policy Guidelines and Framework for the Second National Development Plan (NDP II)*. Windhoek, 23 August

— (undated/2002), *Second National Development Plan (NDP2) 2001/2002–2005/2006*; 4 volumes. Windhoek: National Planning Commission

Nel, Philip (2005), 'Democratization and the Dynamics of Income Distribution in Low- and Middle-income Countries,' *Politikon*, Vol. 32, Mo. 1, pp. 17–43

NEPRU (1999), *Can Namibia do Better? Policies to Improve Economic Performance. Reducing Poverty andIinequality*. Windhoek: Namibian Economic Policy Research Unit (The Namibian Economy – A NEPRU Viewpoint, 22)

Nujoma, Sam (2003), 'Interview, Namibia Special Report,' *New African*, No. 423, pp. IV–XV

Office of the President (2004), *Namibia Vision 2030. Policy Framework for Long-term National Development (Main Document)*. Windhoek: Office of the President

Philander, Frederick (2006), 'EU's Concerns,' *New Era*, 30 June

Rakner, Lise (2001), 'The Politics of Revenue Mobilisation: Explaining Continuity in Namibian Tax Policies,' *Forum for Development Studies*, Vol. 28, No. 1, pp. 125–45

Republic of Namibia (undated), *Poverty Reduction Strategy for Namibia*. Windhoek: National Planning Commission (Cabinet Decision 34th/01.12.98/002)

—(2002), *National Poverty Reduction Action Programme 2001–2005*. Windhoek: National
    Planning Commission

— (2004), *Namibia Vision 2030. Policy Framework for Long-Term National Development
    (Summary)*. Windhoek: Office of the President

Schade, Klaus (2000), 'Poverty,' in Henning Melber (ed.), *Namibia: A Decade of
    Independence 1990–2000*. Windhoek: Namibian Economic Policy Research Unit,
    pp. 111–24

— (2004), 'Armut nachhaltig bekämpfen,' *afrika süd*, No. 6, pp. 23–27

Schmid, Sabine (2002), *Affirmative Action as a Tool for Transformation. The Cases of South
    Africa and Namibia*. Saarbrücken: Verlag für Entwicklungspolitik (Bochumer
    Schriften zur Entwicklungsforschung und Entwicklungspolitik; 50)

Shigwedha, Absalom (2005), '"Greed monster" is Consuming the Nation,' *The Namibian*,
    Windhoek, 7 September

Shivute, Oswald (2005), 'Greed is the "New Colonialism" Warns President,' *The Namibian*,
    6 May

Sibeene, Petronella (2006), 'Jealousy Breeds BEE Failure,' *New Era*, 1 June

Sida/Embassy of Sweden, Namibia (2004), *Sida Country Report 2003 Namibia*. Stockholm:
    Sida/Department for Africa

Sutherland, Jean (1996), 'One Namibia, Two "Nations" – UNDP Report,' *The Namibian*,
    Windhoek, 17 July

Tjaronda, Wezi (2006), 'Affirmative Action Act Reaps the Opposite,' *New Era*, Windhoek,
    28 June

Tvedten, Inge (2004), '"A Town is Just a Town": Poverty and Social Relations of Migration
    in Namibia,' *Canadian Journal of African Studies*, Vol. 38, No. 2, pp. 393–423

UNDP (1996), *Namibia Human Development Report 1996*. Windhoek: UNDP Namibia

Weidlich, Brigitte (2007), 'Let the Rich Drive Fast: Nambinga,' *The Namibian*, 12 March

Wilson, Francis, Nazneen Kanji and Einar Braathen (2001), 'Introduction: Poverty, Power
    and the State,' in F. Wilson, N. Kanji and E. Braathen (eds), *Poverty Reduction. What
    Role for the State in Today's Globalised Economy?* London/New York: Zed, pp. 1–14

Winterfeldt, Volker (2002), 'Labour Migration in Namibia – Gender Aspects,' in V.
    Winterfeldt, T. Fox and P. Mufune (eds), *Namibia – Society – Sociology*. Windhoek:
    University of Namibia Press, pp. 39–74

Out of order?
The margins of Namibian ex-combatant 'reintegration'[1]

Lalli Metsola

A new ministry of veterans' affairs was created in October 2006, following pressure from a group calling itself the National Committee on the Welfare of Ex-combatants.[2] Their demonstrations and the ensuing government response were just the latest stage in an informal negotiation that has continued since Namibia's transition to independence in 1989. The main players in this negotiation have been former fighters of SWAPO's armed wing PLAN and other former exiles on one hand, and leading members of the ruling Swapo party in government on the other. Consequently, the former have been the main beneficiaries of various 'reintegration' programmes, such as the Development Brigade Corporation (DBC) in the 1990s and the 'Peace Project' job creation scheme since 1998. Other groups of potential 'reintegrees' have occupied a more marginal position in 'reintegration,' with different degrees of inclusion and exclusion. They include former Namibian troops who fought on the South African side as part of South West Africa Territorial Force (SWATF) and the Koevoet paramilitary police unit engaged in the bush war in the northern Owambo regions; formerly exiled youths; and ex-combatants eligible for 'reintegration' benefits but who have decided to avoid them. Additionally, while formerly exiled women have become mainstream 'reintegration' beneficiaries over the past ten years, their relationship to 'reintegration' initiatives has been more ambiguous than for their male comrades.

1. This chapter draws on fieldwork conducted in 2002 and 2003 in Windhoek and the north-central regions of Namibia. Its primary material consists of ethnographic observation and life historical and thematic interviews. Interviews were conducted with 98 ex-combatants and former exiles, 43 state and ruling party officials and 'civil society' representatives, and a few others. Of the ex-combatants, 81 were former exiles and 17 were former SWATF and Koevoet fighters. Of the former exiles, 49 were men and 32 were women. Twenty-eight belonged to the youth, according to the official definition of having been born in 1974 or later, and 53 were older. Ex-SWATF and Koevoet fighters were all men, as no women were recruited into these forces. My sincere gratitude goes to all the informants who shared their experiences and insights and to my research assistants Gideon Matti and Likius Ndjuluwa. I also wish to thank the Department of Sociology of the University of Namibia, to which I was affiliated during fieldwork, and the Academy of Finland and the Kone Foundation for funding.

2. The events related to this latest series of ex-combatant demands and demonstrations have been reported in a number of articles in the local media between June 2006 and July 2007. See especially, 'Ex-combatants' Body Makes Fresh Demands,' *The Namibian,* 21 June 2006; 'War Vets on Warpath,' *The Namibian,* 25 July 2006; 'War Vets Get Own Ministry,' *The Namibian,* 5 October 2006; 'New Ministry for War Veterans,' *New Era,* 5 October 2006.

I have dealt with the general dynamics of 'reintegration' and the specific case of its core target group of former exiles elsewhere (Metsola 2006; Metsola and Melber 2007; Metsola 2007; Metsola 2005).[3] This chapter will concentrate on the making and crossing of boundaries associated with the other groups mentioned above. It aims to describe the classifications that have defined these groups in 'reintegration,' particularly during the 'Peace Project' job creation scheme from 1998 onwards, and their negotiation of entitlements and identities with state and party actors. It further seeks to identify possible reasons these groups' differing relations to 'reintegration.' Finally, this chapter broadly aims at examining the implications of these relations for the particular characteristics of the state and citizenship in Namibia.

By addressing these concerns, it contributes to discussions on statehood as contested and constantly negotiated in the everyday encounters of state agencies and functionaries with the citizenry or population (Steinmetz 1999; Trouillot 2001; Corbridge et al. 2005). It has been argued that drawing lines of inclusion and exclusion and marginalising certain population segments is a fundamental act of sovereign power (Agamben 2005 and 1998; Hansen and Stepputat 2005). On the other hand, marginal people, spaces and practices can interrupt the order of the state as imagined from the political centre (Das and Poole 2004). They come to be seen as problematic or 'out of place,' or, vice versa, things defined as problematic are rendered marginal. The project of the state then becomes a continuous string of responses and adjustments to such problems or anomalies. This interplay between attempts at control and order by the state and the actions and reactions of 'problematic' groups can highlight the ways in which statehood and citizenship are negotiated as historically particular and socially grounded phenomena. The ex-combatants as a whole used to be seen as this kind of problematic group. The former exiles have, by and large, made a transition from social problem to frontline functionaries of the state through public sector employment, but at the same time the particular manner of their inclusion has highlighted other significant distinctions and created forms of further marginalisation. These constitute the subject matter of this chapter.

This chapter does not aim to provide a full comparative picture or complete ethnographies of the groups discussed here, but rather to highlight significant aspects of their relationship to 'reintegration' and the associated effects of marginalisation, inclusion and exclusion. This also means that the focus is only on people who could reasonably be expected to be targeted by 'reintegration' schemes or to seek benefits through such schemes. The elite and educated middle-class former exiles are not discussed. Other groups have also fallen outside the purview of this chapter, most significantly former exiled women. While significant numbers of them have been employed during the Peace Project, their experience of 'reintegration' has been distinct from men's experiences in many ways.[4] Space restrictions also preclude consideration of former SWAPO detain-

---

3. For other general accounts on the ex-combatants and their 'reintegration,' see Preston et al. 1993; Preston 1997 and 1994; Colletta et al. 1996; LeBeau 2005; McMullin 2005; Gleichmann 1994; Tapscott 1994; Tapscott and Mulongeni 1990; Fikeni 1992.
4. As long as the concept of 'ex-combatant' was primarily taken to mean those who had actually been in combat, reintegration favoured men over women. This situation arose from the exile division of labour that placed mainly men as combatants and women mainly in supportive and reproductive roles (Soiri 1996:76–77; Preston 1997:458; Metsola 2001: 78–81). Hence, for in-

ees, disabled ex-combatants as well as those with incapacitating traumas, and the San who served with the SWATF.

'Makakunya' – the ex-SWATF and Koevoet between reconciliation and patriotism

> *"Freedom fighters are not mercenaries and this clearly distinguished Swapo Plan ex-combatants from the South West Africa Territorial Force and Koevoet."*

> *"The Swapo Party Government has a responsibility to promote the welfare of all Namibians, irrespective of colour, race, ethnic origin and political affiliation."*[5]

The 'reintegration' of ex-combatants was mainly justified by framing them as a threat to the security of the state and society. This securitisation led to the employment of thousands of ex-PLAN fighters and former exiles in the government sector, especially in the uniformed services. However, 'reintegration' has not proceeded similarly for their former opponents, the members of SWATF and Koevoet. Theirs is a history of a complicated relationship with 'reintegration.'

In the immediate post-independence period, when the new integrated security forces were formed, the Namibian Defence Force (NDF) and police recruited from both previously opposed forces. However, over time, former SWAPO cadres have come to dominate NDF ranks,[6] while major new drives to recruit ex-combatants into the police, especially the Special Field Force (SFF), have almost exclusively drawn on former exiles. Additionally, both forces take in younger recruits who are not ex-combatants. Similarly, although the Development Brigade Corporation, a 1990s training programme for ex-combatants, was initially meant for fighters from both sides, its membership was eventually almost exclusively drawn from the former ranks of PLAN. (Preston 1997; Colletta et al. 1996: 136, 149, 159; Lamb 2007:167–169; McMullin 2005.) When the Peace Project commenced, it initially targeted former exiles only.[7] Ex-SWATF and Koevoet were included from 1999 onwards, after they, clearly inspired by the successful

---

stance, women were not taken into the army and police to the same degree as men. The different history of men and women in exile is still reflected in patterns of employment: more men than women have been employed in the uniformed services, and more women in other duties than men. Furthermore, the imagery of ex-combatants in national remembrance as liberation heroes remains predominantly masculine.

5. Excerpts from a speech by the Swapo party president and former President of the Republic Sam Nujoma, reproduced as 'Nujoma Lashes Out at Divisive Forces' in *Die Republikein,* 26 July 2006.

6. According to Major-General Shalli, in 2002, approximately 40% of NDF personnel were ex-combatants, of whom approximately one in four were former SWATF fighters (interview with author, 7 November 2002). According to Colletta et al. (1996: 149), approximately 80% of NDF personnel were former SWAPO combatants by 1995.

7. In an exceptionally straightforward admission of considering the political benefits of the proposed programme to Swapo and mixing public good with that of the ruling party, the first report of the Technical Committee on Ex-Combatants notes that "because of correct political understanding, most of the genuine ex PLAN combatants did not participate in any demonstration. They continued to hope that one day, SWAPO shall remember them ... The arrival of the

demands of PLAN ex-combatants and other former exiles, applied similar pressure to the government.[8]

However, the number of registered ex-SWATF and Koevoet fighters was much lower than for former exiles, and far fewer of those registered have been employed than in the case of registered former exiles.[9] Indeed, the overall level of formal employment among former SWATF/Koevoet is considerably lower than among former exiles. According to LeBeau (2005:72–73), 69.2% of former SWAPO combatants are formally employed, compared to 45.6% of former SWATF/Koevoet. Most formally employed SWAPO combatants have a government job, whereas former SWATF/Koevoet are mainly employed by private security companies. Furthermore, the ex-SWATF and Koevoet have been excluded from the war veterans' pension (Republic of Namibia 1999).[10]

What accounts for these differences? First, while the securitising discourse on the threat posed by ex-combatants concerned SWAPO fighters and former SWATF and Koevoet alike, the latter were perhaps not quite as worrying to the political elite as the former. The demonstrations staged by PLAN combatants and other former exiles in the 1990s were large-scale and enjoyed considerable popular support. Furthermore, as former exiles are a key Swapo constituency, there was clearly a need to try to maintain their loyalty. Related to this, there has probably been a concern to neutralise the possibility of their disclosing contentious remembrances of events in exile.[11] Third, former exiles did not merely demonstrate vis-à-vis abstract state structures, but contrasted their lot with that of their now extremely well-off erstwhile comrades, demanding that the latter keep the promises of better life they had made before independence. The demonstrators sometimes backed these demands by direct threats to power holders.[12]

However, such strategic political considerations and binding ties of loyalty and reward between formerly exiled members of the liberation movement are anchored in a version of Namibia's political history that was crafted by SWAPO and its allies well

---

Committee had a pacifying effect on the former combatants and will pay divide[n]d during the forthcoming regional elections." (Republic of Namibia 1998:13).

8. 'Ex-SWATF to March on State House,' *The Namibian,* 2 June 1995; 'Centre Besieged by Ex-Fighters,' *The Namibian,* 26 January 1999; 'Ex-soldiers Stick to their Guns,' *The Namibian,* 27 January 1999; 'Action on Ex-Soldiers,' *The Namibian,* 28 January 1999; 'Ex-soldiers Head Home,' *The Namibian,* 29 January 1999.

9. By November 2000,13,992 former exiles had been registered, compared to 2,420 former SWATF and Koevoet fighters. In November 1999, 7,881 (65.9%) of the then registered 11,956 able-bodied former exiles had been employed, compared to 679 (34.3%) of the then registered 1,980 former SWATF and Koevoet members (Republic of Namibia n.d.:3, 9). The number of SWATF and Koevoet fighters demobilised in 1989 was 25,000 (Colletta et al. 1996:131).

10. This line was duly contested by the opposition. For example, DTA MP Phillemon Moongo argued on 4 March 1999: "The plight of all former fighters who are still unemployed ... is not a joke. But I cannot buy the political nonsense that ex-PLAN members are the only war veterans. A war veteran to me means a person who has grown old or has long experience of military service." Debates of the National Assembly 32/1999.

11. For more on this aspect, see Metsola 2007.

12. For instance, there were incidents where demonstrating ex-combatants took or tried to take government ministers or regional councillors hostage. See *Facts and Reports* 25(U), 27 October 1995, p. 8; 'Hostage drama rocks Oshakati', *the Namibian* 9 July 1997; 'Hamutenya hassled, faces wrath of ex-combatants', *The Namibian,* 8 May 1998. For recent demands, see 'War vets threaten land grab', *New Era* 7 June 2007.

before independence. This narrative serves as the founding myth of the nation and is a cornerstone of the legitimacy of the ruling party. It portrays a fundamental antagonism between colonial rule and liberation, between patriotic Namibians who struggled for independence and the puppets and collaborators of the apartheid regime. Significantly, this narrative is not restricted to accounts of the past. It is regularly reproduced in political leaders' statements on current issues, depicting contemporary social forces as either truly patriotic or the 'enemy' (e.g., secessionists, imperialists, foreign cultural influences, criminals, independent media, human rights activists or the political opposition).

This narrative counterposes SWAPO's ex-combatants and the former SWATF and Koevoet. As, for example, the official commemoration of the liberation struggle at the Heroes' Acre attests, recent history is often portrayed in pronouncedly militarist tones, with SWAPO fighters occupying a central role in this portrayal as heroes prepared to sacrifice life and limb for the nation's freedom. SWATF and Koevoet fighters, by contrast, cannot be seen as anything but traitors or 'mercenaries,' as Nujoma's speech put it, as they fought on the 'wrong side' despite being Namibians. They are an anomaly in the strictly dualist liberation narrative between colonial oppression and a unified nation rising against that oppression.

What this picture omits, or rather forces into the binary imagery of 'us' and 'them,' is the myriad power relations and contradictions within SWAPO as well as in the pre-independence state. During the war, which lasted for decades, very real divisions opened up along multiple fault lines *within* Namibian society, between north and south town and country, educated and uneducated (especially within the liberation movement), and last, but not least, along ethnic lines (Leys and Saul 1995a and 1995b; Brown 1995; Tapscott 1995). SWAPO's membership and support was mainly, though not exclusively, drawn from people of Owambo background. In Owamboland, a 'culture of resistance' to colonial power developed from the 1960s and SWAPO became virtually the only visible and accepted political movement. 'The struggle' became a pervasive condition of local social relations (Soggot 1986; Cliffe et al. 1994). Yet even Owamboland did not simply stand unified against South African rule. The members of the 'homeland' authorities and local military and paramilitary units, as well as a considerable number of their family members, stood to gain directly from the occupation. The 101 Battalion of the SWATF was an Owambo battalion. Likewise, Koevoet was composed of Owambos, many of whom were captured and 'turned' PLAN combatants. Additionally, the war situation could be used to settle parochial scores, for instance by accusing people of 'collaboration.'

In the south, people had more contact with the everyday relations and practices of the colonial administration and its representatives, but repression was not as severe as in the north. Also, SWAPO was not nearly as dominant in politics as in the north. In the early 1980s, compulsory conscription into SWATF was introduced in the south. The army recruited from various ethnic groups, which served to give an ethnic edge to the war. No doubt, the South Africans intended these processes as part of divide and rule, but over time they led to enduring and self-sustaining divisions along ethnic lines.[13] Groups other than the Owambo pursued their own agendas that were not simply pro-

---

13. See e.g., Gewald 2004 for a detailed microhistory of spontaneous conflict breaking out along such lines.

colonial but were attempts to find an alternative political space between colonial power and potential SWAPO rule. There was fear – justified or not – of Owambo dominance if SWAPO came to power.

The former SWATF and Koevoet fighters I met were torn between feeling that such complicated history explains and justifies their military involvement and a pressure to rewrite that history in accordance with the dominant version in order to be accepted as full citizens. They tended to recount that they have been discriminated against in job provision by the government, both during ex-combatant registrations and thereafter. Some had registered as former fighters but had not been called up;[14] some had been recruited into the uniformed services but had faced discrimination and resigned. Most told of having been unemployed most of the time since independence. Indeed, it is easy to imagine the sense of long common history and being 'on the same side' present in the interaction between former exiles and state and party functionaries during registrations. Some former SWATF and Koevoet told of the informal ways by which they were made to feel out of place and inferior, such as making them queue without being attended while former exiles were taken in, or being addressed in a hostile and derogatory manner by officials. Many also complained of their exclusion from the veterans' pension scheme. To be sure, these problems represented actual instances of discrimination, but they also arose out of a fear among former SWATF and Koevoet that coming out into the open could lead to negative consequences. Some said they would not register because they distrusted the intentions of Swapo government. Some of the officials I spoke to referred to this problem when I enquired about the low number of registered SWATF and Koevoet fighters.

On occasions when I observed people from the previously opposed forces meet, there was no visible hostility. However, they tended to favour the company of 'their own.' There were also indications of remaining tensions bubbling under the surface. As Simeon,[15] a friend who had not himself participated in the war on either side, explained:

> [When] we are talking about ex-combatants, basically we are talking [about] people who have been fighting each other ... These wounds [have] not healed in their hearts ... They have been silenced by ... national reconciliation ... They are still thinking of revenge ... [When] we are sitting for instance with Isack[16]... or my brother even ... you hear that ... "these people must ... be thankful to the government. If that national reconciliation was not there you should have seen." Isack for instance ... lost his eye ... one of his legs is crippled, you heard what Mandume[17] said, "this ... mark here is the bullet from first April." When he went into exile he [did] not have such a mark. The spirit ... of revenge will be there ... but there is no other alternative [than] just forget.

---

14. A letter from the 'Committee of Ex Combatants in Caprivi Region,' a group of ex-SWATF fighters, to the prime minister, dated 16 October 1999, complains that while all ex-PLAN combatants have been employed by the government, they have not because they are ex-SWATF, even though they have registered many times. "If you don't want us to work in your army or police you can give us even the civilian jobs ... because this your army of Namibia is not a national army ... but only for the ex-PLAN."

15. His name and the names of the ex-combatants who appear in this chapter have been changed.

16. A former PLAN combatant.

17. Another former PLAN combatant.

On one occasion, I was interviewing a police reservist in the company of a few SFF members, all former exiles. Inspired by the reminiscences of life in exile, they started to sing liberation songs. A colleague of theirs, a former Koevoet, quietly left the scene. Later when I was discussing the issue of SWATF/Koevoet members with Pine, one of the SFF members, he explained that they prefer to avoid public exposure of their past: "If someone knows that his mother is a witch, he won't talk about it." On another occasion, I happened to sit with Laurence, a former SWATF 101 Battalion soldier when three former PLAN combatants entered the house. We entered into a long discussion, with the three ex-combatants vividly recalling their war-time exploits. Laurence hardly said a word, clearly wanting to avoid in any way his own involvement in the war.

Overall, it was clear that many former SWATF/Koevoet were not keen to have public exposure of this aspect of their past. This is obviously known to their families and others close to them, but they do not make it generally known. There are stories of real reconciliation within families and communities, and it also exists as part of the rhetoric of national unity that proscribes open hostilities, but this goes only so far. The antagonism that separates 'patriots' from 'collaborators' and 'traitors' is constantly reiterated in the public imagination, reproducing the pariah status of former SWATF and Koevoet in public discourse. There are differences between communities in this regard: it is clearly different to be a former SWATF/Koevoet for example in the Damara location of Katutura than in Owamboland. In the former, this was a quite common and well-known aspect of community history, whereas in the latter it was taken as much more exceptional and abnormal (cf., Colletta et al. 1996:188–192).

Against this background, it is hardly surprising that the former SWATF/Koevoet did not usually portray themselves as military heroes or even draw attention to that part of their history. They tended to explain military service as something forced on them, either directly by being drafted or out of economic necessity. They longed for recognition and acceptance, and many would have appreciated government employment. "We even voted for them [Swapo] in the first elections," commented Jacob and his Damara friends in Katutura of their optimistic expectations and readiness to be part of the new nation at the time of independence. However, they were now deeply sceptical that they would be incorporated, on account of political considerations. Opposed to the dominant view that depicted them as pariahs and to the heroic self-portrayal of most former exiles, they presented themselves as victims. First the colonial power had dragged them into the army and prevented them from advancing in education or work, and then the Swapo government had refused to look into their situation while adding insult to injury by labelling them traitors and collaborators.

This dual marginalisation is evident in the case of Andreas. An Oshiwambo-speaking townsman from south of the Red Line,[18] he received his conscription papers in 1980, soon after finishing his schooling. He managed to evade the service until 1982 when he was forcibly fetched. He soon deserted but was caught, jailed and later sent to the 101 Battalion. He was wounded in 1985 and resigned in 1986. After a few years of job hunting and stints of casual work, he applied to the new national army in 1990 and was accepted. He served at Grootfontein, but soon ran into problems with his for-

---

18. The Red Line is a veterinary cordon that used to serve as the border between the 'police zone' of white residential and farming areas and the northern reserves or 'homelands'.

merly exiled superior. After further intimidation and the 'accident' that befell a former SWATF colleague, he resigned in 1992.

Non-Owambo former SWATF members easily see their discrimination as not just politically but also ethnically based. For example, Frederick, a former SWATF member living in the Katutura Damara location, explained that the Owambos, particularly former exiles, only seemed to favour each other, and that this could be seen in 'reintegration' too.

Some refused to bow and took an angry stance towards the current government, which they saw as deeply partial, sometimes saying that they wouldn't even accept a job from government. For example, a former SWATF soldier from the same Katutura neighbourhood as my assistant responded angrily when we approached him. Referring to the former exile in the next stall, he said: "I was in SWATF and I'm proud of it. Why don't you ask this terrorist?" Despite the pressures, not all are prepared to give in and rewrite their history, but this is not easy as there is no generally accepted respectable position available to former SWATF/ Koevoet members to draw upon for self-esteem and bargaining power.

In sum, the history of the former SWATF and Koevoet fighters in relation to 'reintegration' is one of partial inclusion and exclusion. The former has been driven by the policy of reconciliation and the associated responsibility of government to "promote the welfare of all Namibians, irrespective of colour, race, ethnic origin and political affiliation," as Nujoma said, as well as by the concerns about the potential threat posed by ex-combatants of both sides. Undoubtedly there are many who genuinely believe in reconciliation. Yet such official neutrality is compromised by the binary imagery of the liberation struggle, which continues to legitimate the exclusion of South Africa's 'allies' (and those considered their heirs and as current enemies). Furthermore, this binary image is often linked to other distinctions, such as ethnicity. In the current political setting, reconciliation often appears to be viewed as necessary to the degree it prevents open conflict, but it does not extend to genuinely overcoming past differences. This would be possible only by revising the notion of 'liberation' and shaking its position as the national foundation more profoundly than has been done. 'Reintegrating' former exiles has involved a combination of techniques such as categorisation, registering, training and work discipline that aim to neutralise the threat to security, and the language of national liberation that elevates them as heroes. This convergence, together with their close historic relationship with those currently in power, has made them the privileged group in 'reintegration.' Positive discrimination in favour of former SWATF and Koevoet can only follow from their securitisation as potentially dangerous and from the language of national reconciliation, but these are always countered by the negative discrimination in the dominant narrative of the history of the nation. Thus, paradoxically, the supposedly unifying language of the nation becomes a way of drawing lines of inclusion and exclusion, separating those who really belong to it from those who have not yet reached full belonging or, worse still, oppose the national fulfilment (cf., Chipkin 2004). The antagonistic imaginary of the nation posits identification with Swapo and its vision of liberation as a condition of real belonging, so that 'all Namibians' easily slips into 'all patriotic Namibians,' a far less inclusive and far more politically charged category. Therefore, it seems that as laudable as the effort to overcome the deep divisions of war and past injustice through reconciliation may be, reconciliation cannot be fully achieved as long as the militant antagonism of liberation stands as the founding myth of the nation.

When the ministry of veterans' affairs was set up, the concept of 'ex-combatant' was given a new, extended definition. In launching the ministry, President Pohamba said: "Our Government regards all those patriotic Namibians who took part in the struggle for national liberation of Namibia, regardless of whether such citizens were in exile or not, as ex-combatants." Henk Mudge, an opposition politician, soon expressed concern about the implications of this for former SWATF and Koevoet members: '"These members were merely professional soldiers ... recruited by a foreign country ... They were intimidated and brainwashed ... exactly the same way in which Swapo brainwashed the Plan fighters." At the time of writing (July 2007), the decision on whether former SWATF/Koevoet would be included as war veterans had not been made, according to Veterans Affairs Minister Tjiriange, responding to questions in parliament by DTA MPs Katuutire Kaura and Phillemon Moongo.[19] The president's formulation rather points towards another twist in the marginalisation of former SWATF and Koevoet.

Youth – unemployment and existential anxiety

Earlier 'reintegration' initiatives were often rather vague in their definition of 'ex-combatant.' However, what was said tended to equate 'ex-combatant' with 'ex-PLAN fighter'. With the Peace Project, the concept 'ex-combatant' was officially extended to cover other former exiles (Republic of Namibia 1998:6), undoubtedly due to the presence of many non-combatant former exiles, mostly women, among the demonstrators demanding jobs and recognition. Due to the unconventional nature of the war and the irregular organisation of SWAPO in exile, it was not easy to differentiate strictly between combatants and non-combatants. The definitional extension also served to recognise the fact that exiled SWAPO members had very limited control over their fates: whatever the movement assigned them to, they had to do. Hence, they were perhaps justified in feeling that responsibility for their consequent life courses did not lie solely with them as individuals, but with their exile leaders. Whatever its rationale, the inclusion of non-fighters opened the door to further demands and problems of demarcation.

By the time the Peace Project commenced in 1998, many under-age exiles who had returned to Namibia had completed their schooling or dropped out. This group of people represented another problem of demarcation over the course of the programme. Initially, the eligibility criteria did not discriminate on the basis of age. Among other former exiles, the circle of ex-combatants was to include "anyone who was born in exile [to] parents who were both or one of them Namibian citizens participating in the liberation struggle" (Republic of Namibia 1998:6).

By the third round of registrations in October and November 2000, this definition had been found to be problematic and cabinet decided that "not everybody who was born in exile during the liberation struggle was an ex combatant and, therefore, entitled to claim a job under the peace project" (Republic of Namibia n.d.:6, 7). Additionally, young people who went into exile in only 1988 or 1989 were to be excluded. Only those

---

19. 'Ministry Still has to Vet the Term "War Veteran",' *The Namibian* 11 July 2007)

born before 1974 would be eligible for benefits, with the exception of war orphans, i.e., those whose parents had died in exile. However, even after the official age-limit was introduced, fairly significant numbers of young former exiles were recruited. According to the final report of the technical committee on ex-combatants, 464 former exiles who had gone into exile in 1988 and 1989 or were born in exile were registered during the third registration exercise.

Once it seemed that the door to employment initially opened by the Peace Project started closing officially again, the youth also tried applying pressure on government, as older ex-combatants had done. A group of youngsters calling themselves 'young Swapo loyalists,' gathered at Swapo headquarters in Katutura in 2001 for several weeks, claiming ex-combatant benefits by virtue of being born in exile or to parents who were there. Government representatives denied their right to such benefits and they were finally arrested and charged with trespass.[20]

The creation in 1999 of the National Youth Service Scheme (NYSS), a quasi-military training programme to counter youth unemployment, can be seen as a response to youth expectations. Sacky Kayone, governor of Omusati region, explicitly tied its establishment to ex-combatant 'reintegration': "The Youth Service Scheme … was initiated because … with the [re]integration process, some of these problems started to crop up."[21] However, the scheme has been modest in scale and has faced problems similar to those faced by the earlier Development Brigade Corporation. Disgruntled NYSS members marched to Windhoek in 2002 to meet President Nujoma with complaints that they had not received the promised jobs and education opportunities. They were accused of indiscipline and threatened with dismissal. The leaders of the group were arrested and expelled from NYSS.[22]

Generally, the protests and demands of the former exiled youths did not garner much public support, unlike those of older ex-combatants.[23] It was argued that these youths faced the same problems as youths or other unemployed people in general, and had the same opportunities to advance in life as those who had grown up in the country. This undoubtedly played a part in the government's turnabout, as it would have been difficult to justify preferential treatment for formerly exiled youths over other young people or the non-returnee unemployed. A development planner in the national planning commission closely involved in the administration of the Peace Project explained: "The Cabinet … realised that we were going into uncharted territory … creating an open-ended situation, because … anybody who had gone in exile up to 1989 would just come and expect to participate."[24]

Minister of Higher Education, Training and Employment Creation Nahas Angula specified in which way the situation was 'open-ended':

---

20. See articles in *The Namibian*, 10 and 15 October 2001; 28 November 2001; 13 and 21 December 2001; 12 April 2002; 12 August 2002.

21. Interview with author, 22 November 2002.

22. Lamb 2007:170–171; see also articles in *The Namibian*, 9 and 11 April 2001; 16, 19 and 20 August 2002; 9, 10 and 16 September 2002; 6 November 2002; 29 January 2003; and 8 April 2003.

23. However, the recent ex-combatant pressure for compensation has met with much less public approval.

24. Michael Kafidi, interview with author, 4 August 2003.

Every young Namibian has to find [his/her] own way of getting integrated in the society. If [there is] a problem, it has nothing to do with … [re]integration … If you give in then you create a situation which you will never solve because every youth, every person who feels that he is marginalised will say "no, I have to come up with something also."[25]

Despite such setbacks, the hopes of the youth to be beneficiaries were not shattered. While the official response to youth demonstrations indicated they did not quite have the muscle or public support required to get their way, the earlier play with official definitions and practical eligibility criteria created a grey area so that one could try to bend the rules in one's favour and wrestle access to benefits. The following two cases illustrate this arbitrary and shifting ground between inclusion and exclusion.

Martha was born in 1974 near Oshikango. She went into exile in 1988 and continued her schooling in Kwanza Sul until 1990. After returning to Namibia, she went to school in the north until she reached grade 12. Since then, she had been staying at the family farm, was unemployed and had a one-year-old daughter. She had taken part in ex-combatant demonstrations and had registered herself, but was later told by officials that her registration had been a mistake and that she was too young to be entitled to ex-combatant status. During my fieldwork, she received temporary employment at a construction site nearby. Nakale was born in 1974 near Ogongo in the Omusati. After going into exile in 1987, he attended school in Kwanza Sul until 1991. After returning to Namibia he continued schooling and matriculated in 1997. Following registration, he was employed in the security forces in 2000.

We have here two people with similar backgrounds but different outcomes in terms of 'reintegration.' This kind of a situation ensured that the feeling of entitlement, based on having been in exile, remained alive. Nearly all the formerly exiled youth I spoke with, men and women alike, would have appreciated government employment or other forms of assistance and felt that if their parents were entitled to these benefits, they should be too. They justified this expectation mainly by arguing that they had lost time and opportunities by moving between countries and education systems and because they had to readjust to life in Namibia. Many of them had registered or tried to register. However, while the youth shared the sense of entitlement with older former exiles, this sense was seemingly not as intense or as important to them.

It is not possible here to chart the multiplicity of the life situations of formerly exiled youths and their experience of 'reintegration.' Instead, I will highlight a few significant features through a more detailed exposition of the history, current situation and ambitions of one of them, Alex. Alex was born in Angola in 1979 and lived there until he was sent to school in Eastern Europe for a few years after his father had died. After his return in 1991, he first went to school in the central part of the country. After moving to Owambo in 1993, he found difficulty in adjusting at first, but gradually slipped into the local lifestyle. Because his father had died in exile, he was granted official war orphan status and his schooling was supported by the Socioeconomic Integration Programme for Ex-combatants (SIPE)[26] until he failed his grade 10, a not uncommon occurrence in Namibia, particularly in remote areas. Since then, he had been staying at the fam-

---

25. Interview with author, 4 November 2002.

26. SIPE is tasked with seeking job and training opportunities for ex-combatants as well as assisting war orphans.

ily homestead, unemployed. During my stay in the field, he got a job at one of the big warehouses in Oshikango. As the work was tough and repetitive and did not earn him much, he kept dreaming of something better.

Alex's mother had been employed at the local government offices after taking part in the big ex-combatant demonstrations of 1997–98. She supplemented her income by buying mahangu from Angola in big bags and reselling it in smaller amounts on the roadside market in Namibia. Alex did not get on too well with her husband and said that this was why he was not staying at his mother's household but with his mother's sister. His mother was having a small house built for him nearby and he said that he would soon like to move so that he would not have to contribute so much of his income to his aunt's household. Now that he had a job, there were also expectations from his mother: "I'm the firstborn so if I got a job I have to help my brothers, because they are still young, they are still going to school … If you have many poor relatives, you will stay poor yourself." By contrast, his aunt was not happy as his full-time job left him much less time to work on the farm and in the household. He appreciated his mother's help but complained about the schism his mother and his aunt had over who should be supporting him and what they should get from him in return.

Alex was also an active football player in the local team. He lived near the football field and went to practice almost every evening. "I'm now a soccer player, but as you know, soccer this side [in the north] does not [earn you] any income, I'm just playing for the purpose of not thinking too much, so that I won't steal," he explained. His football skills also helped him get his job, as it was arranged by Tommy, a team mate who held a senior position in the same warehouse. According to Tommy, Alex was "always asking for ten dollars," so it would be better to give him a chance to earn the money himself.

Alex followed English football and Western popular culture keenly and we often ended up sitting in one of the local bars watching TV together and chatting. Apart from reflecting common Namibian youth concerns, in his case these interests also reflected a longing for 'Europe.' He sometimes talked about friends who had married a European and returned to live in Europe. One way of fulfilling his dream of Europe, he thought, would be to get to play football there. However, more than reflecting a concrete attachment to European ways, 'Europe' was more of an abstract dream of a better life. It was a negation of the very local everyday problems that surrounded him. Life in Namibia was difficult, he said, as there was no work, friends from exile were spread around the big country, there was too much violence and people were too reckless in their sexual behaviour. Also, taking the necessary steps to adulthood seemed difficult: "If I become a family man, I can't support her, I can't support my family because I don't have any work,[27] but … there I can get a job … It's only in Europe you can get money easily." Alex was insecure about his relationship with his girlfriend, as he acutely felt that he could not give enough to her in material terms. However, 'Europe' not only embodied a promise of wealth, but also of modernity and style – and this was true for many of his friends too, who were carefully, within the limits of their means, trying to fashion themselves on a hip hop-based street wisdom.[28]

---

27. This was said before he was employed.
28. Cf., Fairweather (2006) and Behrend (2002) on the importance of style as a youthful way to produce and express identity.

While the above concerns might distinguish Alex from formerly exiled youngsters who never got further than Angola and Zambia, he was by no means removed from local realities and social relations. While he had many former exile friends, he interacted with everybody with equal ease and had been 're-Namibianised' to such a degree that some non-returnees were surprised to hear he had been in exile. Indeed, over time the distinction, evident after the repatriation of exiles, between those exile kids who had lived in SWAPO settlements and those who had spent years studying in other countries[29] has often become blurred and partly replaced by other distinctions. There were also those young former exiles who crafted clearer distinctions through their manner of speech, dress and lifestyle. However, these distinctions were clearly enmeshed with class position and associated with educational achievement, family wealth and urban residence. It seemed to me that the production of distinction was also partly dependent on such resources, as its consumptive requirements would be difficult to fulfil without them.

After failing grade 10, Alex had registered with SIPE for employment in 2000, but was still waiting:

> They said if you fail grade ten or you fail grade twelve they will … give you jobs from like NDF or in Nampol … but [it's] now three years [since] they promised that … Always at the end of the year, they used to come here and make meetings with us … We tell them our problems but they say we have to wait. We'll wait until you get old … I don't even have his[30] phone [number] … Here in Owamboland it is difficult … not like [for] those who are in Windhoek.[31]

Alex was also trying to enlist the support of Shikongo, a high government official who used to be his mother's partner in exile after his father's death, to get a job in the army. Shikongo invited him to Windhoek. He agreed with Tommy that he could go back to work at the warehouse if things did not work out in Windhoek. I met Alex for the last time at a Windhoek petrol station. He had found his way to Shikongo and stayed at his place for a few days. Shikongo had welcomed him warmly but Alex felt that his wife and daughters were annoyed. He said that he couldn't stay long in Windhoek but was hopeful that Shikongo could arrange something. He had promised to try to use his connections. Over half a year later I heard that Alex was back in the north, still without a job.

It is by no means surprising that young former exiles would try to negotiate themselves into the circle of beneficiaries of ex-combatant schemes. As far as they might seem to be from the core definition of ex-combatant, the inflation of the concept to cover all needy former exiles brought them to the threshold of inclusion, with only the arbitrary line of whether one was born before 1974 or after dividing the eligible from the ineligible. It probably did not make much sense to young people born in, say, 1974

---

29. These included most notably two larger groups of Namibian youth educated in Cuba and the German Democratic Republic (GDR). For a case study on the 'GDR kids,' see Kenna 1999.
30. Alex is referring to General Manager Ndilula of SIPE.
31. During my visits to the SIPE head office, I saw youngsters hanging around in the reception. The receptionist confirmed that they had come to ask for jobs. She further told me that it was common for young people, mostly with an exile background, to come for that purpose. It was apparently this kind of persistent pressure to keep one's case alive that Alex thought would be easier to apply in Windhoek than from the north.

or 1975, to see that others from a similar background but a year or two older would be included while they were not. Their understanding was further enhanced by the knowledge that this demarcation has not been consistently followed and that in many cases their parents or friends benefited from the schemes, even though they had never fought concretely in the war.

The recent promise to cover 'all patriotic Namibians' who participated in the struggle, whether in exile or inside Namibia, represents the next step in the blending of new demands into the category of 'ex-combatant.' If such a redefinition actually reaches implementation, we may see an even more radical entanglement of the fault lines of the 'liberation struggle' with current politics of power, citizenship and entitlement, with various new interests rallying under the increasingly vague 'ex-combatant' banner.[32]

However, although Alex and many other youngsters were trying to use their exile past and their connections to gain benefits, their approach to ex-combatant 'reintegration' was a lot more practical than that of many older former exiles. Alex did not have a strong emotional tie to Swapo. On the contrary, he was quite critical of its practices of rule in exile and considered the current political elite self-interested and corrupt.[33] One night he suddenly told me that "most of these ministers killed a lot of people in Angola," a reference to events in the 1980s when SWAPO arrested and mishandled a sizeable number of its own members as suspected spies. He also told of how "PLAN thugs" used to bully schoolboys in the settlements into joining the army instead of going to school.

Indeed, for youths like Alex the prospect of government employment as an 'ex-combatant' was merely one possible future among others. Thus, he also talked admiringly about an Angolan friend who had made a fortune in diamond deals. He had a luxurious house and five cars in Lunda Norte, and lived a flashy life with lots of women and drink. He had invited Alex over for a few days the previous year and Alex was fascinated by the grandiose way of life he had seen. He said that if the friend came again he would leave his work without hesitation and go with him. Still, the youth know their hopes would be easily fulfilled, and are quite prepared to take government employment if the opportunity arises – even if it requires giving up one's youthful style, as in the case of a friend of Alex, who had to cut off his dreadlocks when he joined the police.

All in all, Alex is an example of the unemployed young Namibians lingering between childhood and adult life.[34] For formerly exiled youth, this is heightened by the contrasts between life in exile and Namibian ways and conditions. This anxiety is apparent from how Alex was searching for any way ahead, be it government employment, professional football, other employment or hustling. He was tired of waiting in limbo, yet lacked financial independence to make the transition to adulthood. The themes of blocked social mobility and associated anxiety, distinction vis-à-vis the older generation and the political elite, and the crossing of boundaries between 'state' and 'non-state' domains that emerge here are familiar from other African contexts, despite the fluidity of the concept of 'youth' and the variety of different situations on the continent.[35] There is

32. Cf., Kriger 2003 and 2006 on the conceptual politics of 'ex-combatants' in Zimbabwe.

33. Similar sentiments about politics and especially the current political elite were shared by many of his 'exile kid' friends, as well as other young Namibians.

34. For a general account of the challenges faced by Namibian youth, see Mufune 2002.

35. Abbink 2005; de Boeck and Honwana 2005; Vigh 2006:89–104; cf. Liechty 2003 on youth construction of middle-class modernity in Kathmandu.

a mismatch between actual possibilities and expectations, heightened by relatively high educational levels and imageries of modernity.

This indeterminacy easily leads to identifying the youth as a problem. They are said to be in danger of getting lost to unemployment, alcoholism, HIV/AIDS and severed social ties. There is also a constant worry they will turn to crime.[36] While this discourse is driven by elite security concerns and operates relatively independently of actual crime rates, the imaginaries of success and style associated with a 'thug' lifestyle do appeal to many youngsters, particularly young men. Interestingly, such aspirations can coincide with a readiness to utilise state resources if and when they are available. In Namibia, unlike for instance in West African post-conflict situations (Fithen and Richards 2005; Vigh 2006:105–112; Utas 2005; Olonisakin and Alao 2005; Fitz-Gerald 2005), state-provided livelihoods often do represent a viable option. At the same time, the selectivity of state inclusion helps maintain the appeal of informal, even illegal livelihoods that have a long history in Namibia owing to the starkly exclusionary character of the state during the colonial era.[37]

From an administrative perspective, the question of youth appears different from that of the ex-combatants. Youth is a diverse category and not a strategically positioned interest group like the ex-combatants. At the same time, problems of youth are of a different magnitude, as they not only concern former exiles. It would be difficult to justify differential treatment of exile and non-exile youth and impossible to provide government employment to all of them. It is not easy to predict the future in this regard, let alone provide recommendations. What can be said is that if the extreme of widespread alienation of the youth is undesirable, the other extreme of their militarisation as 'patriots' does not appear to be a lasting solution either.

Avoidance of state capture

The above discussion on youth has already pointed to a concern that has been evident in ex-combatant 'reintegration' but that is actually more fundamental for the construction and maintenance of state power, namely that of capturing populations by institutional arrangements that are conducive to producing compliant subjectivities. Apart from the immediate aim of dispersing the demonstrations, a fear that ex-combatant agency would turn subversive, both in terms of political disloyalty and unrest and conventional crime, clearly motivated the Peace Project. Job provision for the ex-combatants was meant to redirect their agency in ways that would not contest the political regime and could even be useful to it. From this perspective, those who purposely avoid ex-combatant programmes become particularly interesting. Many potential beneficiaries have not registered or taken up the employment offered to them. Many of these people are involved in different forms of self-employment, ranging from small-scale production and trade in agriculture, beverages and food or services such as carpentry and bricklay-

---

36. For recent debate, see Isaacs 2007; Hengari 2007; 'Let's Get AIDS Wise, Urges the President', *The Namibian* 22 August 2007; 'Youth Unemployment a Big Problem: Angula', *The Namibian* 2 July 2007; 'Youngsters of Today Have Some MPs Tugging at Their Grey Hairs', *The Namibian* 23 February 2007.

37. For a historical precedent, see Glaser 2000.

ing to activities considered as illegal or illicit in the eyes of the state, such as smuggling or buying and selling stolen goods. Sometimes these activities are preferred out of cost-benefit calculations in terms of money, comfort and family arrangements. However, for some, self-employment appears as a sphere of freedom and autonomy. It is mainly the latter that I focus on here by way of the cases of a number of childhood friends from the same neighbourhood.

Peach and Manu are Owambo-speaking streetwise men in their thirties from Katutura. They had not registered themselves or sought ex-combatant employment. Peach went into exile in mid-1980s as a schoolboy. He first went to school and then underwent military training in Angola. When meeting him he was running a shebeen and made trips to South Africa, where he bought goods that he then sold in Namibia. He also had regular connections to former SWATF/Koevoet fighters who reside in South Africa, a link that had initially grown through family members in the early 1990s. His lifestyle was closely connected with events of the past. To him, ex-combatant programmes with their requirement of a regimented and dependent way of life was not appealing. Referring to disappearances and the heavy discipline in exile and empty promises at independence, he told of having learned enough about SWAPO in exile to avoid getting captured by 'politics' anymore:

> I don't today believe in Swapo ... not in Boers, nobody ... I believe only in myself. I just work hard for my children ... Doing my business as you know, I'm on my own ... Don't tell me politics, [I'm] no longer interested ... Politics is a dead game ... gambling with other people's lives ... They can steal your heart, to make you feel strong ... but everything [they] said was a lie ... There was a promise [of] free housing, that we are gonna have a free beautiful house in town ... [and] free education ... We were not supposed ... to pay for the hospital. Not even water, not to pay house rent ... There won't be hard things, everything's just gonna be easy like that ... There's many things which happened there ... There are people who schooled with me, till now they are lost. They never came back ... Today everybody says he's been fighting for the country ... If they can make a truth commission like in South Africa it's much better ... We could claim our brothers, those who passed away.

Manu had not been in exile. Instead, he had run away from Windhoek to avoid being captured by the police and joined the SWATF in Owamboland as a way to make money and wait for things to cool down. Although he managed to avoid the law that time, he had later accumulated a criminal record. He explained how he currently made a living: "In life if you are not working, you have many challenges. So ... if somebody stole something, then I can buy from him and resell it to make a profit." He had previously been involved in larger scale operations and enjoyed a more flamboyant lifestyle. However, after a few stints in jail, he now seemed to be keeping a lower profile. Like Peach, he sneered at the prospect of applying for the low-paid, regimented ex-combatant jobs.

Many in the neighbourhood circle of friends to which Peach and Manu belonged were involved in the thriving shadow economy of Katutura that reaches across the borders to South Africa and Angola.[38] Their trade was dependent on a network of informal connections, including strategic relations with state representatives. Here, the official

---

38. According to Grobler (2003) and Goba (2003), the most important goods that cross these borders illegally are diamonds, vehicles, drugs and guns. Involvement in diamond smuggling allegedly extends to people in the highest echelons of politics and society (Grobler 25–32).

aspirations of state power do not appear as a reference for identification. Rather, state agents represent a potentially hostile force to be reckoned with by tactics of avoidance or cooption. Without glorifying this way of life, it does not reflect an amoral position. Rather, the distant relationship to the 'liberation struggle' of people such as Peach, and their disillusioned and sceptical view of the projects of the ruling party and the state arises from a long history of predatory state power, from particular personal histories, and from neighbourhood solidarities and an everyday morality of providing for yourself and those close to you.

Some of those involved in this lifestyle were now trying to find more stable and less risky ways of making a living. Freddy and Kamati had previously operated in the same gang with Manu but had recently tried to enter into more mainstream occupations and were currently struggling in temporary employment. Freddy had also been employed in the Special Field Force for some time. Peach's friend Johnny had spent most of his childhood in exile and completed high school in the north in the late 1990. He had come to Windhoek to search for work but had found none and had instead got involved in the illegal diamond trade. However, he was constantly looking for a 'real' job.

Some young men from the neighbourhood had been employed in the police through the Peace Project. In this way, 'reintegration' placed people who had grown together and shared similar life histories on different sides of the law. However, this division was far from absolute, as the cases of Pine and Peter illustrate. Pine already knew the tricks of the street when he left for exile in the early 1980s. After going to school and receiving military training, he resumed a life of hustling and petty crime after repatriation. In the late 1990s, he was registered as an ex-combatant and became an SFF police officer in the north. His life story is thus an example of multiple movements over the boundaries of legality over time.

In the case of Peter, this boundary was constantly blurred in the present, as he was balanced between the demands of his job and expectations rooted in his old social network. After going to school both in Windhoek and in the north, Peter went into exile in the mid-1980s and joined PLAN. After repatriation, he struggled for a few years without permanent employment and took part in one of the early ex-combatant demonstrations. He was employed in the police after being registered as an ex-combatant. He served in the SFF 'in the bush' for some time, but did not like it, and managed to get a transfer to other duties in Windhoek.

Unlike Pine, who manifested extreme loyalty to the government, the ruling party and President Nujoma, Peter never portrayed himself as a Swapo loyalist. In his case, the job in the police seemed more like a practical survival strategy than an existentially significant attachment. Like Peach, he was also vocal on disappearances and other problems in exile:

> There were many things man ... Someone is just disappearing like nobody's business ... So we were not feeling nice. See? Because ... if you say anything, then you go also. You see? You can't complain. You can complain in your heart but you can't complain in public ... Okay, it was struggle ... but something was not right ... You can't stay for five days without food. Five days, but the superiors, they are eating, full time ... [And] the store room is full of food. They say we can't eat like the country is independent. So we have to wait the country to be independent, then we can eat (laughter).

Peter lived on the same street as Manu and surely knew of his dealings. He also told of another neighbour's diamond deals. Yet business went on as usual. According to Manu, "the police understand ... because we are all from the same background ... If they recover the items they just have to take the[m] back to the owner," but they would not arrest him. Peter was also quite prepared to use his position within the state framework to lubricate not entirely transparent deals. In many cases, the line between legitimate and illegitimate livelihoods is thin and can be crossed situationally due to divided loyalties and trying to make ends meet. At the same time, he had also made enemies as he had had to make arrests in the neighbourhood, and that was why he always carried a gun. It was perhaps because of such contradictions that he hoped to be able to give up his police employment for some other job in the future.

Peach, Peter and Pine come from the same township background. Yet they have adopted different survival strategies, and at the same time, different relations with state power in general and to 'reintegration' in particular. Pine has become a fiercely loyal SFF policeman, a frontline manifestation of state sovereignty. By contrast, Peach is in the opposite position, having grown disillusioned with Swapo and politics in general and seeking to maintain his distance from the state. Peter tries to straddle the two extremes, making strategic use of his ex-combatant status without giving strong allegiance to the current government, while trying to maintain and use his neighbourhood relationships for his own ends at the same time. Such neighbourhood and peer solidarities stretch far back to the time when the colonial state was clearly perceived as the enemy. For various reasons, such as problematic events in exile and the perceived self-serving tendencies of the elite, the current state is seen as a continuation of that history. Local loyalties often crossed both pre-independence enmities and current boundaries of legality. This might be seen as an instance of grassroots reconciliation but perhaps not of the kind that the government would like.

To the neighbourhood 'brothers' discussed here, the legality or illegality of their various livelihoods was not a highly significant distinction, apart from an instrumental sense of having to protect oneself from the unwanted attention of the law. They consider what they are doing to be licit, a conviction that arises from the necessity of making a living in a situation of meagre opportunities (cf., Roitman 2004). As one person from the same neighbourhood told me:

> I grew up in a very rough suburb where the mafias are ... the botsotsos, [they are] my neighbours, even my brothers ... But what can you do? ... How could you report this gentleman to the police if this gentleman is the one bringing bread into your home? You would be stupid to report, then you wouldn't eat.

Yet, these people do not operate from a position where state power is insignificant or merely external. Rather, their personal histories show a multitude of varying engagements with the state, and their current stance towards it is informed both by these personal histories and by the fact that some of their current livelihoods are officially relegated as unlawful (which does not mean that they could not be economically significant or clandestinely tolerated). However, mostly it seems that 'reintegration' in the way it has been carried out cannot capture them, as its ways of constructing the link between the state and the 'reintegrees' does not resonate with their ambitions and sense of self. They might contest state sovereignty in their remembrance, their current stated relations to the state and their deeds, but such contestations remain partial and fragmented and are not likely to form any systematic political 'resistance.'

Conclusion

The relationship of the various groups discussed in this chapter to ex-combatant 're-integration' varies, both between the groups and over time. Throughout the history of 'reintegration,' the very definition of 'ex-combatant' has been a contested category as it has been the key to recognition and material benefits. The ex-PLAN combatants have always been at the core of the concept and therefore also the prime beneficiaries of 're-integration' programmes. The groups discussed here have had a much more ambiguous relationship to 'reintegration.' Theirs is a history of partial inclusions and exclusions, based on both official and unofficial delimitations of eligibility. Such limits have been drawn in both legal and popular discourse, and in the planning and implementation of 'reintegration' and in wider socio-political arenas. They have been drawn both for political reasons, as in the case of former SWATF and Koevoet, and in order to avoid inflating the concept and bloating the base of potential beneficiaries (as in the case of youth).

However, in a significant departure from a narrow definition of 'ex-combatant,' an official decision was made to include not only those former exiles who participated in combat but also all other formerly exiled SWAPO members. This was a response to pressure from demonstrating ex-combatants, who included a considerable number of non-PLAN returnees. In a situation of scarce resources and hampered upward mobil-ity, fulfilling particular demands has opened doors to renewed claims, either by the people who have been preferred (as in the case of recent demands for compensation) or by previously excluded groups who feel that their situation closely resembles that of the favoured. In this way, the apparently distinct bureaucratic operation of 'reintegrating' ex-combatants opens into the broader field of Namibian politics, into arguments over inclusion and exclusion in the political society and national economy. Apart from the demands of formerly exiled youths, the evolution of ex-combatant 'reintegration' might call forth demands, for instance, from unemployed youth in general or from groups who claim to have suffered and sacrificed in the struggle for independence inside Na-mibia. Both demands have been preliminarily recognised through the militaristic youth service scheme and through the promise to extend the concept of 'ex-combatant' to all who contributed to 'liberation.' It remains to be seen what will happen with these initia-tives, but if pursued, they definitely have the potential to radicalise Namibian politics along the fault lines of liberation.

In a contrary response, some potential 'reintegrees' have not sought ex-combatant benefits. Such decisions might indicate a better level of economic well-being than could be offered by ex-combatant employment; in other words, of having become the au-tonomous economic agents that the DBC was, mostly unsuccessfully, trying to turn ex-combatants into. However, avoidance of 'reintegration' often seems to be associated with a critical relationship to the ruling party's version of Namibian nationhood and to the politics of inclusion and exclusion associated with 'reintegration.' For these ex-com-batants and former exiles, modes of 'reintegration' are too deeply immersed in troubled political histories and too heavily loaded with expectations of discipline and loyalty to be appealing.

Hence, the case of ex-combatants demonstrates that the biopolitical or bureaucratic operations of the modern state are not necessarily apersonalised and depoliticising. Rather, they are malleable and can be put to use for various purposes in various contexts. Consistent with this pattern, many of the political effects concerning ex-combatants have been produced through ostensibly neutral administrative techniques and have become part of deeply political processes of selective inclusion (and exclusion) on the basis of particular personal and group histories and political allegiance.

One may ponder whether the prioritisation of ex-PLAN combatants and other adult returnees, mainly based on ad hoc security concerns of the elite, is sufficient for long-term political and socioeconomic stability. In different ways, groups left out of 'reintegration' are examples of tensions beneath the calm surface of Namibian political and social life and may challenge existing power relations in time to come. Furthermore, this challenge might be more difficult to deal with than that of the ex-combatants who demanded (re)inclusion in the state and party ranks through employment and other benefits. In concrete terms, this challenge arises from demographic pressure and large-scale unemployment. However, it also arises from alternative imaginations and social networks that are fed by current material circumstances and the particular histories of the groups concerned.

Notably, the principle of reconciliation has been upheld throughout the years and there is still the possibility that it might be translated into genuinely more inclusive practices of citizenship. However, this requires re-evaluation of the significance of the 'liberation struggle' as the cornerstone of current Namibian nationhood. Those in power would have to seriously acknowledge the heterogeneity of Namibian society as a persistent reality not to be brushed aside by the dictates of unity, and to reconsider the bases of their own legitimacy in the long run. It would also be necessary to resist the temptation to give in to particular popular demands for short-term political gain, in favour of a more balanced assessment of the needs of the various currently disadvantaged groups.

References

Abbink, Jon (2005), 'Being Young in Africa: The Politics of Despair and Renewal,' in Jon Abbink and Ineke van Kessel (eds), *Vanguard or Vandals: Youth, Politics and Conflict in Africa*. Leiden and Boston: Brill

Agamben, Giorgio (1998), *Homo Sacer: Sovereign Power and Bare Life*. Stanford: Stanford University Press

— (2005), *State of Exception*. Chicago and London: University of Chicago Press

Behrend, Heike (2002), '"I Am Like a Movie Star in My Street": Photographic Self-Creation in Postcolonial Kenya,' in Richard Werbner (ed.), *Postcolonial Subjectivities in Africa*. London and New York: Zed

Brown, Susan (1995), 'Diplomacy by Other Means – Swapo's Liberation War,' in Colin Leys and John S. Saul (eds), *Namibia's Liberation Struggle: The Two-Edged Sword*. London: James Currey and Athens, OH: Ohio University Press

Chipkin, Ivor (2004), 'Nationalism As Such: Violence during South Africa's Political Transition,' *Public Culture*, Vol. 16, No. 2, pp. 315–35

Christiansen, Catrine, Mats Utas and Henrik E. Vigh (2006), 'Introduction: Navigating Youth, Generating Adulthood,' in Catrine Christiansen, Mats Utas and Henrik

E. Vigh (eds), *Navigating Youth, Generating Adulthood.* Uppsala: Nordiska Afrikainstitutet

Cliffe, Lionel, Ray Bush, Jenny Lindsay and Brian Mokopakgosi (1994), *The Transition to Independence in Namibia.* Boulder and London: Lynne Rienner

Colletta, Nat J., Markus Kostner and Ingo Wiederhofer with the assistance of Emilio Mondo, Taimi Sitari and Todesse A. Woldu (1996), *Case Studies in War-to-Peace Transition: The Demobilization and Reintegration of Ex-Combatants in Ethiopia, Namibia, and Uganda.* Washington DC: World Bank

Corbridge, Stuart, Glyn Williams, Manoj Srivastava and René Veron (2005), *Seeing the State: Governance and Governmentality in Rural India.* Cambridge: Cambridge University Press.

Das, Veena and Deborah Poole (2004), 'State and Its Margins: Comparative Ethnographies,' in Veena Das and Deborah Poole (eds), *Anthropology in the Margins of the State.* Santa Fe and Oxford: School of American Research Press and James Currey.

De Boeck, Filip and Alcinda Honwana (2005), 'Introduction: Children & Youth in Africa,' in Alcinda Honwana and Filip De Boeck (eds), *Makers & Breakers: Children & Youth in Postcolonial Africa.* Oxford: James Currey, Trenton, NJ: Africa World Press and Dakar: Codesria

Fairweather, Ian (2006), 'Heritage, Identity and Youth in Postcolonial Namibia,' *Journal of Southern African Studies,* Vol. 32, No. 4, pp. 719–36

Fikeni, Somadoda (1992), 'Exile and Return: The Political Economy of Namibia's Returnees,' Unpublished master's thesis, Queen's University, Canada

Fithen, Caspar and Paul Richards (2005), 'Making War, Crafting Peace: Militia Solidarities & Demobilisation in Sierra Leone,' in Paul Richards (ed.), *No Peace, No War: An Anthropology of Contemporary Armed Conflicts.* Athens, OH: Ohio University Press and Oxford: James Currey

Fitz-Gerald, Ann M. (2005), 'Disarmament, Demobilisation and Reintegration Interrupted: The Three-phased Experience in Sierra Leone,' in Ann M. Fitz-Gerald and Hilary Mason (eds), *From Conflict to Community: A Combatant's Return to Citizenship.* Shrivenham: Global Facilitation Network for Security Sector Reform

Gewald, Jan-Bart (2004), 'Who Killed Clemens Kapuuo?' *Journal of Southern African Studies,* Vol. 30, No. 3, pp. 559–76

Glaser, Clive (2000), *Bo-tsotsi: The Youth Gangs of Soweto, 1935–1976.* Portsmouth, NH: Heinemann, Oxford: James Currey and Cape Town: David Philip

Gleichmann, Colin (1994), 'Returned Exiles in Namibia: The Dynamics of Reintegration and Political Change,' Unpublished master's thesis, University of Hamburg, Germany

Goba, Ray (2003), 'Money Laundering Control in Namibia,' in Charles Goredema (ed.), *Profiling Money Laundering in Eastern and Southern Africa.* Pretoria and Cape Town: Institute for Security Studies

Grobler, John (2003), 'Namibia,' in Peter Gastrow (ed.), *Penetrating State and Business: Organised Crime in Southern Africa,* Volume One. Pretoria and Cape Town: Institute for Security Studies

Hansen, Thomas Blom and Finn Stepputat (2005), 'Introduction,' in Thomas Blom Hansen and Finn Stepputat (eds), *Sovereign Bodies: Citizens, Migrants, and States in the Postcolonial World.* Princeton and Oxford: Princeton University Press

Hengari, Alfredo Tjiurimo (2007), 'Let Us Tear Down the "Herero Mall",' *The Namibian,* 31 August

Isaacs, Denver (2007), 'The Rise and Rise of Youth Violence in Namibia,' *The Namibian,* 27 July

Kenna, Constance (1999), *Homecoming: The GDR Kids of Namibia.* Windhoek: New Namibia Books

Kriger, Norma (2003), *Guerrilla Veterans in Post-War Zimbabwe: Symbolic and Violent Politics, 1980–1987.* Cambridge: Cambridge University Press

— (2006), 'From Patriotic Memories to "Patriotic History" in Zimbabwe, 1990–2005,' *Third World Quarterly,* Vol. 27, No. 6, pp. 1151–69.

Lamb, Guy (2007), 'Militarising Politics and Development: The Case of Post-Independence Namibia,' in Lars Buur, Steffen Jensen and Finn Stepputat (eds), T*he Security–Development Nexus: Expressions of Sovereignty and Securitization in Southern Africa.* Uppsala: Nordiska Afrikainstitutet and Cape Town: HSRC Press

LeBeau, Debie (2005), *An Investigation into the Lives of Namibian Ex-fighters Fifteen Years after Independence.* Windhoek: PEACE Centre

Leys, Colin and John S. Saul (1995a), 'Introduction,' in Colin Leys and John S. Saul (eds), *Namibia's Liberation Struggle: The Two-Edged Sword.* London: James Currey and Athens, OH: Ohio University Press

— (1995b), 'Swapo inside Namibia,' in Colin Leys and John S. Saul (eds), *Namibia's Liberation Struggle: The Two-Edged Sword.* London: James Currey and Athens, OH: Ohio University Press

Liechty, Mark (2003), *Suitably Modern: Making Middle-class Culture in a New Consumer Society.* Princeton and Oxford: Princeton University Press

McMullin, Jaremey (2005), 'Far from Spontaneous: Namibia's Long Struggle with Ex-Combatant Reintegration,' in Ann M. Fitz-Gerald and Hilary Mason (eds), *From Conflict to Community: A Combatant's Return to Citizenship.* Shrivenham: Global Facilitation Network for Security Sector Reform

Metsola, Lalli (2001), 'The Liberation Narrative and the Post-return Life Stories of Namibian Former Exiles,' Unpublished master's thesis, University of Helsinki, Finland.

— (2005), 'From a "Social Problem" to Frontline Functionaries – The Core of Namibian Ex-combatant 'Reintegration,' Paper presented at the Nordic Africa Days, Uppsala, Sweden, 30 September – 2 October 2005

— (2006), '"Reintegration" of Ex-combatants and Former Fighters: A Lens into State Formation and Citizenship in Namibia,' *Third World Quarterly,* Vol. 27, No. 6, pp. 1119—35

— (2007), 'The struggle continues? The spectre of liberation, public memory, and ex-combatant "reintegration" in Namibia,' Paper presented at the AEGIS European Conference on African Studies, Leiden, The Netherlands, 11–14 July 2007

— and Henning Melber (2007), 'Namibia's Pariah Heroes: Swapo Ex-combatants Between Liberation Gospel and Security Interests,' Lars Buur, Steffen Jensen and Finn Stepputat (eds), *The Security–Development Nexus: Expressions of Sovereignty and Securitization in Southern Africa.* Uppsala: Nordiska Afrikainstitutet and Cape Town: HSRC Press

Mufune, Pempelani (2002), 'Youth in Namibia – Social Exclusion and Poverty,' in Volker Winterfeldt, Tom Fox and Pempelani Mufune (eds), *Namibia, Society, Sociology.* Windhoek: University of Namibia Press

Olonisakin, Funmi and Abiodun Alao (2005), 'Explaining Disarmament, Demobilisation and Reintegration in Liberia,' in Ann M. Fitz-Gerald and Hilary Mason (eds), *From Conflict to Community: A Combatant's Return to Citizenship.* Shrivenham: Global Facilitation Network for Security Sector Reform

Preston, Rosemary (1997), 'Integrating Fighters after War: Reflections on the Namibian Experience, 1989–1993,' *Journal of Southern African Studies,* Vol. 23, No. 3, pp. 453–72

Preston, Rosemary (1994), 'Returning Exiles in Namibia since Independence,' in Tim Allen and Hubert Morsink (eds), *When Refugees Go Home: African Experiences.* Geneva: UNRISD, Trenton, NJ: Africa World Press and London: James Currey

— et al. (1993), *The Integration of Returned Exiles, Former Combatants and Other War-affected Namibians.* Windhoek: University of Namibia, Namibian Institute for Social and Economic Research

Republic of Namibia (1998), *Report on the Registration, Verification of, and Investigations into the Condition of Ex-PLAN Combatants.* Technical Committee on Ex-Combatants

— (1999), 'War Veterans Subvention Act (Act 16 of 1999),' *Government Gazette of the Republic of Namibia,* No. 2211, 20 October

— (no date [2001]), *Final Report of the Technical Committee on Ex Combatants to the Cabinet Committee on Defence and Security (CCDS).* Technical Committee on Ex-Combatants

Roitman, Janet (2004), 'Productivity in the Margins: The Reconstitution of State Power in the Chad Basin,' in Veena Das and Deborah Poole (eds), *Anthropology in the Margins of the State.* Santa Fe and Oxford: School of American Research Press and James Currey

Soggot, David (1986), *Namibia: The Violent Heritage.* London: Rex Collings

Soiri, Iina (1996), *The Radical Motherhood: Namibian Women's Independence Struggle.* Uppsala: Nordiska Afrikainstitutet

Steinmetz, George (1999), 'Introduction: Culture and the State,' in George Steinmetz (ed.), *State/Culture: State-Formation after the Cultural Turn.* Ithaca, NY and London: Cornell University Press

Tapscott, Chris (1994), 'A Tale of Two Homecomings: Influences of the Economy & State on the Reintegration of Repatriated Namibian Exiles, 1989–1991,' in Tim Allen and Hubert Morsink (eds), *When Refugees Go Home: African Experiences.* Geneva: UNRISD, Trenton, NJ: Africa World Press and London: James Currey

— (1995), 'War, Peace and Social Classes,' in Colin Leys and John S. Saul (eds), *Namibia's Liberation Struggle: The Two-Edged Sword.* London: James Currey and Athens, OH: Ohio University Press

— and Ben Mulongeni (1990), *An Evaluation of the Welfare and Future Prospects of Repatriated Namibians in Northern Namibia.* Windhoek: Namibian Institute for Social and Economic Research, University of Namibia, research report 3

Trouillot, Michel-Rolph (2001), 'The Anthropology of the State in the Age of Globalization,' *Current Anthropology,* Vol. 42, No. 1, pp. 125–38

Utas, Mats (2005), 'Building a Future? The Reintegration & Remarginalisation of Youth in Liberia,' in Paul Richards (ed.), *No Peace, No War: An Anthropology of Contemporary Armed Conflicts.* Athens, OH: Ohio University Press and Oxford: James Currey

Vigh, Henrik (2006), *Navigating Terrains of War: Youth and Soldiering in Guinea-Bissau.* New York and Oxford: Berghahn

Imagining post-apartheid society and culture
Playfulness, officialdom and civility in a youth elite club in northern Namibia

Mattia Fumanti

People who are considered youth form an increasing proportion of the Namibian population. According to UN statistics, the population growth rate in Namibia is 2.9% per annum. The decrease in infant mortality rate, combined with a high population grow rate, has resulted in the largest single sector of the population in Namibia, 42.6%, being under 15 years of age, compared to a mere 2.8% being 65 years or older[1]. Youth are therefore preponderant numerically and these demographic shifts are accompanied by a series of reconsiderations of the wider categories of child, youth, adult or elder. For this reason, the category of youth must be understood as relational, that is as constituted and reconstituted constantly in every social encounter (Durham 2000), and as a social and culturally constructed category and not simply a biological one. This soon becomes very apparent to researchers carrying out fieldwork in Namibia or in other parts of Africa, since people who are considered youths can be between the age of 5 and 45 years according to a series of different definitions, such as their social position, their marital status, their reproductive capacities, their public behaviours or the social context in which they find themselves. There are also great differences between the rural and the urban contexts. With the term youth, I refer in this paper to people who are publicly recognised as youth according variably to age, to local cultural idioms and to their social position in the society they live in.

The youth in Namibia:
Challenges, constraints and state discourses

The youth in post-apartheid Namibia are confronted with many of the problems and challenges that affect their counterparts in other parts of Africa (see Mufune 2002). These problems appear to be very acute given the dramatic demographic, social and cultural changes that have taken place Namibia's post-independence era. First, there is the soaring unemployment rate[2], which primarily affects Namibia's young population, leaving it in a very vulnerable and marginal position (Mufune 2002:184–5). In a country where new socioeconomic and racial inequalities are emerging alongside the old ones, the impact of neoliberal economic policies and their new regime of governmentality (Ferguson and Gupta 2002) have created further discriminatory practices in the

---

1. Human Development Reports, UNDP, 2005, www.hdr.undp.org
2. 'Jobless youth a time bomb,' *The Namibian,* 24/06/2004

employment sector for the young population. Following the demands of the international market, the shift is towards a new workforce that is flexible, educated and highly technical, and incidentally easily dismissible and precarious. Within this context, the Namibian government, more and more constrained by the economic dominance of South Africa, has failed to respond to the challenges and guarantee access to the job market to a greater proportion of its population. Only education, with all its recent problems[3], has paradoxically remained one of the few avenues for upward mobility for many young Namibians (Fumanti 2006, 2007). Excluded from the productive sphere, the youth are in turn excluded from the consumer culture so pervasive in post-apartheid Namibia and Africa at large, and are left facing disenchantment and more often despair and alienation. Second, the high prevalence of the HIV/AIDS pandemic has brought with it dramatic changes on a demographic, social, cultural and economic level reconfiguring the way in which people conceptualise and understand the categories of gender, sexuality and age (Pinkowsky-Tersbol 2002; Talavera 2002). Third, the level of violence is on the increase in the country and the youth, who are often the most vulnerable and excluded in post-apartheid Namibia, emerge at times as victims and at other times as perpetrators[4].

Given this scenario, the youth in Namibia are increasingly seen as a problem that needs to be policed[5]. The circulation of alarming statistics on violence, AIDS and unemployment reinforces the public perceptions of youth as potentially dangerous and amoral agents, lacking the desire to participate in the wider post-independence project as responsible citizens through commitment, hard work and sacrifice. As the 'future leaders of the nation,' so goes the official rhetoric, they are supposed to be trained and educated in civic and national matters in order to guarantee economic development and nation-building[6]. These are discourses that bring to bear and reinforce new generational cleavages alongside old ones and a certain language inherited from the struggle against apartheid (Melber 2003b). While the youth who grew up under apartheid and fought in the liberation struggle are seen as a positive model, post-apartheid youth are seen as morally loose, spoiled and only interested in consumer goods and fashion. It is no surprise that within these emerging discourses the government has recently introduced a National Youth Service with the aim of giving the 'lost generation' the values of a responsible citizenry, to instil the lost sense of sacrifice and provide technical know-how to face the demands of the job market[7]. Yet beyond this initiative, many see a return to the anti-colonial rhetoric and a dangerous step towards the introduction of Zimbabwe-style youth training camps, and the images of youths in uniforms marching before the Namibian head of state, waving their fists and chanting SWAPO songs in the recently established youth camp at Berg Aukas are certainly not encouraging[8].

3. 'Failure of education system in spotlight,' *The Namibian*, 02/02/2006
4. 'WAD says media must find the causes of violence,' *The Namibian*, 09/02/2005
5. 'Youth bill through NA,' *New Era*, 16/03/2005
6. 'Unam has duty to educate youth on civic matters,' *New Era*, 19/05/2006
7. 'President wants a creative youth,' *New Era*, 10/02/2006
8. 'Youth bill upsets Cod,' *New Era*, 10/03/2005

Alternative visions of youth in the making of post-apartheid society and culture

Yet here I aim to move beyond the official narrative of youth as a problem and focus on the way in which Namibian youth participate in the making of Namibia's post-apartheid society and culture. I here build my argument on a more recent academic debate on youth in postcolonial Africa. Flowing from the fresh interest in the studies of youth in Africa (Carton 2000; Glaser 2000; Gondola 1999; McKittrick 2002; Richards 2002), several scholars have pointed out that in the fast changing socioeconomic and cultural context brought forward by demographic changes, encroaching capitalism and the HIV/AIDS pandemic the old ways of thinking about age, generations and social reproduction are no longer adequate to understanding life in contemporary Africa (Simpson 2003; Sharp 2003; Durham 2000). Whereas race, class and gender are still fundamental tools for thinking about the process of cultural difference and change, we need to take age and intergenerational relationships as the primary locus through which other social and economic processes are reconfigured in postcolonial Africa and beyond. Moreover, there is the need to undermine a more recent set of discourses, too often conveyed in media representations, which can be found in the social and cultural imagination of Africa. In these discourses, youths are seen exclusively as victims and/ or cruel perpetrators of unimaginable violence. In these accounts, the youth enter the public space of Africa under the control of the elders and leave behind only violence, destruction and uncivil practices (Richards 2002; Abbink and Van Kessel 2003; Richards and Peter 1998). On the contrary, as Durham argues, we need to explore the real extent to which youth participate in the political space of Africa:

> Traversing these notions, youth enter the political space as saboteurs; their potential for political sabotage comes from their incomplete subjugation to contexts and co-opters, and to their own power for action, response, and subversion in contexts of political definition (2000:113).

The need is therefore to reconsider the role and contribution of youth in Africa in the making of colonial and postcolonial life and to look at the ways in which youth stands at the centre of wider conjunctures of history and globalisation, how they move through them and how by negotiating continuity and change they reconfigure webs of power, reinventing personhood and agency.

In Namibia's context one has to think, for example, of the growing local music industry and the participation by many youths in Namibia's civil society. This cultural revival and active engagement in societal and political affairs is testimony of youthful agency and of cultural creativity. Improvised recording studios are set up literally in people's backyards in many Namibian towns and new artists emerge overnight selling their CDs in local shops, open markets and shebeens, thereby providing an alternative avenue for income and upward mobility for young men and women alike. On my most recent visit to Namibia, I was surprised by the increasing number and popularity of local kwaito, gospel and RandB musicians such as Stanley, Jossy Josh, Gall Level, Sunny Boy and Gazza. Creating hybridised musical genres that cut across Europe, Africa and the US, and borrowing from, among others, the style and image of Black American rappers and South African kwaito artists, these musicians address many issues of interest to Namibian youth. Often singing in their local idioms, their songs speaks of love and relationships, sex and HIV/AIDS, violence and crime, success and conspicuous consumption, but also of religion and morality, kinship and generational relationships, and capture well the hopes and aspirations of Namibia's youth for a modern and cosmopolitan life as well as their daily concerns. "Where will all this lead us?" asks Wernelly, a popular gospel artist from Rundu, in one of his recent hits[9]. These musicians are now household names and their role in Namibia's public sphere has become very prominent through their attendance at public events and state ceremonies and their constant appearances in the media[10]. Their success has become an inspiration to many youths and the ministry of education has been quick to exploit this popularity by appointing Gazza as a cultural ambassador in various schools across the country[11]. Similarly, the youth participate in post-apartheid Namibia's civil society through their role in association life, with youth clubs being a prominent feature in the country. These clubs are very diverse and cover many aspects of urban social life, providing valid alternatives to its youth population. Church associations, gospel and dance clubs, sports clubs, ethnic clubs, cultural clubs and multi-interest clubs constitute part of the life of urban and rural Namibia (for a comparative analysis elsewhere in African, see Gable 2001; La Fontaine 1970; Lentz 1995; Mayer and Mayer 1970; Møller and Nthembu 1991; Rea 1998; Tostensen, Tvedten and Vaee 2001). In these spaces, the youth are able to exert their agency, imagine and foster citizenship and contribute to the society at large by making and remaking cultural and social values. Further, they are fundamental spaces for the formation of youthful subjectivities whose values represent the changing sociocultural and economic context of post-apartheid Namibia.

The Shinyewile Club: Officialdom, playfulness and the emergence of a youthful elite in Rundu

The aim of this paper is to introduce further complexity into this recent debate by looking at the way in which a youth elite in Rundu, a small town in northern Namibia, by combining ethic and civic consciousness, appeals to the rights of citizens and the public good in a post-apartheid society. Heirs in certain cases to local dynasties whose influence stretches from precolonial to postcolonial times, this youth elite is more and more disenchanted with the directions taken in nation-building. The expectations raised at independence are still high, but the accomplishments are seen by the youth elite to fall short of the objectives. In their moral reasoning, they see themselves as possessing the right skills and qualities, moral and professional, to contribute to Namibian post-apartheid society. Yet they feel blocked in their careers and excluded from the public sphere by SWAPO's party elite. While some of these youths are employed as civil servants in

---

9. This is my translation from Ru-Kwangali, 'Kupi Ngatu Yitwara.' 'Where will all this lead us?' is the title of a song on Wernelly's latest album, 'Nsigwe' (the Orphan).

10. 'Young, musical and talented,' *Insight Magazine,* March 2006

11. 'Gazza reaches out to youth,' *New Era,* 07/03/2006. Similarly, in last year's election campaign President Pohamba and ex-president Sam Nujoma encouraged people to vote by lending their voices to a kwaito musical compilation entitled 'Omalaeti o'Swapo' (Swapo Fellas) in *New Era,* 21/10/2004

the ministerial offices of Rundu, others, unlike the elite in power that dominates the public sector, have taken careers in the private sector, working for international NGOs and private companies where they see the possibility for upward mobility and career advancement. To the SWAPO ruling elite's post-independence rhetoric of sacrifice and the work ethic, which pervades the public sphere at both local and national levels, they oppose a moral discourse on the delivery of governance and the public good, on what constitutes capable leadership and the making of moral beings (see Fumanti 2003 for a wider discussion on the public sphere).

In this paper, I show how this youth elite negotiated their emergence in the public sphere of Rundu through the creation of a youth club, the 'Shinyewile Club.' The nickname 'Shinyewile' does not exist as an ordinary word in the local dialects spoken in the Kavango area. It is a distorted form of a Ru-kwangali verb kunyeura, which literally means to pull down one's own foreskin[12]. This nickname became popular and controversial when it was adopted by the somewhat outrageous and jokey Shinyewile Club.

This youth club, formed spontaneously on the initiative of a small group of male friends already known in town through their successful careers and family legacies, became popular in a short time through its capacity to organise successful youth events and for its very distinctive sociality and conviviality. The group of friends, all civil servants in their twenties and early thirties, were able to combine official, formalised and standardised performances with an ironic and playful atmosphere, thus giving to the club its distinctive identity. Over the course of a year, the club organised two youth events, a youth festival and beauty pageant, alongside a more socially responsible clean up and a history symposium. By drawing on these achievements, the Shinyewile Club became central for this youth to assert its own role in public, to perform its professional knowledge and to reflect upon and express its personal trajectories and accomplishments. This was achieved in an urban context in which associational life is largely dominated by the senior SWAPO generation in power and from which they felt excluded on generational and political grounds. With the notable exception of two former SWAPO student activists, the club could not draw its legitimacy either from participation in the liberation struggle or from its contribution to education in the region (Fumanti 2006, 2007). As I show elsewhere (Fumanti 2003, 2004a), these are decisively important factors for access to the town's public life.

Of course the Shinyewile Club is not the gathering of a powerless and marginal youth whose only instrument of opposition is mockery addressed in good measure against a distant and foreign power. On the contrary, in this case there is no 'mimesis and alterity,' as in Taussig (1993): here the youth are young civil servants, many with a tertiary education and a command over technology, both in the Foucaultian sense (1977) and as in information technology. Yet the creation and the activities of this youth club help to capture well a certain post-apartheid mood of disenchantment and disappointment with the recent political climate and the current economic situation. More specifically, the club underlines a youthful desire to reach the status of modern and cosmopolitan elites in the context of a generational struggle situated in the emerging social, economi-

---

12. Ru-Kwangali is the language of the Va-Kwangali and is the most widely spoken language in the Kavango region of Namibia. This region has a population of 180,000 divided among six major ethnic groups, Va-Kwangali, Va-Mbunza, Va-Sambyu, Va-Gciriku, A-Mbukushu and Va-Nyemba. These ethnic groups speak different languages closely related to one another.

cal and political cleavages across the country and the Southern African region. It was one of the most junior club members who, reflecting on the club's activities, told me how for him the club was a major achievement because, contrary to other associations in town, its activities were not based on seniority or on the holding of formal titles or political affiliation, but more on an egalitarian and collegial form: "You see a lot of these people in town. These big people, they don't really open it up. They feel somehow superior. Don't give chances. But our club was different."[13]

In order to unpack the political message of the club, I focus my paper on the formality and officialdom, on the inner sociality and conviviality of this group of young civil servants (see Pons 1959 for comparative analysis). In my analysis, I reveal how distinction (Bourdieu 1986) exemplified in the use of formal titles, in the command of officialdom and bureaucratic language are important aspects of this youth subjectivity. Their use of officialdom and bureaucratic language echoes their practices in their daily work. Jokes and mockery are also part of the activities of the club, yet in order to claim their share in Rundu public life the Shinyewile Club made 'concrete facts' the mark of its distinction, and the reproduction and enactment of officialdom played a central part in the sociality of the club. I call this 'the culture of officialdom.' With this expression, I want to capture the highly formal and standardised style in which public occasions, gatherings and events are represented and celebrated in performance in post-apartheid Namibia. This 'culture,' drawn from state public representation and bureaucratic formalism, is very pervasive and covers almost any social event, even rites of passage, with its rich texture. Further, it is a culture that the post-apartheid Namibian elite use as a mark of their distinction and hierarchical position (Fumanti 2006).

It is this shared culture of officialdom between two different generations of the elite and their quest for distinction that bring fresh problematics into Namibia's post-apartheid governance and the process of elite formation. Officialdom in Namibia is a highly ritualised culture and to master this culture is a mark of one's own education and distinction. In visiting the offices of the local elite in Rundu, I was always struck by the quasi-religious dimension of this experience, what Weber aptly described as "the charisma of the office" (Weber 1967). The display of certificates, of mottoes and wise words and the emphasis on professionalism, individual achievement and sacrifice in these officials' discourses provided a symbolic aura around their official persona (Fumanti 2006:95–6). Further, it represented, through a symbolic play, how a certain form of ritualised officialdom becomes a self-evident guarantee of basic governance (Spencer 1968:2–3). The competition over this form of knowledge and its correct performance between two generations of elites was at the core of the Shinyewile Club's activities. And yet, in the process of legitimating themselves as moral players in Rundu's public sphere, this youth elite undertakes an intergenerational dialogue with the senior elite in power.

In my analysis, a double movement is seen in the club's performances. Although the youth elite distances itself from the senior generation by pointing out its ineffectiveness in delivering officialdom, their intergenerational dialogue remains confined within the realm of civility. There is in public the appearance, and in good measure the actual enforcement, of an assumption of agreement between the youth and senior generations.

---

13. Interview with M 001

The members of this youth elite are conscious of the symbolic continuity between the respectful and those who would be respected. In this sense, the process of elite formation, although it is the expression of different generational experiences and career choices, remains inscribed in powerful local idioms of respect and civility. These idioms are not the expression of fear for authoritarian practices, but are based on the public recognition, despite the recent disclosures and government blunders, of the senior elite's contribution to the liberation struggle, the building of postcolonial educational institutions and the wider process of nation-building (Fumanti 2006). Further, they are the expression of a local culture in which generational relationships are regulated in public through respectful behaviour, what in Ru-Kwangali is known as *efumano*, respect. To have, acquire and perform *efumano* is central to the making of Kavango personhood and regulates social relationships across age and gender (Fumanti 2003). In the case of the Shinyewile Club, the disappointment and disenchantment with the state of post-apartheid Namibia was expressed in the club through careful and ambiguous performances balancing respect and playfulness.

I call these youthful performances evocative transcripts, after Caroline Humphrey's usage: "The term evocative indicates a text that is intended to elicit or evoke a particular interpretation beyond the surface meaning. Evocative transcripts are ambiguous by design" (1994:23). Writing on post-socialist Mongolia, Humphreys demonstrates that the 'evocative transcript' does not operate behind the scenes, as Scott suggests for the hidden transcript (1990). Instead, it "operates openly, but through duality and equivocation, and it was a common resource for all, if only in their imagination" (1994:23). Furthermore, according to Scott's notion, the social reproduction of texts occurs in social gatherings where people of a certain social class can express themselves solely to one another. This has an empowering effect, which rests on concealment from the other side. The 'evocative transcript,' Humphreys argues, has its main form in "the throwing in the social arena, as it were, of texts that are memorably ambiguous" (1994:25). In accord with that, the word 'Shinyewile' ambiguously entering the social arena of Rundu through the activities of the youth club bearing its name, allowed this youth elite to participate in the public sphere of Rundu without taking a confrontational attitude and within the realm of civility and respect. This took place through the use of a language that, in Humphreys terms, "is in a sense – but not in a very strong sense – the preserve of the other side" (1994:27).

Here I will give an actual example of the ambiguous nature of the name Shinyewile, because it illustrates the way these youths managed their club name in the public sphere. Other peers and senior elite members often confronted club members on the meaning of the word Shinyewile. On one of these occasions, a senior SWAPO member argued that the name was definitely an insult and it was shameful that people could use such a name to promote their club activities. After this elder finished his tirade, one youth, without losing his composure and looking as serious as possible, replied: "As you know very well there is not such a word in our languages, whether Ru-kwangali, Ru-Gciriku, Ti-Mbuskushu or even Ru-Nyemba. And you know that. This word is just a joke and does not mean anything. So?"[14] The elder, looking rather puzzled at the youth's answer,

---

14. Ru-Gciriku, Ti-Mbukushu and Ru-Nyemba are the languages spoken by the Va-Gciriku, A-Mbukushu and the Va-Nyemba respectively.

added: "It might not exist, or might not mean anything, but it does not sound nice." The club's name is deliberately ambiguous, something that can be detected by the elite in power but not completely, leaving space for manoeuvre.

Joking and playfulness in the Shinyewile Club

There is a great deal of joking and playfulness among the Shinyewile friends. The bureaucratic language is treated to something of a 'post-mortem.' The everyday expressions of bureaucracy and official gatherings are subjected to dissection and dismembering. They are ridiculed, even to the extent of blasphemy, in the most mundane activities.

To ask someone for a beer becomes "can we address the issue of beers?" Very often, periphrasis and metonymies are used to display skill in language playfulness. The above expression would become "can we address the issue of some of this locally brewed stuff?" Most often, this linguistic ability is directed towards the speech at official gatherings. Also, there was a playful use of certain expressions, with 'to shine' being the ultimate words to describe everything. It can be used to describe various occasions and, in every context, it assumes a different meaning: to shine at work means to have a rewarding day; to shine on a project, means to implement a project successfully; to shine on beers, describes a heavy and joyful drinking session; to shine on someone means to give someone a hard time; to shine each other means to have sex. All in all, the expression 'to shine' implies a sense of excellence and of accomplishment, and it suits both the playfulness, and at the same time, the high expectations of this youth elite.

The language playfulness has its rich repertoire of metonymies and metaphors and the ability to create neologisms or draw from unusual English words to describe mundane activities. In a recent phone call, I was told that the word 'shine' was paired with the expression 'quaff,' signifying the distinctiveness of the youth club. The youth club is exclusive not only because of the high social capital of these young men, but also because of their ability to speak English, the official language of the Namibian state. In this respect, their ability to command the new language of the state sets them in opposition to the old generation, who came to learn English at a later stage in life and are now in a linguistically disadvantaged position vis á vis this youth elite.

In one episode that circulated for months among this youth elite, an incident in the parliament highlighted the founding SWAPO generation's inadequacy in mastering the official language. During a debate on the national budget, a member of the opposition addressed a female SWAPO MP as "blowing hot air." This gave rise to an equivocal interpretation. The SWAPO MP in question, not knowing the meaning of this English expression, asked the speaker of the parliament to impose a limit on the offensive language of the opposition MP: "How can he tell a woman like me that I am blowing hot air?" The discussion in parliament became very heated when male members of the ruling SWAPO party stepped in to defend her. "Yes, how can you dare saying to our female MP that she is farting?" was the final word of one MP[15]. By dissecting and re-proposing this episode ad libitum, the Shinyewile friends distance themselves from the inadequate and embarrassing public performances of the SWAPO elite. In contrast to SWAPO's failure to command the new language of 'officialdom,' they aim to bring to

---

15. 'Hot air raises stink,' *The Namibian* 03/04/2001

the fore their own sophistication in their ability to use and master this language, both in its written and spoken form.

It is not by chance that the preferred target for these jokes is in fact the former president of Namibia Sam Nujoma, 'His Excellency' as he is referred to in the official language of the Namibian state[16]. The episodes around his persona are infinite, a huge repertoire of mistakes or embarrassing statements and performances. That is the way they describe his mistakes, as blunders. His colourful expressions have become a source of great laughter and are dissected and extrapolated from their original context until they inhabit the playful world of youth jargon as familiar linguistic expressions. Here I list a few examples: "UNITA bandits will feel the pinch of their own undertaking," has become the expression to refer to a great drinking session: "Last night I felt the pinch of my own undertaking"; "I will use the same tactics used in the liberation struggle," refers to any aim the person might have, whether the successful courting of a woman or the implementation of some of the programmes of the club. Even more illuminating is the presence within these jokes of past and present African leaders, in particular Canaan Banana, Amin Dada, Mobutu Sese Seko, Kenneth Kaunda, Jean-Bedel Bokassa and Robert Mugabe. These historical figures inhabit and are present in the jokes of the members of the club. Their grotesque, obscene and colourful expressions are similarly dissected and laughed at, and mockery is directed towards their vulgarity and obscenity (Mbembe 1992a, b). Members of the club would endlessly joke about the story of Banana raping his bodyguard. Some of the members saw a connection between this and Mugabe's anti-homosexual campaign: "I think the guy [i.e., Mugabe] these days, he is so angry with homosexuals because he was 'shined' by Banana and he is trying to hide his homosexuality." Amin, Bokassa and Mobutu were simply remembered for their brutal methods and their madness: "These guys were crazy." In one particular case, I was given a copy of a speech that was circulating among these friends and allegedly given by Amin Dada and entitled "A tongue similar to English."

> *After a luncheon hosted by the Queen in London in his honour the former President of Uganda, Field Marshal Alhaji Amin Dada, had this say for his vote of thanks. Mr Queen Sir, horrible Ministers, invented guests, ladies under gentlemen, I thank the Queen very plenty for what she has done to me. I tell you I have eaten so much that I am now completely fed up with malicious meal. Before I continue, I would kindly ask you to open the windows so that the climate may get in plentily. But before I go back, I must invite Mr Queen to my country and I can assure you, Mr Queen, that when you come, I shall revenge to you. You will eat a full cow. You will enjoy yourself to the top and I will work very difficult to make sure that you will go back with a very full stomach. For now, I am sorry to tell you that I have just made a short call on you. The next time, I will make a long one possible for a full moon. Thank you very much for letting me undress you in front of all the disgusting people.*

It is worth noting that the linguistic playfulness, as in the name of the club itself, draws elements from the local cultural context. It was not directed only towards the officialdom of the state. In particular, as in the example above, there is a rich repertoire of nicknames and jokes. Almost everybody in this club and the wider circle of friends within

---

16. His Excellency (H.E) is a common title for state presidents in Southern Africa.

this group of youths has a nickname: 'the hippo,' because of a loud snoring habit; 'the giraffe,' because of his long neck, height and slim body; Nkwapa (armpit) because of a sore armpit; and 'the diamond,' because he had two red spots on his neck. One favourite term is Lichiti. Lichiti, I was told, is the creature of the wild, a mysterious creature living in the bush and associated with witchcraft (see MacGurk 1981). These youths would refer to each other as 'ove lichiti' (you, lichiti), just out of playfulness.

Sometimes, they would draw their repertoire from kinship terms. In particular, they would often refer to each other as *tamwei*, male in-law of the generation above or below ego, and when talking to a girl with whom they have familiarity they would address her as *ngumwei*, female in-law of the generation above or below ego. Also, other terms such as *Vashe*, maternal uncle in *Ru-Gciriku*, or *janane*, brother, were commonly used. Even the attribute of the chief, *hompa*, can be used to 'slag each-other off' as in *tate kuru*, the old first one. This is an interesting aspect of their sociality that is worthy of some comment. The members of this youth elite bring in kinship terminology to convey quasi-kinship bonds with each other. It is also important to recall here that many of these youth informants have kin members within their circle of closest friends. Moreover, some of their friends are people who grew up in the same village, or are fellow tribesmen. Elsewhere (Fumanti 2003), I have shown the way in which these young urbanites have kept their links with their villages of origin, and the way in which the 'rural' shades into the urban and vice versa.

This playful and jokey practice in the club is best understood when it, and the club itself, is seen to be deeply intertwined with and derived from officialdom, the significant other of the club. To shift the metaphor, one might say that the club and its practices form the mirror image of officialdom, rather than being an original with its own autonomous existence. Furthermore, the pull of officialdom is seen in the fact that, for all the playfulness of its genesis in Shinyewile, the creation of the club became a serious endeavour. To think of it as an excuse to meet each other and simply continue with jokes and laughter would be a mistake. Admittedly, its nature is playful, but the formality of the club is equally important to the Shinyewile club's sociality and its genesis.

Creating a youth club: formality, officialdom and 'facts'

Placing great emphasis on officialdom, the club organisation and its activities were conducted after quasi-maniacal research into the use of official details. Everything was formalised and given an official form. The constitution, written in a standard format copied from an Internet web-site called "the league of gentlemen," was divided into the following sections: operating principles, service to members, aims, structures and aims, membership, objectives, membership fees, rights of the members, obligations of the members, termination of membership, the executive, election of the office bearers, and term of office. The following text reproduces some of the main points as stated in the original constitution.

THE CONSTITUTION OF THE SHINYEWILE CLUB

AS APPROVED BY THE ANNUAL GENERAL MEETING, JULY 2000 OMASHARE RIVER LODGE

Introduction

Generally speaking, the club is viewed as a non profit institution brought into existence to serve certain prescribed ends. Those who need such an institution agree to pay a fixed subscription at periodic intervals to meet the cost of maintaining it.

Structure aims and benefits

The club comprised a group of people who join together to save money, start businesses, make loans to each other at low rate of interest share and are united by a common bond of interest and purpose.

Membership

Anyone who falls within a common bond and whose written application to join the union is:

Recommended by at least two members of the union

Approved by the committee

Objectives

To encourage regular saving of money among members

To create a source of credit for productive and providential purposes at a fair and reasonable rate of interest

To foster human and social development within the broader community

To help members use their resources to the best advantage

To support the well-being, defend and promote the economic conditions of its members

To promote and foster togetherness among its members

To arrange and promote income-generating activities, exhibitions, symposia, lectures, and advertising campaigns with a view to improving the league

To promote and distribute different forms of information so as to keep the club members aware of current life conditions and markets, impending legislation, new business methods and techniques

The club meetings were called weeks in advance through the presentation of letters of invitation. The letters would be drawn up using computer software and following a rigorous formalism. Also, the venue of these meetings played a relevant role, as in the above example, which took place at a Rundu lodge that is very popular among government officials as a preferred venue for workshops and official meetings. The agenda would follow the usual protocol for official government meetings: opening remarks, reading of minutes of previous meeting, points of discussion and concluding remarks. Even the positions of the members would be delineated. The meeting would be conducted in a collegial and democratic manner. All the points would be discussed among the members and voted on by raising hands. The club officers were chosen in open votes and the appointments to posts would be formalised through letters of appointment and consequent acceptance, as in the following cases:

> *Shinyewile Club*
> *Rundu 24/07/2000*
>
> *Dear Sir/Madam,*
> *We wish to inform you that, following the meeting of the Shinyewile Club on 23/07/2000, you have been appointed with immediate effect to the position of additional member of the Executive Committee of the Club.*
> *You are required to confirm in writing to the Executive Secretary of the club your decision concerning the above mentioned post.*
> *The answer should be delivered within three days from the receiving of this notice.*
> *We sincerely hope you will accept this position in the true spirit of the Shinyewile Club.*
>
> *Yours sincerely,*
>   *The Executive Secretary*   *The President*

> *To: The President*
> *Attention: The Executive Secretary*
>
> *Re: acceptance of appointment*
> *Subsequent to the receipt of your letter dated 24 July, 2000 refers.*
> *I have the honour and privilege to inform you that I have accepted my appointment as an additional member of the Shinyewile Club.*
>
> *Yours faithfully,*

The club meetings were recorded in minutes, which would then be circulated among the club members. Finally, special care was taken regarding the financial side of the club. In drawing up the club structure at the first meeting, great emphasis was placed on finance. The club members decided to appoint a treasurer and, in recognition of 'the very delicate nature of this post,' they decided to appoint two financial advisors to monitor the treasurer's activities. Also, since the club finances were to be collected through a monthly membership fee, there was a need to open a bank account. In order to maintain transparency and accountability, three people had signing rights at the bank. I still remember the hours they spent filling in papers and having their signatures checked at the local branch of First National Bank of Namibia when they opened the account.

Besides the rather vague and ambiguous nature of the club as stated in the constitution, I want to argue here that the punctilious emphasis on producing facts, the quasi-maniacal care for details, the minutes, the formal organisation of the meetings, and the collective decisions of the club were all set in opposition to the 'charade of officialdom' performed by the power elite. The correct usage of the written material became associated with facts, as if the correct performances of officialdom would allow the delivery of governance. "We have to produce facts" was the constant refrain during these meetings and the club's members were invited to be "seriously committed" to achieving the club's objectives. The club's achievements, 'the facts,' became the most important thing to be mentioned ("we have proven ourselves good") and were set in opposition to the failure of past and present associations in town.

On many occasions during my fieldwork, the youth elite reminded me of the failures of previous projects and local NGOs. Two of them, in particular, were always mentioned as bad examples, not to be followed (see Fumanti 2004a). To give a brief example here, when the activities of the Shinyewile Club almost came to a standstill due to a falling off in enthusiasm and personal disagreements, several meetings were called to redress the situation. However, the quorum necessary to implement future plans was difficult to achieve. On one of these occasions, a club member addressed the meeting in the following terms, calling for more responsible behaviour: "Come on guys, let's not fuck this thing again. Let's not do like the other projects in town. We cannot embarrass ourselves like this".

As the ethnographic example illustrates, there was a very strong association between the written forms and the idea of facts. By facts, the Shinyewile friends would mean not only the practical accomplishments of the club, but also the written material, the documentation they would produce, which would stand against any possible future accusations. This was a further reason for the club to prove its transparency and accountability: the club had to avoid accusations of corruption. For this very reason, these guys kept the club as exclusive as possible. The fear of being associated with the wrong people was very strong, since such association could place the future of the club at risk. Shinyewile Club members are people who look keenly at the means and methods for the reproduction of the elite. For them, social performance gives them a mark of personal distinction. They have their eyes on upward mobility, a reachable good in their view. They have in mind a process of social formation, and what they are concerned about is *finesse*, the artfulness of social life as it is respectfully managed in public performance, and they know about the pitfalls and the risks of being associated with the wrong people. They have a very strong sense of social accomplishment. The members of this youth elite are therefore living within a world of accomplishment, indeed an achiever's world.

Officialdom, civility and respect in the organisation of a successful history symposium

In this section, I consider the problematic relationship between the founding SWAPO elite and the youth elite generation of the Shinyewile Club by describing the club's organisation of a public event, the 'Rundu History Symposium.' In this event, officialdom, as well as respect and civility in the public space, play a fundamental role that affects the successful organisation of the event.

In June 2001, as part of its activities, the Shinyewile Club organised a history symposium. When the president of the club announced the idea of the symposium in February 2001, club members reacted enthusiastically as they saw the project as a way to enter Rundu public space and to give notoriety and public esteem to the club. As one of the youth commented: "I think it is a great idea. We will invite a lot of people, these academics, church leaders, traditional leaders and so on. And we will show them that the Shinyewile can organise any event." Up to that moment in fact, club activities had been limited to the organisation of two youth events, the Miss Kavango Beauty Pageant and the Rundu Beach Festival. Both events had been very successful. In particular, the beach festival, which took place over the Christmas season of 2000 at Rundu beach, a popular spot on the Okavango River, attracted large crowds of youths who travelled across the region to attend the event. For two weeks, it provided an alternative for the town's and region's youth to the few nightclubs and other entertainments. Nevertheless, because of their youthful character, these events failed to attract the esteem the youth were aiming to secure from the founding elite, who, up till then, had seen the club's activities as those of nothing more than a club of 'youngsters,' if not ignoring them all together.

Organising the symposium became a four-month endeavour in which the club members gave great prominence to formalities and officialdom. Club meetings were called on a regular weekly basis to discuss over and over what the youth alternatively defined, using official jargon, as 'the operationality' or 'technicalities' of the events. With these two terms, club members had in mind both the logistics of the events, such as the venue and the sponsorship, as well as the formalities, the event programmes, the list of panellists, the letters of invitation. Since the symposium was seen as an important event for the recognition of the club it was essential that every detail should be continuously checked and collegially approved according to its 'seriousness.' 'Seriousness,' the main expression used in the course of these club meetings, became dialectically opposed to the playfulness and jokey atmosphere of the off-stage youth gatherings. Contrary to the mockery and laughter, 'seriousness' was perceived as the only possible attitude for the successful organisation of the symposium, to prove, as it were, the ability of these young men to deliver in contrast to and in opposition to the failures of the founding elite.

The programme of the event was constantly drawn and redrawn. Although the original intent of the symposium was to focus exclusively on the early colonial history of Rundu, on its foundation and origin, in the course of these meetings it was decided to widen its content. Under the ambitious title of 'Rundu in the New Millennium. Facing the Future through the Prism of the Past,' the conference was divided into four major panels: 'Precolonial and Early Colonial History of Kavango,' 'Labour Migration in the Kavango Region,' 'Pre and Post-Independence Education in the Kavango region' and 'SWAPO, the Church and the Liberation Struggle in the Kavango Region.'

The reasons for this wider programme were twofold. On the one hand, the aim was to cover the greater number of historical events that club members saw as the most significant in the history of Kavango and Namibia at large: "Come on guys," one youth commented, "We cannot organise a history symposium and not talk about the role of the church, the struggle and even of education. We cannot embarrass ourselves like this. This is the history of this region and of this country." On the other hand, it had practical and strategic motivations too. With the ambitious intention of "making an impact in the community," as one youth said, the club members became aware that the senior SWAPO elite generation should be given the appropriate space in the symposium, "We have to include these SWAPO guys here and give them some space. I am sure they would like to talk about the post-independence period." Not inviting the SWAPO elite was seen as both an open and defiant act *vis à vis* the senior generation and also as a dangerous political confrontation with the SWAPO establishment: "We should make sure these SWAPO guys do not think that we have a hidden agenda. You know they are so wary these days." Yet the programme was carefully drawn up so as not to turn the symposium "into a SWAPO party rally," as one youth put it, or as a further occasion for the legitimation of the senior SWAPO generation. The choice of the speakers and the composition of the panel then became very important so as to counterbalance the prominent role of the SWAPO elite.

The two panels on the colonial history of the region and labour migration became exclusively youthful terrain. All the speakers, with the notable exception of me, were BA or MA students in the department of history at the University of Namibia and members of the UNAM History Society, then presided over by Dr. Jeremy Silvester. All originally from Kavango, the students presented the results of their own fieldwork on a wide range of topics to the conference, from the role of the Catholic missionaries in the region to the establishment of the *Vakwangali* kingdom, from the establishment of labour migration in the region to the Angolan immigration into Rundu. Although not part of the club, the speakers were known to the club members and in some cases were their kin. Further, the panel on education, although chaired by the deputy director of education in the Kavango region and having among its panellists the director of education and the regional cultural officer, also included Mr. C, a retired school principal and a member of the apartheid-era Kavango cabinet. Mr. C, who served in the Kavango legislative council in different portfolios, is in fact another respected member of the *ancien régime* generation to whom this youth elite often refers in their intergenerational dialogue with the founding SWAPO elite (see Fumanti 2003, 2004a). By inviting members of the older generation to share a panel on education with the founding SWAPO elite, this youth aimed to concretise the dialogue between the three generations. Also, rather ambitiously, they thought it possible to foreground an alternative narrative in the public space and to undermine the rhetoric of the founding generation elite on schooling during apartheid: "It would be good to have some of these old people. So we will all know how these guys really got their degrees." Although other eminent figures of that older generation were invited to the symposium, such as the former minister of education in the Kavango cabinet and the former minister of health and social services in the Kavango cabinet, only Mr. C was able to attend the conference.

The club members brought great skill to the formal organisation of this event. The letters of invitation were written with great care, with a quasi-obsessive concentration on details. The language and the phrasing used in these letters were relevant in showing their command over officialdom. Moreover, the right order of speakers and their role in the symposium were issues widely discussed in these meetings. For this youth, it was important that people were given adequate space and time, according to the relative prestige and prominence of their positions. Who should be the master of ceremonies as opposed to who would give the keynote address? Who would chair the various panels as opposed to who would give the concluding remarks? These questions widely debated. As young civil servants and employees of foreign-based organisations and NGOs, all of them have a great deal of experience of symposia and workshops and know a great deal about the expectations of the guests, panellists and convenors. Workshops, or "talkshops," as one member of this youth elite defined them rather dismissively, are an important feature of post-independence Namibia. Organised over two- or three-day periods, these occasions involve a huge expenses, partly funded by government and partly by foreign donors. Usually these seminars are held in very exclusive tourist lodges and participants' full expenses, including travel, accommodation and extras, are covered. A great concern in the successful organisation of the event is to provide 'the dignitaries,' as the elite are often referred to, with all the comforts. Long and frequent coffee breaks and large amounts of food should be offered to the guests. A complete and sumptuous lunch with several courses should be a priority, with no regard for the budget involved, because conviviality and sociality are important aspects if an event is to be successful.

Thus, catering and the choice for the venue became a great concern for this youth group. Aiming to lay 'a milestone in the history of Rundu,' the club members decided to organise the symposium at one of the local lodges, as is usual for such events in Rundu. The chosen venue, the Omashare River Lodge, a Portuguese-owned lodge in town, is a regular venue for government and NGO workshops alike, and, because of its exclusive ambience, possesses the favourite bar of the founding SWAPO elite. Nevertheless, after unsuccessful attempts to raise enough funds for the event from local white business-men, the club had to find a more affordable alternative. Following one member's suc-cessful intervention, Lux-Development, the Luxemburg-government funded develop-ment agency, agreed to offer a space for the venue and to cover the catering expenses. The symposium would take place at Rundu Open Market, which had in recent years become a venue for various public events, such as beauty pageants, concerts and work-shops. With great reluctance, the club members accepted the offer. The Open Market was seen as 'unsuitable' for a serious event such as a symposium, and some club members feared a possible failure. As one youth put it: "We cannot afford to embarrass ourselves. Please guys let's make sure this thing will work out."

The day of the symposium, I arrive at the market in the early hours of the morning and find one youth wearing a very elegant suit with the brand label ostensibly sewn on his sleeves in the Namibian fashion style. He looks excited. "Man you look very elegant," I say to him. "What else!" he replies, looking rather surprised by my obvious remark, "I am here to receive the dignitaries." "By the way," he comments *en passant*, "some of them are here already and are complaining because of the place, I told you guys it was not the right place ... But anyway ..." He throws in this last remark shrugging his shoulders.

I walk to the back of the market where the symposium has been scheduled to take place. As promised, all the covering boards have been put in place and the guests are starting to arrive and, directed according to the efficient protocol, are proceeding with registration. After a half hour delay and a strong wind that blows off some of the boards, the panel discussion gathers momentum. From time to time, I look around and meet the gaze of the other club members. They wink at me, looking satisfied. The lunch is served on time and the guests indulge for a while in amiable conversation while eating the large amount of *mutete* (wild spinach), *yisima* (mahangu porridge), fried fish and chicken brought in for the occasion.

The event ends with a very convivial braai (barbecue), which some of the SWAPO elite members attend. The braai becomes an occasion for me to see civility and respect in public at play. The two generations sit around different braai stands and somehow keep themselves apart from one another, both maintaining a serious and respectful attitude.

That night, none of my friends ventures on to the dance floor and, most interestingly, they drink very few beers: "You cannot shine when these guys are around."

Conclusion

In Rundu, as in more of postcolonial Africa than has hitherto been recognised, play-fulness and officialdom are deeply intertwined. The former provides an instrument for distancing oneself from the way leaders perform in public, establishing what should not be done. The latter, by contrast, reminds citizens and even the officials themselves of the officials' command of technology, in Foucaultian terms, as a prerequisite to delivering services in the highly bureaucratic arena of Rundu. Much criticism, even by the officials themselves, especially the young elite, is not directed at officialdom as such, but at the way it is commanded. Officialdom is not a self-evident authority. It is perceived as having authority if correctly conducted. In the perception of this youth elite in Rundu, the correct performance of officialdom leads to delivery and civility, which in turn brings social accomplishment. There is in this sense a moral distinction between successive generations with regard to the way governance in post-apartheid Namibia is understood. For these youths, who have been educated in a post-apartheid Namibia and work for foreign NGO's and the private sector, the language of officialdom has been enriched with the new terminology of accountability, delivery and sustainability. This new language, as I show in this paper, goes beyond the self-evidence of authority embraced by SWAPO at independence.

In support of my argument, made more explicit through my ethnography, I turn to a dissonance between the centre and the periphery of the Namibian nation-state and to the increasing process of 'Swapo-isation' of politics. For this purpose, I paraphrase Norma Kriger's label for a trend in similar post-independence political life in Zimbabwe (1995). Swapo-isation, advanced by official state gatherings and a strong rhetoric of self-legitimation and moral unchallengeability, has led, I argue, to the creation of an idea of authority as self-evident. By this, I mean an authority which is represented as obvious and as therefore needing no further proof besides SWAPO party membership and self-defined professionalism.

More and more often, the government is drawing its legitimacy from the moral weight of the nationalist past, especially from the heroics of the liberation struggle. The structures within the party are divided into ranks according to seniority, that is according to party members' involvement in the liberation struggle or their long-term commitment to party politics. The debate on 'who owns the heroes' (see the debate on ownership and state memorialism: Kriger 1995; Werbner 1998) has acquired a wide public dimension with the inauguration in August 2002 of a massive Heroes Acre in the capital Windhoek[17] and more recently with the building of the controversial new state house[18]. Furthermore, military events in Caprivi, Angola and the DRC have provided

---

17. 'Heroes acre: their blood waters our freedom' special supplement in *New Era,* 23–30 August 2002; 'Heroes Day supplement', *The Namibian,* 26/08/2002.

18. 'State House costs: guess!' *The Namibian,* 09/07/2007

fertile opportunities for drawing the country into a renewed heroisation of SWAPO[19] (see Melber 2003a).

Recent political events and their consequences, being central to the daily debates and the discussions of these youth, affect much of their moral reasoning and political sensitivities. In a recent contribution on youth subjectivities in Africa, Durham argues that:

> New forms of political participation and authority exclude and include youth in novel ways, and debates about those forms are debates about the nature of citizenship, responsibilities and the moral, immoral and amoral nature of social action, issues particularly acute for youth, whose memberships are rapidly changing and multiple (2000:114).

Following this suggestion, I want to clarify how, in Rundu, issues of leadership, succession and inheritance are important for a youth staking their claims to be the future elite of Rundu. Their moral reasoning reflects much more than the disenchantment of young bureaucrats over the difficulties in their career advancement. Their moral reasoning arises within the wider context of the recent economic and social transformations and the post-apartheid political climate so pervasive across the country. These changes are affecting the Namibian youth in often unprecedented ways, bringing to the fore a new generational rift between the SWAPO anti-apartheid generation now in power and the current and future generations educated and raised in an independent nation. This rift cuts across the emergent class structure as the youth elite in Rundu shares a similar disenchantment and concern for the current situation with the rest of the Namibian youth. Of course the instrument and the motives to challenge the generation in power will vary across class, age and gender, from personal recognition and upward mobility, to a better education, employment, leisure activities, and also for women's representation and gender equality. As I show in this paper, being employed, educated and being able to master the old and new language of officialdom is certainly an advantage that only a few youth have in Namibia. And yet beyond the increasing polarisation in Namibia's society, the lack of political representation and the official narrative of violence, the marginality and despair, the youth in Namibia are asserting their agency in the making of post-apartheid society and culture through their different involvements in the country's public sphere. Often the outcomes of these initiatives are only ephemeral and inscribed within powerful idioms of respectability and civility, and yet they are fundamental for the making of youthful subjectivities and the process of self-fashioning different from the one proposed in the dominant discourses. Here I have examined how a group of youth elite through the careful negotiation of playfulness, civility and officialdom try to assert their role in Rundu's public sphere and rob the founding elite, but only within the club's exclusiveness, of the unchallengeable mantle of the past built upon the destabilised and traumatic experience of the liberation struggle and of apartheid education (Fumanti 2006). In the process, they form a youthful subjectivity directed towards imagining post-apartheid Namibia in moral terms as a society constructed around the force of ethics, good governance and the public good.

---

19. See 'The Namibian' archive for the period 1999–2000. www.the namibian.com.na

References

Abbink, J. and I. Van Kessel (eds), 2005, *Vanguards or Vandals. Youth, Politics and Conflict in Africa.* African Dynamics Vol 4. Leiden and Boston: Brill

Bourdieu, P. (1998), *The State Nobility.* Harvard: Polity Press

— (2006), *Distinction. A Social Critique of the Judgement of Taste.* New York and London: Routledge

Carton, B. (2000), *Blood from Your Children: the Colonial Origins of Generational conflict in South Africa.* Charlottesville: University Press of Virginia

Durham, D. (2000), 'Youth and the social imagination in Africa' in *Anthropological Quarterly,* 73(3):113–120

Foucault, M. (1977), *Discipline and Punish.* Harmondsworth: Penguin

Fumanti, M. (2003), *Youth, Elites and Distinction in a Northern Namibian Town.* Unpublished PhD Thesis. University of Manchester

—(2004a), 'Elites, Sport and the State: The Ministry of Basic Education, Sport and Culture and the Building of Public Life in Post-Apartheid Rundu,' in *BAB working paper series,* Vol. 1:2004

—(2004b), 'The Making of Fieldwork/er: debating agency in elite research,' in *Anthropology Matters,* Vol. 6:(2)

— (2006), 'Nation Building and the Battle for Consciousness: Discourses on Education in Post-Apartheid Namibia,' in *Social Analysis* 50(3):84–108

— (2007), 'Burying E.S.: Educated Elites, Subjectivity and Distinction in Rundu, Namibia,' in *Journal of Southern African Studies,* 33(3):469–83

Gable, E. (2000), 'The culture development Club: Youth, Neo-Tradition and the Construction of Society in Guinea Bissau,' *Anthropological Quarterly,* 73(3):195–203

Glaser, C. (2000), *Bo-Tsotsi. The youth gangs of Soweto 1935–76.* Oxford: James Currey

Gondola, D. (1999), 'Dream and Drama: The search for Elegance among Congolese Youth,' *African Studies Review,* Vol. 42(1):23–48

Humphrey, C. (1994), 'Remembering an "Enemy". The Bogd Khaan in Twentieth Century Mongolia,' in R.S. Watson (ed), *Memory, History and Opposition Under State Socialism.* Santa Fe: School of American Research Press

Kriger, N. (1995), 'The politics of creating National heroes,' in Ngwabi Bhebe and T. Ranger (eds), *Soldiers in Zimbabwe's Liberation War.* London: James Currey

La Fontaine, J.S. (1970), 'Two types of Youth Group in Kinshasa (Léopoldville),' in P. Mayer, *Socialization: the Approach from Social Anthropology.* London: Tavistock

Lentz, C. (1995), '"Unity for Development": Youth Associations in Northwestern Ghana,' *Africa,* Vol. 65(3):395–429

Mayer, P. and I. Mayer (1970), 'Socialization by Peers: The Youth Organization of the Red Xhosa,' in P. Mayer, *Socialization: the Approach from Social Anthropology.* London: Tavistock

Mbembe, A. (1992a), 'Provisional Notes on the Postcolony,' *Africa,* 62(1):3–37

— (1992b), 'The Banality of Power and the Aesthetics of Vulgarity in the Postcolony,' *Public Culture,* 4(2):1–30

McGurk, C. (1981), 'The Sambyu,' in G. Gibson, T.J. Larson and C.R. McGurk C.R. (eds), *The Kavango People.* Wiesbaden: Franz Steiner Verlag

McKittrick, M. (2002), *To Dwell Secure: Generation, Christianity and Colonialism in Owamboland.* Heinemann: Georgetown

Melber, Henning (2003a), '"Namibia, Land of the Brave": Selective Memories on War and Violence within Nation Building', in J. Abbink, M. de Brujin, and K. van Walraven (eds), *Rethinking Resistance: Revolt and Violence in African History*. Leiden and Boston: Brill, African Dynamics n.2, pp. 305–27.

— (2003b), "Limits to Liberation. An Introduction to Namibia's Postcolonial Political Culture", in H. Melber (ed), *Re-Examining Liberation in Namibia. Political Culture since Independence*. Uppsala: Nordiska Afrikainstitutet

Møller, V. and T. Mthembu (1991), 'Stairway to Success. Youth Clubs in Greater Durban,' in V. Møller (ed), *Lost Generation Found. Black Youth at Leisure*. Indicator SA Issue Focus. Pretoria: Indicator Project South Africa and Youth Centre Project

Mufune, P. (2002), 'Youth in Namibia. Social Exclusion and Poverty,' in T. Fox, P. Mufune and V. Winterfeldt (eds), *Namibia, Society, Sociology*. Windhoek: University of Namibia Press

Peters, K. and P. Richards (1998), '"Why we Fight": Voices of Youth Combatants in Sierra Leone,' *Africa*, 68(2):183–210

Pinkowksy-Tersbol, B. (2002), 'How to Make Sense of Lover Relationships- Kwanyama Culture and Reproductive Health,' in T. Fox, P. Mufune and V. Winterfeldt (eds), *Namibia, Society, Sociology*. Windhoek: University of Namibia Press

Pons, V. (1961), 'Two small-groups in Avenue 21: Some aspects of the system of social relations in a remote corner of Stanleyville, Belgian Congo,' in A. Southall (eds), *Social Change in Modern Africa*. Oxford: Oxford University Press

Rea, W.R. (1998), 'Rationalising culture. Youth, elites and masquerade politics,' *Africa*, Vol. 68(1):98–117

Richards, P. (2002), *Fighting for the Rainforest: War Youth and Resources in Sierra Leone*. Portsmouth, NH and Oxford: Heinemann/James Currey

Scott, J.C. (1990), *Weapons of The Weak. Everyday Forms of Peasant Resistance*. New Haven and London: Yale University Press

Sharp, L.A. (2003), 'Laboring for the Colony and Nation: The historicized political consciousness of Youth in Madagascar,' *Critique of Anthropology*, Vol. 23(1):75–91

— (2002), *The Sacrificed Generation. Youth, History, and the Colonised Mind in Madagascar*. Berkeley, LA and London: University of California Press

Simpson, A. (2003), *Half-London in Zambia. Contested Identities in a Catholic Mission School*. Edinburgh: Edinburgh University Press

Spencer, H. (1969), *Principles of Sociology*. London: Macmillan

Talavera, P. (2002), 'Sexual Cultures in Transition in the Northern Kunene: Is there a Need for a Sexual Revolution in Namibia?,' in T. Fox, P. Mufune and V. Winterfeldt (eds), *Namibia, Society, Sociology*. Windhoek: University of Namibia Press

Taussig, M. (1993), *Mimesis and Alterity: A Particular History of the Senses*. New York: Routledge

Tostensen, A., I. Tvedten and M. Vaa (2001), *Associational life in African cities: popular responses to urban crisis*. Uppsala: Nordiska Afrikainstitutet

Weber, M. (1967), *On Charisma and Institution Building*. Chicago and London: University of Chicago Press

Werbner, R. (1998), 'Smoke from the Barrel of a Gun: Postwars of the Dead, Memory and Reinscription in Zimbabwe,' in R. Werbner (ed), *Memory and the Postcolony. African Anthropology and the Critique of Power*. London: Zed

Regional development and decentralisation

Graham Hopwood

Thirteen years after Namibia's system of regional government was put in place, the 13 regional councils have very little meaningful power. The Regional Councils Act (Act 22 of 1992) stated that regional councils are responsible for planning the development of regions, but otherwise gave them mainly advisory powers. At the end of 1996, the cabinet adopted a decentralisation policy and this was launched as a decentralisation programme for Namibia in March 1998. The policy was given legal force through a series of new laws introduced in 2000, most notably the Decentralisation Enabling Act (Act 33 of 2000). But six years after this act became law, and despite much groundwork being undertaken, no function of central government had been decentralised in the manner envisaged by the act.

In 2000, then Deputy Minister of Regional and Local Government and Housing (MRLGH)[1] Professor Gerhard Tötemeyer (2000–04) (2000a:95) wrote: "Namibia's history of democratic decentralisation is still in its infancy. Any value judgement on its possible success would be premature. Comments can thus only be made on its contents, intentions, objectives and feasibility." In an interview with the Institute for Public Policy Research in August 2001, then Minister of Regional and Local Government and Housing Dr. Nickey Iyambo (1996–2002) (Keulder 2001:1) predicted that the introduction of legislation would speed up the decentralisation process. When asked about the time lapse between the launch of the policy and its implementation, he said: "The reason for it taking so long was that at the time of formulating the policy, the law that will govern and administer the implementation of the policy in terms of legislative procedures was not in place." The legal framework for decentralisation has now been in place for nearly five years, yet policy implementation is still widely seen as proceeding at a slow pace. In an article published to mark Namibia's 15th independence anniversary, the MRLGH concluded that the lack of a timeframe for decentralisation "seems to lead to some relaxation and lack of commitment to implement the policy as a whole" (MRLGH 2005b:68).

This chapter is the edited version of an earlier publication (Hopwood 2005). It begins with an overview of the historical context of decentralisation, since events prior to Namibia's independence have shaped the regional governance system in Namibia and defined the parameters of public debate about it. The implementation of decentralisation since the inception of regional councils in 1992 is then considered, focusing on the

---

1. On 21 March 2005 the name of the ministry was changed to the Ministry of Regional and Local Government, Housing and Rural Development. In this chapter, the ministry is referred to by the abbreviation MRLGH in connection with its activities before 21 March 2005 and by the new title in relation to its programmes and plans after this date.

progress made and the obstacles that remain. The prospects for effective decentralisation of powers to regional councils are then considered in terms of Namibia's current
political situation, particularly SWAPO's dominance and the recent commitment to
clamping down on wasteful government spending. Finally, some conclusions are offered
concerning both the discourse about decentralisation and the practical implementation
of the policy.

Historical context

Any analysis of the development of regional governance in Namibia cannot be divorced
from the country's painful history of colonialism and apartheid. The German empire
occupied what was then known as South West Africa in 1884, as European powers
scrambled to carve up sub-Saharan Africa. During 29 years of German rule, parts of the
indigenous population were forced out of their traditional areas (particularly in central
and southern Namibia), most notoriously during the 1904–07 war against the Herero
and the Nama people. The German occupation ended with military defeat in 1915, as
South Africa, representing the allied forces in the First World War, took over the territory. South Africa continued the practice of seizing farmland in central and southern
Namibia, while restricting the indigenous population to 'native reserves.' In 1962, Pretoria established the Odendaal Commission, which followed the apartheid thinking
of the time and recommended dividing Namibia along racial and ethnic lines into ten
'homelands.' The recommendations were implemented from the late 1960s onwards,
partly through the forced removal of communities.

In 1966, the South West Africa People's Organisation (SWAPO), which had been
formed six years earlier, launched an armed struggle for the independence of Namibia
(accepted by the United Nations as the name of the country in1968). SWAPO consistently campaigned for Namibia to become an independent unitary state and opposed the
policy of setting up homelands (also known as bantustans) through the popular slogan
'One Namibia, One Nation.' Many of the homeland 'governments' were dominated
by tribal chiefs or headmen. The homeland system was replaced by 11 ethnic administrations in 1980, known as second tier authorities. The legislative assemblies of these
authorities were dominated by political parties such as the Democratic Turnhalle Alliance (DTA), which would become the official opposition in 1990. In December 1988,
South Africa agreed to withdraw from Namibia and allow a United Nations peace plan
to be implemented. After a century of colonial occupation and a 23-year liberation war,
Namibia held its first democratic elections, under the auspices of the United Nations,
in November 1989. A constituent assembly consisting of 72 members was elected, with
SWAPO gaining the majority of seats but not a two-thirds majority that would have
enabled the party to write the constitution on its own. In February 1990, the constitution was unanimously adopted and Namibia became independent on 21 March 1990.
The system of regional councils, set out in the constitution, was established through the
Regional Councils Act (Act 22 of 1992) and the first regional council elections were
held from 30 November to 3 December1992. SWAPO has dominated every election
– at local, regional and national levels – since independence, and since 1994 the party
has held a two-thirds majority in the National Assembly, giving it the power to change

the constitution. The second chamber of parliament, the National Council, which reviews legislation after it has passed through the National Assembly, is made up of two regional councillors from each of the 13 regions. They are nominated to serve in the National Council by their fellow regional councillors.

Namibia is constituted as a "sovereign, secular, democratic and unitary state" (Republic of Namibia 1997:1). A unitary state is run by a centralised, national government and any decentralisation of powers, responsibilities and functions to lower tiers of government can be revoked by the central government. A federation, in contrast, consists of self-governing regions operating under a central government. The governing powers of the regions are usually constitutionally entrenched and cannot easily be overriden by central government. The homeland policy of the South African apartheid government designated areas for black people, usually along ethnic lines. These bantustans, as they became known, were reviled by the indigenous population and never recognised internationally even though some were given an 'independent' status by Pretoria. In Namibia, South Africa's homeland policy transmuted into the creation of 11 ethnic administrations in 1980. SWAPO's antipathy towards these creations of apartheid partly accounts for the lingering doubts about the role of regional councils and the policy of decentralisation.

To understand the ambivalence and suspicion that still exists in some quarters about the policy of decentralisation, it is necessary to examine how Namibia's system of regional government came about. The regional councils were born out of the spirit of compromise that characterised the sittings of Namibia's constituent assembly in late 1989 and early 1990. In 1989 the SWAPO manifesto (SWAPO 1989:18) stated: "Under a SWAPO government independent Namibia will have democratically elected local authorities, both in rural and urban areas, in order to give power to the people at grassroots level, to make decisions on matters affecting their lives." However, the powers of such local authorities were not spelled out. During debate in the constituent assembly there was little direct discussion of regional councils. Instead, the debate was framed by two concerns: firstly, whether Namibia should have a unicameral or bicameral system, and secondly, that the administration of Namibia's future regions should not resemble the much hated bantustan system of ethnic government imposed before independence. In his seminal work, *Namibia's Post-Apartheid Regional Institutions: The Founding Year*, Joshua Bernard Forrest (1998:4) notes that: "As a consequence of the history of apartheid in Namibia, the notion of a regional division of power or regional political structures carries a negative, pro-apartheid connotation for most post-independence government officials and for most Namibian citizens."

SWAPO went into the constituent assembly with commitments to a unicameral system and the holding of national elections based on single member constituencies, which would have put regional representation at the heart of the National Assembly. However, uppermost among SWAPO's concerns was the need to create a strong executive presidency. As a result, the party was prepared to compromise with the DTA and other opposition parties, which wanted a bicameral system and proportional representation (PR) for the National Assembly election. Early in the constitution-making process, on 12 December 1989, the standing committee on standing rules and orders and internal arrangements on constitutional matters reported to the constituent assembly that common ground had been reached on several issues, including the setting up of regional councils. On 29 January 1990, SWAPO's then secretary for legal affairs, Ngarikutuke Tjiriange, told the constituent assembly that SWAPO would not press the issue of single member constituencies and would instead accept PR as the electoral system for the National Assembly. He also indicated that the party was prepared to compromise on the issue of the National Council, saying, "we can live with the idea of a second house in spite of its obvious shortcomings" (Republic of Namibia 1990a:163). On 31 January1990, the constituent assembly passed the sections of the constitution that deal with local and regional government (Chapter 12) with little discussion. In one of his rare contributions to constituent assembly debate, SWAPO President Sam Nujoma sought to clarify the role of the chairpersons of regional councils by saying (Republic of Namibia 1990a:325): "There is a need for a governor to be appointed from Windhoek to the region or we can have a regional commissioner who will interpret the laws as they are passed here in parliament to the regions." Nujoma's comment underlined the thinking at the time that central control would be all-important for the new governing party and that concepts such as decentralisation, never mind devolution, were far from the policy agenda.

Regional councils were established through chapter 12 of the constitution, although the details of how they might function and their powers were left to future acts of parliament. Article 108 of the constitution states that regional councils shall have power to "exercise for the region within which they have been constituted such executive powers and such duties as may be assigned by an Act of Parliament" (Republic of Namibia 2002:55). Article 108 also gives regional councils the power to "to raise revenue or share in the revenue raised by central government within the regions for which they have been established" (ibid.).

The policy of decentralisation was never explicitly discussed during any of these debates and although commentators such as Tötemeyer argue that a commitment to decentralisation is embedded in chapter 12 of the constitution (Tötemeyer 2000a:95), such a concept was not included in chapter 11, which outlines the principles of state policy. Forrest (1998:8) comes to the conclusion that it was unclear whether any kind of meaningful decentralisation was intended: "The policy outputs regarding the creation of regional institutions in Namibia during the 1989–90 Constituent Assembly do not make clear whether the government had in fact adopted a policy of decentralisation."

Decentralisation first entered Namibia's political parlance in 1991, when the first delimitation commission, set up under the constitution (article 104) to establish regional boundaries, delivered its report. The first delimitation commission, which proposed 13 regions and 95 constituencies, made it clear that it had sought to promote decentralisation when demarcating the 13 regions. The report, which was accepted by cabinet in July 1991, attempted to create regions that moved away from the pre-1990 carve-up of Namibia along ethnic lines by incorporating factors such as transport and economic integration. As a result, Kunene region incorporated Ruacana, which had traditionally been seen as part of Owamboland, while the Oshikoto region bound communal farming areas to the heartland of white commercial agriculture. With some regions this was more difficult. For example, Caprivi could hardly have been merged with Kavango. As a result, it remained geographically and ethnically distinct and remote from the political centre in Windhoek[2]. The first delimitation commission (Republic of Namibia 1991:29) said decentralisation was "not only desirable but inevitable to ensure that administration is responsive to the real needs and aspirations of the people." It defined decentralisation as the "devolution of greater responsibility to the local administration." It is pertinent to note that one of the three members of the first delimitation commission was Gerhard Tötemeyer, who from 2000 to 2004 spearheaded the policy of decentralisation as deputy minister of regional and local government and housing.

Despite the talk of decentralisation, the new regional bodies were given very limited powers in the Regional Councils Act (Act 22) of 1992. Most significantly, regional councils were given the task of planning development in their region. Otherwise most of the envisaged roles were advisory or vague. They included:

- to perform duties and functions delegated by the president
- to establish, manage and control settlement areas
- to make recommendations to the minister of RLGH
- to make submissions to the cabinet and/or ministries
- to assist local authorities in the performance of any of their duties

The limited powers were indicative of the scepticism in central government about the function of regional councils. Even Minister of Local and Regional Government and Housing Dr. Libertina Amathila (1990–96) made no attempt to hide her doubts, telling the National Assembly in 1992 "half of these councils will have nothing to do" (cited in Forrest 1998:70). Suggesting that local authorities should have been strengthened instead, she added: "Maybe after five years we will scrap the whole Regional Council story" (cited in Forrest 1998:70). Even with the lack of clarity about the role of regional councils, Namibians leapt at their second chance to vote in free and fair elections when the first regional council and local authority elections were held simultaneously at the end of 1992. Some 81% of registered voters turned out for the election. Despite predictions that the first-past-the-post, single member system used might favour the DTA, SWAPO won 67% of the votes and 71 of the 95 constituencies. The party controlled nine councils, while the DTA took three. In the Kunene region there was no overall majority. To some extent, SWAPO started to warm to the regional government system after the party's strong performance in the 1992 elections (and during subsequent regional elections), but the MRLGH remained convinced that it had to lay down clear parameters on regional governance.

The lowly status of regional councils was confirmed when the ministry ruled in 1993 that councillors were only considered as 'part-time' politicians and were to receive allowances rather than salaries. In March 1994, Minister Amathila was quoted in New Era as saying she regarded regional councils as "experiments" that still had to prove their worth (cited in Forrest 1998:85). By the mid-1990s, there was a sense that more needed to be done on decentralisation and a policy review was initiated with the intention of advancing the process. Dr. Nickey Iyambo was appointed as minister of re-

---

2. The is little evidence that Namibians identify strongly with their regions. Rather, national, ethnic and political affiliations still hold sway. The annual soccer tournament, the Namibian Newspaper Cup, is one of few occasions when Namibians demonstrate enthusiasm for their regional bases.

gional and local government and housing in September 1996 and two months later the decentralisation policy was published. Cabinet approved the policy in December 1996 and in the following year it was tabled in and subsequently adopted by the National Assembly. The decentralisation programme for Namibia was officially launched in March 1998. The policy documents produced in 1996 and 1997 set out in great detail how the decentralisation process would proceed, but significantly no timeframe was attached. Instead, there were repeated warnings about the slow and potentially difficult nature of the process. It was also clear that central government would control the speed and nature of implementation (MRLGH 1997:14):

> How much decentralisation is contemplated, what form it is envisaged to take and at what pace it should proceed, are not established in the Constitution or the Act of Parliament, leaving it in the domain of the executive policy process.

Clearly, a long haul was anticipated, but would the lack of deadlines make it even longer? The documents also contained an essential contradiction – that the process of decentralisation would be tightly controlled from the centre. Forrest (1998:57) described the system of regional government in Namibia as "decentralisation reform with a strongly centralist character." The justification for this central control was the need to proceed within the framework of a unitary state. Fears of federalism and the return of bantustanisation appeared to fuel suspicion about regional councils – a suspicion that could only be quelled by a strong emphasis on central control. Minister Nickey Iyambo proved a far more enthusiastic champion of decentralisation than his predecessor, but he also expressed his doubts at times. In 1997 he told the association of regional councils meeting that the Khomas and Erongo regions probably did not require regional councils as they operated in urban areas where their functions were mainly carried out by local authorities. According to former Deputy Minister Gerhard Tötemeyer, the minister of regional and local government and housing "walks a tightrope trying to satisfy both supporters and opponents of decentralisation in his own party ranks" (2000a:100). In October 1998, Minister Iyambo surprisingly introduced a proposal that the president should directly appoint regional governors, who would then be answerable to the head of state. Until then, regional councillors had chosen governors from their own ranks. Iyambo later withdrew the amendment, saying the time available for debate on the change was too short (at the time the National Assembly was preoccupied with a proposal to change the constitution to allow President Sam Nujoma to stand for a third term in office). But the very fact that the idea had been raised indicated once again that Namibia's decentralisation process sometimes veers towards becoming a centralisation process. Despite the tensions within SWAPO over the issue of centralised control,[3] by 1998 it was clear that the decentralisation process had gained significant momentum. Speaking shortly before the launch of the decentralisation programme, Minister Iyambo said, "The policy for decentralisation in Namibia is one that has been endorsed by the highest political will in this country. Therefore there is no turning back" (Inambao 1998).

---

3. Most pointedly illustrated in a clash between Nickey Iyambo and then Minister of Higher Education Nahas Angula in parliament in 2002 when Angula stated that the subject of "regionalisation" reminded him of the former ethnic administrations in Namibia. Iyambo said Angula's comments were unfair and unpatriotic (Amupadhi 2002).

In the 1998 regional council elections, the ruling party SWAPO maintained its dominance,[4] but perhaps more significantly turnout slumped to 40% of registered voters. While turnouts in local and regional elections are usually lower than national elections, the lack of clarity about the role of regional councils and their limited powers was unlikely to convince the majority of voters that this was a tier of government worth supporting.

The activity of 1996 and 1997 produced a raft of legislation in 2000 when a series of bills were passed with the aim of facilitating the decentralisation process, including the Decentralisation Enabling Act (Act 33 of 2000); the Trust Fund for Regional Development and Equity Provisions Act (Act 22 of 2000); and the Regional Councils Amendment Act (Act 30 of 2000). The Decentralisation Enabling Act (Act 33 of 2000) provides for and regulates the delegation and devolution of functions vested in line ministries to regional councils and local authority councils. The Trust Fund for Regional Development and Equity Provisions Act (Act 22 of 2000) sets up a fund to provide regions and local authorities with technical and financial assistance for development projects. The Regional Councils Amendment Act (Act 30 of 2000) gives the regional administrator the status of chief regional officer while paving the way for other new appointments.

The implementation phase

According to former Deputy Minister Tötemeyer (2000b:112), "decentralisation shifts decision-making power, of no matter what degree, to sub-national administration and political units." Decentralisation is often seen as closely connected with democratisation, and this is often how it has been portrayed in Namibia. The concept was articulated by Minister Iyambo (1996–2002) when he introduced the decentralisation policy in parliament in 1997 (MRLGH 1997:1): "Decentralisation therefore provides an opportunity for people to have access to relevant participative decision-making, extending democracy to people as a right based on national ideas and values."

Decentralisation is generally seen as having three stages of development:

1. deconcentration
2. delegation
3. devolution

Under deconcentration, the powers of the central authority are spread to the regions, where agents of the centre remain in control of decentralised functions. In Namibia this happens when ministries decentralise their staff to the regional level, ostensibly to be closer to the people they serve. This may allow greater contact between citizens and government, but does not necessarily entail grassroots participation in decision-making. At its worst, deconcentration has been criticised as a means whereby central government extends its power base without creating greater accountability. Authoritarian govern-

---

4. SWAPO's dominance in regional elections largely followed the trend in national elections. The party had won a two-thirds majority in the 1994 national elections and would go on to increase its number of votes in elections in 1999 and 2004.

ments are unlikely to go beyond the deconcentration stage of decentralisation. Under delegation, the central authority allocates some of its functions to sub-national levels but retains ultimate responsibility. The Decentralisation Implementation Plan (DIP) issued in September 2001 states:

> Delegation means the decentralisation of a function from a line Ministry to enable and em-power Regional Councils or local authorities to perform the function as an agent on behalf of the line Ministry. This means that the Ministry is still accountable for the performance of the decentralised function, including all aspects of budgeting and planning. (Republic of Namibia 2004a:13)

In Namibia's decentralisation policy, the delegation stage is seen as a stepping-stone towards full devolution of powers. With devolution, the central authority gives full responsibility and public accountability for certain functions to the sub-national level. Regional councils and local authorities will have full decision-making, budgeting and planning powers and the line ministries will become the responsible agencies for policy making, setting of standards, monitoring and evaluation, and providers of technical assistance and training. Unlike a federal system in which devolved powers are usually constitutionally enshrined, in Namibia devolved powers can be withdrawn by the central government.

Progress since the year 2000

The laws[5] passed in 2000 prepared the legislative platform for decentralisation. Since then, significant progress has been made on a number of complex administrative is-sues, particularly concerning finance and coordination. In 2004, regional councils were given the funds to expand their staff complements in anticipation of the transfer of central government functions. The process is guided by the DIP, which was revised and updated in 2004. The DIP is overseen by the decentralisation policy implementation committee, which consists of permanent secretaries chaired by the secretary to cabinet. However, by early 2006 no function had yet been decentralised in terms of the Decen-tralisation Enabling Act (Act 33 of 2000). As one senior official in the MRLGH who prefers to stay anonymous commented, "No ministry has decentralised in terms of the legal framework set down. What we have seen is a deconcentration not within the legal framework" (interview with author, April 2005).

The MRLGH's directorate of decentralisation has been working with other minis-tries on the preparation of their Decentralisation Action Plans (DAPs). Cross-ministe-rial task forces have been set up to iron out a series of potential problem areas, including personnel issues, training, financial management, development planning, harmonisa-tion of legislation, and housing and office matters. These task forces are developing a number of guidelines and manuals on issues such as delegation of staff and budgeting. In addition, the MRLGH has set up special bank accounts into which funds for decen-tralised functions will be paid.

---

5. The Decentralisation Enabling Act (Act 33 of 2000); the Trust Fund for Regional Development and Equity Provisions Act (Act 22 of 2000); and the Regional Councils Amendment Act (Act 30 of 2000).

The regional development and equity provision fund has been set up and a board of trustees appointed with the aim of financing equitable development across the 13 regions. Regional tender boards are being set up in all 13 regions to procure goods and services for regional councils. These structures are intended to give regional councils more control over their capital projects and boost local contractors. The status and remuneration of regional councillors and regional council employees has also been improved ahead of the delegation and devolution of central government functions. Regional councillors have been salaried and regarded as full-time politicians since 2001; chief regional officers were appointed at the end of 2003; and the status of regional governors was elevated in 2001. The appointment of chief regional officers and other top officials was not without controversy. Initially, the incumbent chief executive officers in the regions opposed the plans for their posts to be abolished and took the government to court (Maletsky 2003). The matter was settled amicably, but there was also disagreement in Hardap and Omaheke regions over the MRLGH's imposition of successful candidates for top posts against the regional councils' wishes (Maletsky 2004 and Kuteeue 2004). The dispute again underlined central government's desire to keep tight control on the decentralisation process and its lack of trust in regional councils. The staffing structure of regional councils was expanded in 2003–04 to include 13 chief regional executive officers, 13 directors of general services, 26 deputy directors of finance and personnel and six directors of development planning. The increased capacity of regional councils means they are now more likely to be in a position to take on delegated functions, although it is difficult for the directorate of decentralisation to assess their readiness when many ministries have yet to submit DAPs.

Sub-national levels of government in Namibia have been dogged by reports of maladministration and corruption. While poor financial management by local authorities has received most of the media attention, regional councils may only have received less coverage because of their low profile. The last reports by the auditor-general on regional council finances were published in late 2004 but cover only the 1997–98 financial year. In several cases, the financial statements of regional councils for 1997–98 were only finalised in 2002 or 2003 – leaving a worrying (and illegal) four- or five-year time lag. According to the Regional Councils Act (Act 22 of 1992), the accounting officers of regional councils are supposed to submit their reports to the auditor-general within three months of the end of the financial year. The findings of the auditor-general were perhaps more worrying than the delays. Of the latest reports available, the auditor-general declined to express an opinion on the accuracy of accounts from the regional councils in Hardap and Ohangwena regions due to serious accounting errors or omissions (Auditor-General's Office 2004c and 2004d). These included councils making payments without invoices, failing to keep a fixed asset register and a basic lack of income and expenditure records. The auditor-general also gave only qualified opinions of the accounts of the Erongo and Caprivi regional councils, as basic accounting principles were ignored (Auditor-General's Office 2004a and 2004b). The auditor-general pointed out that the Caprivi Regional Council did not keep minutes of its meetings for the whole year under review (Auditor-General's Office 2004b). Unfortunately, the auditor-general's reports for later years are not yet available, making it impossible to say whether the situation has improved or worsened.

Central government transfers to regional councils have increased significantly in recent years, particularly in 2004–05 when the new staffing structures came into effect. Current MRLGH Permanent Secretary Erastus Negonga indicated in early 2005 that financial controls in regional councils had improved after the ministry approved regional council budgets for the first time in 2004. In contrast to the often disparaging comments from the ministry about the performance of regional councils, Negonga went on to say, "the Ministry has expressed its satisfaction in the able manner Chief Regional Officers are managing and controlling their funds since their appointments in December 2003" (MRLGH 2005a).

Impediments in the way

Despite the progress made in the five years since the Decentralisation Enabling Act (Act 33 of 2000) came before parliament, significant impediments remain in the way of decentralisation. One of the main problems, which is referred to in almost all the official literature about decentralisation, is a lack of cooperation from ministries. The Vision 2030 document (Republic of Namibia 2004b:206) is fairly blunt about this:

> Despite line Ministries having been asked by the Secretary of Cabinet way back in 1998 to identify the precise operations to be decentralised, and the staff and resources to accompany delegation, only very few Ministries have prepared themselves for the implementation process.

The slowness of the ministries to respond can be explained by at least two factors: the long-standing scepticism among some ministers and top officials about the decentralisation project and the inevitability that officials find it difficult to draw up arrangements that effectively cede their powers to another agency. Officials are unlikely to be enthusiastic if the lines of command are not clear. For example, in a devolved structure is a chief regional officer accountable to central government (which is not real devolution) or the regional councils (which may not have the expertise to play a supervisory role)?

The MRLGH has no special powers to force ministries to comply with cabinet decisions. Ultimately only cabinet and the president himself can do this. It may be that a more vigorous enforcement of cabinet decisions is required. At the same time, the functions to be decentralised may need prioritisation if the process is to be efficacious.

While some of the capacity issues have been addressed by the expansion of regional council structures, the staffing issue remains a concern. The MRLGH has stated (2005b:66):

> There is insufficient human resources capacity to cope with the multiplicity of tasks that have to be carried out more or less simultaneously. This picture applies to the Ministry of Regional and Local Government and Housing, line ministries across the board as well as Regional Councils.

Despite a recent upsurge in subsidies to regional councils, funding remains a problem area. Ultimately, regional councils are supposed to raise a significant portion of their own income, but for the moment this remains a distant and potentially unpopular prospect. The Pohamba administration's determination to clamp down on wasteful spending, as made clear in the new president's address on Independence Day (Maletsky 2005), will create an extra but necessary pressure on regional councils to create sound financial management systems. The MRLGH has already indicated that it will adopt a 'carrot and stick' approach by releasing funds to councils that are well-managed, but hold back support when there are reports of mismanagement and corruption (MRLGH 2005c). The timeframe for decentralisation sometimes appears non-existent and at other times extremely elastic. Former Deputy Minister Gerhard Tötemeyer comments (2000a:101): "The timeframe for completion of the implementation process varies between the year 2005, as announced by the Minister of RLGH, and 2030 as indicated by the Deputy Minister of RLGH." While 2005 was clearly unrealistic, the deadline of 2030 is too far away to generate a sense of urgency and commitment to the policy.

It is pertinent to mention how government's policies towards traditional authorities have developed in parallel with the stalling of the decentralisation process. Although a council of traditional leaders was envisaged in the constitution, this did not become a reality until enabling legislation was passed in 1997. The council is empowered to advise the president on communal land issues and other matters the president refers to it. Since its inaugural meeting in 1998, the council has played a low-key role, often being preoccupied with disputes between traditional authorities rather than questioning government policy or even its own possible role within the decentralisation process. Traditional leaders have not come into open conflict with regional councillors, possibly because regional councils have so little power at present. The most obvious strategy for a traditional leader with a concern about regional policies would still be to go straight to the executive in Windhoek. There have, however, been disputes between traditional leaders and local authorities concerning the allocation of land for industrial use and other development purposes (reflecting the fact that local authorities wield more power than regional councils).

Political considerations

Much of the case for regional councils is pinned on the claim that they strengthen and deepen Namibia's democracy. Regional councils do, after all, have the only representatives in the country that are directly elected by constituents. However, the power of regional councils has been so circumscribed that to some extent this undermines the potential benefits of a regional councillor's ties to his or her community. The authentic democratic nature of regional councils does not simply depend on the fact that they are elected. Regional councillors must be able to work for improvements and development for their constituencies and regions. With regional councils having primarily planning and advisory roles, it is certainly not easy for regional councillors to be effective on a broader level. Even those regional councillors who are selected for the National Council seem to have little opportunity (or possibly inclination) to advance the case for development in their region on the national political stage.

While regional councillors might be expected to keep close contact with their constituents for reasons of political survival (certainly in areas where there is some contestation between parties), there is also a need for workable structures that promote grassroots participation. So far the successful implementation of regional development coordinating committees, constituency development committees and settlement committees appears to have been patchy.

Of all Namibia's political institutions, regional councils have the potential to be the closest to the country's citizens and their aspirations, but this 'closeness' will not be significant unless regional councils have structures that reach the grassroots and perceptible power to effect improvements for local communities. As such, it would seem the decentralisation of functions and power is necessary, if only to give a greater degree of legitimacy to Namibia's system of regional governance. The obvious alternative would be to abolish regional councils altogether (and it seems that in the first five years of independence this was a consideration) and replace them with regional development bodies that would be accountable to central government and linked to local authorities for administration and consultative purposes. While such bodies do exist in countries such as the United Kingdom, they are often criticised for being undemocratic and unresponsive to grassroots sentiment. If democratisation is a core principle of the decentralisation project, then the system of regional councils is fundamental to the implementation of the policy. As such, as Minister Iyambo said in 1998, there can be no turning back (Inambao 1998).

However, there are still potential threats that could undermine the case for decentralisation to regional councils. While it has been argued that in the long run the decentralisation of functions to sub-national levels will be cost-effective,[6] for the moment the process is a costly one for central government. In the 2004–05 national budget, an amount of N$141.9 m was set aside as a subsidy to the regions, a massive increase on the N$20 m appropriated in 2003–04 (Republic of Namibia 2004c:234). The level of subsidy for regional councils in 2005–6 was N$141.144 m and increased to over N$150 m for the next two financial years (Republic of Namibia 2005a:246 and 2005b:238). With revenue forecasts down and President Hifikepunye Pohamba declaring a war on wasteful spending, it is inevitable that subsidies to regional councils will come under closer scrutiny. If regional councils are found to have poor financial accountability and ineffective service delivery outputs, then the argument for meaningful decentralisation will be weakened.

The second challenge to the existence of regional councils may become a factor only in the longer term. When regional councils were first posited, some opposition politicians felt such a system would give their parties a greater political role and a base from which to challenge SWAPO's dominance. This might also explain why some SWAPO politicians did not want a second chamber of parliament drawn from regional representatives. In fact, SWAPO confounded the pundits and did extraordinarily well in regional council elections in 1992, 1998 and 2004. As a result, SWAPO has also dominated the regional government system and the number of councils controlled by the opposition has dwindled from three in 1992 to none in 2004. The fact that SWAPO dominates both the national and regional levels of government has meant that conflicts between regional councils and central government have been minimal. Regional councils have largely been quiescent in the face of criticism from the MRLGH about their shortcomings.

---

6. While many of the decentralisation policy documents take this as a given, there appears to have been no attempt to work out the exact costs of decentralisation and how savings could be made.

On a political level, regional councils have not mounted serious challenges to central government on policies they feel might be detrimental to their regions. However, if the scenario was different and some regional councils did become power bases for opposition parties or heterodox elements of the ruling party, would ruling party enthusiasm for decentralisation be much reduced? The financial dependence of regional councils on central government inevitably tends to limit the scope for establishing separate positions on policy. But if regional councils start raising significant amounts of their own revenue, as is envisaged in the decentralisation policy, this is likely to bring an end to the 'he who pays the piper calls the tune' mentality. All long-term policies such as decentralisation should stand the test not only of the immediate political environment, but also of fluctuations in political support over time. Otherwise the strata of regional government could simply be done away with at some point in the future by a ruling party that does not like the political complexion of sub-national levels. This kind of issue will have an early examination when it is decided to whom officials handling decentralised functions will be responsible – the chief regional officer operating under the regional council or the line ministry? At the moment, it would seem that potential conflicts between central authority and regional units have not been fully considered, partly because the current pliant nature of regional councils does not throw up such contradictions.

The successful implementation of policies can often be attributed to backing from a charismatic political personality or an influential powerbroker. Does decentralisation have a champion who is prepared to reach out to the unconverted on the issue and push government to keep to the cabinet commitment to the policy? Once again, the Ministry of Regional and Local Government, Housing and Rural Development will have to take a leading role. However, other figures who could act as driving forces for the policy may be lacking. Former Deputy Minister Gerhard Tötemeyer (2000–04), who has been the most articulate spokesman for decentralisation since the early 1990s, has now retired from government. Without some strong backing from cabinet members, it is possible that the decentralisation process could stall. However, the SWAPO manifesto of 2004, which government has adopted as its programme, made clear that the ruling party remains committed to decentralisation (SWAPO Party 2004:12):

> The SWAPO Party and its government are fully committed to developing a number of functions and services from the central government to the lower levels of state authority in order to maximise participation of our communities in planning for development, decision making and the running of government affairs that affect their lives on a daily basis.

Decentralisation has not proven to be an election issue so far, even though some opposition parties want to see decentralisation speeded up. The National Unity Democratic Organisation (Nudo) has been the most outspoken on the issue. Nudo leaders have called for Namibia to become a federal state (Kuteeue 2003), although in its 2004 election manifesto the party did not urge constitutional change, calling instead for decentralisation to be speeded up and regional councils to be given more powers (Nudo 2004:22). After Nudo, the United Democratic Front (UDF) has been the most outspoken party on the issue of decentralisation. In its 2004 manifesto, the UDF called for ministries to be moved out of Windhoek to regional centres and for "full rights and responsibilities" to be devolved to regional councils and local authorities (UDF 2004:4). The DTA also called for the transfer of more powers to regional councils (DTA

2004:3), but the Congress of Democrats (CoD), which became the official opposition in 2005, did not mention decentralisation or regional councils in its 2004 manifesto (CoD 2004). It is pertinent to note that two parties with the most pronounced positions on decentralisation are both ethnic parties – with Nudo widely seen as a party for Hereros and the UDF depending on its Damara support base. The fact that both were partici-pants in ethnic administrations before independence (Nudo through its affiliation to the DTA) tends to undermine the credibility of their stances on decentralisation, as they can easily be accused of wanting to take Namibia back to the 'bad old days' before 1990. With weak opposition political parties unlikely to force the pace on decentralisation, it may well be left to regional councils themselves to make much of the running – in both calling for functions to be decentralised and demonstrating they have the capability to take on new responsibilities.

While much of the administrative groundwork has been completed for decentrali-sation to proceed in terms of the Decentralisation Enabling Act (Act 33 of 2000), the process faces a number of immediate and longer-term challenges. How these are dealt with could determine the ultimate success of the policy.

Conclusions

Decentralisation is at a crossroads. The status of regional councils could be enhanced through the gradual transfer of central government functions, which could in turn improve service delivery and grassroots participation. However, the process could also become stymied with little decentralisation taking place and, as a result, the credibility and the purpose of regional councils being brought into question. Thirdly, functions could be delegated but the process could be undermined if regional councils are not ef-ficient and effective in the way they handle their new tasks. As a result, the devolution stage of decentralisation could be delayed indefinitely.

The following suggestions, while by no means comprehensive, are intended to aid the successful implementation of decentralisation to regional councils.

While a hard and fast timetable for such a complicated policy may be impossible, it would seem advisable to attach some deadlines to the consolidated national DAP so that at least there is a prioritisation of the functions to be delegated.

Regional councils will have to articulate their own case for decentralisation in a much clearer and more forceful way. This will mean raising their media profile and be-ing transparent about their achievements, capabilities and plans for the future.

Regional councils will have to demonstrate their financial accountability if they want the devolution stage of decentralisation to proceed. The decentralisation policy could stumble at the delegation phase if government and public confidence in the coun-cils' ability to take on devolved functions is lacking.

The National Council needs to do more to promote debate about development in the regions. Regional councils should produce annual reports, which could be presented and discussed as part of National Council business. Governors could be brought into National Council sessions to answer questions on regional development.

The structures of regional councils, such as regional development coordinating com-mittees, constituency development committees and village and settlement committees need to be working effectively – so that the democratisation component of decentralisation is reality rather than rhetoric.

As former Minister of RLGH Joel Kaapanda has stated (Barnard 2005), regional councillors should be "proactive" in initiating programmes and projects in their regions. Former Deputy Minister Gerhard Tötemeyer's proposal that Namibia looks at introducing a unicameral system in which elected regional members of parliament sit in the National Assembly alongside those chosen through the party list system should be widely debated. While the idea has been received negatively in some quarters because it would mean the abolition of the National Council, it would bring direct regional representation into the National Assembly, which could act as a spur to development in the regions and aid the decentralisation process.

References

Amupadhi, Tangeni (2002), 'Regional moves spark AG8 fear,' *The Namibian*, 30 September

Association of Regional Councils (1998), *Association of Regional Councils Conference, Mariental 9–12 October 1997*. Windhoek: Association of Regional Councils, Namibia Institute for Democracy, Konrad-Adenauer-Stiftung

Auditor-General's Office (2004), *Report of the Auditor-General on the Accounts of the Regional Council for the Erongo Region for the Financial Year ended 31 March 1998*. Windhoek: Republic of Namibia

— (2004), *Report of the Auditor-General on the Accounts of the Regional Council for the Caprivi Region for the Financial Year ended 31 March 1998*. Windhoek: Republic of Namibia

— (2004), *Report of the Auditor-General on the Accounts of the Regional Council for the Ohangwena Region for the Financial Year ended 31 March 1998*. Windhoek: Republic of Namibia

— (2004), *Report of the Auditor-General on the Accounts of the Regional Council for the Hardap Region for the Financial Year ended 31 March 1998*. Windhoek: Republic of Namibia

Barnard, Maggi (2005), 'Regional Councils "lack vision",' *The Namibian*, 28 January

Boer, Martin (2005, *Taking a Stand: Comparing Namibia's Political Party Platforms*. Windhoek: Namibia Institute for Democracy

Congress of Democrats (CoD) (2004), *CoD's Programme for a Better Namibia*. Windhoek: CoD

DTA of Namibia (2004), *You Deserve Better – Election Manifesto of the DTA of Namibia 2004*. Windhoek: DTA

Dobiey, B. (2000), 'Decentralisation/regionalisation in Namibia and the role of the Association of Regional Councils (ARC),' in *The Constitution at Work: 10 Years of Namibian Nationhood*. Windhoek: University of Namibia

Forrest, Joshua Bernard (1998), *Namibia's Post-Apartheid Regional Institutions: The Founding Year*. Rochester, New York: University of Rochester Press

Godana, Tekaligne and Erwin Naimhwaka (2002), *Decentralisation of Capital Projects*. Windhoek: Namibian Economic Policy Research Unit (Nepru)

Hopwood, Graham (2005), *Regional Councils and Decentralisation: At the Crossroads.* Windhoek: Namibia Institute for Democracy and Konrad Adenauer Foundation

Inambao, Chrispin (1998), 'Decentralisation on track,' *The Namibian,* 6 March

Keulder, Christiaan (1999), *Voting Behaviour in Namibia II: Regional Council Elections 1998.* Windhoek: Swedish International Development Agency, Friedrich-Ebert-Stiftung

— (2001), *Interview on Decentralisation with Dr. Nickey Iyambo, Minister of Regional and Local Government and Housing.* Windhoek: Institute for Public Policy Research (IPPR)

— (2002), *To PR or To Ward? Notes on the Political Consequences of Electoral Systems in Namibia.* Windhoek: Institute for Public Policy Research (IPPR)

Kuteeue, Petros (2003), 'Herero chief wants federal system,' *The Namibian,* 15 August

— (2004), 'Omaheke Council in financial straits,' *The Namibian,* 15 June

Larsen, Anne (2002), *Decentralisation in Namibia: A Case Study of the Erongo Region.* Aalborg: Aalborg University

Maltestky, Christof (2003), 'Regional CEOs throw down gauntlet,' *The Namibian,* 25 July

— (2004), 'Hardap Regional Council caves in to Govt pressure,' *The Namibian,* 2 August

— (2005), 'New Era Dawns,' *The Namibian,* 22 March

Ministry of Regional and Local Government and Housing (2005a), 'Statement by the Permanent Secretary of the Ministry of Regional and Local Government and Housing, Erastus Negonga,' during the Consultative Meeting with all Chief Regional Officers and their staff on 21 January 2005. Windhoek: MRLGH

— (2005b), 'Decentralisation On Course – Bracing Multiple Challenges,' in *15 Years Of Independence.* Windhoek: New Era

— (2005c), 'Address by Honourable Joel Kaapanda at the official opening of the Induction Course for Regional Councillors,' 26 January 2005. Windhoek: MRLGH

Mwilima, Fred (1994), 'Councils: Time for Judgement,' *New Era,* 24–30 March

National Unity Democratic Organisation (Nudo) (2004), *2004 Election Manifesto.* Windhoek: Nudo

New Era (1992), 'Regional Councils: An Afterthought,' *New Era,* 13–19 August

Republic of Namibia (1990a), *Constituent Assembly Debates, 21 November–31 January. Volume 1.* Windhoek: Republic of Namibia

— (1990b), *Constituent Assembly Debates, 1 February–16 March. Volume 2.* Windhoek: Republic of Namibia

— (1991), *Report by the First Delimitation Commission of Namibia on the Determination of Regions, Constituencies and Local Authorities.* Windhoek: Republic of Namibia

— (1992), *Regional Councils Act (Act 22 of 1992).* Windhoek: Office of the Prime Minister

— (1997), *A Decentralisation Policy for the Republic of Namibia – Decentralisation, Development and Democracy.* Windhoek: Ministry of Regional and Local Government and Housing

— (1998), *Decentralisation in Namibia – Situation Analysis.* Windhoek: Ministry of Regional and Local Government and Housing

— (2000), *Regional Councils Amendment Act* (Act 30 of 2000). Windhoek: Office of the Prime Minister

— (2000), *Decentralisation Enabling Act* (Act 33 of 2000). Windhoek: Office of the Prime Minister

— (2000), *Trust Fund for Regional Development and Equity Provisions Act (Act 22 of 2000)*. Windhoek: Office of the Prime Minister

— (2001), *Second National Development Plan (NDP2) 2001/2002–2005/2006*. Windhoek: National Planning Commission

— (2002), *The Constitution of Namibia*. Windhoek: Ministry of Regional and Local Government and Housing, Namibia Institute for Democracy

— (2004a), *The Decentralisation Implementation Plan*. Windhoek: Ministry of Regional and Local Government and Housing

— (2004b), *Namibia Vision 2030, Policy Framework for Long-term National Development*, Main Document. Windhoek: Office of the President

— (2004c), *Estimate of Revenue and Expenditure for the Financial Year 2004/05*. Windhoek: Ministry of Finance

— (2005a), *Estimate of Revenue and Expenditure for the Financial Year 2005/06*. Windhoek: Ministry of Finance

— (2005b), *Medium Term Expenditure Framework for 2005/06–2007/08*. Windhoek: Ministry of Finance

South West Africa People's Organisation (1989), *SWAPO Election Manifesto*. Windhoek: SWAPO Directorate of Elections

SWAPO Party (2004), *SWAPO Party Election Manifesto 2004*. Windhoek: SWAPO Party National Elections Committee

Tötemeyer, Gerhard (2000a), 'Decentralisation for Empowerment of Local Units of Governance and Society – A Critical Analysis of the Namibian Case,' in *Regional Development Dialogue,* Vol. 21, No. 1, Spring 2000. Nagoya: Regional Development Dialogue

— (2000b), 'Democracy and State-building at the Local Level,' in Christiaan Keulder (ed.), *State, Society and Democracy: A Reader in Namibian Politics*. Windhoek: Gamsberg Macmillan, Namibia Institute for Democracy, Konrad-Adenauer-Stiftung

— (2003), *The Politics of Namibia – From Bantustan to the Positioning of Ethnicity in a Unitary State*. Windhoek: Republic of Namibia

United Democratic Front (UDF) (2004), *Manifesting National Movement for Common Sense*. Windhoek: UDF

United Nations Institute for Namibia (1986), Namibia: Perspectives for National Reconstruction and Development. Lusaka: United Nations Institute for Namibia

Wiese, Tania (2003), *Bringing Down The House? Bicameralism in the Namibian Legislature*. Windhoek: Institute for Public Policy Research (IPPR)

Caprivi under old and new indirect rule
Falling off the map or a 19th century dream come true?

Wolfgang Zeller and Bennett Kangumu Kangumu

The Anglo-German agreement of 1890[1] created an unmistakeable feature on the political map of Africa. The literature on the famous access corridor to the Zambezi is full of references to its resemblance to a finger or an arrow pointing towards the interior of Southern Africa.[2] Generations of colonial and postcolonial cartographers and administrators have puzzled over the best solutions to incorporate the territory nowadays known as the Caprivi region of Namibia into their maps and bureaucratic procedures. For decades, adventure-seeking travellers, journalists and academics have assigned to Caprivi the role of the exotic other: a peripheral and inaccessible territory in the heart of Southern Africa.

Since independence in 1990, the role of Caprivi in Namibian public debate as somewhat different from the rest of the country has been consolidated by the news and policy issues associated with the region. Two seemingly contradictory views can be identified in these discourses. On the one hand, Caprivi is perceived as a body politic under attack. The Caprivi secessionist movement is just the most prominent example. Other threats emerge from powerful forces of sometimes biblical proportions: record floods, droughts and forest fires, wildlife and livestock epidemics, locust plagues, Namibia's highest HIV infection rate and lowest Human Development Index (HDI),[3] power outages and a dysfunctional town council in the regional capital. It appears as if Caprivi is not just sticking out, but in danger of falling off the map of Namibia. If central government fails to 'rein in' Caprivi, the success of the Namibian nation-building project as a whole could be in jeopardy.[4]

Competing with this bleak portrayal is a purposeful optimism regarding Caprivi that is discernible in various discourses of the Namibian government and civil society, as well as of foreign donor agencies. If only it is managed right, some argue, this region, with its abundant water, fertile soil, forests, fish and wildlife could be 'Namibia's breadbasket' (cf., *The Namibian* 17/5/2006, *New Era* 5/7/2006, Mendelsohn and Roberts 1997). Richness in natural beauty and culture and the proximity to the Victoria Falls and Chobe Park make Caprivi a top spot for the tourism industry. In May 2004, a

---

1. Widely known as Heligoland-Zanzibar Treaty.
2. One recent high-profile example is an article published on 21/11/1998 in *The Economist*.
3. In 2000, the Caprivi region had the lowest HDI among Namibia's 13 regions (UNDP 2000). A recent study states that "Caprivi is the poorest region in the country with a Human Poverty Index (HPI) of 36 per cent compared to an overall HPI average of 24.7 per cent for Namibia" (National Planning Commission 2006).
4. See *The Namibian* 21/7/2006 and *New Era* 5/7/2006 for two recent reports reiterating most of these points.

new bridge across the Zambezi closed the last gap in a 2,500 kilometre-long tarmac band stretching from the Copper Belt of Zambia and DRC to the deep-sea port of Walvis Bay. With its recently upgraded container shipping, dock and dry port facilities, Walvis Bay is one of the top gateways for trade between Southern Africa, Europe and the Americas (Namibian Port Authority 2007). Through this and other infrastructure developments in the region, Caprivi and its neighbour, the Sesheke district in Zambia's Western Province, have emerged from relative obscurity. The inaccessible hinterland is no longer a freak of history with unrealised potential. Caprivi is now on the map of global marketplaces and economic opportunities.

In this chapter, we neither reconcile these opposing views of Caprivi nor predict which of them will prevail. Our aim is rather to demonstrate that both have striking similarities, and in two ways that are regularly overlooked. First, we find historical continuities in the actions precolonial, colonial and postcolonial administrators have taken in Caprivi. These actions, we argue, were always grounded in a perception of the territory as both a place of danger as well as of opportunities. Second, we argue that the measures taken by powerful external actors in Caprivi have to this day always been aimed primarily at satisfying external interests in the region, with little to no concern for the priorities of the area's population. To expose both continuities, we shift the analytical focus. Instead of lamenting or disputing how separate Caprivi is from the rest of Namibia, we examine the processes of its incorporation into the changing power structures that have sought to rule the area, both historically and in the present. We argue that this enables us to gain insight into past and present processes of political and economic marginalisation within Caprivi. In this sense, the case of Caprivi is anything but peripheral or exceptional. In the same way as margins constitute the centre (compare Das and Poole 2004), Caprivi's past and present reveal the fissures that are at the very heart of Namibia's colonial and postcolonial society as a whole. Conversely, the case of Caprivi also illustrates how colonial subjects and postcolonial citizens have worked with, around and against the imposition of external control over their lives and resources.

Our chapter will be divided into five parts, each of which addresses one major phase of the exercise of external rule in Caprivi. We begin with a short account of the 19th century Lozi kingdom's use of the area to fend off neighbouring enemies and gain access to tribute, labour and natural resources. We then briefly sketch out the time of German administration following the area's partitioning from the Lozi kingdom in 1890 by the European colonial powers. The German efforts to police and administer the perceived hideout for white outlaws with a minimal budget and methods of indirect rule will be contrasted with their futile hopes of incorporating Caprivi into ambitious colonial projects. From the German loss of the territory in the First World War, we fast-forward to the South African apartheid regime's development of Caprivi from the mid-1960s onwards. We show how changing priorities turned the emerging bantustan project into a military launch pad for South Africa's cross-border incursions into Zambia and Angola against SWAPO's guerrilla fighters. In the final sections, we highlight some of the key developments in Caprivi since Namibian independence. The secessionist movement will be described in relation to processes of economic and political marginalisation and the SWAPO state's politics of recognition of Caprivi chiefs. We finally contextualise the current economic boom in the region's new strategic relevance for transnational investors in the global race for Africa's mineral resources.

On the verge of Bulozi[5]

Most historiography on south-central Africa treats the area nowadays known as Namibia's Caprivi region as an insignificant appendage of the Lozi kingdom and instead focuses on the processes of state and elite formation at the centres of Lozi power (e.g., Mainga 1973; Caplan 1970; Gluckman 1959).[6] This approach neglects a marginal yet vital aspect of Lozi state formation, the resistance of some of the kingdom's subject peoples against the centre. From the opposite perspective, the rule of the Lozi overlords is but one, albeit significant, aspect of Caprivi's history prior to European colonisation. Located on the fringes of Bulozi's waxing and waning sphere of power, Caprivi was for a long time mainly a source of human and natural resources (Flint 2003:401). It was loosely controlled through raids and shifting alliances with more or less loyal local leaders. In times of internal turmoil at the centres of Lozi power, this set-up had the tendency to quickly turn against its makers. The most prominent example is the Kololo invasion and subsequent transformation of the Lozi kingdom from c.1840 to 1864. This was an offshoot of the Mfecane crisis that rippled through Southern Africa in the first half of the 19th century.[7] The invaders from the south were quickly able to establish a stronghold on Bulozi's southern fringes. The area's population had mixed loyalties to the Lozi overlords, a decisive factor in the Kololo's conquest of their kingdom (Flint 2004:70f.). After the Kololo's demise, a crucial aspect of Lozi King Lewanika's centralised project of Lozi state formation was therefore to strengthen and control the southernmost frontier of Bulozi (Flint 2003:402, 406). In appointing Simataa Mamili as chief of Linyanti, Lewanika placed a trusted old ally over the former Kololo stronghold in Caprivi. Mamili's task was to keep the Tawana and other possible intruders from the southwest in check. Lewanika's son Litia was posted at Sesheke.[8] His key role was the control of the southeastern frontier of Bulozi, from which direction the Matebele and Tonga posed a threat (Mainga 1973:123, 133–5,154; Flint 2004:114, 256).

From the late 1880s onwards, southern Bulozi gained new importance for the kingdom's centre as a gateway for trade. More and more European frontiersmen and missionaries found their way to the upper Zambezi (Flint 2003:410). Lewanika, however,

---

5. 'Bulozi' refers to the historical and present area of settlement of the majority of the Lozi people, situated in the upper Zambezi floodplain and its hinterland.

6. Trollope refers to the Subiya and Fwe as "... vassals and hangers-on of other tribes" (Trollope 1937:19).

7. The Kololo presence impacted heavily on both the Lozi and their various subject groups in Caprivi. As elsewhere in Southern Africa, the Mfecane crisis and migration played an important role in establishing the framework of political and cultural life in a number of modern African states (Omer-Cooper 1966). The Mfecane was characterised by warfare, population flight, social dislocation and conquest resulting in more densely constructed political units with greater levels of cohesion and organisation becoming established throughout the region (du Toit 1995).

8. Not to be confused with the current Sesheke across the Zambezi from Katima Mulilo, this place is nowadays known as Old Sesheke or, more commonly, as Mwandi, the town across from Schuckmannsburg.

regarded the increasing German and Portuguese presence in the region as potential threats. He sought to offset this danger by entering into alliances with the British, following the advice of resident missionary Francois Coillard. Through the 1890 Lochner concession and other contracts, Lewanika gradually traded the kingdom's sovereignty for political-military and material protection by the British (Mainga 1973:171). Exactly four days after Lewanika had signed the Lochner concession, and without his approval or knowledge, the Heligoland-Zanzibar treaty sealed the Lozi kingdom's loss of Caprivi. This had no tangible effect on the ground until 1909, when the German administration finally arrived at the Zambezi. As late as the 1950s, decades after the separation of Caprivi from Bulozi-proper, Lozi royalty continued to enjoy special concessions allowing them to use Caprivi's abundant natural resources for hunting, fishing and securing construction materials.[9]

From 1909, existing and new elites in Caprivi were able to dissociate themselves from the Lozi and consolidate their new status under German protection. For them and their subject population, the new situation was an opportunity to break free from domination of the Lozi overlords, albeit in exchange for new ones.

Outlaw frontier and access corridor: The Caprivizipfel under German administration

Bulozi's southern fringes were largely a *terra incognita* to the Germans when they acquired their access corridor to the Zambezi in 1890. Germany, nevertheless, had large-scale strategic interests in the territory. The corridor represented the last chance to negotiate a direct land connection from the existing protectorate of German Southwest Africa to the interior of Southern Africa. The country's colonial lobby hoped that through a rail link or shipping route via the Zambezi, the German territories in Southwest and East Africa could eventually be connected.[10] German Southwest also needed water and labour resources, and both seemed available in great abundance via the corridor.

Reality soon grounded this high-flying colonial utopia. Reaching the Zambezi from the established German outposts proved much more difficult than expected. For the time being, the corridor was left with neither a colonial administration nor a single official name. Instead, a colourful lot of rambling outlaws, frontier businessmen and prospectors found their way into the area. They engaged in a flourishing business involving organised poaching, and trade in animal hides and ivory, weapons and household hardware, beads and alcohol. Wildlife in the corridor was decimated rapidly (*Deutsches Kolonialblatt* 1908:1152). In the colony and the Reich, the value of the unproductive backwater on the Zambezi was openly questioned (*Allgemeine Zeitung* 1907–08). A scapegoat was found in Count Leo von Caprivi, the German chancellor (1890–94), whose signature appears on the Heligoland-Zanzibar treaty. Already in 1890, the treaty had met with great opposition from the hawks of German foreign policy, who denounced

---

9. The relevant administrative arrangement became known as the 'Barotse privilege' (Hangula 1993:71; Fisch 1996:150).

10. Sandner and Rössler have argued that, as with the other major colonial powers of the era, "geography provided a continuous and deep-seated language for German imperialism" (Sandner and Rössler 1994:115).

Caprivi as being too lenient with his British counterparts. Caprivi was an outspoken sceptic about Germany's colonial ambitions and had fallen out of favour with Kaiser Wilhelm II by the time he resigned in 1894. The count withdrew from the public eye and died five years later. In the following years, parts of the German public regarded the Zambezi corridor as synonymous with Caprivi's legacy of allegedly poor statesmanship. The name *Caprivi Zipfel* (alternatively *Caprivizipfel* or *Caprivi-Zipfel*) was never officially proclaimed with the purpose of honouring Count von Caprivi (compare Seiner 1909b:417). Rather, it was a form of popular mockery arising from the circumstances of Germany's gaining access to the area and emerged during the early years of the 20th century. The name appeared in newspapers, maps and colonial literature around 1900, first in quotation marks. More official sounding names were in use at the time, but none of them became the norm (e.g., *Hukwefeld, Deutsch Bechuanaland, Deutsches Barotseland, Deutsche Sambesiregion*). In 1909, several publications by Seiner (Seiner 1909a, 1909b, 1909c) established the name *Caprivizipfel*. From then on it came into full official use in maps, documents and other publications (e.g., Streitwolf 1911). The undertone of ridicule borne by the original name was lost in the later translations of the word *Zipfel*[11] into the English *strip*[12] and Afrikaans *strook*.

From 1905 the aggressive military and political expansionism of Kaiser Wilhelm II led to a more vigorous exploration of the potential of Reich's overseas territories for raw material production and trade (Sandner and Rössler 1994:118). German interest in the access corridor to the Zambezi was rekindled and more reliable scientific data was in high demand.[13] By 1908, several events added urgency to this endeavour: after the genocidal war against the Herero and Nama, German settlement surged in Southwest Africa. The colony urgently needed to increase its indigenous labour force. There was public speculation about possible coal, diamond and copper deposits in the Caprivizipfel (*Allgemeine Zeitung* 1908–09; *Deutsches Kolonialblatt* 1907:25, 73; Fisch 1996:16). During the same period, the British high commissioner in South Africa repeatedly demanded that the German authorities establish police control and enforce hunting restrictions in Caprivi (Fisch 1996:52). A British offer to swap the corridor for a piece of the Kalahari was rejected by the Germans. Instead, they sent Hauptmann Kurt Streitwolf with 17 troops on a mission to establish the German presence on the Zambezi. After an arduous three-month journey, the German flag was hoisted at Schuckmannsburg in February 1909. Besides policing, Streitwolf was tasked with setting up a functioning administration and exploring the territory's geography and economic potential, in particular, mineral and labour resources (Streitwolf 1911). Streitwolf was strongly influenced by the British concept of indirect rule and was restrained by a tight budget and difficult transport access. To administer Caprivi, he identified what he regarded as two sufficiently coherent cultural-linguistic native groups, the Fwe and the Subiya. He then oversaw the installation of two paramount chiefs with equal status under the German resident. His ef-

---

11. *Zipfel = appendix, end*, as in *Wurstzipfel*, the titbit end of a sausage. In colloquial German, *Zipfel* can also refer to a (usually small or young boy's) penis.

12. The English name 'Caprivi Strip' is based on the original wording of the English version of the Anglo-German agreement of 1 July 1890, Article III. 2: "a strip of territory". The German version used the term "Landstreifen".

13. This was the rationale for Seiner's expedition to the Okavango and Zambezi in 1905–06 (Seiner 1909a; Fisch 1996:16).

forts were initially hampered by widespread fear of the Germans. These subsided when Streitwolf used careful negotiation and benign measures in dealing with the population. Streitwolf also claimed progress in policing Caprivi and expelling illegal white settlers. He reported no traces of minerals for commercial exploitation, a dangerous climate for European settlement, but good farmland, wildlife and forest resources and the Zipfel's potential as a labour reserve. Difficult transport access remained the decisive constraint in realising this potential, however (Streitwolf 1911:229–34).

The Caprivi Zipfel had returned to relative obscurity even before the brief German regime came to a sudden end. On 21 September 1914, the German resident at Schuckmannsburg surrendered without fight to British forces and the access corridor became the first German loss of territory in the First World War (Fisch 1996:147). The German period, nevertheless, represents an important legacy for Caprivi and its inhabitants: it was the beginning of a new phase of external domination that was to continue and to radically intensify half a century later.

A military launch pad: The Caprivi bantustan under apartheid rule

Between 1914 and 1939, the administration of the Caprivi Strip changed repeatedly between various governments of the surrounding British colonies. This bears testimony to both the low priority and the continuing difficulties of access to the territory during that time. In 1939, administration of the eastern Caprivi Strip was once again transferred, this time to Pretoria. The strategic location of the strip in the heart of southern Africa was central to Pretoria's interests at the outbreak of the Second World War (Kangumu 2000). In 1940, a special company of the Native Military Corps was formed in the Strip as a strategic backup for the protection of the Victoria Falls Bridge. From 1940, the South African Defence Force (SADF) used the first air strip at Katima Mulilo for military and air training exercises. Plans existed to build a tropical military school in Caprivi in the 1950s.

South Africa's administration perceived the Caprivi Strip as unsuitable for white settlement and reserved its natural resources for the exclusive use of its inhabitants. Due to Caprivi's low commercial potential, government's priority was to avoid heavy administrative expenditure and encourage labour migration. Local government therefore was based on the continuity of Streitwolf's model: indirect rule through the Few and Subiya chieftaincies under the supervision of one white government officer. Virtually no government-induced development took place during this first period of South Africa's direct administration from 1939 to 1964. The provision of education and health services was left in the hands of missionaries, first the Seventh Day Adventists and then the Catholic Holy Family Mission. Learners and patients from both sides of the Zambezi were allowed to cross the border routinely and visit schools and hospitals or attend to other matters of daily life. Thus the people of Caprivi kept very close contact with their kin in Northern Rhodesia/Nyasaland. Labour migration further strengthened and expanded these ties geographically. A fair number of young men went periodically to

Livingstone, the Line of Rail and the Copper Belt in Northern Rhodesia or the Rand mines in the Union.[14]

The year 1964 was a turning point in the history of Caprivi. The Odendaal Commission recommended a roadmap for a self-governing homeland and the South African administration began to implement large-scale plans for direct government-driven development in the Strip. Educated Caprivi residents were sent to South Africa to be trained as teachers, veterinarians, nurses, agricultural extension workers, policemen or soldiers. The Katima Mulilo hospital was expanded and recognised as a training facility. Ngweze was developed as a residential area for blacks near Katima Mulilo, which itself was developed into an administrative and housing centre for whites. In the rural areas, government built up health services, road infrastructure, fire and wildlife management, animal husbandry, boreholes and irrigation. In 1972 Eastern Caprivi was finally inaugurated as a South African bantustan with a legislative council. Eventually, a Caprivi 'government' was formed in 1976, complete with regulations for Caprivi citizenship and symbols of state: a flag, an anthem and a constitution. The legislative council consisted of the Fwe and Subiya chiefs and their councillors, who received salaries.

The seemingly benign character of the early phase of strong government-driven development in Caprivi was accompanied by political and military concerns that gradually moved centre-stage. Already in 1963, the Caprivi African National Union (CANU) had been formed with the purpose of achieving a black self-government for the Caprivi Strip. CANU's first president, Brendan Simbwaye, was arrested in 1964 and subsequently disappeared in the hands of the South Africans (Flint 2004:174). Another leading member of CANU and a prominent member of the Fwe royal family,[15] Mishake Muyongo, and other CANU activists escaped arrest and fled to newly independent Zambia. In November 1964, they met leading members of SWAPO in Lusaka. Muyongo agreed to a SWAPO-CANU merger, but maintains that SWAPO President Sam Nujoma made a promise that Caprivi would be granted either special political status or complete autonomy after Namibia's independence (United Democratic Party 2005; Flint 2004:188). SWAPO disputes this claim today, but the issue played a vital role in the emergence of the secessionist movement in the late 1990s.

SWAPO's military wing, the People's Liberation Army of Namibia (PLAN), employed hit and run tactics such as ambushes, laying landmines and general sabotage of military installations and infrastructure in Caprivi from the late 1960s onwards. South Africa responded with a heavy military build-up in the region. Major army bases were constructed in Caprivi, including the Mpacha military air field outside Katima Mulilo and the Omega III base in Western Caprivi. The Caprivi Strip played an important role in South Africa's destabilisation policy in the sub-region. Training of specialised secret military units took place in the area, cross-border operations into Zambia and bombing raids into Angola were launched. The military build-up further fuelled ongoing service- and infrastructure development.

---

14. By 1962, the number of migrant labourers to the Rand mines had increased to an average of 30 per month (Kruger 1984:10).

15. Muyongo is a direct descendant of Fwe chief Simataa Mamili, who had been appointed by Lewanika and was recognised by Streitwolf as the first Fwe chief in Caprivi in 1909 (Fisch 1999:42).

The shift of SWAPO's headquarters from Lusaka to Luanda in the mid-1970s diminished the role of Muyongo and others from Caprivi within the liberation movement, which became increasingly intolerant of internal dissent. Muyongo left SWAPO in 1980 when its hard core accused him of trying to revive CANU (Hopwood 2004:198). Other former CANU activists within the liberation movement were allegedly expelled from SWAPO, detained, interrogated or disappeared in unclear circumstances (compare Fosse 1997:441).

Caprivi's new outlaws in the first decade of Namibian independence

The extent to which Caprivi's economy had been dominated by the apartheid military's massive presence became apparent when the SADF withdrew its troops in the run-up to Namibian independence in 1990. The deployment of new Namibian Defence Forces troops was a buffer for only a fraction a fraction of these changes and a significant share of employment and income opportunities in the region was lost.[16] The trend was compounded by the return of hundreds of exiles with Caprivi background from Zambia and other countries in the early 1990s. This development stood in stark contrast to the promises of economic well-being with which the long-awaited independence transition had become associated, not least due to the official SWAPO rhetoric of the time. Fwe residents of Caprivi argued that the distribution of government employment (especially in the educational sector) and other benefits unfairly favoured the Subiya population and other supporters of the ruling party (Fosse 1996:165). Oshivambo-speakers were enviously watched as they took up jobs (especially in the state security services) and established ethnically segregated neighbourhoods around Katima Mulilo. Allegations of a perceived 'Owambo invasion' circulated among the regional population and added to the frustrated expectations and competition for scarce opportunities. Long-standing rifts between 'traditional' and political party leaders and their supporters in Caprivi became more pronounced and soon broke out into more or less open forms of violence (Fosse 1996:165–8; Flint 2004:244, 66).

One issue of hot contestation that emerged soon after independence was the recognition of chiefs in Caprivi. Streitwolf's indirect rule arrangements and his dual Fwe and Subiya chieftaincy had essentially functioned since 1909 through the various phases of German, British and South African administration. In the case of the Subiya, a rather coherent identity and internal hierarchy had been constructed and continues to exist to the present day. The Fwe chieftaincy was less homogenous from the start. Several groups with more or less clearly pronounced ideas of a separate identity traced their existence back to the times before 1909 (compare Streitwolf 1911:126). The Yeyi are one of these groups. Early attempts by Yeyi chiefs to dissociate themselves more strongly from the Fwe emerged in the late 1950s, but the South African authorities were not supportive of this endeavour. In the 1972 Caprivi constitution, the Yeyi were not officially recognised as distinct from the Fwe and their name was dropped from the previous official title *Mafwe-Mayeyi*. Yeyi complaints over insufficient autonomy under the Fwe grew into

---

16. For the effects of the exodus of SADF from West Caprivi on the Khwe, see Taylor (forthcoming 2008).

open demands for dissociation around the time of independence. In August 1992, a Yeyi faction elected its own chief. This move led to a number of violent confrontations between Fwe and Yeyi supporters and took on a party-political dimension. The Fwe under their chief, Bwima Mamili, had been supporters of the Democratic Turnhalle Alliance (DTA) party since before independence. The political career of Mamili's cousin, Mishake Muyongo, did not end when he fell out with SWAPO during his time in exile. He instead became a leading member of DTA. The new Yeyi leadership openly associated with SWAPO, however. When the Namibian government officially recognised the Yeyi chieftaincy in December 1995, Chief Mamili accused SWAPO of political motivations in breaching the law.[17] At least two other controversies over SWAPO's politics of recognising chiefs in Caprivi have since emerged. One was the attempted establishment of a chieftaincy by the Khwe San in Western Caprivi, which the SWAPO government has so far rejected.[18] The other is the emergence of a new chieftaincy which claims to represent the 'true Mafwe' (*The Namibian* 5/8/2004 and 9/8/ 2004).

For the Fwe leadership, the Yeyi defection opened a new front in a long-standing rivalry with the Subiya that had already surfaced during the apartheid era. For several decades, members of the Fwe and Subiya elites unsuccessfully tried to claim superiority over each other in Caprivi (Fosse 1996). Significant in this context is the strong support for SWAPO since independence among the Subiya leadership and their followers. By the mid-1990s, the previous majority vote in Caprivi in favour of DTA was swinging towards SWAPO. Muyongo regarded SWAPO's post-independence politics in Caprivi as the continuation of the perceived Owambo dominance that he had allegedly experienced during his time in exile (Fisch 1999:20). During the 1990s, a group of educated and politically active Caprivi men formed around the veteran politician. As SWAPO's electorate and influence over traditional leaders in the region increased, Muyongo and his associates saw their room for political action in Caprivi shrinking. They questioned the inclusion of Caprivi in the Namibian state formation project and instead identified with an alternative idea of statehood, which drew ideological strength from two sources. One was Caprivi's cultural and historical distinctness from Namibia based on the area's inclusion in the precolonial Lozi kingdom. Speculation that the Caprivi secessionists cooperated with like-minded Lozi nationalists in Zambia and/or UNITA in Angola have so far not been substantiated. Muyongo's own statements never indicated a wish for Caprivi to become part of a resurrected Lozi kingdom (see also Flint 2003:427). The Lozi heritage, however, provided a powerful background in terms of which secessionists could label alleged 'Owambo invaders' as 'foreigners.' The other source included a more explicitly territorial claim. The secessionists imagined a self-governing state of Caprivi that would exist as the continuation of the bantustan declared in 1972 yet fully independent from any external control. To what extent this vision was fully formed in the minds of the Caprivi secessionists is difficult to ascertain. It is, however, clear that

---

17. Referring to the Traditional Authorities Act of 1995.
18. The Khwe argue that SWAPO is politically biased in this issue, due to the services provided by many Khwe to the South African military during the armed struggle for Namibian independence and their alleged support of the CLA. Khwe demands for an official recognition of their traditional authority have also been consistently undermined by the leadership of the Mbukushu, whose controversial chief Erwin Mbambo displays great loyalty to SWAPO (Taylor forthcoming 2008).

several of the leading members of the movement had been educated within the South African programmes that aimed at increasing black self-administration of the Caprivi bantustan (compare Melber, forthcoming 2008). For several years, they were groomed for careers in the apartheid regime's imposed state-formation project, which eventually failed. These personal histories appear to have provided fertile ground for the secessionists' ideas to take root at a time when the Namibian state formation project had not yielded the results they desired. During the high treason trials, this became evident in the refusal by some defendants to accept the jurisdiction of Namibian courts on the grounds that they were "Caprivians and not Namibians" (*The Namibian* 2/2/2005 and 14/6/2007).

By 1998, the secessionists' ideas had ripened and led to organised action. Namibian security forces discovered a training camp of the newly-formed Caprivi Liberation Army (CLA) in the Mudumu Game Park near the Botswana border. The largely Oshivambo-speaking security force members used heavy-handed methods on the civilian population of the greater area in their search for suspected members and sympathisers of the CLA and its political base. Allegedly escaping torture, rape and intimidation, some 2,500 people, mostly Fwe and Khwe, subsequently fled to Botswana where they found shelter in the Dukwe refugee camp. Fwe Chief Bwima Mamili and Khwe Chief Kipi George, as well as Mishake Muyongo and Caprivi Governor John Mabuku, were among them. Mamili and Muyongo were soon transferred to Denmark as political refugees under UNHCR protection, while several hundred others were voluntarily repatriated to Namibia in the following months. A majority remained in Botswana, however, and a hard core of CLA members managed to regroup on Angolan and Zambian territory. On 2 August 1999 they launched poorly coordinated attacks on government installations around Katima Mulilo. These were quickly beaten back by the Namibian army and police but resulted in 15 casualties. During the ensuing state of emergency, Namibian security forces again reportedly used unlawful methods to interrogate suspects and the wider civilian population in Caprivi, this time in some of the SWAPO-voting areas as well.

The SWAPO government's proclaimed project of nation building through peace and reconciliation had been stained by the events surrounding the secessionist attacks. Soon the northeast of the country again became a site of organised violence. In late 1999, the Namibian government officially granted Angolan government forces permission to launch a massive military operation from Namibian soil against the rebel UNITA[19] movement and its legendary leader Jonas Savimbi. In the following months, scattered groups of armed UNITA fighters sporadically crossed the border into Namibia's Kavango region and Western Caprivi, robbing and killing borderland villagers and motorists travelling the Trans Caprivi Highway. For weeks, the Caprivi region was inaccessible by road, except in the relative safety of military convoys. Caprivi's tourism industry and various other businesses and development projects came to a standstill. The Namibian army and Special Field Force targeted suspected illegal immigrants from Angola living on the Namibian side of the border. Dozens of persons were arrested and interrogated. Some were reportedly tortured and killed during these operations (Amnesty International 2001).

---

19. União Nacional para a Independência Total de Angola

Caprivi in the 21st century: A 19th century dream come true?

After Savimbi's death in 2002 and the peace agreement in Angola, the cross-border raids and Namibian counter-operations ended. The stains on the Namibian security forces' human rights record remained. The SWAPO government, however, has since been able to make headlines with its benign, rather than coercive, interventions in Caprivi. Most prominently, the Namibian authorities successfully conducted major relief operations during the 2003, 2004 and 2007 Zambezi floods. In all cases, thousands of people were evacuated and provisioned for up to several months by the Namibian government in co-operation with the Red Cross. The Caprivi region appears to have calmed down politically in recent years. Replacing his predecessor, who remains in exile, George Simasiku Mamili took over the Fwe chieftaincy in 1999. He is politically closer to SWAPO and his appointment was ratified after only three months by the Namibian government authorities. In the 2004 regional council elections, SWAPO candidates won in all six Caprivi constituencies. The secessionist agenda of a separate state of Caprivi occasionally resurfaces on the internet[20] and in the Namibian press,[21] but the radical core of the movement appears to be a spent force whose leadership is either dead, in exile or on trial in drawn-out court cases bogged down by endless technicalities. Meanwhile, Caprivi is making very different headlines.

On the heels of peace, an economic boom has come to Angola, northern Namibia and southwestern Zambia. It manifests itself in new large-scale infrastructure developments, a flourishing cross-border trade and border towns flush with new investments and opportunities.[22] Between Katima Mulilo and its Zambian neighbour Sesheke a new bridge now arches across the Zambezi. The state-of-the-art concrete structure leads to a freshly rebuilt asphalt road from Sesheke to Livingstone. The bridge and road were designed and built by German engineers and construction companies and largely financed by the German KfW Bankengruppe[23] as part of a bilateral development project with Zambia (JBG Gauff Ingenieure 2004:5). At the official opening ceremony on 13 May 2004, Germany's ambassador to Zambia, Erich Kristof, stressed the role of infrastructure development as the basis for bringing "progress", "private sector growth"

---

20. The re-formed United Democratic Party (UDP) under its president, secessionist leader-in-exile Mishake Muyongo, maintains a website, which claims to be an official mouthpiece for the cause of Caprivi secessionism. In 2003, a now-defunct website of a 'Caprivi Government-in-Exile' appeared on the internet. Behind its detailed constitution and policy declarations was apparently a one-man-show run by Edward Ndopu, a former journalist-turned 'President General' of what he claimed was a resurrected CANU party (cf., also *The Namibian* 9/4/2003).

21. Examples are a pro-secessionist opinion piece published in *Caprivi Vision* 1/9/2005, the controversy over the revival of the United Democratic Party (UDP) (*The Namibian* 28/7/2006 and 8/9/2006, *Allgemeine Zeitung* 4/9/2006, *New Era* 4/9/2006 and 5/9/2006), the surfacing of a document that Caprivi separatists claim proves that the 1964 CANU-SWAPO merger was agreed on the condition that Caprivi would become an independent state separate from Namibia (*The Namibian* 24/1/2007), and the repeated public claims by accused and acquitted high treason suspects that Caprivi is historically "not part of Namibia" (*The Namibian* 2/2/2005, 17/1, 17/4 and 14/6/2007).

22. Oshikango and Rundu are experiencing developments similar to Katima Mulilo's.

23. KfW stands for Kreditanstalt für Wiederaufbau. The *Reconstruction Credit Institute* was formed after the Second World War as part of the Marshall Plan and is under the shared ownership of the German federal (Bund) and state (Länder) governments.

and "sustainable development" to the rural poor. The ambassador then pointed out the significance of the bridge as the missing link in a new transport route connecting the Copper Belt of Zambia and Congo (DRC) to the Namibian deep-sea port at Walvis Bay (Kristof 13/5/2004), the so-called Trans Caprivi Corridor (TCC).

Largely due to China's vigorously growing demand, the world market price for copper has been steadily rising in recent years.[24] Zambia's privatised copper mines are back to their former record production levels of the 1970s (*Namibia Economist* 30/7/2004; *The Post* 27/12/2006). How to transport the copper from the landlocked deposit sites to the overseas consumers is therefore a vital question around which the interests of a broad range of parties converge. From the point of view of Western industrialised nations, the port of Walvis Bay has a significant advantage compared to Dar es Salaam and Durban, so far the main exit ports for the mining output from the Copper Belt (*Namibia Economist* 2/5/2003). The Namibian port is five to seven shipping days closer to Europe and America. Copper was not the only consideration when the TCC was designed in the early 1990s.[25] The Zambian capital Lusaka is a major consumer market and site for manufacturing. Livingstone is the Zambian tourist Mecca. Tsumeb in central-northern Namibia is the location of the country's largest copper mine and a major copper smelting plant. Walvis Bay has salt refineries, fish factories and a shipping industry. Altogether, these towns dot the corridor like pearls waiting for a string. Work on the Namibian section of that string began after independence and was completed by 2004 with various upgrades of the Walvis Bay port and Namibia's road infrastructure. The financiers of these projects are largely the EU and some of its individual member states, in particular Germany (German Embassy Lusaka 2004; *Namibia Economist* 12/12/2004 and 13/2/2004).

Why Germany? As Ambassador Kristof stated, regional integration and rural development are declared goals of Germany's development policy, and infrastructure development is one way the country's government expects to achieve them. Germany's diplomatic relations with Namibia are built on the premise that the former colony is entitled to development assistance from the former motherland and the fact that even now a German-speaking minority of approximately 13,000 lives in Namibia, many of them maintaining close personal and economic ties with Germany. German companies[26] benefit from the corridor development directly through building contracts[27] and indirectly through improved access to markets and products in and from the corridor's

---

24. On 7 April 2006 the *Financial Times* reported that the price of copper had hit an unprecedented $6,000 a tonne, double the average price in 2004. The International Herald Tribune attributes this price hike largely to the rapidly growing demand from China, which in 2003 passed the United States as the world's top consumer of copper.

25. Other commodities which the Walvis Bay Corridor Group lists for present and future import into and export from Zambia are: Namibian fish, salt and cold drinks; European and American fertiliser, agricultural and mining equipment; Zambian timber products, fruit and vegetables, coffee and tobacco (Walvis Bay Corridor Group 2004).

26. Examples are the German engineering company JBG Gauff Ingenieure, which designed the Zambezi bridge, and Concor (until February 2005, 44.99% owned by the German-based construction multinational Hochtief), which built the bridge, Livingstone-Sesheke road and several other sections of the corridor road.

27. This has been a cornerstone of German development policy since its inception after the Second World War.

catchment area.[28] Germany had already assisted Namibia in the upgrading of the 400 kilometre Trans-Caprivi Highway, another major section of the TCC. By financing the bridge at Katima Mulilo and the Livingstone-Sesheke road, the German government completed what it had started.

A steady stream of trucks has been rolling across the new bridge since May 2004 and Katima Mulilo is changing fast.[29] Namibian, South African, Chinese and Malaysian investors have constructed new supermarkets, hardware stores, warehouses and petrol stations with long-distance truck facilities. The Namibian government and private investors are developing a prominent section of Katima's Zambezi river shore into a waterfront park with shopping and tourism facilities. Sesheke is undergoing similar changes, and on both sides of the Zambezi investors are currently developing or exploring opportunities in commercial agriculture and the tourism and timber industries (*New Era* 27/7/2006, Barotse Development Trust 2006). But the combination of fast economic development and new opportunities for long-distance mobility for the regional population also attracts growing numbers of small-scale entrepreneurs, smugglers, sex workers and illegal migrant labour, which state authorities regard as potentially dangerous. Katima Mulilo has experienced a steady and rapid increase in its population in recent years. Already in 2002 the mayor admitted openly that the growth of new squatter areas outpaced the formalisation of old ones (Mudabeti 5/9/2002). Infrastructure for communications, electricity, water supply and some government services have been expanded around Katima Mulilo and in the vast rural areas of Caprivi. These changes have, however, been concentrated in Caprivi's regional centre, where they remain less than sufficient. The Katima Mulilo town council is evidently not capable of keeping pace with the rapid change. It is weighed down by scandals, internal feuds and limited management skills. The administration can hardly collect the revenue necessary to pay its employees and the various parastatal service providers. This has resulted in prolonged shut-downs of water and electricity supplies for the entire town, including major institutions such as the Katima hospital (*The Namibian* 16/10/2000, 23/7/2003). On several occasions, the ministry of regional and local government and housing had to intervene directly to force administrators and their finances back on track (*The Namibian* 31/5/2002, 12/12/2003, 4/6/2004 and 4/8/2004).

A look beyond Katima Mulilo's sprawling town limits deepens the understanding that any impression of the current breathtaking progress of development must be checked against the context of Caprivi's broader socioeconomic realities. Hardly a year goes by without a major natural disaster. Record floods alternate with droughts and crop failures. Forest fires, insect plagues and livestock epidemics are decimating what relative wealth and material security many rural dwellers manage to accumulate. The rural population's access to shops and markets, health, education and other government services remains very limited. The Khwe San of Western Caprivi endure particularly poor living and health conditions. Their situation that has not been aided by their low standing with government authorities, where some still regarded them as former enemies from

---

28. Germany's electrical and engineering industries are major consumers of copper.
29. Namibia's Investment Newsletter reported in June 2004: "The mere 20–30 vehicles per day which braved the pontoon ... have now been replaced by a traffic flow of over 60 heavy vehicles each day. And these are but early days."

the liberation struggle (compare Taylor forthcoming 2008).[30] Among Namibia's 13 regions, Caprivi has the lowest Human Development Index (HDI). The population's poor health status is critical to this result. Malaria, tuberculosis and malnutrition conspire with the AIDS pandemic as major killers. At 43% among pregnant women, Caprivi's HIV infection rate is the highest in Namibia and nearly double the national average of 22.5%. Infection rates in areas across Caprivi's borders with Zambia, Botswana, Zimbabwe and Angola are either known or estimated to be above 40%. The longstanding and close personal ties of Caprivi's population with the people in these areas are believed to enhance the spread of the virus (*IRIN News* 30/5/2006).

Conclusion

After the formal end of colonialism in Africa, certain fundamental economic realities have not ceased. With global demand on the rise, there is currently a remarkable revival of the logic of extraction. Mineral resources from African hinterlands are transported via well-developed infrastructure, and with little or no value added on the continent are exported to industrial centres and consumers overseas. 'Regional integration,' 'rural development' and 'poverty reduction' feature prominently in the policy guidelines of the SADC and donors such as Germany or the EU. The difference between these words and concrete infrastructure development, however, lies in hard economic facts, such as the geographical location of the Copper Belt and the rising price of copper on world commodity markets.

On 13 May 2004, 114 years after its inception, the 19th century colonial dream of an access corridor to the interior of Southern Africa finally came true at Katima Mulilo. Caprivi is now connected to the world of global commerce as a thoroughfare for long-distance traffic. The region's peripheral character within Namibia seems to have been reversed. Caprivi suddenly appears central for ongoing developments in the Southern African regional context. The new corridor route to Walvis Bay is only one aspect of this shift. Caprivi is located at the crossroads of several ongoing long-distance infrastructure projects[31] and there are efforts to manage the greater region's water and wildlife resources on a cross-border basis (*The Namibian* 10/10/2006). These developments do not exclusively benefit Big Business. They have already positively affected the lives of

---

30. After years of pressure from development aid donors and NGOs, President Pohamba's administration has introduced new measures with regard to the San people in Namibia. In 2006, a special task force in the office of Deputy Prime Minister Libertina Amathila was established to coordinate government, donor and private sector efforts (*Namibian* 13/6/2007, 6/11/2006). Apart from occasional charity events, small-scale projects and scattered training workshops, one of government's achievements is a decision taken in parliament in 2006 to provide coffins for the San people "so that they don't have to bury their deceased in plastic bags anymore" (*Namibian* 20/11/2006).

31. The reconstruction of the Sesheke-Senanga-Mongu road and other infrastructure projects aimed at linking Zambia's Western Province with the Trans Caprivi Corridor are under way with funds provided by the Danish development aid agency DANIDA (*The Post* 18/12/2006). Japanese investors are financing the construction of a road bridge from Zambia to Botswana at Kazungula (REDI 2005). Namibian energy parastatal NAMPOWER is constructing a 'Western Power Corridor' through Caprivi to upgrade Namibia's links with the power grids of other countries in the region (*Creamer Media's Engineering News* 15/6/2007).

many inhabitants of Caprivi, Zambia's Western Province and beyond. But with the newly arising opportunities a new threat for Namibia emerges from Caprivi: the rapid boom of recent years has also produced socioeconomic changes that are of great concern to the local, regional and national state authorities. The extremely high HIV infection rate evokes fears of Caprivi as a breeding ground and conduit for the further spread of a pandemic that has already had devastating effects on all aspects of social and economic life in Namibia and its neighbours (*IRIN News* 30/5/2006; Lebeau 2006). With Walvis Bay harbouring ships and sailors from around the world, the dangerousness of Caprivi is globalised as well (compare Keulder and Lebeau 2006). Is Caprivi once again becoming a threat to a distant state authority that has vested interests in the region but lacks sufficient knowledge of local realities and the administrative muscle to steer them?

While there are clearly good reasons to be alarmed about this, our study has shown that the currently emerging dualism with regard to Caprivi is just the latest chapter in a story that goes back further than the actual creation of the territory during European colonialism. We have traced this history from the time of the precolonial Lozi kingdom through the German and South African periods to Caprivi's present in independent Namibia. In all these periods, a pattern has repeated itself with regard to Caprivi's relevance for the changing powers that ruled over it: Caprivi has always represented both a potential danger and an opportunity. The priorities of Caprivi's external rulers have naturally been to minimise or block the dangers and to unlock the opportunities. Perceptions of Caprivi have oscillated between a strategically located thoroughfare versus a buffer zone, between a breeding ground for lawlessness and disease versus a labour reserve and natural resource pool. Phases of heightened attention to Caprivi have alternated with periods of administrative idleness during which the region's inhabitants were largely left to their own devices.

The governmental techniques through which Caprivi's external administrators have sought to control the territorial boundaries, inhabitants and resources of the land have always combined coercion with more benign methods, but with changing emphasis. When the interests of the SWAPO government clashed with some among the political elites and inhabitants in 1998–99, the postcolonial state authorities asserted their monopoly of violence. To what degree these actions can be regarded as legitimate remains an issue of contestation. A weak or nonexistent assertion of the postcolonial state's central power in 1998–99 could have jeopardised the still nascent nation-building project of Namibia. Excessive use of the state's coercive force poses the same danger, however, particularly in combination with the political and socioeconomic marginalisation that some among the Caprivi region's population experience. There are many examples of the benign and careful use of state power in the region, often, we should add, in cooperation with and strongly dependent on international donor agencies. The successful establishment of community-based game and forest conservancies in recent years is but one example.

The recent awakening of powerful transnational players' economic interests in Caprivi provides a welcome opportunity for the SWAPO government to work towards the improvement of living conditions of the area's population. But will this opportunity last? The SWAPO government cannot expect its new-found allies to remain committed indefinitely to an alliance that seems largely motivated by business interests. Investors and their capital are extremely mobile and the next bust must eventually follow the current boom. Alternative routes for the extraction of mineral resources from Africa are constantly evolving. The resources themselves are limited and their prices fluctuate.[32] The international tourism business is also highly sensitive to sudden changes in demand. Such developments are not only entirely realistic, but also well beyond the influence of any present or future Namibian government. The proximity of a transnational road transport corridor, supermarkets full of unaffordable products and luxury lodges is hardly sufficient for the majority population of Caprivi to feel included in the Namibian nation-building project. Social unrest along the corridor route, recurring natural disasters and a powder keg mixture of epidemic disease and illegal cross-border migration – these are all plausible scenarios for Caprivi's future with precedents in the recent past. Caprivi then could quickly again become a dangerous liability for the SWAPO government, and a cause for the central state to assert the monopoly of violence by means other than 'development.'

The cartographic metaphor of Caprivi's distinctively penetrating shape is thus bidirectional. The arrow or finger pointing the way to the opportunities in the interior of the continent is also pointing towards the dilemmas and potential pitfalls that will remain of central importance for the ongoing formation of the postcolonial Namibian state.

Acknowledgements

Wolfgang Zeller would like to acknowledge generous funding from the Academy of Finland, the Nordic Africa Institute, the Finnish Graduate School for Development Studies and the Graduate School of International Development Studies at Roskilde University.

Bennett Kangumu Kangumu would like to acknowledge generous funding from the Carl Schlettwein Foundation and the Basler Afrika Bibliographien (BAB).

References

Anglo-German Agreement of 1 July 1890

Caplan, Gerald Lewis (1979), *The Elites of Barotseland, 1878–1969*. London: Hurst

Das, Veena and Deborah Poole (2004), 'State and Its Margins. Comparative Ethnographies,' in Veena Das and Deborah Poole (eds), *Anthropology in the Margins of the State*. Santa Fe: School of American Research Press and Oxford: James Currey, pp. 3–34

Fisch, Maria (1996), *Der Caprivizipfel während der deutschen Zeit 1890–1914*. Köln: Rüdiger Köppe Verlag

— (1999), *The Secessionist Movement in the Caprivi: A Historical Perspective*. Windhoek: Namibia Scientific Society

---

32. The Benguela railway line is currently under reconstruction and a newly planned 'Copper Corridor' through Angola is supposed to connect Zambia's major Copper mines directly to the Angolan port of Lubito by 2010 (Bundesagentur für Außenwirtschaft 12/5/2006).

Flint, Lawrence (2003), 'State-Building in Central Southern Africa: Citizenship and Subjectivity in Barotseland and Caprivi,' *Journal of African Historical Studies*, Vol. 36, No. 2, pp. 393–428

— (2004), *Historical Constructions of Postcolonial Citizenship and Subjectivity: The Case of the Lozi Peoples of Southern Central Africa*. Unpublished Ph.D. thesis, University of Birmingham

— (1996), *Negotiating the Nation in Local Terms*. Unpublished MA thesis, University of Oslo

Fosse, Leif John (1997), 'Negotiating the Nation: Ethnicity, Nationalism and Nation-Building in Independent Namibia,' *Nations and Nationalism*, Vol. 3, No. 3, pp. 427–50

Gluckman, Max (1959), 'The Lozi of Barotseland in Northwestern Rhodesia,' in E. Colson and M. Gluckman (eds), *Seven Tribes of British Central Africa*. Manchester: Manchester University Press

Government Gazette of Namibia (1995), *Traditional Authorities Act* (No. 17 of 1995). Windhoek: Government Printer

Hangula, Lazarus (1993), *The International Boundary of Namibia*. Windhoek: Gamsberg Macmillan

Hopwood, Graham (2004), *Guide to Namibian Politics*. Windhoek: Namibia Institute for Democracy and Institute for Public Policy Research

Kangumu, Bennett (2000), *A Forgotten Corner of Namibia: Aspects of the History of the Caprivi Strip, c. 1939–1980*. Unpublished MA thesis, University of Cape Town

Keulder, Christiaan and Debbie Lebeau (2006), *Ships, Trucks and Clubs: The Dynamics of HIV Risk Behaviour in Walvis Bay*. IPPR Briefing Paper No. 36. Windhoek: Institute for Public Policy Research

Kruger, C.E. (1984), *A History of the Caprivi*. Unpublished manuscript, National Archives of Namibia, A472

Lebeau, Debbie (2006), *Turning Corridors of Mobility into Corridors of Hope: Mapping the Link between Mobility and HIV Vulnerability in Namibia*. Geneva: International Organization for Migration

Mainga, Mutumba (1973), *Bulozi Under the Luyana Kings. Political Evolution and State Formation in Pre-colonial Zambia*. London: Longman

Melber, Henning (forthcoming 2008), 'One Namibia, One Nation? Regional Identities and the Central State – The Case of Caprivi,' in Björn Lindgren and Maria Heimer (eds), *Politicizing Governance: New Ethnographies of Power and Economy in the Global South*. Uppsala: Uppsala University Centre for Sustainable Development

Mendelsohn, John and Carole Roberts (1997), *An Environmental Profile and Atlas of Caprivi*. Windhoek: Gamsberg Macmillan

National Planning Commission (2006), *Caprivi Poverty Profile*. Windhoek: National Planning Commission

Omer-Cooper, John (1966), *The Zulu Aftermath: A Nineteenth-Century Revolution in Bantu Africa*. Evanston: Northwestern University Press

Seiner, Franz (1909a), 'Ergebnisse einer Bereisung des Gebietes zwischen Okawango und Sambesi (Caprivi-Zipfel) in den Jahren 1905 und 1906,' in *Mitteilungen aus den Schutzgebieten*, Vol. 22 (1), pp. 2–106

—(1909b), 'Die wirtschaftsgeographischen und politischen Verhältnisse des Captivizipfels,' *Zeitschrift für Kolonialpolitik, Kolonialrecht und Kolonialwirtschaft*, Vol. 11 pp. 417–65. Berlin: Deutsche Kolonialgesellschaft

— (1909c), 'Der Caprivizipfel. Erlebnisse mit den Eingeborenen,' in *Kolonie und Heimat*, Vol. 24. Berlin: Verlag Kolonialpolitischer Zeitschriften

Streitwolf, Kurt (1911), *Der Caprivizipfel*. Berlin: Süsseroth

Taylor, Julie (forthcoming 2008), *The Politics of Identity, Authority and the Environment: San, NGOs and the State in Namibia's West Caprivi*. Ph.D. thesis, University of Oxford

du Toit, Pierre (1995), *State-Building and Democracy in Southern Africa: A Comparative Study of Botswana, South Africa and Zimbabwe*. Pretoria: HSRC

Trollope, W. E. (1937), *Inspection Tour 1937*, National Archives of Namibia, 2267, A503/1–7

United Nations Development Programme (2000), *Namibia Human Development Report 2000*. Windhoek: UNDP Namibia

Vertrag zwischen Deutschland und England über die Kolonien und Helgoland vom 1. Juli 1890

Newspapers

Allgemeine Zeitung 1906–09, 2006

Caprivi Vision 2006

Deutsches Kolonialblatt 1907–08

The Economist 21/11/1998, *Africa's Pointing Finger*, Vol. 349, No. 8095, p. 48.

The Namibian 1998–2007

Namibian Economist 2004–06

New Era 2001–06

The Post 2006

Internet sources

Amnesty International (2001), *Annual Report 2001: Namibia*. Retrieved 15 May 2005 from http://www.web.amnesty.org/web/ar2001.nsf

Barotse Development Trust (2005), Projects. Retrieved 29 November 2005 from http://www. barotsedevelopmenttrust.com/projects.html

Botschaft der Bundesrepublik Deutschland Lusaka (2004), *Nachrichten aus dem Gastland. Zambezi Brücke eröffnet*. Retrieved 15 August 2005 from http://www.lusaka.diplo.de

Bundesagentur für Außenwirtschaft (12/5/2006), *Sambia plant "Kupfer Korridor" durch Angola*. Retrieved 4 August 2006 from http://www.bfai.de

Creamer Media's Engineering News 15/6/2007), *NamPower set to start construction on Caprivi transmission link*. Retrieved 26 June 2007 from http://www.engineeringnews.co.za

IRIN Plusnews (30/5/2006), *NAMIBIA: Curbing HIV/AIDS along a transport corridor*. Retrieved 10 July 2006 from http://www.plusnews.org

Namibia's Investment Newsletter (2004), *Frontiers of Commerce Expanded*. In issue 5/2004. Retrieved 18 July 2005 from http://www.mti.gov.na/nic_newsletter/nic5_2004.pdf

Namibian Port Authority (2007), *About Namport*. Retrieved 10 June 2007 from http://www.namport.com

REDI news (April 2005), *Kazungula bridge: Regional trade link across the Zambezi*. Retrieved 20 June 2007 from http://www.sardc.net/Editorial/Newsfeature/05400405.htm

United Democratic Party (UDP) (2005), *Caprivi Zipfel: The Controversial Strip*. Retrieved 17 July 2007 from http://www.caprivifreedom.com/history.i?cmd=view&hid=23

Walvis Bay Corridor Group (2004), *Trans Caprivi Corridor. Trade Potential*. Retrieved 20 October 2005 from http://www.wbcg.com.na/wbcg/tcc/tcc.htm

Public Speeches and Interviews

Erich Kristof, Ambassador of the Federal Republic of Germany to Zambia, 13/5/2004, Wenela border post.

Michael Mudabeti, Mayor of Katima Mulilo, 5/9/2002, Katima Mulilo.

Ideas about equality in Namibian family law

Dianne Hubbard

Namibia has introduced some far-reaching law reforms on gender issues in areas such as affirmative action and gender-based violence. And yet, like many other countries, it is a socially conservative society where the home is the last bastion of patriarchy. Men who support gender equality in other spheres are reluctant to countenance such equality in the home.

Men in Namibia are by and large very defensive about law reforms that they feel may somehow discriminate against or disadvantage men. Religious and customary law justifications have been advanced in parliament as arguments for clinging to the status quo. Even where progressive law reforms have been enacted to advance gender equality, the key points of debate in parliament and among the public at large have almost always been based on concerns about the preservation of male power and proprietary sexual control over women. At the same time, supreme court rulings on gender equality issues have shown a tendency to be deferential to 'public opinion' as expressed in parliament and in other male-dominated institutions shaped by Namibian's patriarchal past, thus further entrenching inequalities based on current norms.

This chapter begins with a brief overview of family law reforms since independence. It will then look at three key family law cases decided by the Namibia's supreme court, to examine the legal meaning of equality in Namibia. Next it will examine debates around the meaning of equality in the context of the Children's Status Act, and explain how the South African courts have dealt with similar equality issues.

An overview of family law reform in Namibia

Prior to independence, family law issues were governed primarily by inherited Roman-Dutch common law, an ancient set of legal rules that evolved in highly patriarchal societies. Those who supported the liberation struggle showed little public interest in incremental law reform on gender issues, as the legal system was viewed primarily as a colonial tool of repression.[1] Furthermore, issues of sexual equality were consciously subordinated to the larger objective of national liberation, which was viewed as the necessary enabling condition to advance all forms of political and social equality (Becker

---

1. While some lawyers and judges applied the law in ways that provided a degree of protection for peaceful political protest, the legal system embodied the framework of apartheid, institutionalised repression and established a contract labour system that ensured a controlled supply of cheap labour.

1995:143ff). After independence, there was genuine political will to promote gender equality, even though this objective conflicted with some community and religious traditions and individual beliefs. The resulting contradictions were evident in the parliamentary debates on gender-related law reform, particularly in the family sphere.

Married Persons Equality Act

The first major family law reform in post-independence Namibia was the Married Persons Equality Act 1 of 1996, which eliminated the discriminatory Roman-Dutch law concept of marital power. It was this 'marital power' that placed wives in civil marriages in a similar position to minors, with husbands having the right to administer the property of both spouses. Couples married in community of property must now consult each other on most major financial transactions, with husbands and wives being subject to identical powers and restraints, while husbands and wives married out of community of property now have the right to deal with their separate property independently.[2]

Indications are that the Act is seldom utilised in practical terms. However, the symbolic import of this Act is probably even more important than its practical provisions, as it sends out a clear message that the law will no longer recognise husbands in civil marriages as 'heads of household.'

This aspect of the law generated much controversy both inside and outside parliament. In fact, debate on this point was so fierce that additional language was added to the original draft to emphasise the fact that the removal of the legal designation of head of household would not interfere with a family's private right to treat the male as the head of the household.[3]

Family law issues in rape and domestic violence laws

The next set of law reforms affecting family life centred on the problem of violence against women and children.

The Combating of Rape Act 8 of 2000 is one of the most progressive pieces of rape legislation in the world. It introduces a broad, gender-neutral definition of rape and moves the focus away from the 'consent' of the rape victim to the force or coercion used by the perpetrator. This law reform generally garnered strong political and public support, but the most contentious issue was marital rape.

The Bill contained a provision that removed the previous bar to a wife laying a charge of rape against her husband – a point that inspired long and heated discussion. Many parliamentarians expressed fears that the new rule would be misused by women

---

2. The gender-based inequalities in customary marriage, which stem from a different source, were not addressed by this law – aside from giving husbands and wives in both civil and customary marriages equal powers of guardianship in respect of children of the marriage.

3. The original Bill stated that one effect of the abolition of marital power was that "the common law position of the husband as head of the family is abolished." Parliament added the proviso that "nothing herein shall be construed to prevent a husband and wife from agreeing between themselves to assign to one of them, or both, any particular role or responsibility within the family."

to gain power over their husbands, or asserted that there can be no such thing as rape in marriage because a husband has a 'right' to sexual intercourse with his wife.

These parliamentary attitudes mirror more widespread public opinion. Various studies show that rape within marriage and other intimate relationships is common in Namibia (Becker, Claassen 1996; LeBeau 1996; Rose Junius 1998; LeBeau 1999; Talavera 2002). Even more disturbingly, one recent national study indicates that a significant number of both men and women believe that married women have no right to refuse sex with their husbands. It appears that there is still a widespread perception that women are subordinate to men in marriage, with decision-making – at least about sexual matters – still based on patriarchal constructs (MoHSS 2003:40–5).

The new law on rape was followed by a companion piece of legislation on domestic violence, the Combating of Domestic Violence Act 4 of 2003. This law covers a range of forms of domestic violence, including sexual violence, harassment, intimidation, economic violence and psychological violence. It covers domestic violence between husbands and wives, parents and children, boyfriends and girlfriends and other family members.

The law gives those who have suffered violence alternatives to laying criminal charges, by setting up a simple, free procedure for getting a protection order from a magistrate's court. A protection order is a court order directing the abuser to stop the violence. It can also prohibit the abuser from having any contact with the victim. In cases of physical violence, it can even order the abuser to leave the common home.

No new crimes are created by the law, but existing crimes between persons in a domestic relationship are classified as 'domestic violence offences' with special provisions that encourage input from the victim on bail and sentencing, and protect the victim's privacy by prohibiting publication of information that might reveal the victim's identity.

In parliament, male fears and defensiveness were again evident in this debate, with some men worried that the gender-neutral Bill did not do enough to protect men – especially against forms of 'violence' such as wives who deprive their husbands of sexual relations or use 'witchcraft' to interfere with their husband's sexual functions.[4]

Maintenance – paid by men and abused by women?

The next major family law reform to come through parliament was the Maintenance Act 9 of 2003. The difficulty of securing child support from absent fathers has been regularly cited as a key issue affecting children's welfare and women's economic independence. The Maintenance Act made significant changes to the maintenance system to make it more efficient, but most of the basic principles around maintenance remained the same. The new law provides for the first time for the sharing of expenses incurred during pregnancy and gives clear guidelines for deciding how much maintenance should be paid. It also provides new methods of enforcement to use when maintenance orders are not obeyed.

---

4.   There were proposals to amend the Bill to cover these two issues, but they did not succeed.

During the parliamentary debates, there were repeated allegations that women mis-use the maintenance system – by having children just to get maintenance payments, by spending maintenance money on themselves or by demanding payment from men who are not in fact the fathers of the children.[5]

Many parliamentarians – including women – were concerned about what they per-ceived 'gender neutrality' to be. The maintenance system under both the old law and the new one is gender-neutral on its face, but in practice is used almost exclusively by moth-ers seeking maintenance from absent fathers. Some MPs tried to even the score by citing failings by mothers to counterbalance the Bill's obvious emphasis on fathers' failure to take financial responsibility for their children. The search for a sense of even-handedness eventually moved to reciprocity between parents and children, instead of between men and women, and an amendment was eventually added to the Bill to clarify the duties of children to maintain elderly parents.

Equal rights to communal land for women

The Communal Land Reform Act 5 of 2002, although not primarily a family law re-form, was a large step forward in protecting women's rights to communal land tenure. In terms of this law, if a husband dies, his widow has a right to remain on the land if she wishes and is entitled to keep the land even if she re-marries. (The law is actually worded in gender-neutral fashion, but widowers were not historically forced off their land when their wives died.) If there is no surviving spouse when the holder of the land right dies, then the land will be reallocated to a child of the deceased identified by the chief or tra-ditional authority as being the rightful heir. There was little parliamentary debate about gender, as the discussions centred on race and class issues, with little acknowledgement of the intersection of these points of discrimination with gender discrimination.

One flaw in this law is that it fails to address the disposition of the land in the case of a polygamous marriage. Another problem is that it is not being uniformly implemented in practice, with some incidents of land-grabbing still occurring. Yet it constitutes a radical departure from previous practice. Because most Namibian communities are pat-rilocal, it was previously the case that a widow was expected to return to her parents' home. This law reform thus implicitly recognises women as autonomous actors, rather than as dependents of their husbands or fathers.

However, there is a danger of a reaction against the advances for women contained in this law. The ministry of lands and resettlement announced in 2006 that it is propos-ing to amend the Act. At present, any person irrespective of gender can apply for a cus-tomary land right within the communal area where he or she resides. This provision has recently received some criticism, especially from men, who have suggested that married woman should not be able to apply for land in their own right. Others have said that

---

5. Such objections were anticipated, and the initial Bill already contained provisions which crimi-nalise abuse of maintenance money as well as providing false information in connection with a maintenance claim. The Bill also included a counter-balancing criminal offence for anyone who tries to intimidate someone into not filing a maintenance case by means of any kind of threat, including the use of witchcraft.

single women should not be given land rights either, because of fears about what would happen to a woman's land when she marries and relocates to her husband's homestead.

Foot-dragging and fears

One prominent theme that runs through these various law reform debates is a male reluctance to contemplate any form of 'power-sharing' – particularly in sexual or economic spheres. Equality is not the universal goal. And even where equality is the genuine goal, there are fears that this will result in unfair treatment of men by empowering women to take unfair advantage of men in family contexts.

One problem is that parliament has sometimes applied simplistic understandings of sexual equality to issues of family law reform, without a sensitive analysis of the complex social context in which the legal rules will be applied. Namibian court cases on gender have also struggled with this challenge.

What is the legal meaning of sexual equality?

There is only a small body of jurisprudence on sexual equality in Namibia. However, the decided cases have, on the most controversial issues, given a surprising amount of weight to 'public opinion' as a source of values to guide constitutional interpretation.

The Müller case

Article 10 of the Namibian Constitution states that "(1) All persons shall be equal before the law" and "(2) No persons may be discriminated against on the grounds of sex, race, colour, ethnic origin, religion, creed or social or economic status." In interpreting this provision, the Namibian courts have drawn a distinction between 'differentiation' and 'discrimination.'

The leading case on equality under Article 10(2), *Müller v President of the Republic of Namibia*, followed precedent in other jurisdictions by holding that "an element of unjust or unfair treatment" is inherent in the meaning of the word "discriminate." Differentiation on one of the prohibited grounds will not amount to "unfair discrimination" if it bears a "rational connection" to a "legitimate purpose."

The judgment gave a detailed explanation of how courts should determine whether unfair discrimination is present:

> In this regard, the Court must not only look at the disadvantaged group but also the nature of the power causing the discrimination as well as the interests which have been affected. The enquiry focuses primarily on the "victim" of the discrimination and the impact thereof on him or her. To determine the effect of such impact consideration should be given to the complainant's position in society, whether he or she suffered from patterns of disadvantage in the past and whether the discrimination is based on a specified ground or not. Furthermore, consideration should be given to the provision or power and the purpose sought to be achieved by it and with due regard to all such factors, the extent to which the discrimination

has affected the rights and interest of the complainant and whether it has led to an impairment of his or her fundamental human dignity. (*Müller:*203A–B)

The subject of the *Müller* case was a gender question. When Mr. Müller married Ms. Engelhard, he wanted to take on her surname so that the two of them could operate their jewellery business under her more distinctive and well-established business name. Under Namibian law, she could have simply started using his surname if she wished – but he could assume her surname only by going through a formal name change procedure that involved extra effort and expense.

The supreme court ruled that this particular differentiation did not amount to unfair discrimination. Key factors were the findings that the complainant, a white male, was not a member of a prior disadvantaged group;[6] that the aim of the name change formalities was not to impair the dignity of males or to disadvantage them; that the legislature has a clear interest in the regulation of surnames; and that the impact of the differentiation on the interests of the applicant was minimal since he could adopt his wife's surname by a procedure involving only minor inconvenience. The court noted that the legal provision in question "gave effect to a tradition of long standing in the Namibian community that the wife normally assumes the surname of the husband," with the government being unaware of any other husband in Namibia who wanted to assume the surname of his wife (*Müller:*204B). Thus, the court gave particular weight to the status quo.

The matter was subsequently referred to the United Nations committee that oversees the International Covenant on Civil and Political Rights. This committee ruled in March 2002 that the different procedures for dealing with surnames *do* amount to unfair sex discrimination in terms of the international covenant, noting that long-standing tradition is not a sufficient justification for differential treatment between the sexes. The committee gave the Namibian government 90 days to report on what it had done to rectify the problem. Mr. Müller had already changed his name to Mr. Engelhard by that stage (under the laws of his home country of Germany), but the underlying law has, more than five years later, still not been changed to remove the sex discrimination that was identified.[7]

The Frank *case*

The next major gender issue to be considered by the Namibian courts concerned a lesbian relationship. In the case of *Frank v Chairperson of the Immigration Selection Board*, the supreme court rejected the argument that the immigration board had violated the applicants' fundamental rights to equality by failing to accord their lesbian relationship equal status with the relationships of men and women who are legally married.

---

6. The outcome might have been different if the argument had raised the corresponding discrimination to the wife of the applicant. (See Bonthys 2000)
7. The Committee said: "In view of the importance of the principle of equality between men and women, the argument of a long-standing tradition cannot be maintained as a general justification for different treatment of men and women, which is contrary to the Covenant" (*Müller & Engelhard*, 2002: para. 6.8; see also Menges 2002).

The supreme court's approach to constitutional interpretation here was to start with the 'plain meaning' of the words in the relevant constitutional provision, guided by "the legal history, traditions and usages of the country concerned," followed by a "value judgment" in any case where the constitutional provision is not "absolute" (*Frank*:133B–136A).[8]

In making such a value judgment, the court stated that it must look to the "contemporary norms, aspirations, expectations, sensitivities, moral standards, relevant established beliefs, social conditions, experiences and perceptions of the Namibian people as expressed in their national institutions and Constitution" (*Frank*:135G–H, 135J–136A, 136J–137A).[9] The court noted that it is also appropriate to consider the emerging consensus of values in the international community, although local traditions and values should be given precedence to avoid creating a perception that the courts are imposing foreign values on the Namibian people (*Frank*:141I–142B; 135H–I).

The court identified "the Namibian parliament, courts, tribal authorities, common law, statute law and tribal law, political parties, news media, trade unions, established Namibian churches and other relevant community-based organizations" as sources of expressions of Namibian values, saying that "parliament, being the chosen representatives of the people of Namibia, is one of the most important institutions to express the current day values of the people." (*Frank*:137H–I)[10]

However, the court also expressed the need to exercise caution when considering the value of public opinion in constitutional interpretation:

> It is not a question of substituting public opinion for that of the Court. It is the Courts that will always evaluate the public opinion. The Court will decide whether the purported public opinion is an informed opinion based on reason and true facts; whether it is artificially induced or instigated by agitators seeking a political power base; whether it constitutes a mere 'amorphous ebb and flow of public opinion' or whether it points to a permanent trend, a change in the structure and culture of society ... The Court therefore is not deprived of its role to take the final decision whether or not public opinion, as in the case of other sources, constitutes objective evidence of community values ... (*Frank*:138F–H)

Applying a value judgment to the issue before it, the court found that the Namibian constitution makes no provision for the recognition of homosexual relationships as being equivalent to marriage, and that the constitutional term "family" clearly does not contemplate that a homosexual relationship could be regarded as a "natural" or "funda-

---

8. The court cited the portion of Article 6 that prohibits the death penalty as an example (*Frank*:137E).

9. Other cases have also indicated that constitutional interpretation must be carried out in the context of Namibian values. For example, Berker, CJ, in a concurring judgment in a 1991 case on corporal punishment, stated that "the one major and basic consideration in arriving at a decision involves an enquiry into the generally held norms, approaches, moral standards, aspiration and a host of other established beliefs of the people of Namibia" (*Ex Parte Attorney-General, Namibia*:197H–J; see also *Namunjepo*).

10. The court also listed as sources of information about values "debates in parliament and in regional statutory bodies and legislation passed by parliament; judicial or other commissions; public opinion as established in properly conducted opinion polls; evidence placed before Courts of law and judgments of Court; referenda; publications by experts" (*Frank*:138C–D). The *Namunjepo* case similarly cites the importance of parliament as a source of values.

mental" group unit. In ruling that Article 10 does not protect homosexual relationships, the court found that "Namibian trends, contemporary opinions, norms and values tend in the opposite direction." The main evidence cited for this conclusion was absence of a legislative trend towards the recognition of same-sex relationships in Namibia, and statements by the president and one male member of parliament that motivated against the recognition of such relationships.[11]

The court concluded that discrimination on the basis of sexual orientation in the context before it is not "unfair discrimination" according to the *Müller* test: "Equality before the law for each person, does not mean equality before the law for each person's sexual relationships." However, the court emphasised that "nothing in this judgment justifies discrimination against homosexuals as individuals, or deprives them of the protection of other provisions of the Namibian Constitution" (*Frank*:155E, 156H).

The Myburgh *case*

The 'absolute' approach to constitutional interpretation was taken in the *Myburgh* case, which concerned a husband's marital power over his wife. In this case, the supreme court held that this discriminatory concept was already automatically invalid by virtue of its unconstitutionality, even before it was overruled by parliament with the Married Persons Equality Act. Here the court found unfair discrimination on the grounds of sex, without finding it necessary to make any value judgement.

The court noted that the differentiation in question is based on stereotyping "which does not take cognisance of the equal worth of women," thus impairing the dignity of women as individuals and as a group.[12] The court concluded that this was "not an in-

---

11. "[T]he President of Namibia as well as the Minister of Home Affairs, have expressed themselves repeatedly in public against the recognition and encouragement of homosexual relationships. As far as they are concerned, homosexual relationships should not be encouraged because that would be against the traditions and values of the Namibian people and would undermine those traditions and values. It is a notorious fact of which this Court can take judicial notice that when the issue was brought up in parliament, nobody on the Government benches, which represent 77 percent of the Namibian electorate, made any comment to the contrary." (*Frank*:150D–F). This suggests that the ruling party's perspective could guide constitutional interpretation whenever there is some ambiguity.
   The Court looked to international law as well: "The 'family institution' of the African Charter, the United Nations Universal Declaration of Human Rights, the International Covenant on Civil and Political Rights and the Namibian Constitution, envisages a formal relationship between male and female, where sexual intercourse between them in the family context is the method to procreate offspring and thus ensure the perpetuation and survival of the nation and the human race" (*Frank:*146F–H). The court also stated that the International Covenant on Civil and Political Rights specifies "sex" but not "sexual orientation" as one of the grounds on which discrimination is prohibited. In fact, in March 1994 (before Namibia's ratification of the covenant) the human rights committee charged with monitoring the covenant stated that the references to "sex" in the provisions on discrimination are "to be taken as including sexual orientation" (*Toonen*: para. 8.7).

12. The court noted that "the differentiation takes no cognisance of the fact that in many marriages in community of property the intelligence, training, qualifications or natural ability or aptitude of the woman may render her a far better administrator of the common estate than the husband …" (*Myburgh*:266B–I).

stance where meaning and content must still be given to the provisions of the Constitution," stating that "no value judgement is necessary" to see that the common law rules on marital power are discriminatory (*Myburgh*:268D–E).

Some comments on the Namibian jurisprudence

These three cases (decided by a judiciary which is almost exclusively male) each give a different role to tradition and public opinion, thus giving us poor guidance as yet on when existing notions of sexual roles and relationships will prevail over a new world refashioned in light of constitutional ideals. All the institutions cited in the *Frank* case as sources of Namibian values are male-dominated institutions that have been shaped by patriarchal cultures, meaning that the courts are likely to be looking to 'male' public opinion for guidance.

This approach also raises the danger of a circular and mutually-reinforcing dialogue between the courts and parliament: the court looked to parliament's lack of support for homosexual relationships in the *Frank* case, and parliamentarians have subsequently cited the court's judgment in the *Frank* case as a justification for continuing to exclude homosexual relationships from the protection of the law.

Constitutional analysis in other jurisdictions has pointed out that constitutional protections enforced by the judiciary are particularly necessary to protect the *unpopular* rights of the minority. Parliament, as the representatives of the majority, can in theory be relied upon to enact laws based on the will and values of the majority. But the constitution and the courts should be the source of protection for the rights of those who are most vulnerable – often because they want to express an opinion or engage in a practice that *departs* from society's existing norms.[13]

For example, in South Africa the constitutional court decided a case that was very similar to Namibia's *Frank* case, yet with an opposite outcome, holding that it is unconstitutional for immigration law to favour non-citizen spouses over non-citizen same-sex partners. The constitutional framework is different in South Africa, where discrimination on the grounds of sexual orientation is explicitly forbidden. But in contrast to the *Frank* case, the South African court did not look for the endorsement of public opinion, but on the contrary found that it is especially important to afford constitutional protection to those who are already vulnerable because of societal stereotyping or prejudice.[14]

---

13. This idea has often been espoused in respect of the US Constitution by Harvard Law School Professor Lawrence H. Tribe. (See, for example, Tribe 2003.)
   The right to freedom of speech is a good example – it seldom needs to be invoked to protect people who are agreeing with the prevailing views of those with power in society, but is usually asserted rather to safeguard the rights of those who want to challenge prevailing views or power structures.

14. This judgment stated: "Society at large has, generally, accorded far less respect to lesbians and their intimate relationships with one another than to heterosexuals and their relationships." Quoting Canadian jurisprudence, the court noted that "it is easy to say that everyone who is just like 'us' is entitled to equality. Everyone finds it more difficult to say that those who are 'different' from us in some way should have the same equality rights that we enjoy" (*National Coalition for Gay and Lesbian Equality*:28C–29D). Unlike the Namibian court, which looked to parliament as one source of societal norms, the South African court noted that although the South African parliament had shown a legislative trend in the direction of equality for all sexual orientations,

It is unthinkable that tradition would be cited by the Namibian courts to uphold any form of racism. Apartheid Namibia certainly had a long tradition of racism, and sadly, there is still public opinion that would support discrimination on the grounds of race or ethnicity in some quarters – but this would surely never be relied upon by the courts as a relevant factor in determining whether Article 10's prohibition against race discrimination is applicable.[15] For example, in the case of *S v van Wyk*, Namibia's high court held that it was permissible to consider racism as an aggravating factor in sentencing for a racially-motivated crime, even though the culprit's racism had been conditioned by a racist environment. Here, one of the judges drew an analogy between racism and sexism:

> At different times in history, societies have sought to condition citizens to legitimise discrimination against women, to accept barbaric modes of punishing citizens and exacting brutal retribution, and to permit monstrous invasions of human dignity and freedom through the institution of slavery. But there comes a time in the life of a nation, when it must and is able to identify such practices as pathologies and when it seeks consciously, visibly and irreversibly to reject its shameful past. That time for the Namibian nation arrived with independence (*S v van Wyk*:456I–457A, concurring opinion of Judge Mohamed).[16]

Unfortunately, the analogy referred to is not being fully observed in practice.

Notions of 'equality' in the Children's Status Act

Particularly pointed examples of how notions of equality affect law-making can be found in debates around the Children's Status Act, first introduced into parliament in 2003 and passed after several heated rounds of debate in late 2006.

Custody – joint, equal or one at a time?

One of the topics addressed by the Bill is parental rights over children born outside marriage. The Bill initially proposed that the mother would have sole custody of such children from birth, then mothers and fathers would automatically acquire joint custody when the child reached the age of seven. Many NGOs objected that such a rule

---

it had not yet gone far enough in recognising same-sex life partnerships as relationships in law (*National Coalition for Gay and Lesbian Equality*:25D–E).

15. Race and sex discrimination are treated identically by Article 10, as well as in the preamble of the constitution, which states that the "inalienable rights of all members of the human family" include "the right of the individual to life, liberty and the pursuit of happiness, regardless of race, colour, ethnic origin, sex, religion, creed or social or economic status." Article 23 of the constitution gives special emphasis to both race and sex discrimination., noting that "women in Namibia have traditionally suffered special discrimination and that they need to be encouraged and enabled to play a full, equal and effective role in the political, social, economic and cultural life of the nation."

16. See also the *Kauesa* case, which upheld the constitutionality of portions of the Racial Discrimination Prohibition Act 26 of 1991. Several of the passages supporting the court's decision equate several forms of discrimination, including racism, sexism and attacks on the basis of "sexual identity." (The high court decision was subsequently overruled by the supreme court on other grounds.)

would be unworkable in practice, as well as contrary to the best interests of children in many situations.

The inspiration for the Bill's approach seemed to be the fact that married parents have joint custody of children born of the marriage, but unmarried parents cannot be said to be similarly situated, especially where they are not cohabiting. Persons who are joined in marriage are bound by a number of reciprocal legal rights and responsibilities. In particular, married couples do not have the power to bring the marriage to an end without supervision. In the case of civil marriages, a court must make sure that the best interests of the child are protected. In the case of customary marriages, the relationship is regulated by a body of custom and negotiated by the extended family unit. None of these things applies to unmarried parents. Therefore, it did not make sense for the law to afford married couples and unmarried couples identical treatment.

In the wake of extensive public hearings throughout the country convened by a parliamentary standing committee, the debate became so tangled that the Bill was intentionally allowed to lapse – at a time when a new president was scheduled to take office shortly, raising the possibility of a cabinet reshuffle.[17]

A revised version of the Children's Status Bill was tabled by the new minister of the newly renamed Ministry of Gender Equality and Child Welfare in October 2005. The revised Bill jettisoned joint custody in favour of equal custody for both parents from birth unless one parent applied to a children's court for sole custody. The revised Bill was passed by the National Assembly very quickly, with relatively little debate, leading to a public demonstration by representatives of the NGO community appealing to Namibia's second house of parliament, the National Council, to give further scrutiny to the Bill. The National Council referred the Bill to its own standing committee, which held additional public hearings in Windhoek.

Many NGOs asserted that equal custody, like joint custody, would be unworkable in practice. Because the social reality at present is that single mothers tend to take responsibility for the day-to-day care of children born outside marriage, equal rights on paper for single mothers and single fathers would be unlikely to translate into equal practice.

Debates around this issue replayed some familiar themes. In public hearings before the National Assembly committee, some people advocated joint custody from birth on the grounds that men might otherwise be reduced to 'cheque book fathers.' However, there were more concerns that parents (and fathers in particular) might want to exercise their custody rights purely to avoid paying maintenance, with the result that the child would end up as a weapon in the 'tug of war' that might ensue. (NA 2005: para. 6.5.1; *The Namibian*, 1/12/2005; *New Era*, 24/2/2006).

---

17. As a result of debates between the parliamentary committee and the minister of women affairs and child welfare, two contradictory committee reports were issued, with both purporting to represent the views of a majority of the persons consulted. The first report, following the lines of a joint submission by a large coalition of NGOs, recommended that sole custody of a child born outside marriage should vest in the mother, with the father having automatic rights of access and the right to make application to a children's court to become the child's custodian. The minister favoured "equal rights to custody" for both parents simultaneously from the child's birth, and this approach was recommended in the second committee report (MWACW 2005; Dentlinger 2005).

A large group of NGOs pointed out that children born outside marriage are usually born to parents who are not living in the same household, meaning that their situation is similar to that of children of divorced parents. In divorces under both civil law and customary law, custody of the children is usually given to one parent while the other parent has rights of contact and access. This arrangement helps to prevent disputes. Submissions made to parliament argued that children born outside marriage are entitled to the same degree of clarity about parental rights and responsibilities as children born to married parents. If the proposed law did not give this same degree of protection to children in both situations, it would continue to discriminate against children born outside marriage.

One proposed solution was to provide different approaches for unmarried parents, depending on whether or not they were cohabiting. It was suggested that cohabiting parents should be allowed to have joint custody and equal guardianship if they wished (subject to court approval), just like married parents. But where parents were *not* sharing a common home, then one parent must take primary responsibility for the daily care of the child while the other parent would have access rights, just like children of divorced parents. Both parents would have an equal right to become the child's custodian, thus providing a level playing field as a starting point. If the parents could not agree between themselves on who would act as the primary custodian, then the children's court could decide the question, based purely on the best interests of the child. The NGOs suggested that the mother could be the temporary custodian of the child until a parental agreement is registered or until a court decides the matter, since the mother (for obvious biological reasons) will definitely be present at the child's birth.

This proposal was not ultimately accepted, although it appeared to find favour with the minister of gender equality at one stage. The approach ultimately adopted by parliament, after the Bill was considered by a parliamentary committee for a third time, was a mechanism for choosing a single primary custodian for all children of unmarried parents. Unmarried parents can make an oral or written agreement between themselves on who will act as the primary custodian. If no agreement is made, either parent (or someone acting on behalf of the child) can apply to the children's court for the appointment of a primary custodian. The person with physical custody of the child can make an application to any court (including a traditional tribunal) for a quick order for interim custody if the child's best interests are at risk. This interim order will remain in effect until the same court makes a final decision on custody. There is no default position. If the parents make no agreement and no one approaches the court to request legal custody of the child, then the child will remain in legal limbo, without a legal custodian or guardian to make decisions on behalf of the child.

This final approach seems to bend over backwards to pretend that children have two identical parents, instead of a mother and a father. It is arguably 'gender-neutral' to a fault, despite the fact that childbearing and childrearing are not gender-blind activities in Namibia. In addition to the sex-based biological facts of childbearing and breastfeeding, societal problems such as domestic violence and the failure to provide child maintenance continue to have a gendered nature. The law is not yet in force, so it is too soon to assess how it will play out in practice.

The rights of rapists

Another contentious equality issue in the Children's Status Act brought up the topic of rape – and marital rape – once again. The original Bill included a provision stating that "male perpetrators of rape which results in the conception of a child born outside marriage" would have no parental rights over the child but could be required to pay maintenance.

One concern that arose here was gender neutrality. Since the Combating of Rape Act is gender-neutral, it is possible for women to be convicted of rape – although this usually involves a woman who acts as an accomplice to a male rapist or commits a sexual act other than intercourse (for obvious biological reasons). A submission based on input from 31 NGOs supported the reference to male rapists on the grounds that it would be very rare for a pregnancy to result from the actions of a female rapist, and that even in such a rare event, there might be a need for the female rapist to care for the child for a time for the purposes of breastfeeding (LAC 2006).

But parliamentarians generally felt that any exclusion of rights based on a pregnancy resulting from rape should apply equally to male and female rapists. For example, one asked: "Why this discrimination: are men being punished because they are men? ...We have had many incidents where women raped men" (*The Namibian*, 4/3/2004). In fact, in a sample of 409 rape dockets examined by the Legal Assistance Centre from locations around the country covering the period since the new rape law came into force, there were only 3 female perpetrators among the 477 perpetrators – and none of these women was convicted (LAC 2007:176).

The parliamentary committee which initially studied the Bill recommended that the provision should be reworded in gender-neutral terms (NA 2004: paragraph 6.10).[18] However, the revised version of the Bill tabled in 2006 instead eliminated the restriction on the rights of rapist fathers altogether – which sparked further debate.

A second equality concern that arose around this issue related to rape inside marriage versus rape outside marriage. Because the Bill at hand concerned custody and guardianship rights for children born outside marriage, the proposed exclusion of rapists' rights logically applied only to children born outside marriage. On this point, the submission based on input from 31 NGOs stated:

> We do not propose limiting the rights of all fathers who are convicted of rape (or any other crime). But the situation is different where the ONLY connection between the child's mother and father is that he is the rapist and she is the rape victim. (LAC 2006)

In any event, rape in marriage could be a basis for divorce proceedings, which would settle the question of custody.

This approach inspired strong objections. For example, one parliamentarian complained about this source of inequality, saying that "a husband who rapes his wife inside marriage has custody over his child, but a father who rapes a mother of a child born

---

18. Some who made representations to the committee felt that if a rapist father can be required to pay maintenance, then he should also have parental rights. Astonishingly, the suggestion was put forward that a woman who falls pregnant from a rape should choose in the early stages of pregnancy either to reconcile with the rapist father so that he could have parental rights, or to have an abortion.

outside marriage would not have such a right to custody" (National Council debate, 27/2/2006). What is interesting about this argument is that whereas many male parliamentarians were reluctant to recognise the existence of marital rape in 2000, in 2005 they were not only admitting the existence of marital rape but worrying about the relative rights of marital rapists.

A third aspect of the equality debate raised involved the distinction between men who father a child by means of rape and other criminals. One local NGO, the National Society for Human Rights, asserted that there should be no distinction "between a father and a mother who is a convicted murderer and one who is a convicted rapist!" (NSHR: para.2.6.3). Many other NGOs felt, on the contrary, that there is a very important distinction between a parent who commits a crime and a parent *who causes the conception of a child* through a heinous crime against the other parent. One of the most disturbing aspects of the latter situation, for example, was the idea that a woman who has fallen pregnant by means of rape might actually have to get the *consent of the rapist* to put the child up for adoption.

After considering this range of viewpoints, the National Council's parliamentary committee recommended that the law should restrict male perpetrators from having rights of custody, guardianship or access over a child born of the rape unless a court has specifically approved such rights (NC 2006: para.1.8). However, the National Council as a whole rejected this proposal (National Council debate, 27/2/2006).

After hearing strong objections on this point from the NGO community, the minister tabled an amendment in July 2006 that inserted a gender-neutral restriction on the parental rights of any persons who cause a pregnancy through rape, requiring a court order to authorise any rights over the child in question (*The Namibian,* 13/7/2006 and 17/7/2006). This amendment was incorporated into the final version of the law.[19]

The role of social realities in considering equality

One question implicit in the discussions around the Children's Status Act was what weight to give to current social reality. Women's groups pointed to statistics indicating that only 4% of Namibian children under the age of 15 live with their fathers but not their mothers while both parents are alive, and only 0.4% live with their fathers even after their mothers have died (MoHSS 2003:11–12).[20]

It was contended that the fact children born outside marriage are generally cared for by their mothers and not their fathers justifies giving mothers a procedural advantage over fathers by giving them custody as a starting point – as long as fathers had the right to approach a children's court and request custody, with the ultimate decision being

---

19. In terms of the final law, people who have caused the conception of a child by means of rape have no rights to custody or access in respect of that child without explicit court approval. The rapist may not inherit from the child in the absence of a will. The child, on the other hand, may inherit from the rapist parent, and the rapist parent is legally liable to bear a share of the child's maintenance expenses just like any other parent.

20. Many children were living with someone other than a parent. One-quarter of children under age 15 were living with both parents, one-third with their mothers only (even though their father was still alive) and one-third with someone other than a biological parent (even though both parents were in most of these cases still alive).

based solely on the best interests of the child. Asking fathers to be the ones to go to court if they really want custody was asserted as being the best way to avoid placing an impossible burden on Namibia's already overstretched courts. This procedural difference would be a variation of the one upheld by the court in the *Müller* case, although it could be argued that such an approach gives too much weight to the status quo.

The South African constitutional court considered precisely this issue in the 1997 *Hugo* case. In 1994, South African President Nelson Mandela pardoned certain categories of prisoners who had not committed very serious crimes. A blanket pardon was given to mothers with minor children under the age of 12, while fathers of young children were eligible to apply for remission of sentence on an individual basis. The justification for the different procedures was that only a minority of South African fathers are actively involved in childcare. A male prisoner challenged the pardon on the grounds that it was unfair sex discrimination and the constitutional court found that the different pardon procedures were not unconstitutional.

According to the South African court, it is necessary to look at the practical considerations involved. Since male prisoners outnumber female prisoners almost fifty-fold in South Africa, releasing the fathers of young children as well as the mothers would have meant the release of a very large number of prisoners. This might have produced a public outcry. And because fathers play a lesser role in childrearing, the release of male prisoners would not have contributed very significantly to the president's goal of serving the interests of children. In other words, the costs of such a move would have outweighed the gains. The president's pardon did not restrict the rights of any fathers permanently: it did not stop any of them from applying to the president for an individual remission of sentence on the basis of their own special circumstances. So the court found that there was discrimination in the sense that mothers and fathers were treated differently, but that this discrimination was not unfair – and therefore not unconstitutional. The different treatment was justifiable as a reasonable way to serve the best interests of the children involved.

One concurring justice argued that society must move away from gender stereotyping, which has prevented women from "forging identities for themselves independent of their roles as wives and mothers" and discouraged fathers from participating in childrearing, to the detriment of both the fathers and their children. This justice therefore concluded that the presidential pardon constituted unfair sex discrimination, but found that it was nevertheless justifiable on practical grounds (*Hugo*:41G–H;42B).

Another justice rooted her opinion in social realities. She asserted that the discrimination in question was not unfair, even though it was based on a gender stereotype, because that stereotype is a social fact:

> In this case, mothers have been afforded an advantage on the basis of a proposition that is generally speaking true. There is no doubt that the goal of equality entrenched in our Constitution would be better served if the responsibilities for child rearing were more fairly shared between fathers and mothers. The simple fact of the matter is that at present they are not. Nor are they likely to be more evenly shared in the near future. For the moment, then, and for some time to come, mothers are going to carry greater burdens than fathers in the rearing of children. We cannot ignore this crucial fact in considering the impact of the discrimination in this case. (*Hugo*:49E–G)

One justice disagreed, saying that although it is true that women actually bear a dispro-portionate burden of child rearing in society, it is not fair to base a legal distinction on this fact (*Hugo:*36C). He argued that the view of women as the primary care-givers for children relegates women to a "subservient" and "inferior" role which is part of the old system of patriarchy rejected by the new constitution, and may hamper the efforts of those men who want to break out of the stereotypical mould and become more involved with their children. In his view, the presidential pardon thus reinforced existing "gen-der scripts," whereas "whatever tradition, prejudice, male chauvinism or privilege may maintain. Constitutionally the starting point is that parents are parents" (*Hugo:*37E–F, 38C–F; 39D–E).[21]

The roles of mothers versus fathers were also considered in the *Fraser* case in South Africa, where an unmarried father challenged the constitutionality of a statute which required that married mothers and fathers must both give consent to put their child up for adoption, while only the mother's consent was required in cases where the parents of the child were not married. The court agreed that this distinction was an unfair form of discrimination between married fathers versus unmarried fathers, and between unmar-ried mothers versus unmarried fathers. The court gave parliament two years in which to develop an alternative approach, but warned that a blanket rule that treated all parents equally would be just as unlikely to produce the desired result:

> Why should the consent of a father who has had a very casual encounter on a single oc-casion with the mother have the automatic right to refuse his consent to the adoption of a child born in consequence of such a relationship, in circumstances where he has shown no further interest in the child and the mother has been the sole source of support and love for that child? Conversely, why should the consent of the father not ordinarily be necessary in the case where both parents of the child have had a long and stable relationship over many years and have equally given love and support to the child to be adopted? Indeed, there may be cases where the father has been the more stable and more involved parent of such a child and the mother has been relatively uninterested in or uninvolved in the development of the child. Why should the consent of the mother in such a case be required and not that of the father? (*Fraser:*283E–H)

The court noted that statutory and judicial responses to these problems in other juris-dictions are "nuanced," having regard to factors such as the duration and the stability of the relationship between the parents, the age of the child, the intensity or otherwise of the bonds between parent and child, the reasons the relationship between the parents was not formalised by marriage and the best interests of the child. The court also urged parliament to be "acutely sensitive to the deep disadvantage experienced by the single

---

21. Two commentators criticised the court's analysis for failing to give proper recognition to the complexities of situations where fathers are in fact acting as primary care givers: "The Court seems unable to see Hugo as both part of an advantaged group of fathers, and as distinct from that group, because of his location within the sub-group of disadvantaged fathers or the groups of primary care-giver parents. The problems of application faced by the Court arise where the Court tries to relate the complainant to a particular group but loses sight of the overlapping na-ture of social groups." They suggest that the discrimination should have been found to be unfair, but nevertheless justifiable (Albertyn, Goldblatt 1998:264–5). For another useful analysis of the *Hugo* case, see Kende 2000.

mothers in our society" and to ensure that law reforms on the issue did not "exacerbate that disadvantage" (*Fraser*:282C–D).[22]

Other equality cases decided by the South African constitutional court give good examples of sensitive considerations of the social context of discrimination and the social impact of specific legal rules – although sometimes in the dissenting judgments rather than the majority judgments.[23]

Unfortunately, this kind of nuanced analysis is what is, to date, often missing in Namibian jurisprudence and parliamentary debate.

The question of how to promote equality in an unequal world is a vexed one. As the debates discussed above illustrate, parliament has sometimes applied simplistic understandings of sexual equality to issues of family law reform. Treating people equally does not mean treating everyone in exactly the same way. It means treating people who are in similar situations in a similar way, but like a hall of mirrors this gives rise to additional questions about who is similar to whom in what ways.

Legal analysis often distinguishes between two kinds of equality: 'formal' versus 'substantive.' Formal equality means adopting gender-blind rules which eliminate all gender distinctions. Substantive equality means looking at laws in their social context – a context formed by race, sex and class inequalities – to see what approaches will best advance meaningful equality in real life. One South African commentator gives this explanation of the differences between the two concepts of equality:

> [F]ormal equality is blind to entrenched structural inequality. It ignores actual social and economic disparities between people and constructs standards that appear to be neutral, which in truth embody a set of particular needs and experiences which derive from socially privileged groups. Reliance on formal equality may therefore exacerbate inequality. Substantive equality, on the other hand, requires courts to examine the actual economic and social and political conditions of groups and individuals in order to determine whether the Constitution's commitment to equality is being upheld. (De Vos 2000:67)[24]

An analysis based on substantive equality seeks to compensate for past inequalities, and recognises that applying formal equality to an unequal reality may simply entrench the existing situation.[25]

---

22. The South African parliament has applied a succession of rules that have tried to capture some of these nuances. See the Natural Fathers of Children Born out of Wedlock Act 86 of 1997, the Adoption Matters Amendment Act 56 of 1998 and the Children's Act 38 of 2005.

23. Good examples of such analysis can be found, for example, in the dissenting judgment of Justice O'Regan in *Harksen*:333ff and the dissenting judgments of Justices O'Regan and Sachs in *S v Jordan*:656ff.

24. See also Cassidy 2002:58. The South African *Hugo* case explained the distinction this way:
    [A]lthough a society which affords each human being equal treatment on the basis of equal worth and freedom is our goal, we cannot achieve that goal by insisting upon identical treatment in all circumstances before that goal is achieved. Each case, therefore, will require a careful and thorough understanding of the impact of the discriminatory action upon the particular people concerned to determine whether its overall impact is one which furthers the constitutional goal of equality or not. A classification which is unfair in one context may not necessarily be unfair in a different context. (*Hugo*:23E–G)

25. Ideas about substantive equality are inherent in arguments for Black Economic Empowerment, although these arguments usually focus on race inequality to the exclusion of class inequalities.

Of course, a law that takes account of unequal realities must also try to move towards the ideal of sexual equality. Achieving this delicate balance in complex family situations will be very difficult.

Similar issues will probably arise in future in other contexts. For example, the deputy minister of labour recently announced that his ministry was hard at work on introducing leave proposals for paternity leave to correspond with the paid maternity leave already provided for mothers, on the grounds that "men should also have the right to obtain leave to look after their babies" (*The Namibian,* 10/7/2006).[26] However, proposals for paternity leave may founder on the twin shoals of biological fact (given that there is no limit to the number of children a man can father over any particular time period) and social reality (given that most Namibian men are not involved in the day-to-day care of their children, no matter how much one might wish for the situation to be different). The debate on when and in what ways women and men are similarly situated on this issue, and on how to tailor such a law to encourage more involvement between fathers and children in reality, will be interesting.

Moving forward

There is a large plain of uncharted territory between the ideal and the actual. For example, during the debates about child custody in relation to the Children's Status Act, many women expressed their hope that some day men and women in Namibia would play a genuinely equal role in childcare, but pointed to the dangers of legislating today for a social ideal that is perhaps still several generations away. The law can lead, but not if it moves so far ahead that the public can no longer see its light.

Men in many parts of the world are struggling to adapt as definitions of masculinity are in a state of transition (Kaufman 1993). Namibia has seen a number of far-reaching social changes since independence, so it is not surprising that changes in the home are particularly frightening to some. It is natural for people to be fearful of change, and particularly when they believe that the change in question will lead to a reduction in their personal power and status.

This is not to imply that men are the sole source of resistance to changes in the direction of gender equality. Some women are exploiting the situation – for example,

---

26. The Labour Act 6 of 1992 currently in force provides for three months of maternity leave for any woman who has been employed for at least one year by the same employer (section 41), with maternity benefits (80% of full pay up to a ceiling of N$3,000) financed by matching employer and employee contributions through the Social Security Act 34 of 1994. Neither Act makes any provision for paternity leave or parental leave. The Labour Bill 2007, which is before parliament at the time of writing, would provide improved provisions on maternity leave, but still makes no provision for paternity leave. (See also *The Namibian,* 31/3/2004 and Burnett 2004a & 2004b.)

Previously, after Deputy Minister of Higher Education Hadino Hishongwa called for the introduction of paternity leave, Director General of National Planning Commission Saara Kuugongelwa-Amadhila jokingly expressed the hope that "our very sensible men" will soon get the benefit of paternity leave "so that they can have more time to go to kambashus (shebeens) and come back and harass wives and their newborn babies who disturb them in the night" (*The Namibian,* 8/5/2002).

by bringing false charges of rape – and some are as reluctant as men to change familiar relations between the sexes. Another problem is the 'sugar daddy' syndrome (where young girls give sexual favours to older men in exchange for money and luxuries). This type of relationship reinforces stereotyped ideas that girls are dependent on males for their success and security, while the age gap works against any form of equality in the relationships. This also suggests that sex is the main attribute of value that girls have at their disposal, and that men are to be valued not in themselves but only in terms of what material goods they can provide. In this way, sugar daddy relationships can undermine the self-respect of both parties involved.

One root of the problem seems to lie in public perceptions of power within families as a finite resource, so that the empowerment of women is viewed as leading ineluctably to the disempowerment of men.[27] If family issues are to move forward effectively, it will be helpful for men and women to understand different interpretations of power and how increased sexual equality can be an economic and emotional gain for the entire family. To this end, public awareness efforts on family law issues should not focus only on information about new laws, but also on influencing attitudes that affect the acceptance of new approaches.

It is also important for the courts, the legislature and the public to develop deeper understandings of sexual equality. The goal should not be to ensure that every law in Namibia is gender-neutral, but rather to ensure that past discrimination is remedied and harmful stereotypes and practices are eliminated.

There is at present increased attention to gender issues in Africa – at least in terms of rhetoric if not yet in reality. The Protocol to the African Charter on Human and People's Rights on the Rights of Women in Africa – ratified by 21 nations and signed by a total of 43 of the 53 members of the African Union as of June 2007 – takes a very progressive stance on a range of family law topics ranging from polygamy to the rights of widows. At the same time, Namibia's parliament and other national institutions are constantly acquiring experience, and hopefully increased maturity. It would not be unreasonable to hope that these developments will lead to more subtle understandings of equality as a complex concept.

References

Albertyn, Cathi and Goldblatt, Beth (1998), 'Facing the Challenge of Transformation: Difficulties in the Development of an Indigenous Jurisprudence of Equality,' *South African Journal of Human Rights,* Vol. 14, p. 248

Becker, Heike (1995), *Namibian Women's Movement 1980 to 1992: From Anti-Colonial Resistance to Reconstruction.* Frankfurt: Verlag für Interkulturelle Kommunikation

---

27. For example, a study based on interviews with urban men in Katutura, Khomasdal and Windhoek, and rural men in northern Namibia concluded that many men feel that gender-related laws discriminate against men in favour of women. They feel that "men and women should have equal laws," but believe at the same time that "the law protects women mostly" (Lebeau/Spence 2004:30).

— and Claassen, Pamela (1996), *Violence against Women and Children: Community Attitudes and Practices*. Report prepared for the Women & Law Committee of the Law Reform and Development Commission, unpublished mimeo

Bonthys, Elsje (2000), 'Deny Thy Father and Refuse Thy Name: Namibian Equality Jurisprudence and Married Women's Surnames,' *South African Law Journal*, Vol. 117, p. 464

Burnett, Matthew (2004a), 'Is Namibia Prepared For Paternity Leave?' *The Namibian*, 25 June

— (2004b), 'Pros And Cons To Paternity Leave,' *The Namibian*, 2 July

Cassidy, Elizabeth (2002), *A Delicate Balance: Equality, Non-Discrimination and Affirmative Action in Namibian Constitutional Law – as compared to South African and US Constitutional Law*. Unpublished Master's thesis, University of Stellenbosch

Dentlinger, Lindsay (2005), 'Minister 'stuns, surprises' NA with Children's Bill Objections,' *The Namibian*, 17 February

De Vos, Pierre (2000), 'Equality for All? A Critical Analysis of the Equality Jurisprudence of the Constitutional Court,' *Tydskrif vir Hedendags Romeinse Hollandse Reg*, Vol. 63, p. 62

Kaufman, Michael (1993), *Cracking the Armour: Power, Pain and the Lives of Men*. Toronto: Viking

Kende, M. (2000), 'Gender Stereotypes in South African and American Constitutional Law: The Advantages of a Pragmatic Approach to Equality and Transformation,' *South African Law Journal*, Vol. 117, p. 745

LeBeau, Debie (1996), *The Nature, Extent and Causes of Domestic Violence against Women and Children in Namibia*. Report prepared for the Women & Law Committee of the Law Reform and Development Commission, unpublished mimeo

— et al. (1999), *Taking Risks – Taking Responsibility: An Anthropological Assessment of Health Risk Behaviour in Northern Namibia*. Windhoek: Ministry of Health and Social Services

— and Spence, Grant (2004), 'Community Perceptions on Law Reform: People Speaking Out,' in Justine Hunter (ed.), *Beijing + 10: The Way Forward – An Introduction to Gender Issues in Namibia*. Windhoek: Namibia Institute for Democracy

Legal Assistance Centre (LAC) (2006), *Proposed Amendments to the Children's Status Bill*, Submission to the National Council Standing Committee on Gender, Youth and Information

— (2007), *Rape in Namibia: An Assessment of the Operation of the Combating of Rape Act 8 of 2000* (Full Report). Windhoek: LAC

Menges, Werner (2002), 'Swakop Man Makes Gender Equality History,' *The Namibian*, 11 July

Ministry of Health and Social Services (MoHSS) (2003), *Namibia Demographic and Health Survey 2000*. Windhoek: MoHSS.

Ministry of Women Affairs and Child Welfare (MWACW) (2005), *Comments of the Ministry of Women Affairs and Child Welfare on the Report of the Committee on the Children's Status Bill*, 16 February

National Assembly (NA) (2004), *Report on the Children's Status Bill* by the Parliamentary Standing Committee on Human Resources, Social and Community Development

— (2006), *Report on Children's Status Bill* [B. 13–2005] by the National Council Standing Committee on Gender, Youth and Information

National Society for Human Rights (NSHR) (undated), *Submission on Children's Status Bill* [B.13–2005] to National Council Standing Committee on Gender, Youth and Information

Rose Junius, SMH et al. (1998), *An Investigation to Assess the Nature and Incidence of Spouse Abuse in Three Sub-Urban Areas in the Karas Region, Namibia.* Windhoek: Ministry of Health and Social Services

Talavera, Philippe (2002), 'Sexual Culture in Transition in the Northern Kunene – Is There a Need for a Sexual Revolution in Namibia?' in V. Winterfeldt et al. (eds), *Namibia Sociology.* Windhoek: University of Namibia

Tribe, Lawrence H. et al. (2005), 'On Judicial Review,' *Dissent,* summer 2005. Online: www.dissentmagazine.org/article/?article=219 [accessed 25/7/2007]

Cases

Ex Parte Attorney-General, Namibia: in re Corporal Punishment by Organs of State 1991 NR 178 (SC)

Frank v Chairperson of the Immigration Selection Board 2001 NR 107 (SC), overruling 1999 NR 257 (HC)

Fraser v Children's Court, Pretoria North and Others 1997 (2) SA 261 (CC)

Harksen v Lane NO & Others 1998 (1) SA 300 (CC)

Müller v President of the Republic of Namibia and Another 1999 NR 190 (SC)

Müller & Engelhard v Namibia, Communication No. 919/2000, U.N. Doc. CCPR/C/74/D/919/2000 (2002)

Myburgh v Commercial Bank of Namibia 2000 NR 255 (SC)

Namunjepo & Others v Commanding Officer, Windhoek Prison & Another 1999 NR 271 (SC)

National Coalition for Gay and Lesbian Equality & Others v Minister of Home Affairs & Others 2000 (2) SA 1 (CC)

President of the Republic of South Africa v Hugo 1997 (4) SA 1 (CC)

S v Jordan & Others 2002 (6) SA 642 (CC)

S v van Wyk 1993 NR 426 (HC)

Toonen v Australia, Communication No. 488/1992, U.N. Doc CCPR/C/50/D/488/1992 (1994)

HIV/AIDS in Namibia

Gender, class and feminist theory revisited

Lucy Edwards

Western feminist thought has provided the analytical tools for understanding gender inequalities. Throughout Africa, there has been a patriarchal backlash against Western feminism. The central argument is that feminism is un-African and that it undermines African culture. This argument does not take into account the fractured nature of African identities and African culture, nor does it take into account the huge class and gender cleavages that exist on the continent. Often the authority of African culture is invoked to legitimise African patriarchy. While cultures do endure, their mutability is demonstrated by the proliferation of Western consumerism among the African elite and the rapid adoption of Western values of competitiveness and symbols of success (Gucci shoes, Armani suits and SUVs). It is, however, in the area of gender relations that resistance to change is most ferocious.

While Western feminist analysis has thus far failed to explain adequately African women's experiences due to the ethnographic and class roots of its own construction, this criticism should not detract from deep-rooted African patriarchy or the value of feminist analysis in understanding HIV/AIDS. The devastation caused by HIV/AIDS makes the struggle for female emancipation all the more urgent, as the rapid spread of the virus is directly linked to high levels inequality and exploitation.

The irrefutable link between the HIV virus and AIDS should not lead to the medicalisation of the problem. Parallel epidemiological patterns in North America and Asia affirm the linkages between HIV/AIDS, gender and class (Farmer 1993:223 and 1996:37). The recognition that HIV/AIDS is not simply a biomedical problem, but arises out of certain social structural conditions negates dominant racist stereotypes that AIDS is essentially an African disease with black victims. While poverty and social inequalities are the structural drivers of HIV/AIDS, AIDS also reproduces and intensifies poverty and inequalities due to household income loss and increased expenditure related to increased levels of morbidity and mortality.

Epidemiological discourses on HIV/AIDS can be divided into four categories. First, we have the *biomedical* discourse that medicalises HIV/AIDS and locates it within a public health framework. Then there is the *behaviouralist* discourse that individualises HIV/AIDS as a psychological and behavioural problem driven by individual autonomous choice. More recent literature saw the emergence of a *human rights* discourse that asserts certain individual sexual, reproductive, treatment and socioeconomic rights in the context of liberal democracy. Last but not least is the *political economy* discourse that locates the socio-structural dimensions of HIV and AIDS. Feminist analysis that places causality in a socio-structural realm has found the least resonance within policy debates, perhaps because it calls for socially redistributive and transformative interventions.

The HIV virus crossed the species barrier more than 70 years ago (Hunter 2003). The reason we have an epidemic at this historical juncture is linked to how features of precolonial African practices converge with modern patriarchal African political economy. The fact that HIV/AIDS has hit poorer countries and the poor people in those countries hardest is linked to gross inequalities at global, national, local and household levels. The reticence in acknowledging or acting on these inequalities reflects the dominant neoliberal orthodoxy that resists any suggestions of redistributive or socially transformative interventions in response to AIDS.

High HIV prevalence and AIDS death rates come at a time of economic dislocation, mass poverty and high income disparities (Global Fund Secretariat 2002:2). In addition to the high HIV infection rates, Namibia also has the world's highest tuberculosis (TB) rates. The TB-HIV co-infection rates stand at between 50–60% (Sibeene 2007). The broader structural economic features that undermine health and provide conditions for rapid HIV spread are embedded in some of Namibia's key economic indicators (United Nations 2004). Although Namibia is classified as a lower middle income country, average per capita income masks the high levels of income inequality. The Gini coefficient that measures income inequalities currently stands at 0.6 (Namibia Household Income and Expenditure Survey 2003/2004). Caprivi and Ohangwena are Namibia's poorest regions: they also have the lowest level of per capita consumption and the highest level of AIDS-related deaths and therefore high orphan populations (Ruiz-Casares 2007 and Weidlich 2006b).

HIV/AIDS and female dependency

Namibia is ranked amongst the top five AIDS-affected countries in the world (Global Fund Secretariat 2002). The national HIV prevalence rate is 19.9%. There are, however, regional disparities and prevalence rates vary from 39.4% in Katima Mulilo to 7.9% in Opuwo. HIV infection rates are highest in the 25–29 year age group (Report of the 2004 National HIV Sentinel Survey 2005:15). Women bear the greatest HIV burden. They account for almost 60% of new infections (United Nations 2004), and 55% of those living with AIDS (Ngavirue 2006). We are therefore talking about the feminisation of HIV/AIDS because women, particularly poor women, are disproportionately affected when compared with any other social group.

There are biological factors that make women's bodies more susceptible to HIV infection. Higher HIV concentrations in male seminal fluids, the bigger vaginal surface and the higher incidence of vaginal trauma as a result of Sexually Transmitted Infections (STIs) or the insertion of agents to meet male preference for dry sex (Jackson 2002:136) make male-to-female HIV transmission 2–5 times more likely than female-to-male transmission (Farmer et al 1996:47). However, these biological factors must be seen in the context of gender power relationships. Unequal power relationships impede women's ability to protect themselves from HIV exposure. Addressing HIV/AIDS therefore implies policy measures beyond public health or behaviouralist frameworks.

Some of the limitations of Western feminism stem from the dualistic heuristic devices it employs to analyse gender oppression. The production-reproduction, agency-structure, biological-social or subject-object dichotomies do not adequately capture African women's experiences. The feminisation of HIV/AIDS has exposed the overlaps between these categories of abstraction generated by social theory. For example, socialists (Engels 1972; Sacks 1998 and Millet 1998) link women's oppression to the advent of private property and monogamous marriage. However, the Namibian experience shows that African women's oppression is not necessarily an outcome of private property or monogamous marriage, but rather of male control over the means of production and social surpluses. It also shows that patriarchy can constitute itself under different modes of accumulation and family structures. In many parts of Namibia, factors implicated in HIV/AIDS spread have their roots in precolonial African political economy where the primary means of production, land, was not privately owned but communally owned. However, gendered land tenure patterns allowed men to appropriate social surpluses and hence command the labour, sexuality and fertility of women.

Becker (1995:76–7) disputes the notion of women's oppression in 'traditional' Namibian society because of the relative autonomy African women had to control surpluses produced from the plots allocated to them by their husbands and the fact that some women of royal descent had some political influence. Hango-Rummukaien (1998) further argues that the contract labour system introduced by capitalist social relations destroyed the historical control women had over property and social surpluses. Both ignore the fact the female body was exploited in precolonial society and that that women provided the primary source of wealth accumulation and surplus extraction. The gendered patterns of control over primary productive assets created the systemic basis for precolonial patriarchy.

In most of the crop-growing societies of Southern Africa, including parts of Namibia, women provided the primary source of labour (Haviland 1993:221) and their fertility ensured the future labour supply. Despite the communal ownership of land, men controlled land use through gendered land-tenure patterns and surpluses through gendered inheritance systems. The link between sexuality and economy was forged through the institution of marriage. Adult males (and not females) received land from the chief and then in turn granted usufruct to their wife/wives, who produced most of the household food supply. Female livelihoods were therefore primarily predicated upon their sexual relationship with a man (Gordon 1996:290).

Women's bodies provided productive labour. In addition, women's bodies could be exchanged for other forms of wealth such as cattle and land. The payment of bridewealth in the form of cattle was an exchange relationship between the woman's father/uncles and her husband for control over her labour and fertility (Guy 1990:40). Women's fertility reproduced future generations of labour. Control over the female body meant control over a primary source of surplus production (Koopman 1995). The polygamous marriage provided men with increased opportunities for wealth accumulation through their control over multiple female bodies.

In Namibia, as in South Africa, the colonial capitalist economy built itself on the pre-existing gender division of labour found in the precapitalist peasant familial mode of production. The articulation of capitalist and precapitalist modes of production resulted in female labour providing the basis for super exploitation and capitalist accumulation (Guy 1990:43–4 and Gordon 1996:21).

There is a trajectory of female dependency from precolonial modes of production to the present that has and still severely impedes women's sexual and reproductive autonomy. This constitutes causal relationships between production, sexuality and reproduction. The feminist binarisation of production and reproduction presents us with a false dichotomy, for they are integrally linked into the patriarchal political economy.

Biological essentialist arguments are often used to present women's oppression as natural and inevitable. We often hear that men are stronger than women and therefore they are the protectors and providers, while women are the bearers and nurturers of children because they are weaker. Even radical feminists such as Firestone fall into the trap of biological essentialism, for instance when she argues that women's role in biological reproduction creates their dependency on men (Firestone 1998). However, in many Namibian communities the polygamous family historically formed the most basic unit of production and reproduction. Female labour also formed the backbone of the peasant subsistence economy. Women's reproductive functions did not limit them to domesticity, as they worked in the fields throughout pregnancy, resumed work shortly after childbirth, and continued to work in the fields alongside lactation and childrearing and in addition to other domestic responsibilities.

Firestone is thus referring to a white middle class phenomenon of advanced Western capitalist societies. This 'Parsonian'[1] nuclear family gave rise to the phenomenon Betty Friedan termed the "feminine mystique"[2] and differs substantially from most family forms in Namibian society. Historically, African women have always been at the centre of production and played the role of providers despite their biological and social reproduction functions.

What is changing is the fact that with introduction of capitalism and Christianity there has been a decline in the polygamous marriage (Population and Housing Census 2001). This ongoing process results in the economic dislocation of single black women. Despite its inequality and oppressiveness, the polygamous marriage gave women access (though not control) to the primary means of production, namely land.

The decline in formal polygamous marriages does not mean an end to polygamous sexual cultures. The figures seem to indicate a trend towards one formal marriage.[3] This, however, does not preclude multiple partner non-monogamous sexual relations outside formal unions. Formal marital unions were traditional alliances between family groups and carried with them certain obligations that are absent in the non-formal, stable or casual unions. Wives in polygamous unions had powers and responsibilities in accordance with their seniority and were provided with a means of sustaining themselves and their children through their access to land, which women in non-formal unions do not have.

1. Talcot Parsons (as cited in Haralambos, Holborn and Holborn1990:462) identified 'the family' as consisting of two heterosexual parents and their dependent children. This nuclear family has a clear division of labour in terms of which the role of the father is breadwinner and protector and the mother takes care of the socialisation of the young and the stabilisation of adult personalities. Feminism used this family model to construct public-private and production-reproduction dichotomies.

2. Betty Friedan in Feminine Mystique likened the situation of women in white middle class America to a gilded cage. Western feminism tended to universalise these experiences, thereby betraying its own class and ethnographic roots, as pointed out by Angela Davis (1982), Patricia Hill-Collins (1990) and bell hooks (1984).

3. Comparisons between the 1991 and 2001 population census data indicate that marriage rates are on the decline.

The network of multi-partner sexual relationships that arises out of polygamous sexual cultures places formal wives, informal wives and casual partners at risk of HIV infection. This explains why married women are also at risk of HIV infection, even if they are not always recognised as a risk group. An SADC study revealed that HIV infection rates are six times higher among married women than among single women (Tibinyane 2003).

Past studies have linked HIV/AIDS to male sexual promiscuity (Le Beau et al 1999), but with economic displacement women are increasingly forced into multiple sexual relationships as a means of securing livelihoods. This increases the rate of change in sexual partnerships and size of sexual networks that fuel the rapid spread of the disease. Women's unequal status and their dependency constrain their sexual autonomy and their ability to negotiate safe sex.

Single economically displaced women often enter into serial monogamous relationships as a means of economic survival. A study of such relationships in the Ohangwena region of Namibia shows that women will repeatedly enter into relationships that have no formal status. Instead of paying a bride price to the woman's kin, as would have been case in a formal/traditional marriage, the man undertakes to support the woman financially during their union. Often the woman will have children with the man, who later abandons her to raise the children alone. The cycle can be repeated a number of times, as each time the relationship ends the woman has to seek the patronage of another male (Tersbol 2002:353).

Some women will have more than one relationship at the same time to improve their financial position. The ephemeral nature of these sexual unions forces some women into multiple sexual relationships, since they do not have the relative economic stability and access to productive resources that those in traditional polygamous marriages have.

Despite the relatively low marriage rates, the Namibian National Population and Housing Census (2001) statistics classify 43.1% of the economically inactive population as homemakers. Seventy per cent are women. In absolute numbers, this 43.1% amounts to a total of 186,644 people, which is in fact more than the number of formally unemployed persons in the country (185,258). Given the absence of a social security net, this means that a large group of women are not employed on their own account but depend on others for their livelihoods.

Although female rural subsistence farmers are classified as own-account workers, their labour mainly ensures household food supply and does not provide them with cash income. The need for cash becomes more pertinent in an increasingly monetised economy. They rely on remittances from the modern wage labour sector for cash income or they rely on pension payments.

At the beginning stages of capitalist development in Namibia, male labour migration resulted in an increase in women's workloads in the rural subsistence economies (Becker 1994:99). Economic monetisation has also led to the monetisation of gender relations as cash started replacing cattle as a medium of exchange. Control over cash increased male power and female dependency, because restrictions on female migration[4] caused reliance on male cash remittances for interactions with the market economy

---

4. Winterfeldt (2002:48–52) points to the colonial restrictions on labour migration, such as pass laws. The Native Administration Proclamation No11of 1922 restricted the issue of work permits solely to men.

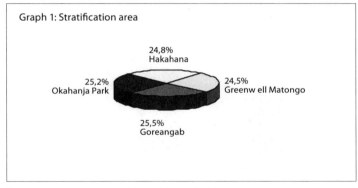

Graph 1: Stratification area

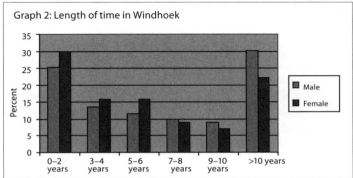

Graph 2: Length of time in Windhoek

(Winterfeldt 2002:48–52). With increased economic displacement and the abolition of influx control legislation, female migration to urban areas has increased significantly since Namibia's independence. However, our research shows that female migrants have difficulty in entering the formal labour market and have to eke out precarious livelihoods in the informal economy or engage in risky sexual behaviour as part of their survival strategies.

Social and economic changes add to the complex structure of society as new classes begin to form. Emerging classes or class fractions are wage workers, informal sector traders, working and non-working poor and urban elites, who by virtue of their privileged positions in politics, the administrative system or business, attain considerable incomes. High-income males from privileged positions often become the sugar daddies to young girls and the partners of unemployed women in transactional sexual relationships.

Our empirical data[5] were collected in the informal settlements of Windhoek. Three data collection instruments were used, namely a baseline survey, focus group discussion and key informant interviews. The baseline survey provided demographic and social economic data that permitted correlations between sexual attitudes, behaviour and socio-cultural circumstances. A total number of 712 interviews were conducted in four different informal settlements, Goreangab, Okahandja Park, Hakahana and Greenwell Matongo as shown in Graph 1. The informal settlements act as the reception centres for new urban migrants and Graph 2 shows an increase in female migration, particularly over the last five years.

---

5. All empirical data cited in this article was collected in 2004 and reported in Edwards (2005).

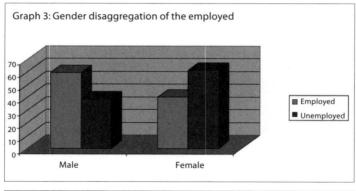

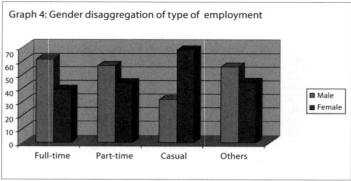

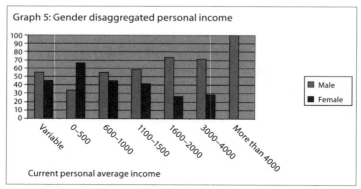

Graphs 3, 4 and 5 show that women face higher levels of labour market exclusion and that when they have jobs, they are most likely to be casual and with lower pay. The study also shows 61.4% unemployment among new female migrants in informal settlements. This is much higher than unemployment in the general population, which, depending on the source, is set at between 19% and 34.5%.[6] In addition, women are more likely to be in casual employment. This implies less job security, no benefits and lower incomes.

---

6. Population and Housing Census of 2001 sets the unemployment rate at 19% but the Labour Force Survey 1997–2000 sets it at 34.5%.

Focus group discussions revealed that men generally have more skills they could use to generate income such as plumbing, electrical repairs and maintenance work. The gender disaggregation of schooling indicates that up to junior secondary level more women have access to education than men. In the senior secondary and tertiary phases, the gender gap reverses in favour of men, who then show higher levels of educational attainment.

Sixty-six per cent of all women reported a monthly income of below N$ 500 a month. The results also show an inverse relationship between gender and level of income, as women were less represented in higher income categories, and the concentration of women is in the lower income categories. Not a single woman reported a personal income of N$ 4,000 or more per month. Besides wages and salaries, respondents were asked to indicate other sources of income in order to establish how income is generated outside formal employment. The majority (34%) reported no other sources of income. Of those who had other sources of income besides wages and salaries, 31.6% of all female respondents cited boyfriends as another source of income.

Although some may see female migration as an expression of human agency and an attempt to escape patriarchal control, our research shows that these women are subjected to new forms of patriarchal control as their bodies become commodified and the means by which they secure their tenuous livelihoods.

Marginalised women's survival strategies are often hailed as an assertion of female agency and testimony of women's ability to negotiate patriarchy at an individual level. This is also seen as evidence of a resisting subject who defies victim stereotypes (Barriteau 1995). The point often overlooked is that survival strategies do not challenge the structural basis of women's marginalisation or exclusion, nor do they challenge the gender and class division of labour and ownership patterns that force many women to eke out a living on the margins of the economy. The ingenuity with which some women at times establish very tenuous livelihoods bears testimony to creative and active subjects. This should not be romanticised as emancipation. It is mere survival.

The socio-cultural construction of sexuality and autonomous, rational choice

Since Firestone, a whole generation of poststructuralist feminist scholarship attempted to overcome the reductionism of the base-superstructure metaphor to explore the multiplicity and intersecting nature of power that is neither essentialist or deterministic. The retreat from structuralism was also an attempt to give an account of the individual human subject that totalising meta-narratives lacked (Weedon 1997 and Hill-Collins 1990). The poststructuralist feminist female subject became a corporeal and sexual subject whose body is the root of subjectivity, and the corporeal manifestation of relations of power (Harcourt 2002:290–2).

This concern with the politics of the body provides new insights into the intersection between the sexual and the social. While the incisiveness of poststructuralist feminist analysis lies in pointing out how women's corporeal experiences are outcomes of relations of power, it does not, however, provide us with a clue as to the causes of these power differentials. The focus on women's diverse experiences occludes any assertions of causality, common interests or collective struggles. It tends to privilege the role of subject and individual agency over social structure. This presents the danger of positioning the struggle for control over the body as an individual one, thus liquidating collective struggles for structural change that will give many poor women the space to control their own bodies.

The feminist argument of the body as a marker of social power and the site of many struggles (Harcourt 2002:293) become very germane when theorising HIV/AIDS. While being transmitted through and acting on the body, the HIV/AIDS epidemic in Southern Africa is an outcome of relations of subjugation and domination. If the retreat from structuralism has underscored the multiplicity and intersecting nature of power, then HIV/AIDS once again foregrounds the structural nature of that power.

The feminist debates around the epistemological location of female oppression are often dichotomised into biological essentialist or social constructivist discourses. However, HIV/AIDS shows the interconnectedness between the socio-cultural and the biological and blurs the boundaries between these theoretical constructs. The dominant biomedical and behaviouralist discourses on HIV/AIDS have ignored the gross class and gender inequalities that spawn its spread. The underlying assumptions of most campaigns are that once individuals have been educated about the modes of HIV transmission and prevention, they will make rational choices about protecting themselves (Fox 2002). Our findings show that the link between knowledge and sexual behaviour modification is not linear or automatic. Sexual and reproductive decisions are not always made out of own volition, as the liberal philosophy of autonomous free choice that underlies the ABC rule seems to suggest.

Farmer et al. (1996:199–200) argues that the epistemic shift towards behaviouralist and individualistic psychological explanatory frameworks tends to atomise and individualise HIV/AIDS. It dis-socialises a very social phenomenon. It also results in a near obsession with knowledge, attitudes and behaviour surveys to identify the causes of HIV spread. The weaknesses of these explanatory frameworks lies not in what they reveal but rather conceal, namely an account of the social-structural factors implicated in HIV/AIDS spread and how those structural factors diminish autonomous choice.

Our research findings show a high level of HIV/AIDS awareness. This is consistent with findings elsewhere that show where there are high levels of HIV prevalence there are high levels of HIV/AIDS awareness (United Nations 2002). Most respondents (99.2%) had heard of HIV/AIDS. Respondents were very aware of how one could protect oneself against HIV/AIDS infection. The majority (84.8%) of respondents knew that there is no cure for the disease. Only 6% felt that a doctor, nurse or traditional healer could cure AIDS. Ninety per cent agreed that HIV infection could be prevented through condom use. When asked what preventive measures they would recommend, 64% said condoms and 19.6% said being faithful to one partner while 13.4% recommended abstinence. People were also very aware of other forms of transmission and prevention such as avoiding contact with contaminated blood and other body fluids. So why then, despite high levels of knowledge and awareness, do we still such a high percentage of new infections?

The link between sex and marriage forged in HIV/AIDS campaigns ignores the socio-cultural construction of sexuality. In Namibia, 19% of the population have marriage certificates. A further 7% are in stable relationships without having gone through

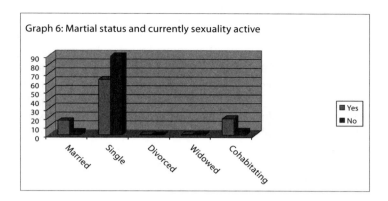

a legal or traditional marriage (Population and Housing Census of 2001). In our study, 13.4% of all respondents reported that they were married and a further 15.5% were co-habiting. Men reported societal and peer pressure to prove manhood by being sexually active. Women reported a lack of sexual autonomy to make decisions about abstinence due to unequal gender power relationships and economic exigencies. As Graph 6 shows, most people engaged in premarital sex despite calls for abstinence.

The 'be faithful' aspects of the ABC rule fly in the face of existing polygamous sexual cultures. Elements of traditional African patriarchal sexual cultures are still widespread and exist alongside Christian patriarchal sexual norms, resulting in a synthesis and a wide range of sexual norms.

The Western Christian notion of being faithful as advocated in prevention campaigns does not carry the same meaning in all cultures. In our research population, some saw it as applicable to women and not to men. Some traditions do not recognise adultery as offensive towards women. It is for this reason that adultery has historically been something that only happens to men. When one man had sexual relations with the wife of another man, then adultery was committed against the male spouse of the woman involved in the adulterous affair and not against the female spouse(s) of the man who had the adulterous affair (Becker 1995:72). With some groups, polygamous male sexuality was and to some extent still is a desirable norm as it signifies social status. Monogamy on the other hand has traditionally been a poor man's burden.[7]

The migrant labour system introduced under apartheid capitalism further contributed to the polygamous sexual cultures, as men entered into additional sexual unions with women where they were based while still conducting relationships with spouses or partners in the rural areas.

Of the three elements of the ABC, rule our study shows condom use to be the most practised prevention strategy. However, gender inequality in decision-making over condom use underlines women's vulnerability. Patriarchal power relations and economic dependency often make it impossible for women to negotiate condom use.

Most women cannot express their own sexual desires or even discuss sexual matters with their partners. Culturally, women are taught to display a passive uninterested

---

7. In our interviews, we wanted to know why men still engage in sexual relations with multiple partners despite the threat of HIV/AIDS. We were constantly reminded that it is the "way of the forefathers."

aloofness about sex to confirm male sexual dominance in relation to female innocence and ignorance (Becker 1995). In addition, widespread gender-based violence creates a culture of fear that inhibits women's ability to express their sexual preferences freely.

Where ideological platforms failed to manufacture female consent to male control, the use of physical violence was an acceptable way of asserting male dominance and control over the female body. Anthropological research (unpublished research reports from a class of sociology students of the University of Namibia in 2005) show that many cultures justified the use of violence if a woman did not accept male authority or did not meet male domestic or sexual expectations. Violence against women is still widespread. The World Health Organization's (2005) country study on violence against women indicate that in Namibia 36% of women experienced some sort of physical or sexual violence at the hands their partners and that as many as 20% reported sexual abuse before they reached the age of 15 years.

Decisions about fertility are often not matters of personal choice, but made to meet family and social-cultural obligations. Fertility desires often outweigh health considerations, be it in relation to HIV exposure or the possibility of mother-to-child transmission (United Nations Secretariat 2002). Fertility desires are still central to social construction of masculine and feminine identities. Fatherhood is often synonymous with manhood and motherhood synonymous with womanhood. This creates pressure to prove fertility through unprotected sex (McFadden 1992). There is further speculation that women may want to prove their fertility and thereby good health to hide their HIV-positive status for fear of abandonment or stigmatisation by their spouses and families. This may explain why some have unprotected sex, risk pregnancy, ill health and possible HIV transmission to their unborn children.

In our research, male condom use was consistently higher than female condom use. Ninety per cent of men and 55% of women reported condom use with casual partners and 93.3% of men and 52.4% of women reported condom use with other partners. The empirical evidence suggests that condom use is relative to male preference. Since female condoms are not as freely available as male condoms and microbicides are still not a reality, women do not have the same degree of choice about condom use and other safe sex technologies.

Despite the polygamous sexual cultures that place women in stable unions at risk, there is still a great deal of ambivalence about a woman's right to protect herself through condom use, as shown in Graph 8 below. Of all men, 73.7% and 43.3% of all women thought that a man has a right to have sexual intercourse with his wife without a condom.

There are other sexual practices that further impede women's sexual autonomy and that increase their susceptibility to HIV infection, such as the practice of dry sex, wife lending,[8] early sexual debut and cross-generational sex, when young girls are offered to maternal uncles or cousins who initiate them into sexual activity or become involved with sugar daddies.

---

8. Talavera (2002:51) refers to the practice of Okujepisa or Oupanga used in Ovaherero and Ova-himba cultures where a man can offer his wife to a friend or person of high office to cement male friendship. Oupanga literally means demonstrating true friendship.

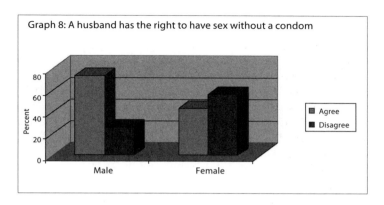

Graph 8: A husband has the right to have sex without a condom

Conclusions

A social-structural analysis of HIV/AIDS will necessarily lead to certain conclusions about the need for socially transformative interventions beyond behaviour change as assumed by most HIV/AIDS prevention campaigns. It in fact calls for action that will challenge the existing class and gender inequalities that fuel the spread of the disease in Namibia. The trajectory that links women's current dependent status has its roots in precolonial political economy. Colonialism exacerbated women's exploitation and post-independence economic policies have failed to address the gender imbalances in the ownership and control of productive assets, hence continuing the trajectory of female dependency that curtails sexual and reproductive autonomy and fuels the HIV spread.

Attempts to label all structural analysis of women's oppression as essentialist or reductionist dissipate when analysing the historical roots of women's dependency on men and how that dependency diminishes women's sexual and reproductive autonomy. Despite attempts to develop a non-economic analysis of power, the epidemiology of HIV/AIDS locates the disease firmly within the realm of structural-level inequalities, of which unequal access to productive assets and unequal resource distribution are the most structuring.

The question of how to tackle the HIV/AIDS spread is linked to how we tackle inequalities. Campaign messages based on assumptions of rational free choice mostly fail to bring about the desired results because they do not take into account the broader social-cultural construction of sexuality. Feminist analysis that points to the political economy of AIDS can help us understand the underlying causes of not only HIV spread, but the feminisation of the disease.

References

Barriteau, E. (1995), 'Postmodernist feminist Theorizing and Development Policy and Practice in the Anglophone Caribbean,' in M. Marchard and J. Parpart (eds), *Feminism Postmodernism Development.* London: Routledge

Becker, H. (1995), *Namibian Women's Movement 1980–92.* Frankfurt/Main: IKO

Berer, M. (1993), *Women and HIV/AIDS: An International Resource Book.* Pandora

Caplan, P. (ed.), (1987), *The Cultural Construction of Sexuality.* London: Routledge

Cranny-Frances et al. (2003), *Gender Studies: Terms and Debates.* New York: Palgrave

Davies, A. (1982), *Women, Race and Class.* London: Women's Press

Edwards, L. (2005), HIV/AIDS, *Patriarchy and Poverty: A gendered perspective.* Windhoek: !Nara Training Centre

Engels, F. (1972), *The Origin of the Family Private Property and the State.* New York: International Publishers

Epinge, S. (2003), 'The Relationship Between Gender Roles and HIV Infection in Namibia,' in B. Otaala (ed.), HIV/AIDS: *Government Leaders in Namibia Responding to the HIV/AIDS Epidemic.* Windhoek: University of Namibia Press

Farmer, P. (1993), 'AIDS and Racism,' *AIDS and Accusation.* Berkeley: University of California Press

— et al. (1996), *Women, Poverty and AIDS: Sex, Drugs and Structural Violence.* Maine: Common Courage Press

— (1999), 'The Persistent Plagues,' in P. Farmer, *Infections and Inequalities.* Berkeley: University of California Press

Firestone, S. (1998), 'The Dialectic of Sex,' in S. Ruth (ed.), *Issues In Feminism: An Introduction to Women's Studies.* California: Mayfield

Fox, T. (2002), 'The Cultures of AIDS: A Cultural Analysis and New Policy Approaches for Namibia,' in V. Winterfeldt, T. Fox and P. Mufune (eds), *Namibia, Society, Sociology.* Windhoek: University of Namibia Press

Fourie, P .(2005), *AIDS in Africa: Three Scenarios by UNAIDS.* Gordons Bay, Workshop Presentation

Frayne, B. and W. Pendleton (2003), *Mobile Namibia: Migration Trends and Attitudes.* Cape Town: Southern African Migration Project

Friedan, B. (1963), *The Feminine Mystique* (Online). Chapter 1. Available from: www.h-net.org/~hst203/documents/friedan1.html and Chapter 2. Available from: www.h-net.org/~hst203/documents/friedan2.html

Gordon, A. (1996), *Transforming Capitalist Patriarchy.* London: Lynne Reinner

Gordon, P. and K. Crehan (1999), *Dying of Sadness: Gender and Sexual Violence and the HIV Epidemic.* New York: UNDP

Guy, J. (1990), 'Gender Oppression in Southern Africa's Pre-capitalist Societies,' in C. Walker (ed.), *Women and Gender in Southern Africa to 1945.* Cape Town: David Philip

Hango-Rummukainen, B. (1998), *Gender and Migration: Social and Economic Effects on Women in Owambo (1890–1940).* Windhoek: UNAM Seminar Paper

Hangula, L. (2003), 'Opening and welcoming remarks at a workshop,' in B. Otaala (ed.), *HIV/AIDS: Government Leaders in Namibia Responding to the HIV/AIDS Epidemic.* Windhoek: University of Namibia Press

Haralambos, M. and M. Holborn (1990), *Sociology: Themes and Perspectives,* 3rd edition. London: Unwin Hyman.

— (1995), *Sociology: Themes and Perspectives*. London: Harper Collins

Harcourt, W. (2002), 'Body Politics: Revisiting the Population Question,' in K. Saunders (ed.), *Feminist Post-Development Thought: Rethinking Modernity, Post-Colonialism and Representation*. London: Zed

Haviland, W. (1993), *Cultural Anthropology*. Florida: Harcourt Brace

Hill-Collins, P. (1990), *Black Feminist Thought: Knowledge, Consciousness, and the Politics of Empowerment*. Boston: Unwin Hyman

Hooks, B. (1984), *Feminist Theory: From Margin to Centre*. Boston: South End

Hunter, J. (ed.), (2004), *Beijing +10 the Way Forward: An Introduction to Gender Issues in Namibia*. Windhoek: Namibia Institute for Democracy.

Hunter, S. (2003), *Black Death: AIDS in Africa*. Hampshire: Palgrave

Global Fund Secretariat (2002), *Namibian Country Co-ordination Mechanism for HIV/ AIDS, Tuberculosis and Malaria*. Windhoek: Funding Proposal

Iipinge, E. and D. Le Beau (1997), *Beyond Inequalities: Women in Namibia*. Windhoek: UNAM/ SARDC

— and M. Williams. M. (ed.), (2000), *Gender and Development*. Windhoek: Pollination

Jackson, H. (2002), *AIDS Africa: Continent in Crises*. Harare: SAfAIDS

Jauch, H. (2003), *The Namibian Labour Market at a Glance*. Windhoek: LaRRI Research Paper

Kemal, M. (2000), 'Reproductive Rights, Policies and Strategies,' in E. Iipinge and M. Williams (eds), *Gender and Development*. Windhoek: Pollination

Koopman, J. (1995), 'Women in the Rural Economy: Past, Present and Future,' in M. Hayman and S. Stichter (eds), *African Women South of the Sahara*. London: Longman

Le Beau, D., T. Fox, H. Becker and P. Mufune (1999), *An Anthropological Assessment of Health Risk Behaviour in Northern Namibia*. Windhoek: Ministry of Health and Social Services

Lash, S. (1990), *Sociology of Postmodernism*. London: Routledge

Loewenson, R. and A. Whiteside (1997), *Social and Economic Issues of HIV/AIDS in Southern Africa: A Review of Current Research*. Harare: SAfAIDS

Marchard, M. and J. Parpart (ed), (1995), *Feminism Postmodernism Development*. London: Routledge

Marshall, B. (1994), *Engendering Modernity: Feminism, Social Theory and Social Change*. Boston: Northeastern University Press

McFadden, P. (1992), 'Sex, Sexuality and the Problem of AIDS in Africa,' in R. Meena (ed.), *Gender in Southern Africa: Conceptual and Theoretical Issues*. Harare: SAPES

Millet, K. (1998), *Sexual Politics in Ruth, S (ed) Issues in Feminism: An Introduction to Women's Studies*. California: Mayfield

Mufune, P. (2002), 'Youth Problems in Namibia,' in D. Le Beau and J. Gordon (eds), *Challenges For Anthropology in the African Renaissance*. Windhoek: University of Namibia Press

Ngavirue, M. (2006), 'United We Win Divided AIDS Wins,' *New Era*, 4/12.2006

Republic of Namibia (1993), *1991 Population and Housing Census: National Report*. Windhoek: National Planning Commission

— (2002), *Report on the 2002 National HIV Sentinel Survey*. Windhoek: Ministry of Health and Social Services

— (2003), *2001 Population and Housing Census: National Report*. Windhoek: National Planning Commission

— (2005), *Report of the 2004 National HIV Sentinel Survey.* Windhoek: Ministry of Health and Social Services

Ruiz-Casares, M. (2007), 'How Did I become the Parent? Gender Responses to New Responsibilities among Namibian Child Headed Households,' in S. LaFont and D. Hubbard (eds), *Unravelling Taboos: Gender and Sexuality in Namibia.* Windhoek: Legal Assistance Centre

Sachs, K. (1998), 'The Class Roots of Feminism,' in S. Ruth (ed.), *Issues in Feminism: An Introduction to Women's Studies.* California: Mayfield

Saunders, K. (ed.), (2002), *Feminist Post-Development Thought: Rethinking Modernity, Post-Colonialism and Representation.* London: Zed

Sibeene, P. (2007), 'Namibia's TD Infection Too High,' *New Era,* 27/03/07

Sommerville, J. (2000), *Feminism and the Family: Politics and Society in the UK and USA.* London: Macmillan.

SWAPO (1984), *Women in Production and Reproduction.* London: Conference Paper

Talavera, P. (2002), *Challenging the Namibian Perception of Sexuality: A Case Study of the Ovahima and Ovaherero Culturo-sexual Models in Kunene North in the HIV/AIDS Context.* Windhoek: Gamsberg Macmillan

Tersbol, B. (2002), 'How to Make Sense of Lover Relationships: Kwanyama Culture and Reproductive Health,' in V. Winterfeldt, T. Fox. and P. Mufune (eds), *Namibia, Society, Sociology.* Windhoek: University of Namibia Press

Tibinyane, N. (2003), 'Are Reproductive Rights Respected and Promoted in Namibia?' *The Namibian,* 9/12/03

United Nations Secretariat (2002), *HIV/AIDS and Fertility in Sub-Saharan Africa: A Review of the Research Literature.* New York: United Nations

UNAIDS (2004), *Report on the Global AIDS Epidemic.* Geneva: United Nations

UNICEF (2005), *Childhood under Threat: The State of the World's Children.* New York: Report

Weedon, C. (1997), *Feminist Practice and Poststructuralist Theory.* Oxford: Blackwell

Weidlich, B. (2006), 'Caprivi the poorest region in Namibia, says report, *The Namibian,* 21/07/06

World Health Organization (2005), *WHO Multi-country Study on Women's and Domestic Violence.* Geneva: World Health Organization

Decolonising sexuality

Suzanne LaFont

Field notes, March 9, 2006: Thursday night at about 9:00 p.m. I walk into a bar on Independence Avenue in Windhoek. All of the bar stools are occupied by young beautiful black women. About thirty minutes later the men begin drifting in. In contrast to the women, many of who could have been supermodels, the men are older, balding, most sporting big beer bellies, and they are white. Subtle and not-so-subtle negotiations begin as the women vie for the men's attention and presumably, the contents of their wallets.

The above scenario, an integrated bar and interracial sexual interaction, would have been illegal under apartheid. Today it is part of what sexuality looks like in postcolonial Namibia. Race and class dynamics from the colonial era have been altered, but not eliminated and 'liberation' is the not first word that comes to one's mind while watching a scene, such as the one described here, unfold.

Independence in Namibia created an opportunity for immense political, economic and social changes. Liberation from colonisation and apartheid offered the hope for the realisation of other forms of freedom, such as the restructuring of gender roles and sexual mores. In many ways, the new constitution and legal reform reflected this atmosphere of equality and the expansion of personal liberty. However, independence has also fostered nationalism, which in turn has fostered self-consciousness about national identity and morality. The struggle for postcolonial national identity has at times involved the rejection of things foreign, including perceived foreign immoral sexual attitudes and practices. At the same time, a reverence for 'traditions,' including those that deny sexual self-determination, are defended under the auspices of nationalism.[1]

The 'new' Namibian morality is often at odds with human rights discourse. There is at once a desire to be both modern and politically correct and Namibian and African. At times it has not been easy to reconcile these sometimes contradictory notions in terms of national identity and statehood. In some cases, perceived Namibian-ness has been given preference over human rights.

Postcolonial debate on issues related to sexuality has been extensive, with topics ranging from HIV/AIDS to gay rights. The HIV/AIDS pandemic has, in some ways, forced sexuality out of the closet, while at the same time state-sponsored homophobia has ensured that many gays and lesbians stay in the closet (or out of the country). This

---

1. The entire notion of 'tradition' has been called into question, because cultures are continually evolving, the concept of 'traditions' is elusive and one has to be careful not to present a snapshot of a culture frozen in a time the 'photographer' deemed traditional (Becker 2000).

paper will begin with a brief description of pre-independence sexuality and then survey various aspects of sexuality and discuss the dynamics of sexuality in Namibia today.

Pre-Independence Sexuality

Christianity, colonisation and the various local sexual ideologies were the three major dynamics that shaped pre-independence sexuality. Colonialism affected sexuality on many levels, affecting gender roles and gender relations. The introduction of 19th century Christian doctrine with its patriarchal and puritanical morality impacted existing sexuality ideologies. Yet despite these hegemonic forces, local traditional sexual ideologies managed to evolve and survive. Iipinge and LeBeau (1995) note that "for many black Namibians, especially in the rural populations, traditional values and norms still apply today."

Traditional Sexualities

It is impossible to discuss comprehensively the sexual ideology of 'a' national culture in Namibia due to the differences in sexual beliefs among the diverse ethnic groups. Cross-cultural comparisons are also difficult because during the pre-independence era data about sexuality were not collected in any systematic way. Despite these disclaimers, the findings from some recent research may shed light on past and current sexual beliefs and behaviour.

Talavera (2007) interviewed three different generations of people in northern Namibia specifically about sexuality. He sought out the elders and asked them about the sexual mores, attitudes and practices that were accepted when they were young. He found that some of Namibia's ethnic groups allowed children to explore their sexuality with little adult interference.[2] However, once young people reached puberty, sexual experimentation, which could then lead to pregnancy, was strictly forbidden. Some ethnic groups had initiation rites to prepare young people for marriage that included basic information about sex. Marriages were arranged and girls were often married at a young age, usually shortly after their first menses. It was not uncommon for husbands to be significantly older than their wives. Wives were not allowed to reject their husband's sexual advances: refusal was seen as justification for a beating. Husbands were formally and informally allowed to have multiple partners, while wives were expected to be monogamous. Men as head of the household were entitled to make decisions about the couple's sexual and reproductive lives.

Despite the sexual freedom allowed some children, sex and sexuality were rather taboo subjects and, in general, parents did not discuss sex with their children. In some cultures, girls did not learn about menstruation until it occurred, and boys knew nothing of wet dreams until they had them. If young people were told about sex, it was often

---

2. Talavera (2007) has reported childhood sexual games among the Himba, Herero, San and people in the Kavango and Caprivi. The presence of institutionalised childhood sexual exploration has not been studied among the Owambo, Damara or Nama.

put in a negative context, for example, penises bite and premarital sex is lethal (Talavera 2007).

Christianity

British (1806), German (1842) and Finnish (1870) missionaries entered into cultural environments where, according to Becker (2007), class and not gender was the defining feature of power and many women held a high position. Christian doctrine from this period was patriarchal and held a primitive view of African sexuality. Many Christian missionaries in Namibia, as elsewhere, believed that African sexuality needed to be contained (Becker 2003). In order to accomplish this, a new moral order was promoted while traditional expressions of sexuality were discouraged. The new religion helped reinforce men's power vis-à-vis women. Namibian men were able to adopt the aspects of Christianity that suited them and further legitimised their power. Missionaries were influential in promoting female chastity, transforming or eliminating rituals related to initiations and eroding women's power.

The introduction of Christianity through missions turned out to be a double-edged sword for Namibians. The German government used their presence as a pretext for sending troops into the country, which led to the loss of land. The church also discouraged 'traditional' practices and beliefs and reinforced the existing silence on sexuality. On the positive side, missionaries had resources and assisted with education and health care and later they participated in the struggle for independence by supporting SWAPO and publicising the plight of Namibians (CSA n.d.). The long-term effects of the introduction of Christianity cannot be overstated and conservative Christian morality is strong and popular today and continues to impact sexual beliefs and practices.

Colonialism

The colonial administration refused to recognise women leaders and manipulated customary laws to suit its needs. Colonial officials promoted Western patriarchy, which reconfigured power within gender relations. Under colonial law, women were classified as minors: they could not vote nor own land and they needed their husband's permission to enter into legal contracts (LeBeau n.d.). Prior to this, many Namibian women enjoyed substantial autonomy in their personal and sexual lives (Becker 2007). Similar to those of the missions, colonial discourses constructed Namibian sexuality as the opposite of their own 'civilised' sexuality, something that needed to be contained and controlled (Becker n.d.).

Apartheid affected sexuality by putting into effect laws prohibiting the social and sexual intercourse between whites and people of other 'races.' The most important pieces of legislation regarding sexuality were the Prohibition of Mixed Marriages Act (No. 55) of 1949, which banned marriage and cohabitation between whites and non-whites and Amendments to The Immorality Act (1950), which went beyond the 1949 legislation and legally forbade sexual relations between whites and non-whites. This act gave police the power to spy on people, hunt them down, invade their homes, enter their bedrooms and confiscate their bed sheets and underwear as evidence: some suspects were forced to undergo physical exams. These insidious methods may have curbed, but did not prevent interracial intercourse. In South Africa, as many as 20,000 people were prosecuted, convicted and jailed under this law until its repeal in 1985 (Iyer 2005).[3] Presumably, this figure represents only the tip of the interracial sexual relations iceberg. Apartheid effectively pushed interracial sexuality underground and much of it remains there today.

Sexuality Today

> If I think young kids are having sex, it might be because of nowadays this television thing. The kids are more attracted to it, see the things on television and say let me give it a try, let me try it out. For example, the advertisement of using a condom, it is very wild. (13-year old boy from Katutura, quoted in Hailonga-van Dijk 2007)

Despite the 'modern' ring to the above quote, young people in Namibia face a conservative government, churches and parents. The young, especially those in urban areas, are caught between the new and the old morality. They are exposed to and must reconcile the in-your-face sexuality of the West with public health campaigns that focus on the dangers of sex and the conservative messages from the church and government. On one hand, there seems to be a reconfiguring of sexual morality due to the desire by the young to be 'modern.' On the other, the elders and their parents emphasize constraint and the importance of 'tradition.'

'Tradition' and Sexuality

The long struggle for independence has fostered a reverence for tradition and nostalgia for recognition of Namibian culture. On the one hand, there is a desire to be Namibian and African. On the other, there are strong desires in the government to be politically correct in terms of gender equality. On this point, some legal reform has been implemented, but the lives of people in rural areas have not been significantly impacted by new laws. Thus, independence has not liberated women from customs that disadvantage them and limit their freedom in terms of sexuality and marriage. Patriarchal practices are defended as 'traditions' and legal reform such as the Married Persons Equality Act 1 of 1996, which dethroned men as the legal head of their household, were fiercely debated and met much opposition before enactment (cf., Hubbard 2007).

One custom practised by many ethnic groups in Namibia that negatively impacts women's sexuality and has contributed to male dominance is *lobola,* the word that is locally used to describe bride price.[4] In Namibia, *lobola* was commonly paid in the form of cattle and was an indication that a man had wealth and, hence, would be able to support his wife. It was also a gesture of respect and gratitude to the bride's family for raising

---

3. According to court records, most cases involved European men and African women. Sentences were usually around six months in jail combined with caning (Farrell 2006).
4. The word *lobola* is Zulu in origin but is used throughout Southern Africa to describe bride price. Bride price was and is still practised in many cultures in Africa. Specific customs vary (e.g., bridewealth and bride service) but in all its forms it involves a transfer of goods and/or services from the groom or his family to the bride or her family.

his future bride. Today, *lobola* is more often seen as payment for a bride, meaning that the husband and his family have purchased the woman, including her future domestic production and children. This relegates wives to a rather powerless position within the family unit and promotes sexual abuse, physical abuse and limits her ability to negotiate safe sex. *Lobola* also creates hardships for men who find it is increasingly difficult to accumulate the necessary wealth to marry. This does not mean, however, that they forgo sex or parenthood: hence it contributes to the number of children being born out of wedlock (Pauli 2007).

Another custom that negatively impacts women's sexuality is polygyny. Twelve per cent of Namibian women live in polygynous unions, 8% report having one co-wife and 4% report having two or more co-wives. Polygamous marriage is illegal under civil law but is legal under some customary laws. Today, polygyny exposes women to HIV/AIDS because it increases the number of her husband's sexual partners, and there has been a move to outlaw it altogether (cf., Hubbard 2007). If outlawed, it would also be the end of levirate, another custom that disadvantages women by denying them sexual autonomy. Levirate, a custom in which the brother of a deceased man 'inherits' his brother's wife, is practised to some extent by most of the cultures in Namibia (except among the Nama). Traditionally, it is based on the benevolent idea of women needing men's protection and it would be cruel of the family to leave a woman without a husband. However, for some women their options are limited and the choice she must make is between a levirate union and abject poverty (Ovis 2005).

Race and Sexuality

As the field notes at the beginning of this chapter suggest, much of today's inter-racial sexual activity is based on mutual exploitation and rarely sees the light of day, despite the fact that laws prohibiting sexual apartheid have been repealed. This is primarily due to vast economic inequalities between blacks and whites and the persistence of social separation between whites and blacks, who often live, work and socialise in separate spheres. This separation is painfully evident in Windhoek. In areas such as Klein Windhoek and Ludwigsdorf, black domestic workers arrive in the morning to clean houses almost exclusively owned by whites. In the evening, they return to the former black township of Katutura, where white faces are a rarity. It is unusual to see interracial couples in town and rarer still is to see them accompanied by interracial offspring. White men and women who become openly involved with black men and women are assumed to be foreigners. Most Namibian-German families, despite having lived in Namibia for several generations, are still intermarrying and producing blond, blue-eyed children.

Wise's (2007) research confirms that racial prejudice still exists among elite Afrikaner men. She found that sexual stereotypes persist alongside the construction of the 'other' in terms of sexual prowess and ability and behaviour. Interestingly, some of Wise's informants appropriated African identity when describing their own sexual prowess – "You know what they say about African men ..." This is a sexual stereotype usually reserved for black, not white, African males. Most rich Afrikaner men claim to avoid sexual contact with black women and when Afrikaner men were presented with hypothetical scenarios of having sex with white and black women, some men admitted that they would not or had not used a condom when having sex with white women, but that they would definitely wear a condom when/if they had sex with black women. This suggests that there is a perception among Namibian elites that HIV/AIDS is a 'black disease,' a factor that could certainly reinforce racial sexual segregation, increase racial prejudice and promote unsafe sex between whites.

In my research with black female sex workers, many of the women discussed their clients in terms of race and emphasised racial differences. They explained that they preferred white clients because they paid better and that they were nicer. These women, however, also underscore that they encounter the 'other' regarding white people's sexuality and believed that white and black people's sexuality differs in terms of preferences and practices.

Sexuality and Economics

Independence has not translated into economic independence for most Namibians. It has resulted in increased urban migration with subsequent decreases in support from the extended family. In addition, persistent poverty has been combined with an increased exposure to consumer goods. Given these circumstances, it is not surprising that a variety of non-marital sexual relationships with economic components are flourishing in the postcolonial era. It is believed that sex work, transactional sex, survival sex, and sugar daddy/mommy and teacher/learner relationships are on the rise. It is, however, difficult to fit this myriad of sexual contacts into neatly labelled boxes. Grey areas are probably the rule rather than the exception, with various levels of emotional attachment, psychological connectedness, physical involvement and economic compensation.

While some men are on the economic receiving end of sex-exchange relationships, overwhelmingly it is women who negotiate, barter and sell sex for economic gain. Therefore, to gain a perspective on sex-exchange in Namibia, we need to examine the economic situation of women. Thirty nine per cent of the urban and 44% of the rural households are headed by women. Female-headed households tend to be the poorest of the poor because they become dependent on one income and child care conflicts with income-producing activities. Single mothers are often compelled to work in the informal sector or take low-paying, dead-end insecure employment, such as the production of handicrafts and domestic work.[5] Iipinge and LeBeau (2005) report that unemployment among women was 64%, and that "women often take advantage of any income-generating activity available to them, regardless of risk or low profit turnover ... women and children have been found working in some of the most squalid circumstances in Namibia."

Many women shoulder the financial responsibility for their children, although their annual income is, on average, 50% less than what men earn. Securing child maintenance payments is notoriously difficult – men deny paternity, many men migrate and connections are lost, and it is difficult to determine a man's income if he works in agriculture or the informal economy. In addition to these problems, the magistrates' courts are understaffed and are often located far from rural areas. Even if a mother is able to

---

5. Domestic workers in Windhoek earn between N$ 50 and N$ 80 per day, which works out to less than 10 Euros per day, or about 163–261 Euros a month.

obtain a court order for maintenance, the average payment per child per month was N$ 76 the last time it was calculated.[6]

Since independence, there has been an increase in unwed teenage pregnancies.[7] This is attributed to the breakdown of 'traditional' sexual mores that forbid premarital sex. It has been reported that in urban areas, some young men insist that their girlfriends prove their fertility by having a baby before they marry. Too often, the young woman finds herself abandoned after the baby is born. When the woman forms a new relationship, she is expected to have another child with her new partner and so on and so on, only to be deserted by father after father (Pauli 2007). Her financial responsibilities grow with the number of children she bears, yet her ability to find employment and remain employed decrease due to increased child care responsibilities.

Transactional and Survival Sex

Edwards (n.d.) found that many women, in addition to income generated from domestic work and petty trading, rely on cash and gifts from boyfriends and other sexual partners for survival. In fact, there is a very fine line between being involved in a romantic sexual relationship and transactional sex. In Namibia, as elsewhere, men are supposed to demonstrate their love by supplying their girlfriends/wives with material goods – often basic items such as soap or food. The transactional aspect of such relationships is not explicit and the sex-for-goods is done in the context of romance and generalised reciprocity.

Intergenerational Relationships

Two forms of exceptionally unequal relationships have received a lot of attention in recent years: sugar daddy/mommy relationships and the sexual relationships between teachers and learners. Although these relationships have been discussed and mentioned in newspaper articles and development reports, there has been no qualitative or quantitative research conducted that allows us to determine the prevalence of or the dynamics involved in such relationships. Information, however, can be inferred from other sources. For example, it is believed that higher HIV prevalence rates among 15–19 year-old girls is due to intergenerational sexual relations. Boys within their own age group have much lower prevalence than older men (Edmondson 2004).

The heightened consumerism that accompanied independence is seen as responsible for the sugar daddy/mommy phenomenon, thus it is assumed that such relationships are on the rise (Hailonga-van Dijk 2007). It is taken for granted that most of these intergenerational relationships involve young girls and older men, although it is also acknowledged that some young men have sugar mommies. Young girls and boys are supposedly seeking out the three Cs: cash, cars and cellphones. On a more modest level, it is believed that they are also involved in these relationships to help support their families and pay their school fees. In addition to the moral issues – the sexual exploitation of young people by older men and women and the fact that most sugar daddies/mommies

---

6. This figure from ten years ago is the latest information available. There is no reason to believe that payments are much higher today.

7. Of women, 45.4% have begun childbearing by the time they reach 19 years of age (Iipinge 2005).

are presumed to be married – these liaisons are also blamed for increasing the transmission of HIV/AIDS because the inequality between the partners makes it difficult for young people to negotiate safe sex (Potkins 2005).

In regard to the sexual relationships between learners and teachers, while speaking at a workshop in 2001, Basic Education Deputy Minister Clara Bohitile said, "The silence and denial surrounding sexual abuse of learners is deafening." (Inambao 2002). She was referring to the fact that although these relationships are a well-known phenomenon, teachers who impregnate their students are not usually disciplined. In contrast, girls who become pregnant must leave school for a full year (Iipinge 1995). According to statistics published by the ministry of basic education and culture, in 2000 around 10,000 female students dropped out of school for various reasons, including pregnancy (Hamata 2001).

While conducting a focus group on sexuality with the San in Tsumkwe, I asked about the quality of sex education in the local schools. An older man laughed and said that their teachers taught the girls about sex by showing them how to do it.[8] The other participants laughed and nodded their heads in agreement. Another participant mentioned a specific incident at their school where a teacher had impregnated a 15 year-old girl and was arrested. Although The Namibian (2003) reported that between 1995 and 2002 114 male teachers had been expelled for impregnating school girls, this seems to be the exception rather than the rule. Of course, these dismissals are only the cases that resulted in pregnancy and complaints being laid. It can be safely assumed that many teacher/learner relationships are never discovered, do not result in pregnancy, or are settled informally with the girl's family because the teacher promises to support the girl and the child.

Sex Work

As noted above, commercial sex work is not as common as other forms of exchange-sex in Namibia. Existing research has not determined how many women are engaged in commercial sex work, and as with other forms of exchange-sex, there are many grey areas and situations in which Namibians have sex for money. For example, in 2006 when I interviewed 65 self-identified female sex workers ranging from age 12 to 55, many of the women and girls admitted that they had sexual intercourse with their clients for as little as N\$ 20 and N\$ 10. They accepted such small fees because they or their children were hungry. One must certainly qualify this as survival sex because these women claim that they have no other way to make money.

The Combating of Immoral Practices Act (No. 21 of 1980), which was passed during the colonial era, has not been repealed. It criminalises soliciting sex, pandering and keeping a brothel. The law is sex-specific, mentioning women but not men as those who potentially sell sex. The move to decriminalise sex work in Namibia has met with strong resistance from the government and church organisations, despite research proving sex workers are at risk of HIV/AIDS (LAC 2003). Morality and national pride seem to be the justification for marginalising these people, who are sometimes forced to have unsafe sex, or suffer from sexual violence and police harassment.

---

8.   I would like to thank Anne Rimmer of LAC for recording our session in shorthand, transcribing the notes and making them available to me.

Human Rights and Personal Liberties vs Morality

As mentioned earlier in the chapter, the discourse on sexual ideologies is usually formulated in two schools, one arguing for the recognition of human rights while the other argues the importance of morality and the rejection of foreign immorality. These conflicting points of view have been used to both justify reform and preserve the status quo concerning reproductive rights and the rights of gay, lesbian, bisexual and trans-gendered (GLBT) people.

Abortion

The colonial-era Abortion and Sterilisation Act of 1975 has not been repealed. This act criminalises abortion except when it is necessary to save a woman's health or in cases of rape where a police report has been filed or if a woman makes an affidavit convincing the magistrate that there was a reason why she did not report it. In reality, obtaining permission to have an abortion is a complicated process that can take a long time – sometimes so long that abortion is no longer an option. Recently, it took two months, with the help of Legal Assistance Centre (LAC), for a 16 year-old rape victim to gain permission for an abortion.

Economic inequality has led to differences in terms of reproductive rights between the rich and the poor. Wealthy women seeking abortions can go to South Africa and receive a safe legal abortion, while poor women who cannot afford to travel often have illegal abortions. The ministry of health released a report in 2002 that revealed 7,147 women had been treated for problems arising from illegal abortions in a three year period. During that same period, only 107 women had received legal abortions (Maletsky 2002). Deaths due to unsafe illegal abortions are thought to contribute to Namibia's high maternal mortality rates (abortion-related deaths are counted as maternal mortality deaths).

Abortion as a reproductive rights issue is not even on the agenda. A draft Abortion and Sterilisation Bill was supposed to be debated in 1996 and after three years of no progress the bill was put on ice due to pressure from church and pro-life groups. In 2002, the health minister announced that abortion would remain illegal for at least another ten years (Maletsky 2002).

Gay Rights

There has been no greater debate regarding sexuality in independent Namibia than the one about gay rights. The move to reform sodomy laws and protect the rights of GLBT people has met with stiff resistance from church organisations and the government. The discourse has focused on homosexuality as a foreign evil, un-African and sinful by those who are hostile to the gay rights movement, while supporters argue that inclusion, tolerance and human rights are important to democracy. There are marked differences between Namibia's ethnic groups in terms of the acceptance and tolerance of GLBT lifestyle and rights. 1Khaxas, researcher and co-founder of Sister Namibia (a feminist/human rights/LGBT rights NGO), notes that the Damara are much more open to homosexuality than some of the other cultures, in particular, the Owambo (!Khaxas/Wieringa 2007).

The Owambo politicians who dominate SWAPO have been at the forefront of gay-hate rhetoric. Verbal attacks have come in waves and the upper echelons of the government began to express their views in 1996 when President Nujoma exclaimed that "homosexuals must be condemned and rejected in our society." Such inflammatory statements were not met with silence. Sister Namibia (headed, at the time by a Namibian lesbian living openly with her European partner), criticised Nujoma and sparked an ongoing war of words.

On 31 January1997, SWAPO, to show support for their president, issued the following statement:

> It should be noted that most of ardent supporters of this perverts [sic] are Europeans who imagine themselves to be the bulwark of civilisation and enlightenment ...

> If there is a matter which must be dealt with utmost urgency, it is the need to revitalise our inherent culture and its moral values which we have identified with foreign immoral values. Promotion of homosexuality in our society scorns many sets of our values ...

> The moral values of our nation, as defended by the President, incorporate the fundamental principles of nature and should not be equated to the vile practices of homosexuals which has a backlash. Homosexuality deserves a severe contempt and disdain from the Namibian people and should be uprooted totally as a practice (HRW 2003).

In response to the onslaught of attacks on the rights of GLBT people, The Rainbow Project (TRP) was formed in February 1997. It remains the only organisation solely focusing on the rights of GLBT people, although it has been supported by several other NGOs such as Sister Namibia and LAC. The project, run primarily by volunteers, holds workshops, organises lectures and does counselling and media work (Titus 1999). However, the periodic assaults by government officials have been somewhat effective. Ian Swartz, TRP's head, explain to me that although the organisation has a large mailing list and some financial support from its members, many gays and lesbian are afraid to come out of the closet.

Despite the formation of TRP and the international outcry condemning such blatant homophobia, SWAPO government officials continued to make anti-gay statements and went so far as to threaten new legislation increasing punishments for gay sex (Maletsky 1998). In 1999, Jerry Ekandjo, the minister of home affairs, announced that the police had been ordered "to eliminate all gays and lesbians" in Namibia.[9] The following year, he claimed that the equality and freedom entrenched in the Namibian constitution does not apply to homosexuals, saying "We never had *moffies* in mind when SWAPO drafted the Namibian Constitution 10 years ago" (The Namibian 2000).[10]

In March 2001, after President Nujoma told university students, "The Republic of Namibia does not allow homosexuality, lesbianism here. Police are ordered to arrest you, and deport you and imprison you too." Hundred of Namibians, including members from 20 civil groups, marched through Windhoek to protest (HRW 2003; Reuters 2001). Interestingly, the rally speeches focused primarily on the rights of minorities: it became a march for human rights.

---

9. According to Phil ya Nangoloh, the executive director of the National Society for Human Rights in Namibia, the police took no action, yet several people were attacked (Simo 2001).
10. *Moffie* is a derogatory word used to describe a male homosexual or effeminate man.

The verbal attacks by politicians continue. In 2005, on Heroes Day, Deputy Minister of Home Affairs and Immigration Theopolina Mushelenga gave a speech blaming gays for the HIV/AIDS pandemic. The latest heated words came from former president Nujoma, now the president of SWAPO, when he called the president of the National Society for Human Rights a homosexual (Isaacs 2006). TRP responded by condemning the statements.

From time to time, the political rhetoric has been accompanied by statements made by religious institutions. In 1998, the Christian Ecumenical Fellowship of Gobabis, which represents several churches of various denominations, submitted a statement formally rejecting gay rights. A portion of it read:

> Not only is homosexuality un-Biblical, it is also in direct opposition to our Namibian culture, indeed all cultures represented in our society. We fail to see why Namibia should be intimidated into accepting it as part of 'democracy.' (The Namibian, 10 July 1998)

The religious homophobia, however, did not last and in 2001 the Council of Churches in Namibia (CCN) released a press statement and "rejected any form of discrimination based on sexual orientation" (IRIN 2001). The statement, while encouraging, did not end the debate within the churches nor was it embraced by all its members. The church continues to be a powerful institution in Namibia and many Namibians believe that homosexuality is a sin (IKhaxas/Wieringa 2007).

Liz Frank, the head of Sister Namibia, reports growing support for the rights of gay and lesbian people in rural areas and the former black townships, the heart of religious Namibia (Rothschild 2000). Personal testimonies of lesbians interviewed by IKhaxas/ Wieringa (2007) support this assertion. Their informants described a variety of experiences in terms of being accepted in and outside the church. One of their informants recounts:

> On the day we met. I said, "Pastor, do you know me?" and he said, "Yes". [And I said] "Pastor, I, Helen, have relationships with women ..." He said that maybe with my way I might bring someone to God and that he does not have any problem with me.

Discussion

In Namibia, sexuality has been constructed and reconstructed by complex historical interactions of racial, political, economic and religious forces. Since independence, various sexual rights have been debated and changes have occurred. However, sexual rights have not necessarily expanded: in some areas they have remained the same and in others areas sexual liberties have actually contracted. Furthermore, legal reform has not necessarily translated into attitudinal and behavioural change. For example, independence brought the end of apartheid and its ban on interracial sex and marriage, yet most interracial relations remain undercover, between unequal partners. The Married Persons Equality Act granted women equal legal status in their households, yet most women do not seem to be benefiting from such legal reform. The Combating of Rape Act 8 of 2000 outlaws rape within marriage, but most men still believe that their wives are obliged to provide them with sex.

Although legal reform has taken place, many of the laws imposed by the white South African government concerning family and 'morality' are still in effect in Namibia today. Abortion, sex work, pornography and gay sex are criminalised under the old laws and the new government seems determined to keep these actions and behaviours illegal and claims that their perspective is from a moral higher ground. Interestingly, the postcolonial South African government that inherited the same laws as Namibia has reformed, repealed legislation and passed new laws expanding personal sexual freedoms.

Supporters of the gay rights movements believe that they have identified a pattern in the government's moral outrage. They suggest that attacking gay rights is a ploy used to draw attention away from larger problems facing the country and the shortcomings of promised economic prosperity. These tactics thwart efforts to investigate the larger systemic problems facing Namibia, such as persistent poverty and racial and economic inequality.

Similarly, the perceived increase in sexual violence is often attributed to alcohol and drug abuse. Sexual violence is often dismissed as individual aberrance rather than produced by socioeconomic circumstances that put young people, women or gays at risk. Young women in particular are at risk of sexual violence. According to a WHO (2004) study, one-third of girls who have had sex before the age of 15 reported that they were forced, another 38% reported that they were coerced, while only 30% of girls who had sex before the age of 15 reported that it was not against their will. Blaming alcohol and drugs for these figures will not help reduce such figures or protect young women. The establishment of the women and child protection units has been welcomed: however, they do not concentrate on prevention of violence. Again, the focus is on individuals rather than on structural, systemic problems that produce violence.

This paper has not dealt with HIV/AIDS per se because it is the topic of the chapter by Lucy Edwards in this volume. Three points, however, need to be made: continued criminalisation of sodomy inhibits gay men from seeking treatment for sexually transmitted infections, including HIV/AIDS. A related point is that although politicians have blamed gays for the HIV/AIDS pandemic, most prevention has focused on heterosexual transmission. Thus, some Namibian men who have sex with men believe that homosexual sex is safer than heterosexual sex (Lowray 2007). Thirdly, the HIV/AIDS pandemic has prompted a discourse that would never have occurred prior to the disease. It has forced dialogue about sexuality and an opening up about sexuality in a country where sex used to be a taboo. And although it remains taboo for some and much of the HIV/AIDS discourse is about the negative consequence of unprotected sex and/or the importance of abstinence, it has put the topic on the table. The response to the HIV/AIDS pandemic has created a space for further and more in-depth public discussions about sexuality and prompted the development of sexual education programmes, even if implementation still seems to be a problem (Gockel-Frank 2007).

Conclusion

The lynchpin of the anti-apartheid movement was that apartheid was a violation of human rights, but now that Namibia has gained independence, human rights in terms of sexual rights is not at the forefront of the national agenda. There is a desire to be modern and politically correct, but there is also a desire to be Namibian and African. In this context, moves to promote a more equal society in regard to the sexuality of women and GLBT people are seen not only as immoral, but also as un-Namibian and un-African. Some Namibians view the international pressure to change their views on gender roles and homosexuality as a form of postcolonial imperialism. In this, Namibia is not unique. Their actions and tactics provide an illustration of the global dialogue that is going on between human rights and sexual rights (Chanock 2000). Sexual rights have not been widely accepted as part of the today's human rights. In fact, they constitute one of the most contested areas of human rights.

Engelke (2007) notes that morality and moral sentiment "constitute a serious obstacle to human rights activism" and "that there are problems with the practice and theory of such a universalising discourse." It is necessary to find a place for cultural difference within the framework of human rights and to recognise that human rights mean different things in different cultures. Yet it is unclear how this will be accomplished. One step is to understand sexuality and treat it as fundamental to, rather than marginal to culture.

Acknowledgements

I would to thank the Board of Trustees of the City University of New York for granting the fellowship leave of absence that enabled me to travel to Namibia. Dr. William Burger, chair of Behavioral Sciences and Human Services at Kingsborough Community College, deserves special thanks for his continued and unwavering support of my research endeavours. I am grateful to Dianne Hubbard for inviting me to be a visiting scholar at the Legal Assistance Centre's Gender Research and Advocacy Project and for her support during and after my residency.

References

Becker, Heike (2000), 'A concise history of gender, "tradition" and the state in Namibia,' in Christiaan Keulder (ed.), *State, Society and Democracy. A reader in Namibian Politics.* Windhoek: Gamsberg Macmillan, pp. 171–99

— (2003), *Imagining tradition and modernity.* Paper presented at the Sex and Secrecy Conference. [online]Available from the World Wide Web: http://wiserweb.wits. ac.za/conf2003/becker.doc

— (2007), 'Making Tradition: A historical perspective on gender in Namibia,' in S. LaFont and D. Hubbard (eds), *Unravelling Taboos: Gender and Sexuality in Namibia.* Windhoek: Legal Assistance Centre

Chanock, Martin 2000, '"Culture" and human right: orientalising, occidentalising and authenticity,' in Mahmood Mamdani (ed.), *Beyond Rights Talk and Culture Talk.* New York: St. Martin's Press, pp. 15–36

CSA (Church of Sweden Aid) (n.d.), *Namibia.* [online] Available from the World Wide Web: (http://www.svenskakyrkan.se/lutherhjalpen/lh50eng/lh50eng9.htm)

Edmondson, Janet C. (2004), *Socio-Cultural Research Support to Unfpa Country Programmes in Namibia, Zambia, Malawi and Mozambique.* United Nations [online] Available from the World Wide Web: (HIV levels among women in Southern African countries remain high)

Edwards, Lucy (n.d.), *HIV and the ABC: A dual between Western-Christian morality and African patriarchy.* Gender and Women's Studies for African Transformation [online] Available from the World Wide Web: (http://www.gwsafrica.org/knowledge/lucy%20edwards.html)

Farrell, C. (2006), *Judicial Corporal Punishment in South Africa World Corporal Punishment Research.* [online] Available from the World Wide Web: (http://corpun.com/jcpza7.htm)

Gockel-Frank, Marina (2007), 'The gift from God: Reproductive Decisions and Conflicts of Women in Modern Namibia,' in S. LaFont and D. Hubbard (eds), *Unravelling Taboos: Gender and Sexuality in Namibia.* Windhoek: Legal Assistance Centre

Hailonga-van Dijk, Pandu (2007), 'Adolescents Negotiating Between Tradition, Modernity, Local And Globalisation,' in S. LaFont and D. Hubbard (eds), *Unravelling Taboos: Gender and Sexuality in Namibia.* Windhoek: Legal Assistance Centre

Hamata, Max (2000), 'Ekandjo elaborates on anti-gay stance,' *The Namibian* [online] November 3, 2000. Available from the World Wide Web: (http://www.namibian.com.na/2000/November/news/00B37E6051.html)

— (2001), 'Nanso appeals to Govt on teenage pregnancies,' *The Namibian* [online] September 26, 2001. Available from the World Wide Web: (http://www.namibian.com.na/2001/September/news/01177CA7A0.html)

HRW (Human Rights Watch) and The International Gay and Lesbian Human Rights Commission (2003), *More Than A Name: State-Sponsored Homophobia and Its Consequences in Southern Africa* [online] Available from the World Wide Web: (http://www.hrw.org/reports/2003/safrica/index.htm)

Hubbard, Dianne (2007), 'Ideas of Equality: Gender, Sexuality and the Law,' in S. LaFont and D. Hubbard (eds), *Unravelling Taboos: Gender and Sexuality in Namibia.* Windhoek: Legal Assistance Centre

Iipinge, Eunice and Debie LeBeau (2005), *Beyond Inequalities: Women in Namibia.* UNAM & SARDC: Windhoek & Harare. [online] Available from the World Wide Web: (http://databases.sardc.net/books/namibia2005/view.php?chapter=7&id=8)

Inambao, Chrispin (2002), 'Silence on sex abuse in schools "deafening",' *The Namibian* [online] March 11, 2002. Available from the World Wide Web: (http://www.namibian.com.na/2002/march/news/024A2B4032.html)

IRIN (2001), *Church Defends Gay Rights.* [online] Available from the World Wide Web: (www.sodomylaws.org/world/namibia/nanews017.htm)

Isaacs, Denver (2006), 'Rainbow Project joins Nujoma fray,' *The Namibian.* [online] August 4, 2006. Available from the World Wide Web: (http://www.namibian.com.na/2006/August/national/063C4901D5.html)

Iyer, Pico (2005), 'A Partial Victory for Romance: Infamous sex laws will be repealed, but apartheid remains intact,' *Time Magazine* [online] April 12, 2005, Available from the World Wide Web: (http://jcgi.pathfinder.com...)

!Khaxas, Elizabeth and Saskia Wieringa (2007), 'Same-sex Sexuality among Damara Women,' in S. LaFont and D. Hubbard (eds), *Unravelling Taboos: Gender and Sexuality in Namibia.* Windhoek: Legal Assistance Centre

Keulder, Christiaan and Debie Lebeau (2006), *Ships, Trucks and Clubs: The Dynamics of HIV Risk Behaviour in Walvis Bay.* Institute for Public Policy Research, IPPR Briefing Paper No. 36. [online] Available from the World Wide Web: (http://www.ippr.org.na/Briefing%20Papers/BP36.pdf)

LaFont, Suzanne (2007), 'Not Quite Redemption Song: Queer Hate in Jamaica,' in D. Murray (ed.), *Homophobias: Lust and Loathing Across Time and Space.* Madison: University of Wisconsin Press

Lowray, Robert (2007), 'Breaking a Public Health Silence: HIV risk and male-male sexual practices in the Windhoek Urban Area,' in S. LaFont and D. Hubbard (eds), *Unravelling Taboos: Gender and Sexuality in Namibia.* Windhoek: Legal Assistance Centre

Maletsky, Christof (1998), 'Govt planning to criminise gays,' *The Namibian* [online] November 8, 1998. Available from the World Wide Web: (http://www.namibian.com.na/netstories/november98/gaycrime.html)

Maletsky, Christof (2002), 'Abortion ruled out,' *The Namibian* [online] November 28, 2002. Available from the World Wide Web: (http://www.namibian.com.na/2002/November/national/029C6A15DC.html)

Ovis, M.H. (2005), Polygamy – To share or not to share? That is the question. Legal Assistance Centre, Gender Research and Advocacy Project. [online] Available from the World Wide Web: (http://www.lac.org.na/grap/Pdf/poligamy.pdf)

Pauli, Julia (2007), '"We all have our own father!" Reproduction, Marriage and Gender in Rural Northwest Namibia,' in S. LaFont and D. Hubbard (eds), *Unravelling Taboos: Gender and Sexuality in Namibia.* Windhoek: Legal Assistance Centre

Potkins, Meghan (2005), 'Research links AIDS to "transactional sex",' *The Gateway,* March, 17, 2005, Volume XCIV Issue 40. [online] Available from the World Wide Web: (http://www.gateway.ualberta.ca/view.php?aid=4217)

Reuters, (2001), 'Namibians March to Defend Gay, Other Minority Rights,' *Sodomy Laws* [online] Available from the World Wide Web: (http://www.sodomylaws.org/world/namibia/nanews018.htm)

Rothschild, Cynthia (2000), *Written Out: How Sexuality Is Used to Attack Women's Organizing.* Center for Women's Global Leadership. [online] Available from the World Wide Web: (http://www.iglhrc.org/files/iglhrc/WrittenOut.pdf)

Shigwedha, Absalom (2000), 'NC contemplates sex and morality,' *The Namibian* [online] March 30, 2000. Available from the World Wide Web: www.namibian.com.na/Netstories/2000/March/News/morality.html

Simo, Ana (2001), 'Namibia: The Bermuda Triangle of African Homophobia,' *The Gully.*com [online] Available from the World Wide Web: http://www.kellycogswell.com/essays/africa/010327gay_na.html

The Namibian (1998), 'Churches Reject Gayism,' November 7, 1998 [online] Available from the World Wide Web: http://www.namibian.com.na/Netstories/Ops8-98/LETS112798.html

— (2003), '114 teachers expelled over school pregnancies,' August 20, 2003. [online] Available from the World Wide Web http://www.namibian.com.na/2003/august/national/03EDF496AE.html

Titus, Zoe (1999), 'Gays, lesbians urged to "come out of the closet",' *The Namibian.* [online] May 3, 1999. Available from the World Wide Web: (http://www.namibian. com.na/Netstories/May99/gays.html)

US Department of the Army (n.d.), *South Africa: Legislative Implementation of Apartheid.* Library of Congress Country Studies/Area Handbook Series [online] Available from the World Wide Web: (http://countrystudies.us/south-africa/25.htm)

Wise, Sheila (2007), 'The Male "Powersexual": An Exploratory Study of Manhood, Power, and Sexual Behaviour among Afrikaner and Owambo Men in Windhoek,' Iin S. LaFont and Dianne Hubbard (eds), *Unravelling Taboos: Gender and Sexuality in Namibia.* Windhoek: Legal Assistance Centre

Biographical notes on the authors

Gregor Dobler studied Anthropology and Political Sciences. He has previously worked at the departments for Religious Studies and Anthropology at Bayreuth University, and is teaching Anthropology and African Studies at Basel University, Switzerland, since 2002.

Lucy Edwards is a lecturer in the Sociology Department of the University of Namibia. She has done research on the Socio-cultural context of HIV and AIDS and gender. She is currently completing a PhD dissertation on the impact of HIV/AIDS related mortality on family structures.

Mattia Fumanti studied Social Anthropology in Manchester where he obtained his doctorate in 2003 after extensive field research in Rundu since 1999. He is a research assistant at the University of Keele and currently pursuing a 30-months ESRC funded research project among African migrants in London.

Graham Hopwood holds a BA Hons degree in English Language and Literature from the University of Liverpool. He heads the Public Dialogue Centre at the Namibia Institute for Democracy (NID) in Windhoek and is co-editor of Insight Namibia, the only current affairs magazine. He was a journalist and sub-editor at The Namibian newspaper from 1992 to 2004.

Dianne Hubbard holds degrees in English literature from the University of North Carolina and Stellenbosch University, and a law degree from Harvard Law School. Since 1993, she has been the Co-ordinator of the Gender Research & Advocacy Project at the Legal Assistance Centre, a public interest law firm based in Windhoek.

Herbert Jauch holds two teaching degrees and a master's degree in Political Sciences. He has been associated with the Namibian labour movement for the past 20 years and was the director of the Labour Resource and Research Institute (LaRRI) from 1998 until 2007. He is currently employed as LaRRI's senior researcher.

Phanuel M. Kaapama is Lecturer in the Department of Political and Administrative Studies at the University of Namibia (UNAM). He is currently pursuing his PhD thesis on Namibia's land policy with the University of Witwatersrand in Johannesburg.

Bennett Kangumu Kangumu studied History, English and Political Science at the University of Namibia, and thereafter obtained an MA degree in Historical Studies at the University of Cape Town, where he is currently finalizing a PhD thesis on Contestations Over Caprivi Identity.

Suzanne LaFont, Ph.D. is an Associate Professor of Anthropology at City University of New York, Kingsborough Community College. She has published several books, numerous articles in scholarly journals and book chapters. Her research interests are the interrelatedness of sexualities, gender, power, and human rights.

Henning Melber studied Political Sciences and Sociology in Berlin and obtained his PhD in Bremen. He was Director of the Namibian Economic Policy Research Unit (NEPRU) in Windhoek (1992–2000) and Research Director of The Nordic Africa Institute in Uppsala (2000–2006), where he is Executive Director of The Dag Hammarskjöld Foundation.

Lalli Metsola obtained a master's degree in cultural anthropology at the University of Helsinki. He is based at the Institute of Development Studies in Helsinki, completing a PhD on state formation, citizenship and political subjectivity in Namibia through the case of ex-combatant 'reintegration'.

Chris Saunders studied History in Cape Town and Oxford, where he obtained his doctorate from St. Antony's. He returned to teach at the University of Cape Town, where he is now Professor in Historical Studies. He has held visiting positions at a number of universities, including Adelaide, Calgary and Yale.

Volker Winterfeldt studied Sociology, German Literature, and Rhetoric. He lectured in Sociology at the University of Tübingen, Germany, from 1984 to 1996. Since 1998 he has been a lecturer at the Department of Sociology at the University of Namibia.

Wolfgang Zeller holds an MA degree in Geography from the University of Helsinki. He is currently finalising his PhD thesis on state formation in the Namibia/Zambia borderland and lecturing at the Institute of Development Studies, University of Helsinki.